THIS HAT BELONGS TO JEFF PETERS

Slight

PUBLICATIONS 2015

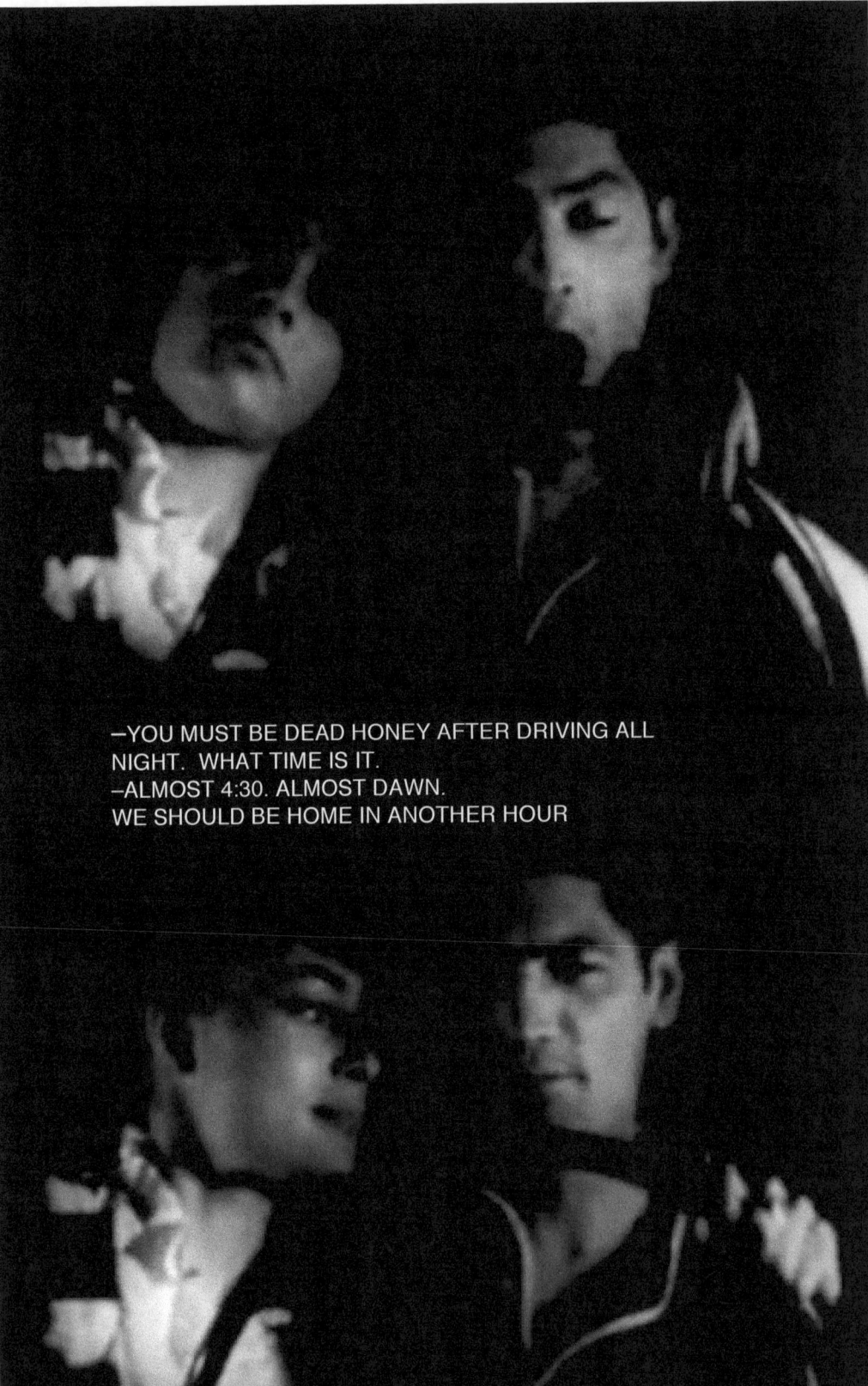

—YOU MUST BE DEAD HONEY AFTER DRIVING ALL
NIGHT. WHAT TIME IS IT.
—ALMOST 4:30. ALMOST DAWN.
WE SHOULD BE HOME IN ANOTHER HOUR

THIS MAN'S NAME IS MARTIN
GORDON THE LOVELY GIRL BESIDE
HIM IS BRETT, HIS BRIDE OF TWO
WONDERFUL WEEKS. ITS LATE
AUGUST AND THEY ARE RETURNING
FROM THEIR HONEYMOON TO THEIR
HOME IN QUIET, PEACEFUL, ANGEL
COUNTY CALIFORNIA. MARTIN'S
UNCLE BEN IS SHERIFF OF ANGEL
COUNTY AND MARTIN IS HIS SENIOR
DEPUTY. MARTIN HAS HIGH HOPES
OF SUCCEEDING HIS UNCLE WHEN
BEN RETIRES BUT FOR NOW, MARTIN
HAS ONLY THE THOUGHTS, EMOTION
AND PRIDE OF A VERY HAPPY NEWLY
MARRIED YOUNG MAN. BRETT IS HIS
AND HE FEELS NO MAN COULD ASK
FOR MORE. NOW WITHOUT
WARNING, THEIR HONEYMOON IS TO
BECOME A NIGHTMARE.

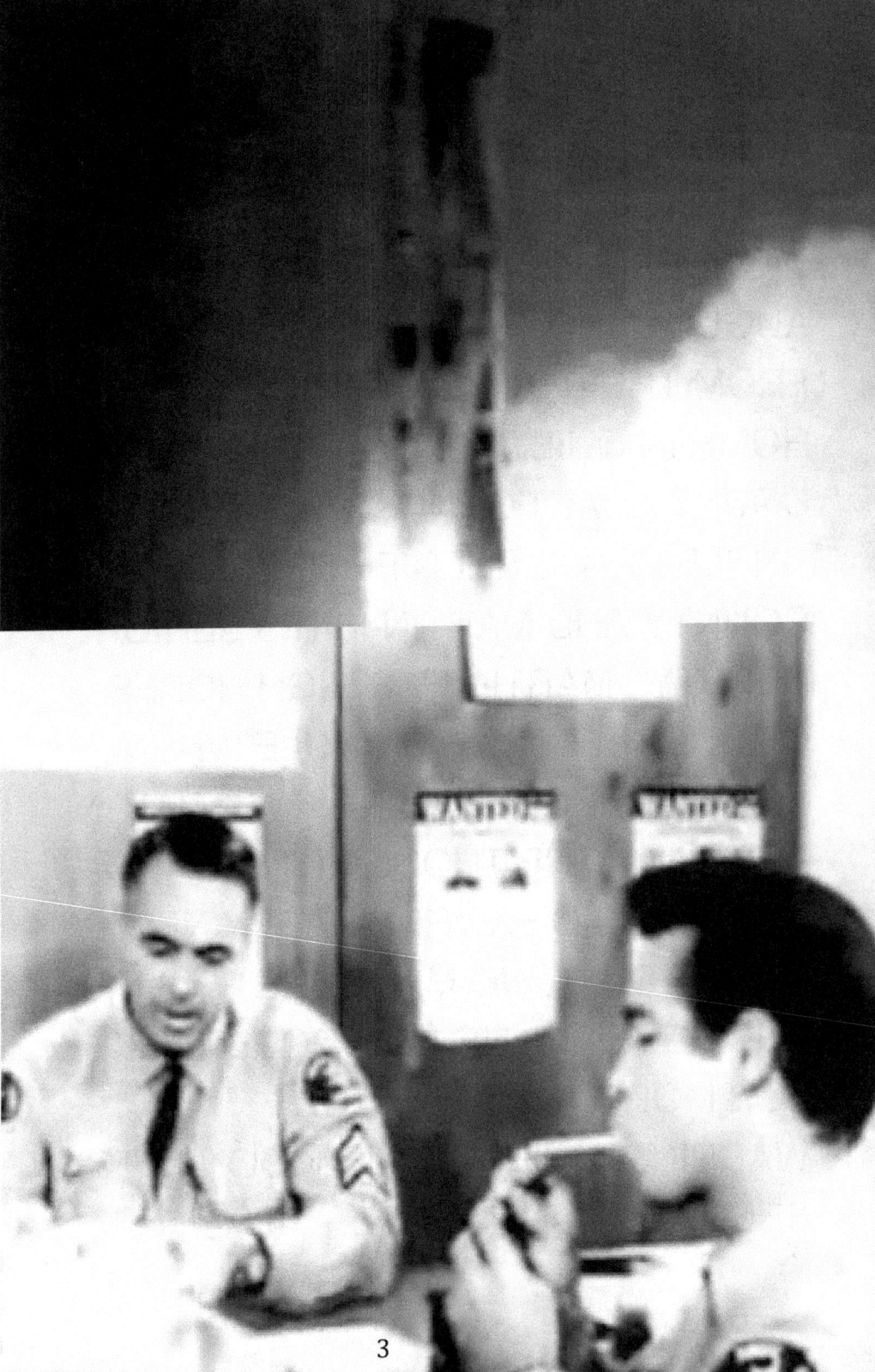

NEITHER MARTIN OF BRETT SAW
THE GLOWING ROCKET DESCEND
THE EARLY MORNING SKIES.
IT WAS REPORTED TO THE
SHERIFF'S OFFICE BY JEFF, THE
COUNTY FOREST RANGER. JEFF
REPORTED TO SHERIFF BEN THAT
A PLANE HAD CRASHED
NEAR WILLOW CREEK AND THAT HE
WAS GOING OUT TO INVESTIGATE.
BEN SAID HE WOULD JOIN HIM AS
SOON AS POSSIBLE. BARNEY,
BEN'S JUNIOR DEPUTY, WAS TO
SUMMON MEDICAL AID AND SEE IF
HE COULD ROUSE SOMEONE AT
THE AIR AUTHORITY IN SAN
FRANCISCO.

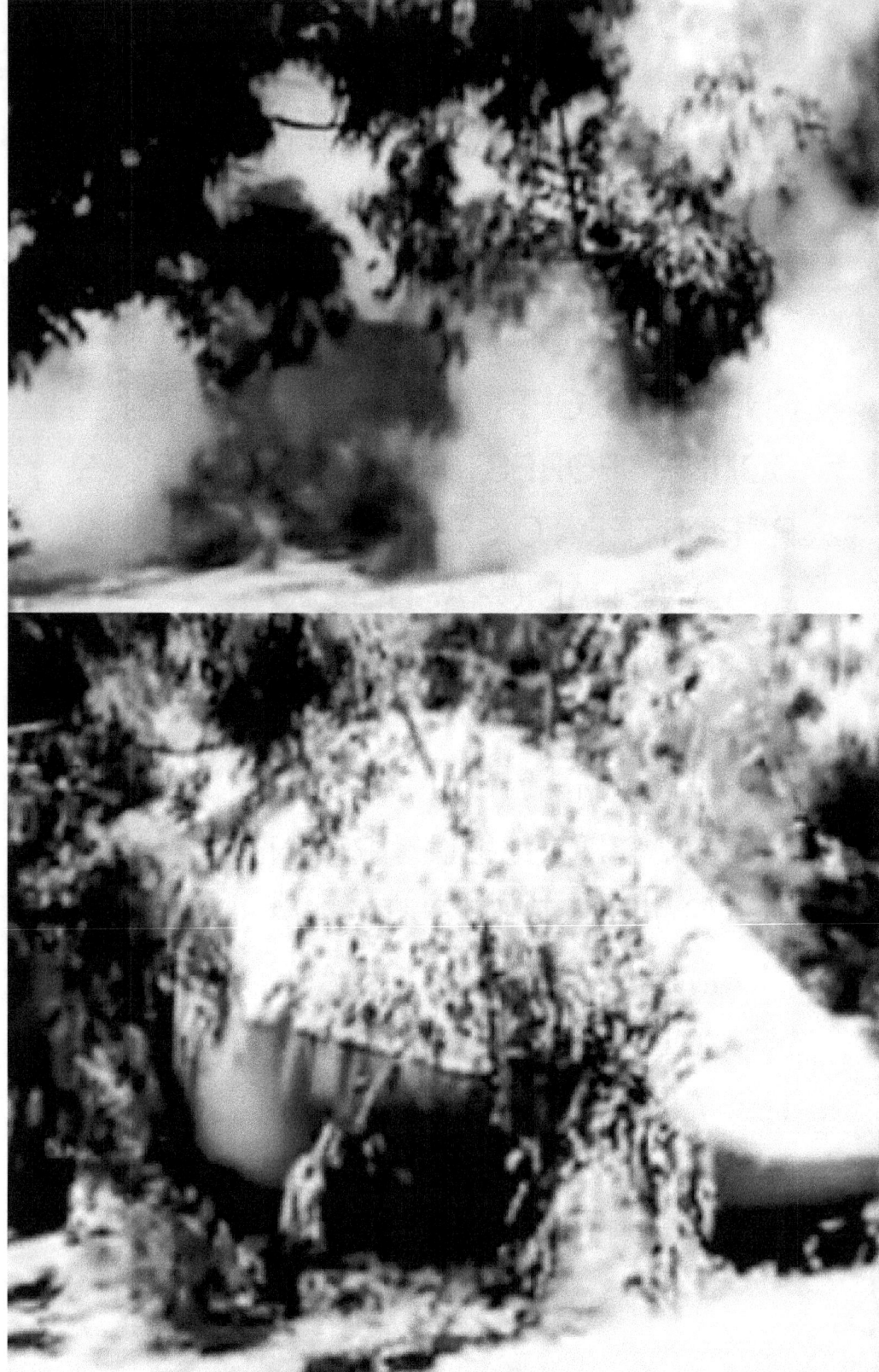

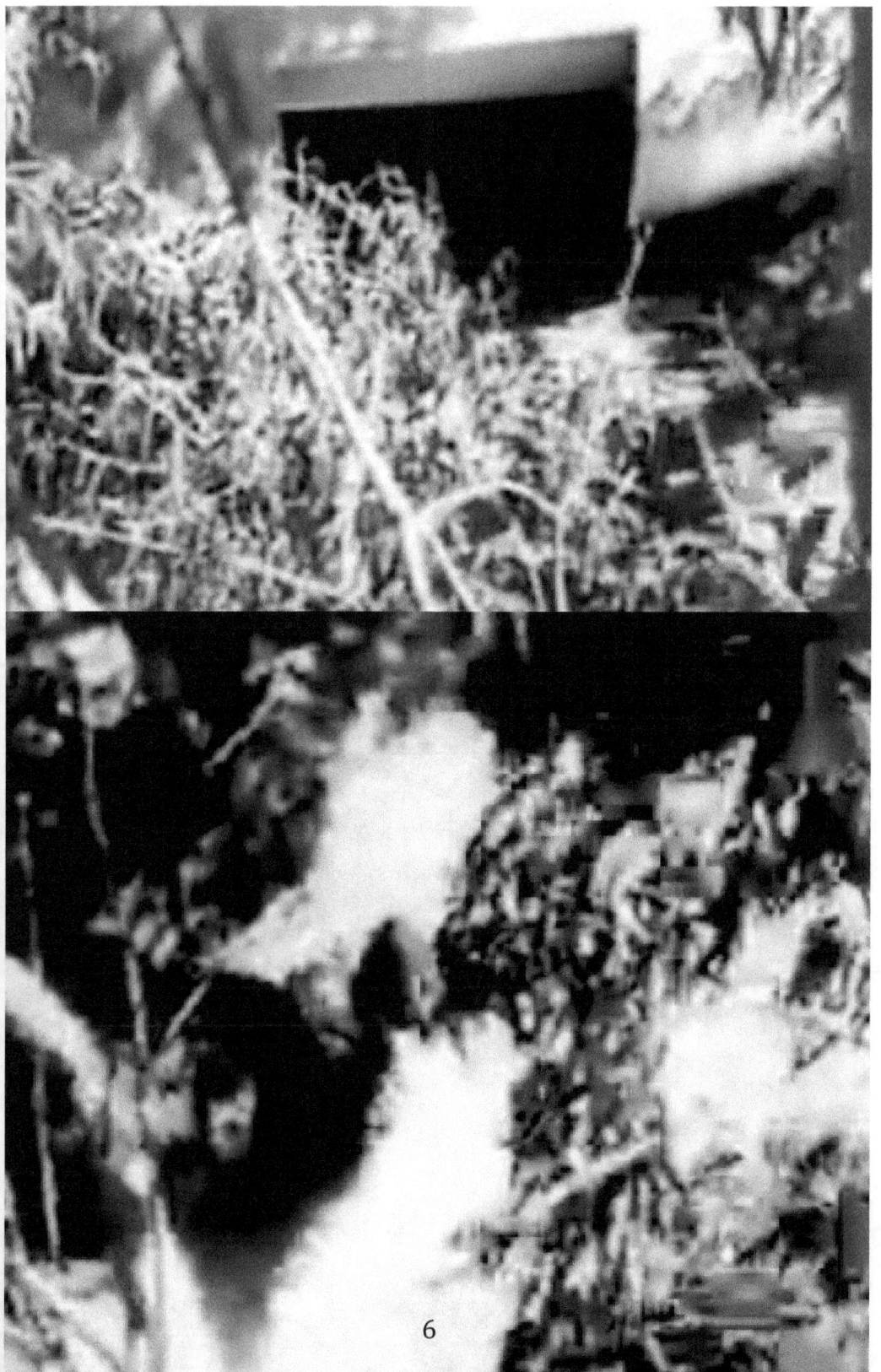

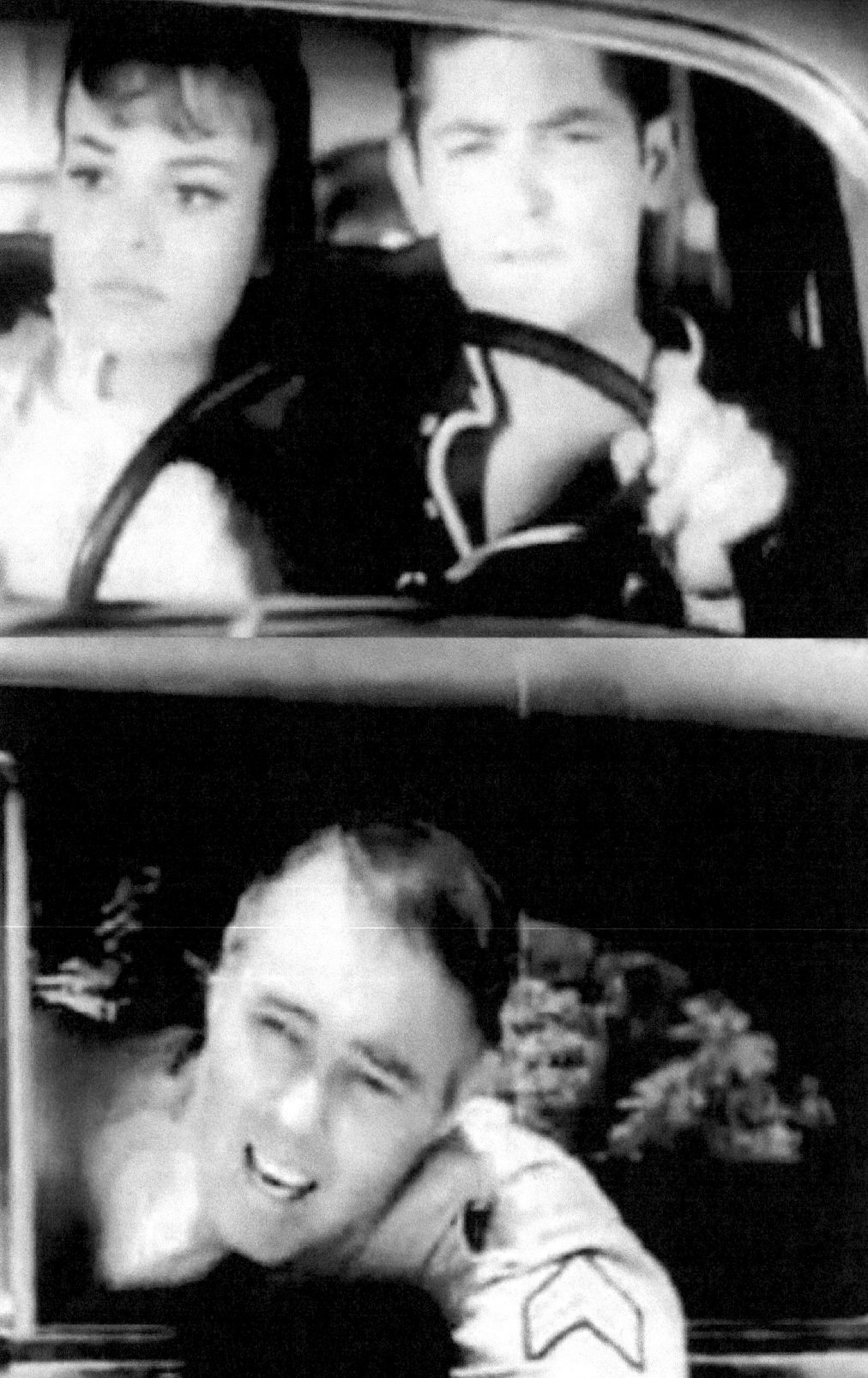

—IT'S UNCLE BEN HONEY.

MUST BE AN ACCIDENT

OR SOMETHING.

—PLANE CRASH

DOWN THE ROAD

A COUPLE OF MILES.

GOING TO BE A LITTLE SHORT

HANDED TILL HELP GETS HERE.

PULL AROUND BACK OF ME.

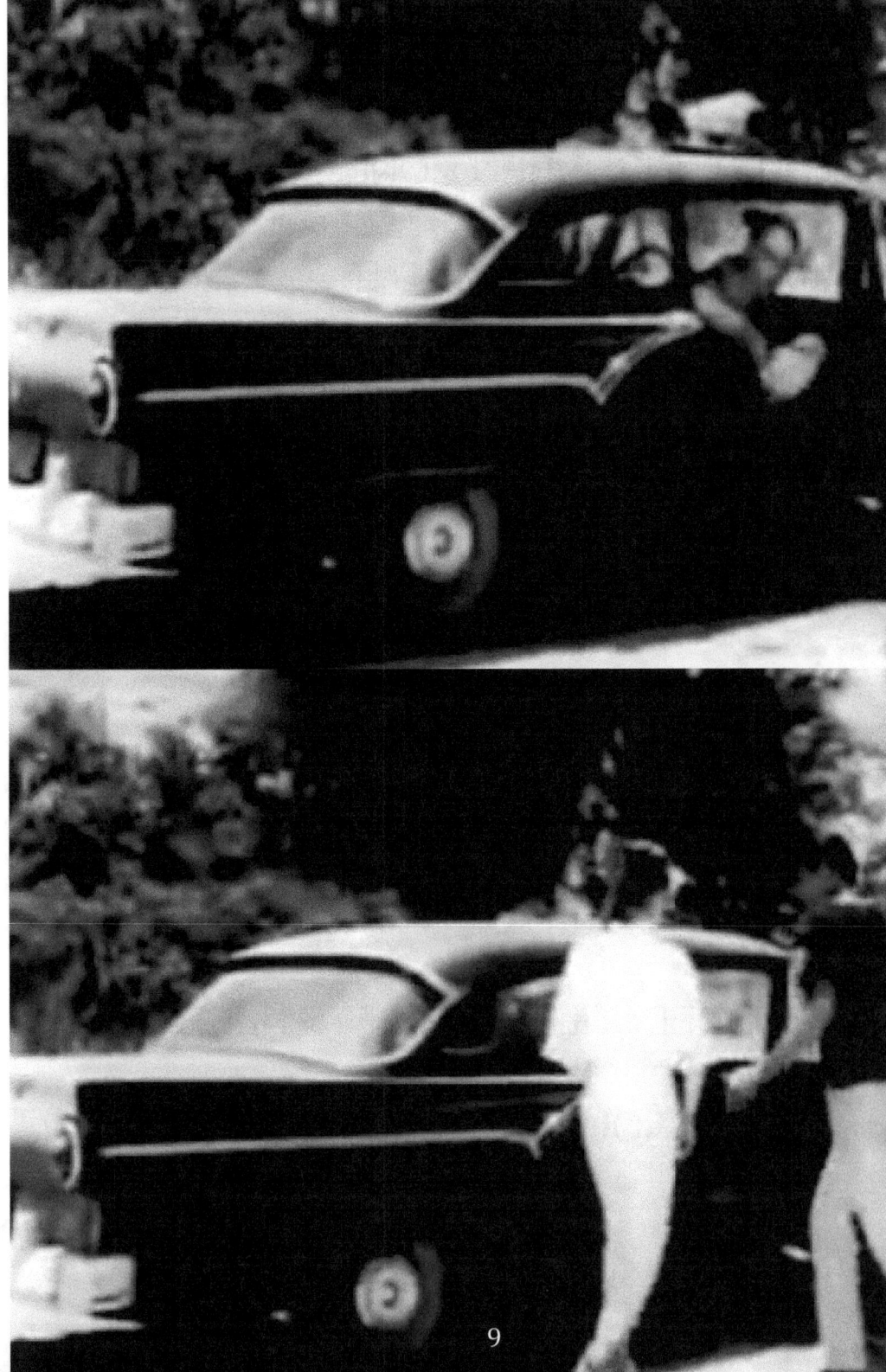

COME ALONG

BOTH OF YOU.

–GET IN, HONEY

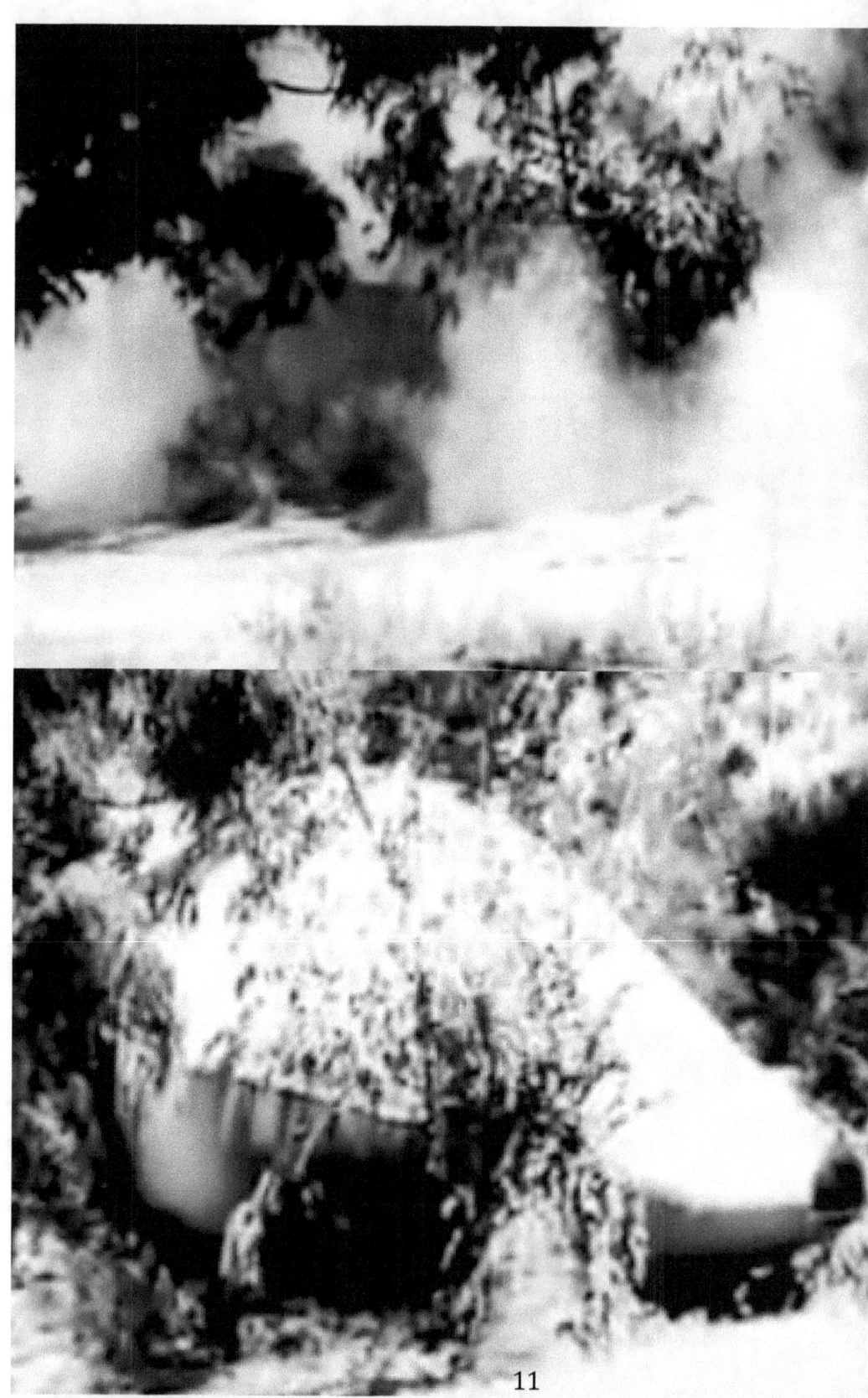

THEY LOOKED AT THE ROCKET IN UTTER

AMAZEMENT

A PUZZLED BEN ASKED MARTIN WHAT

HE MADE OF THE CRASH

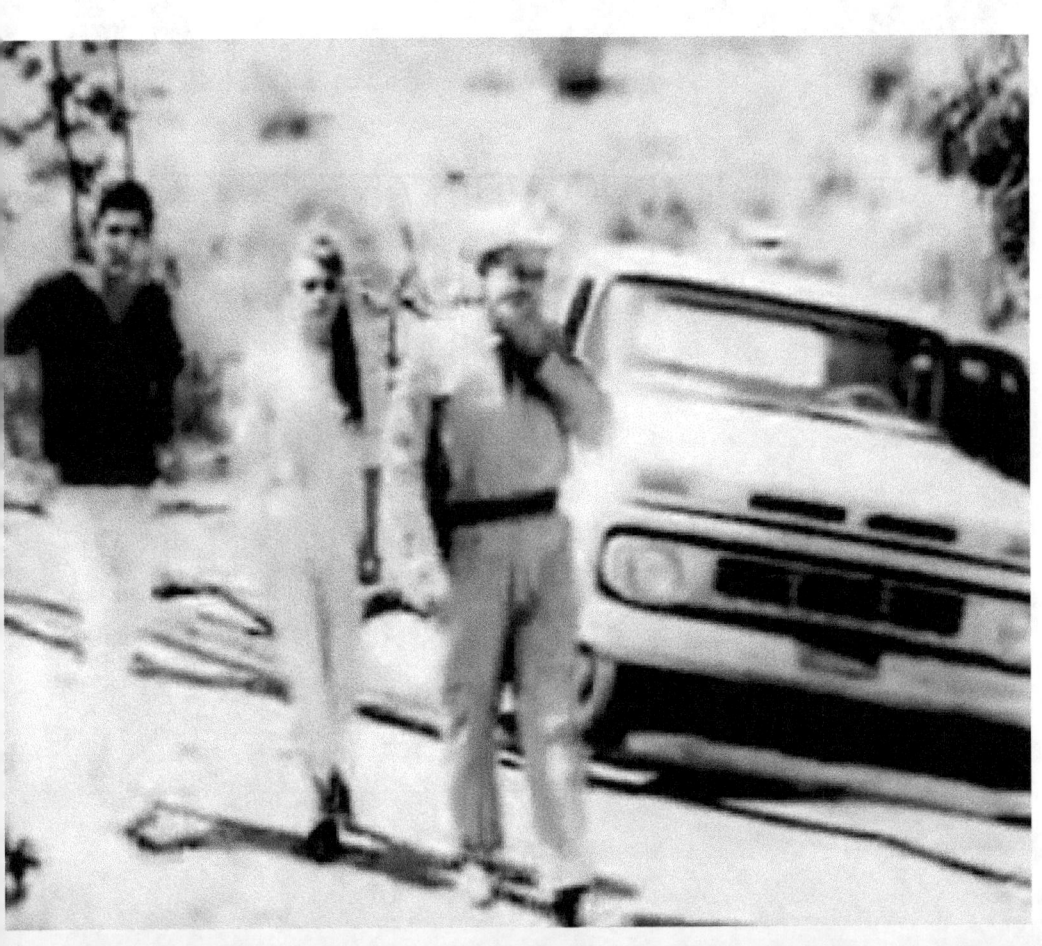

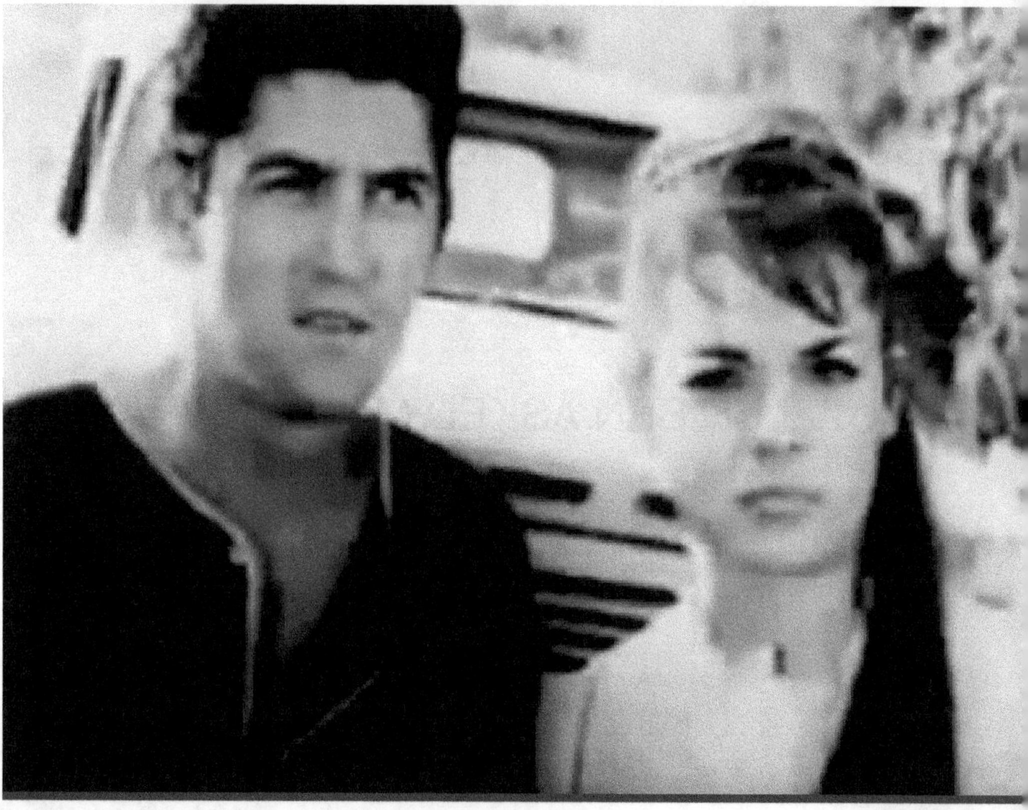

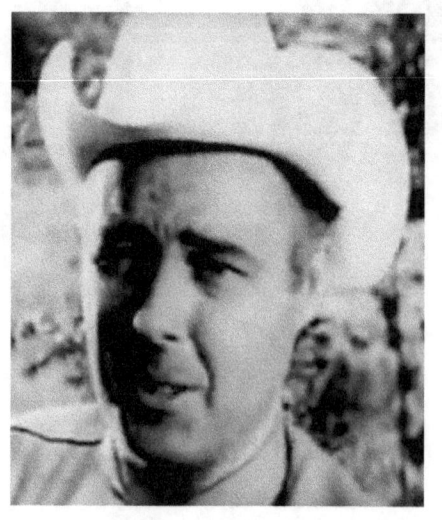

IT'S NO AIRPLANE

COULD BE ONE OF
OUR MISSLES

–OR ONE OF THEIRS said Brett

–YOU COULD BE RIGHT, HONEY

–DON'T THINK WE HAVE ANYTHING THIS BIG said Ben

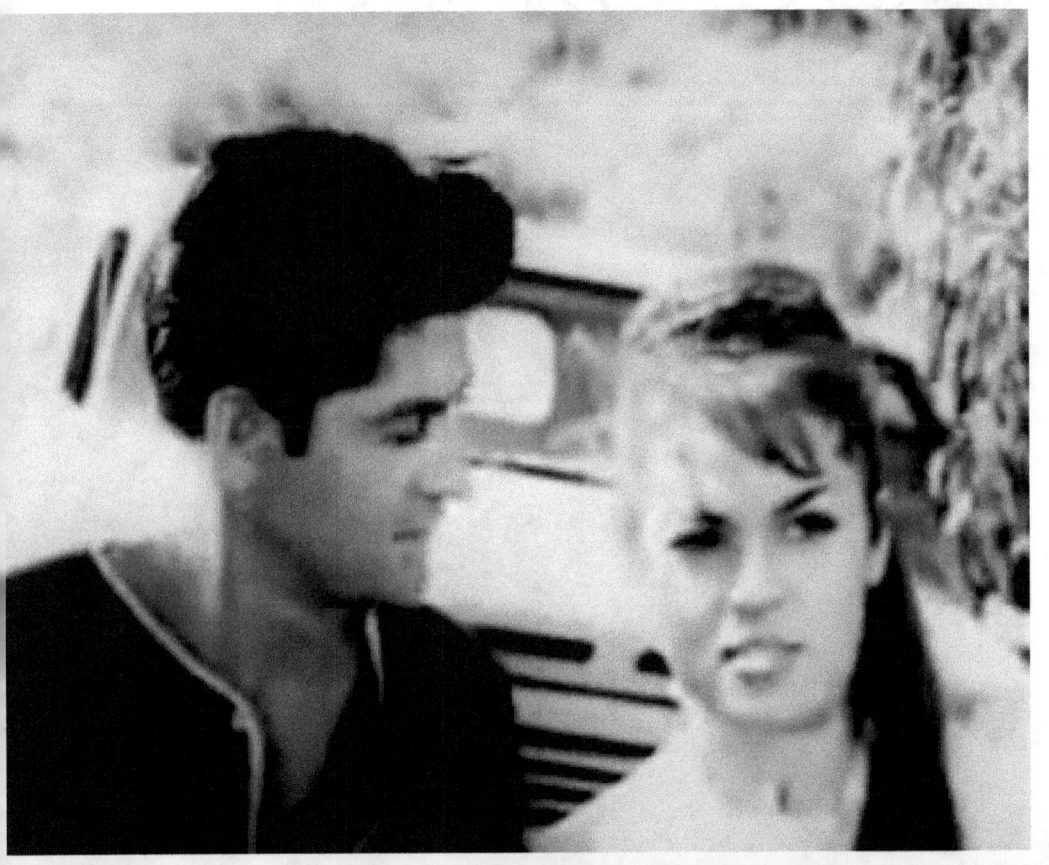

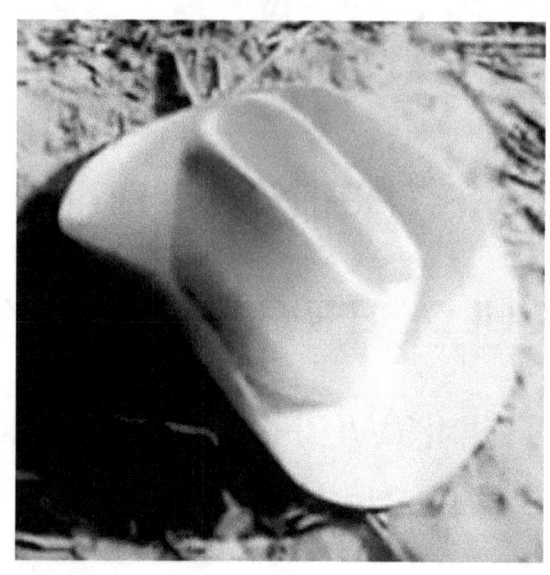

THIS HAT BELONGS TO JEFF PETERS

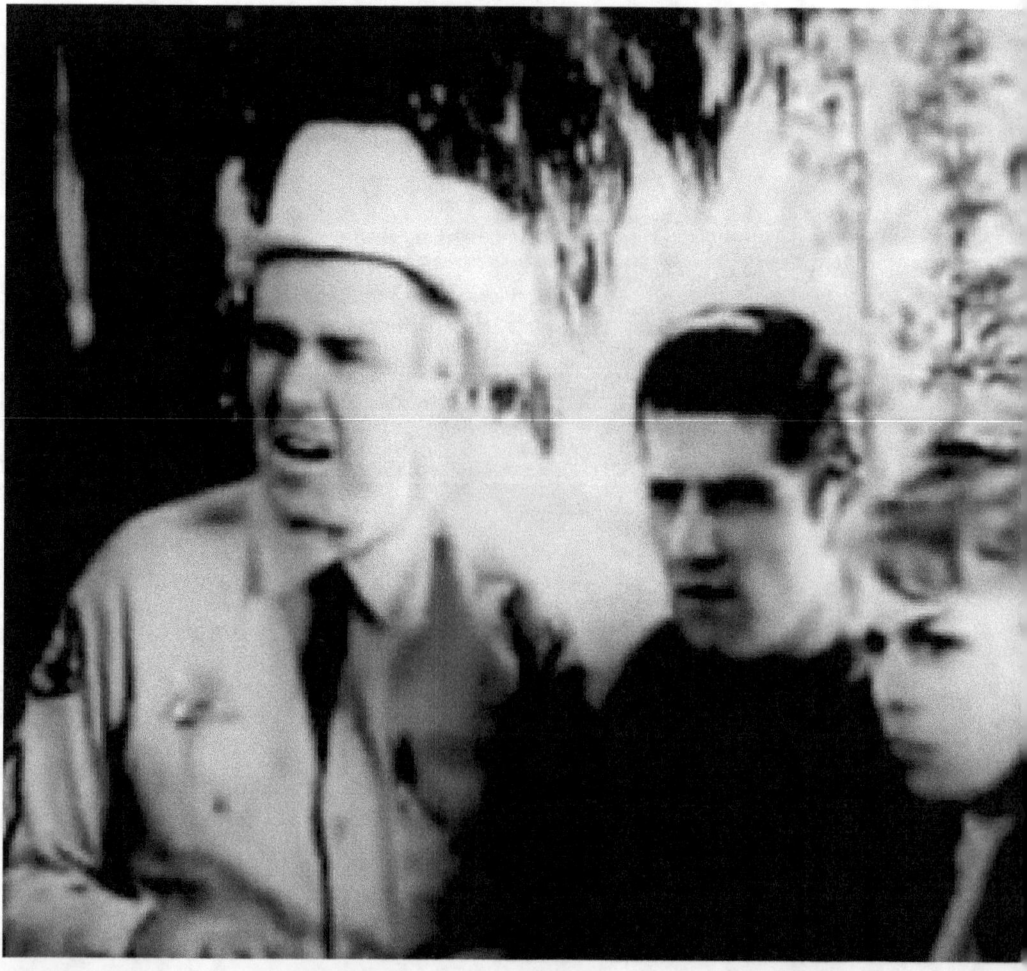

JEFF!
JEFF!
JEFF!
JEFF ARE YOU IN THERE?

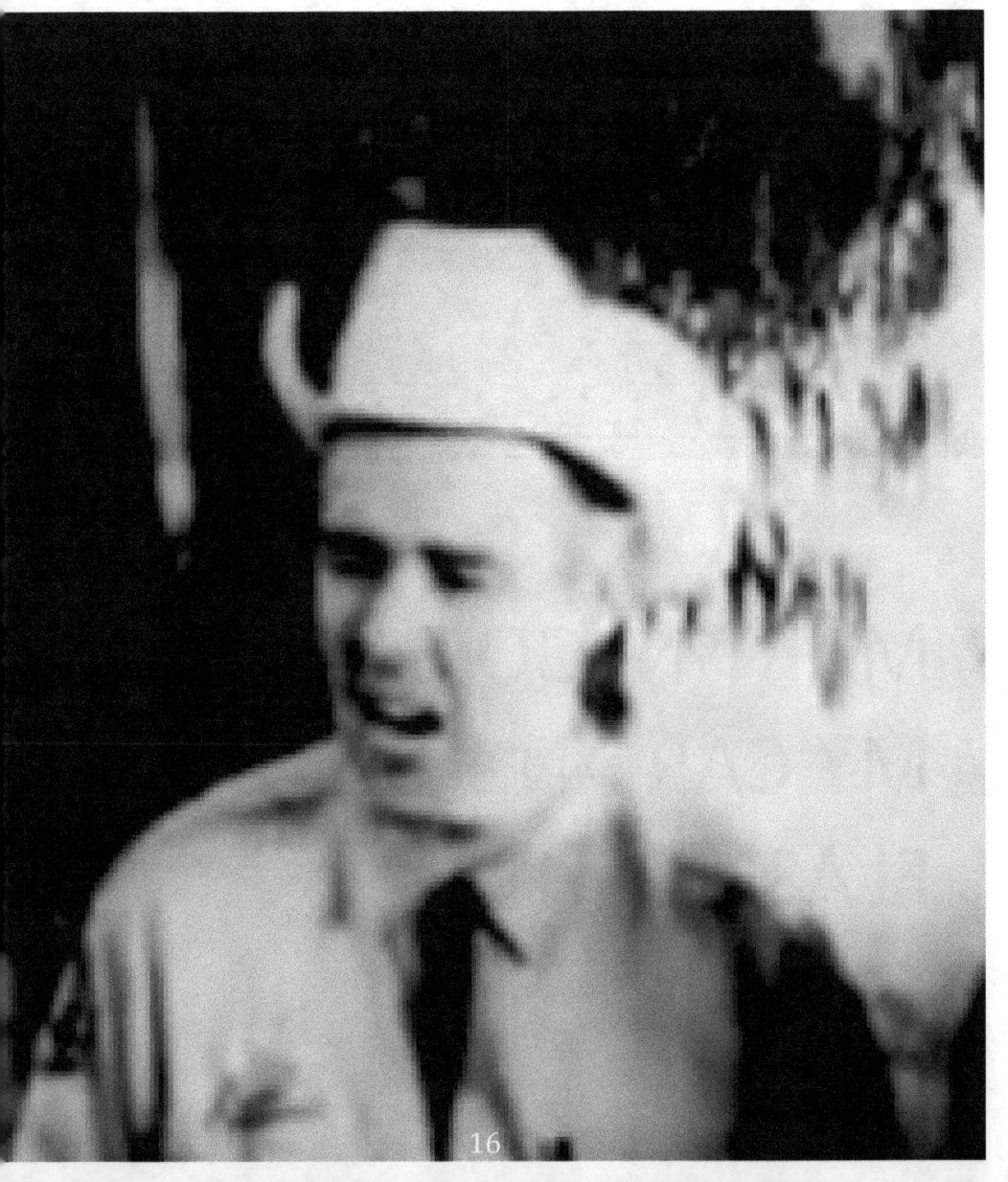

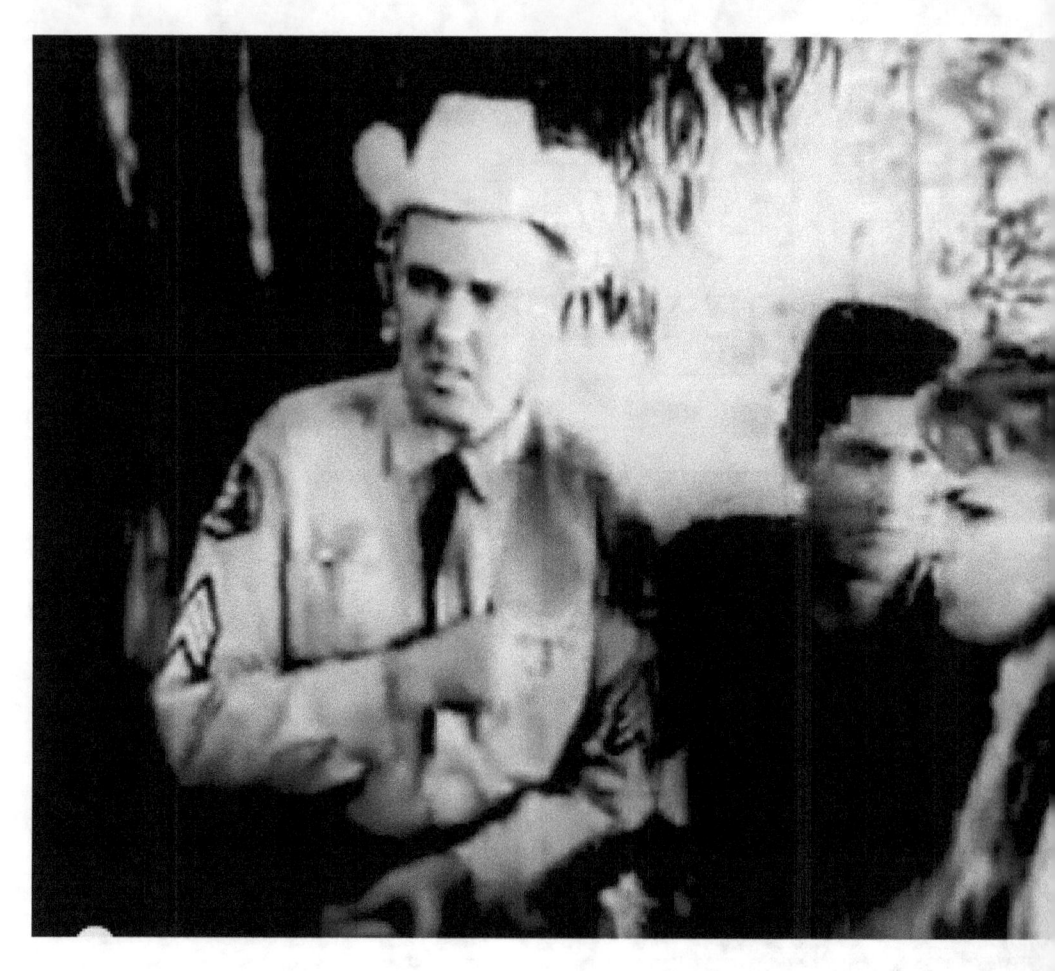

MARTIN, GO BACK TO
MY CAR AND GET MY
FLASHLIGHT

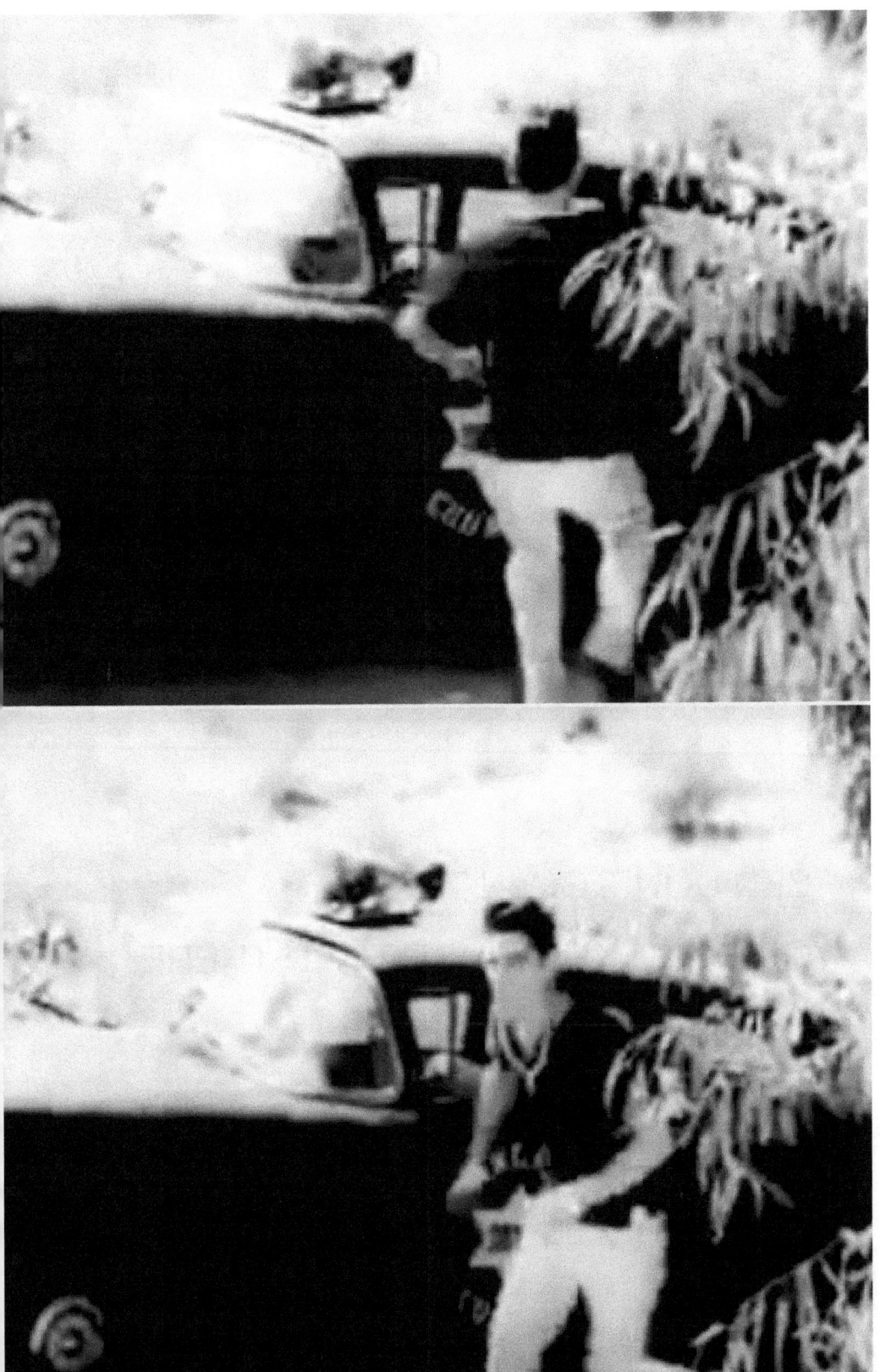

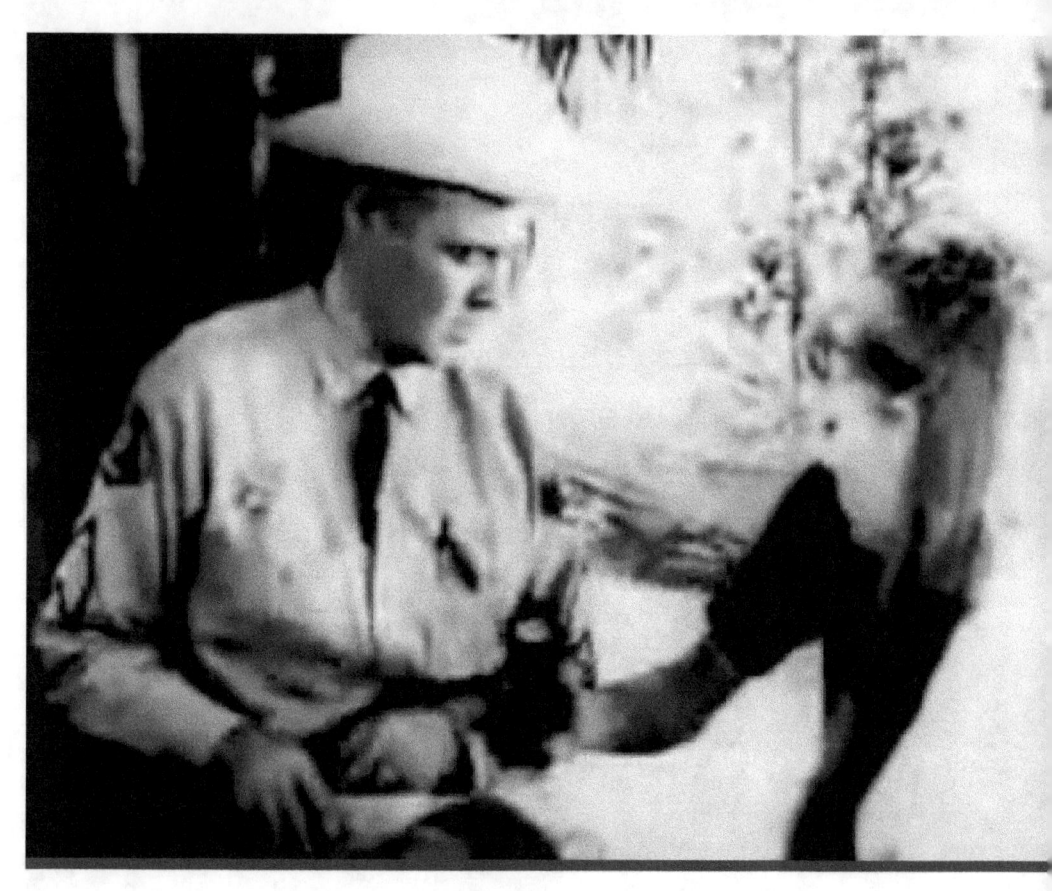

—BEN DON'T GO IN THERE.
YOU DONT KNOW WHAT'S IN THERE.

—I THINK I HEAR HIM MOVING INSIDE.
MAYBE HE'S HURT.

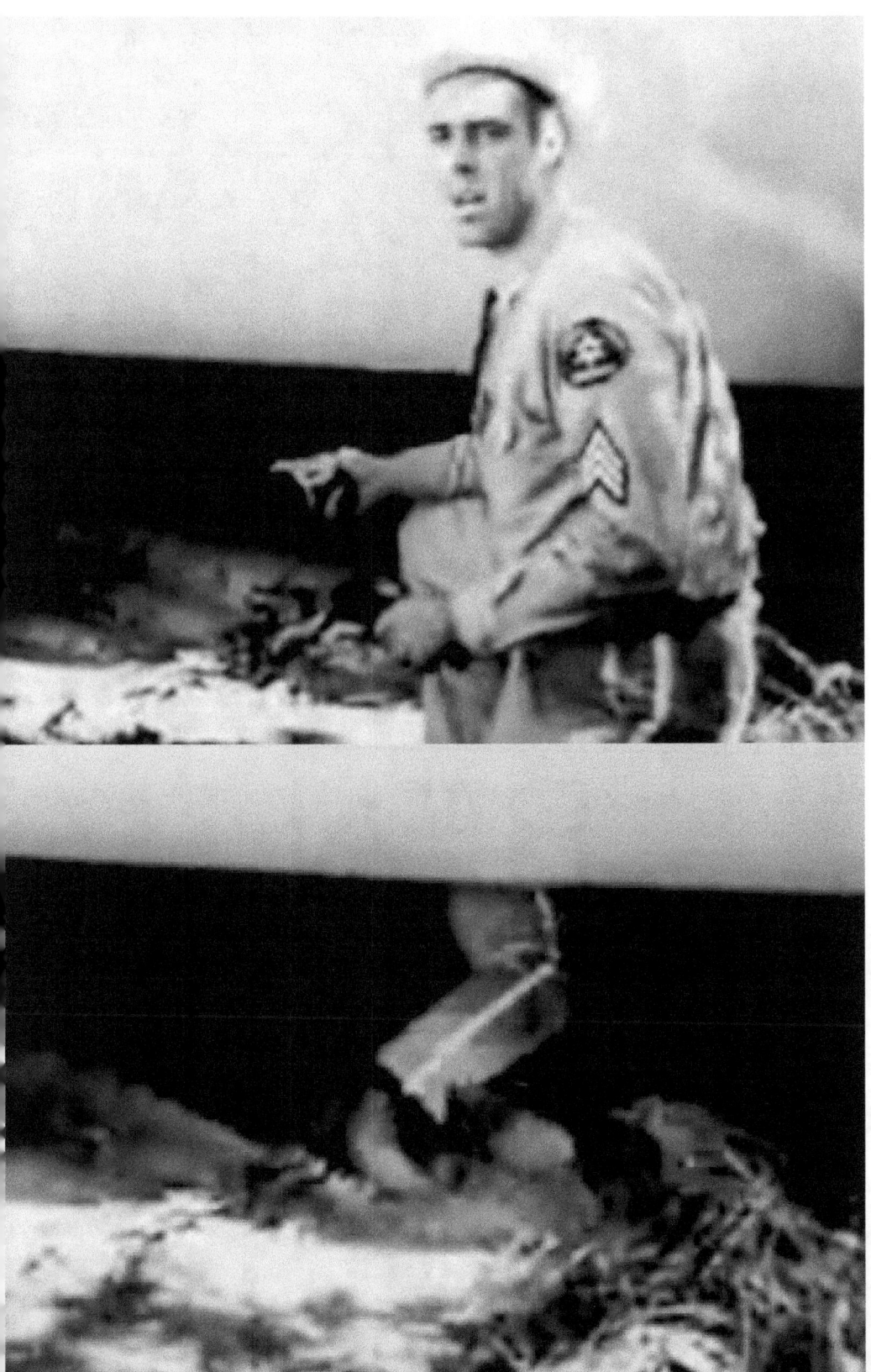

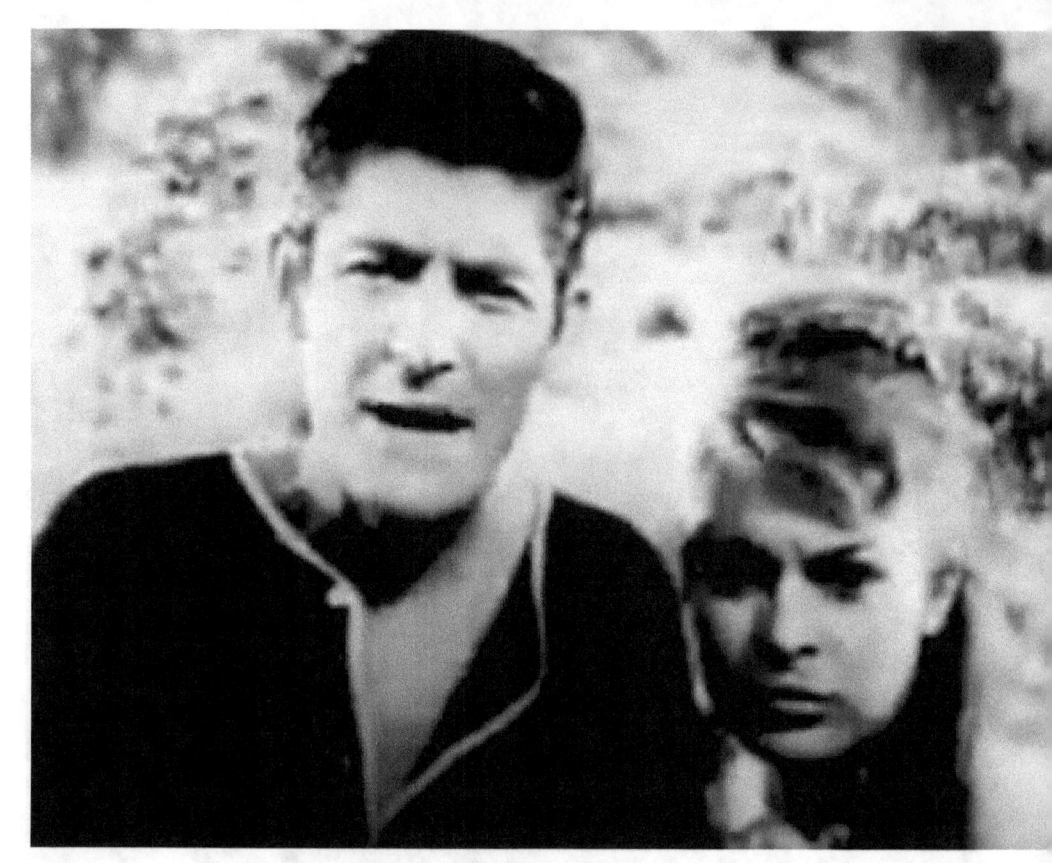

BEN
PLEASE
DON'T

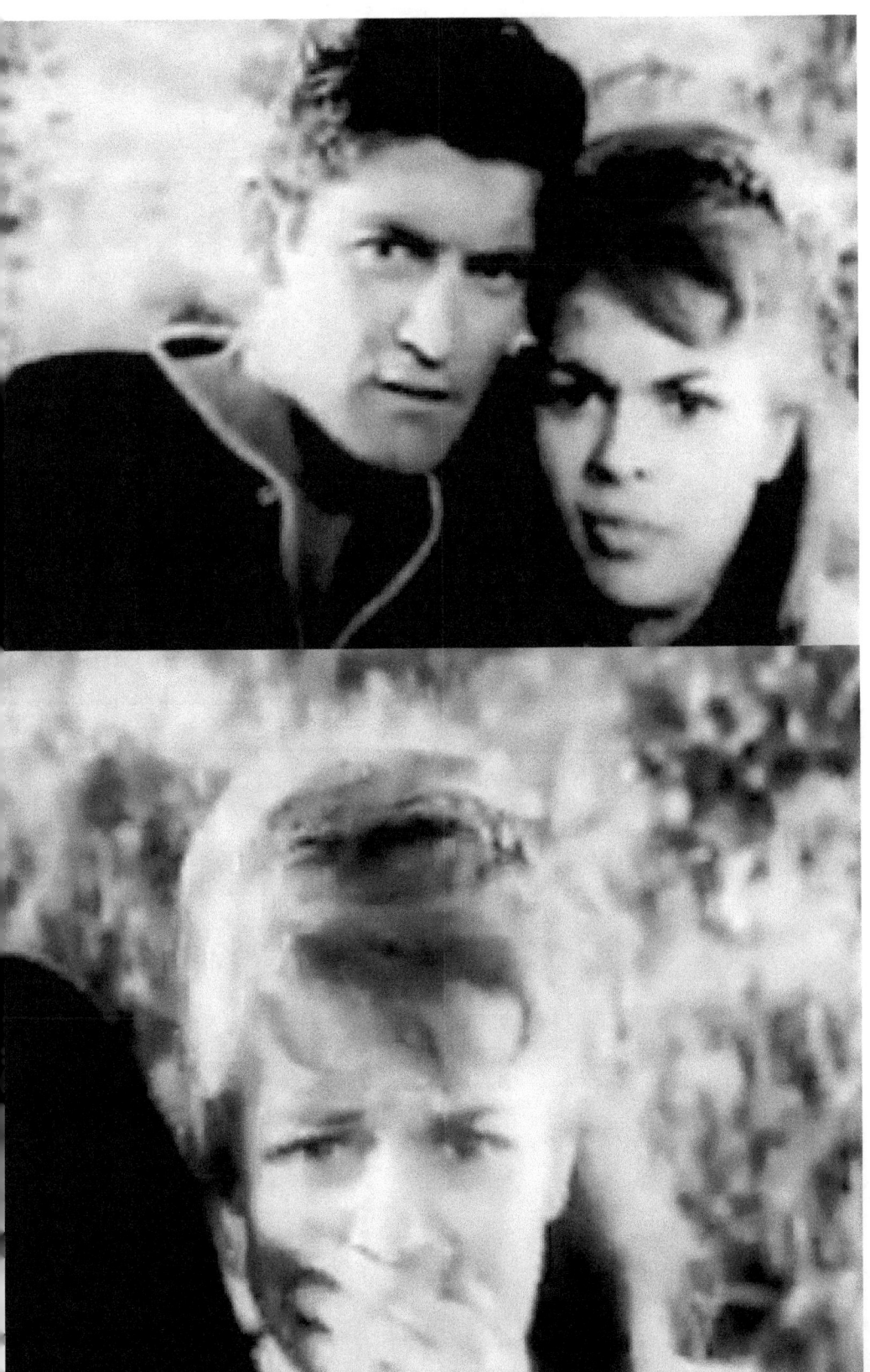

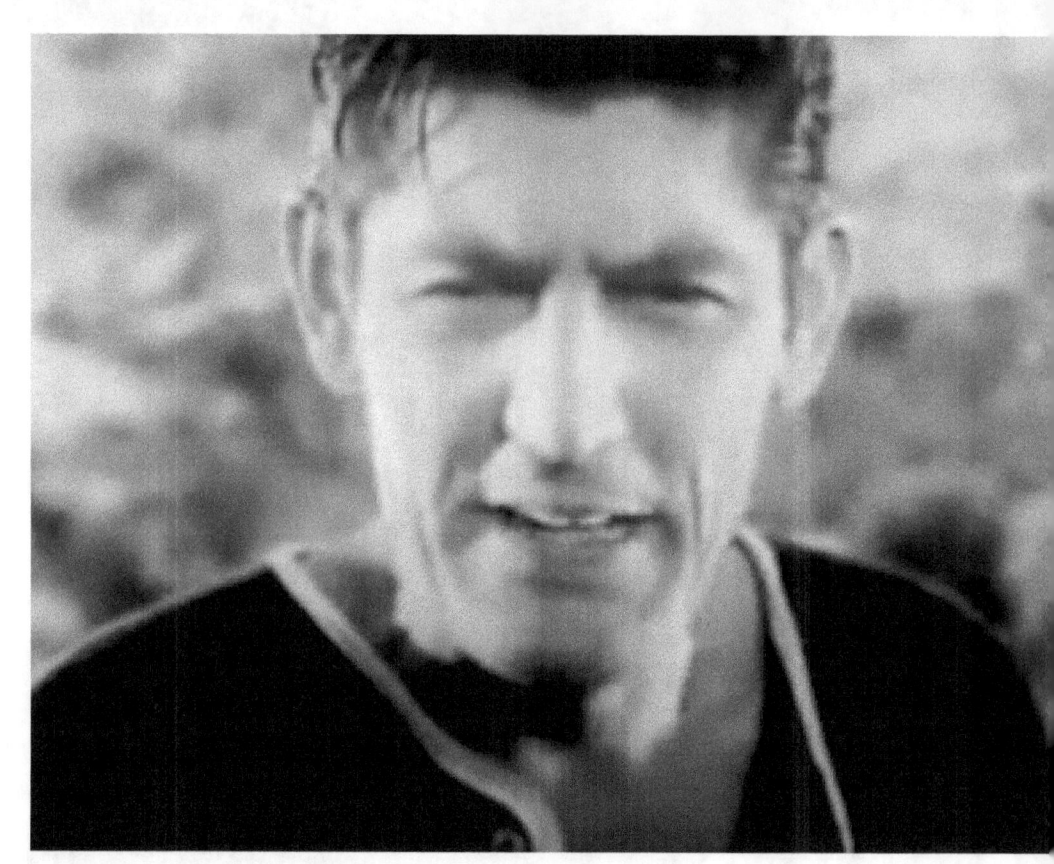

BEN

BEN

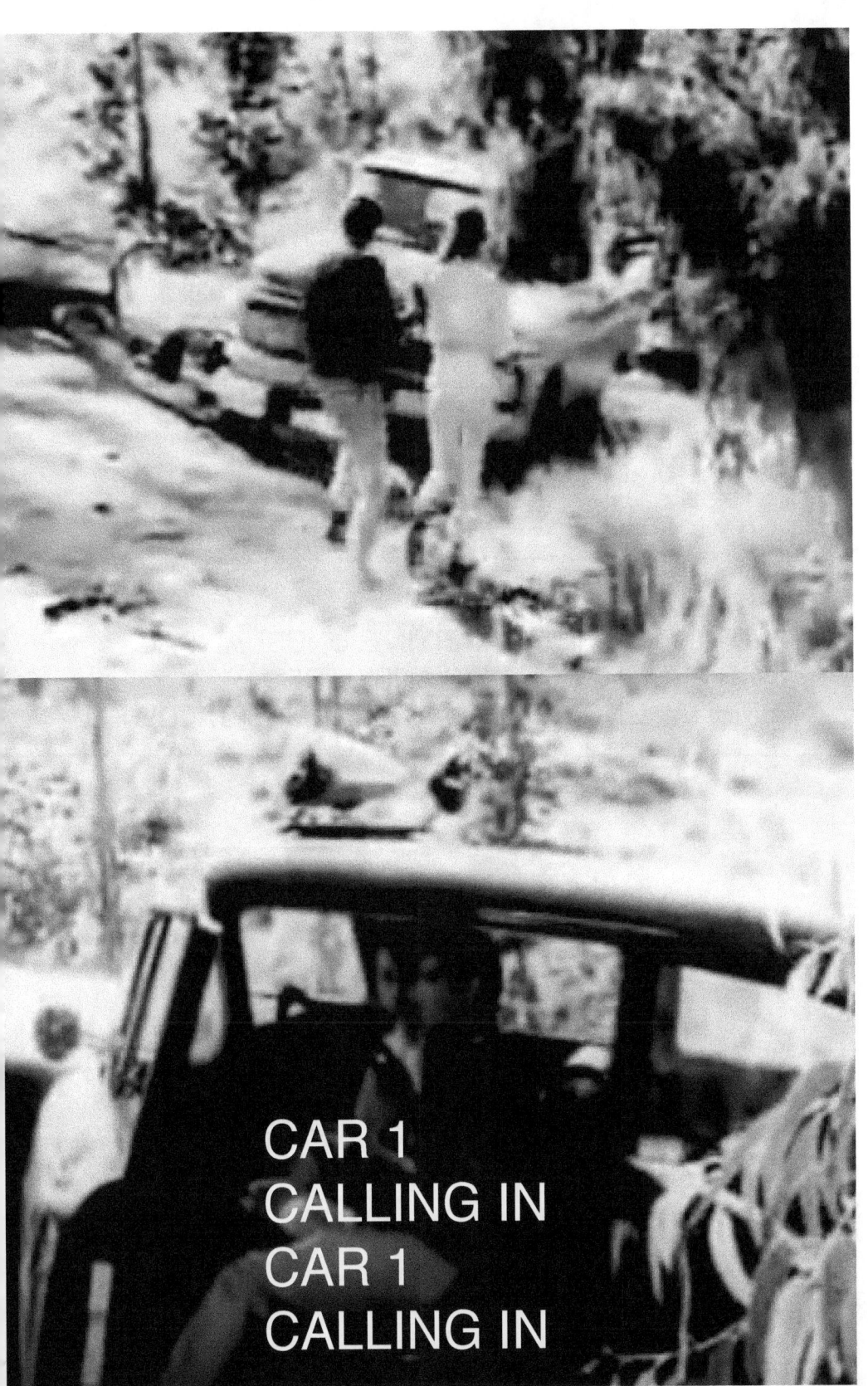

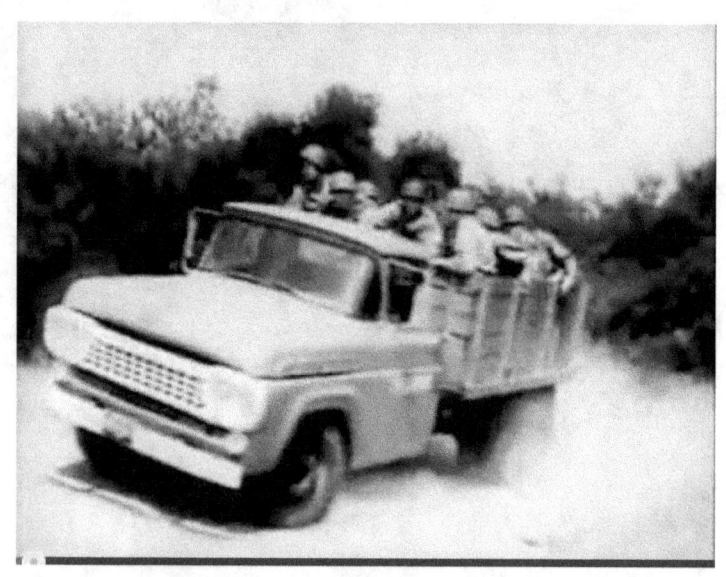

WITHIN THE HOUR MARTIN'S UNUSUAL CALL
FOR ASSISTANCE WAS ANSWERED BY A
SPECIAL UNIT LED BY A COL. JAMES CALDWELL

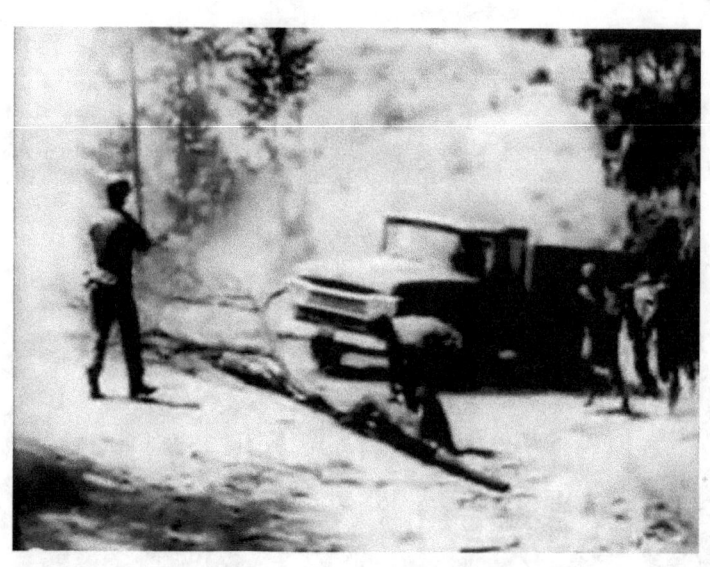

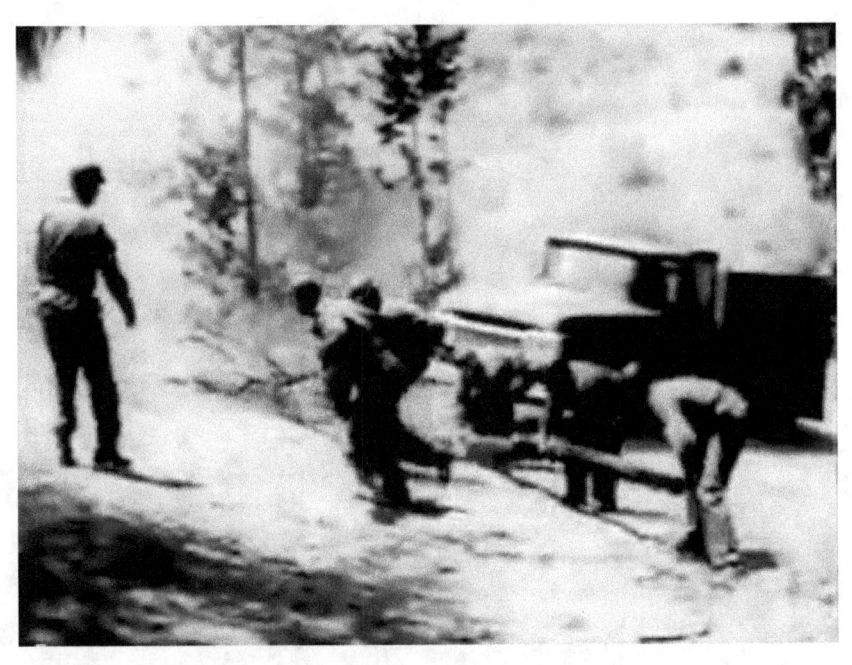

–LETS GET GOING
LETS GO
LETS GO
MOVE IT OVER
LETS GET GOING
LETS GO
ALL RIGHT
BACK ON THE TRUCK
LETS GET GOING
LETS GO

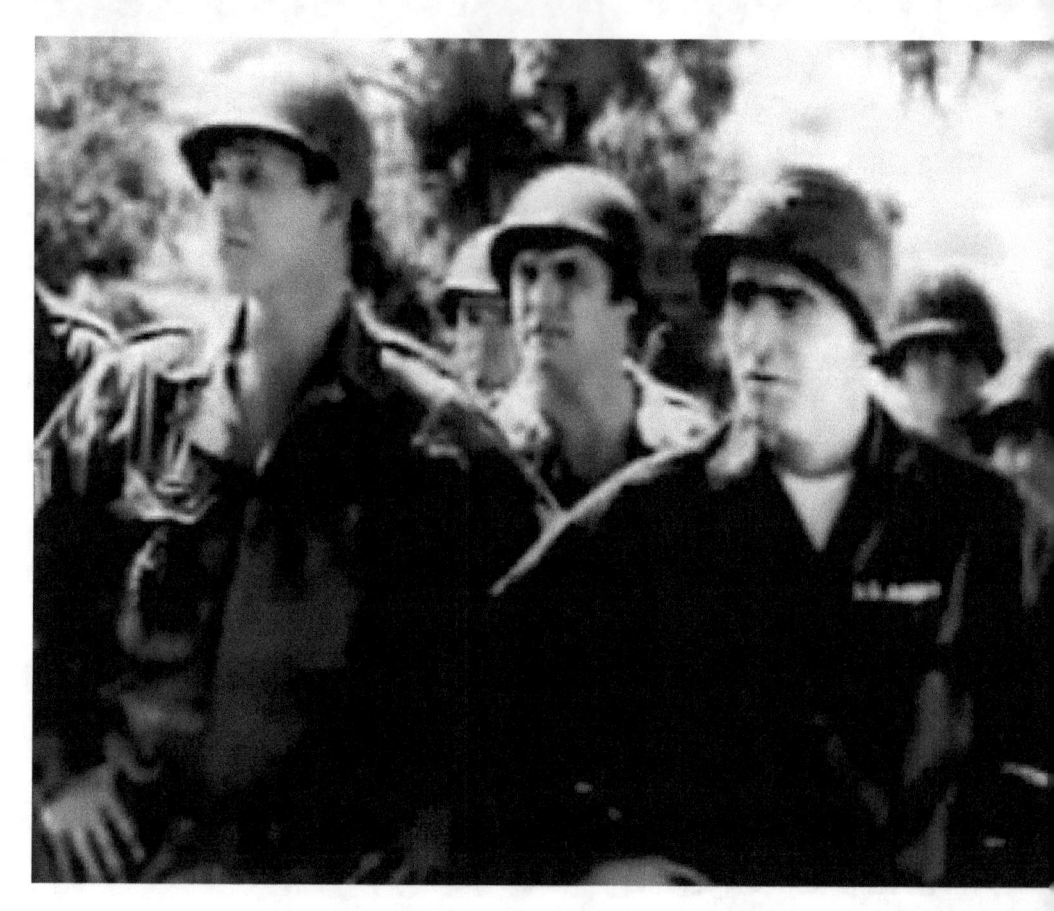

–SERGEANT TAKE ONE MAN

AND CHECK IT OUT

–YES SIR

–OK

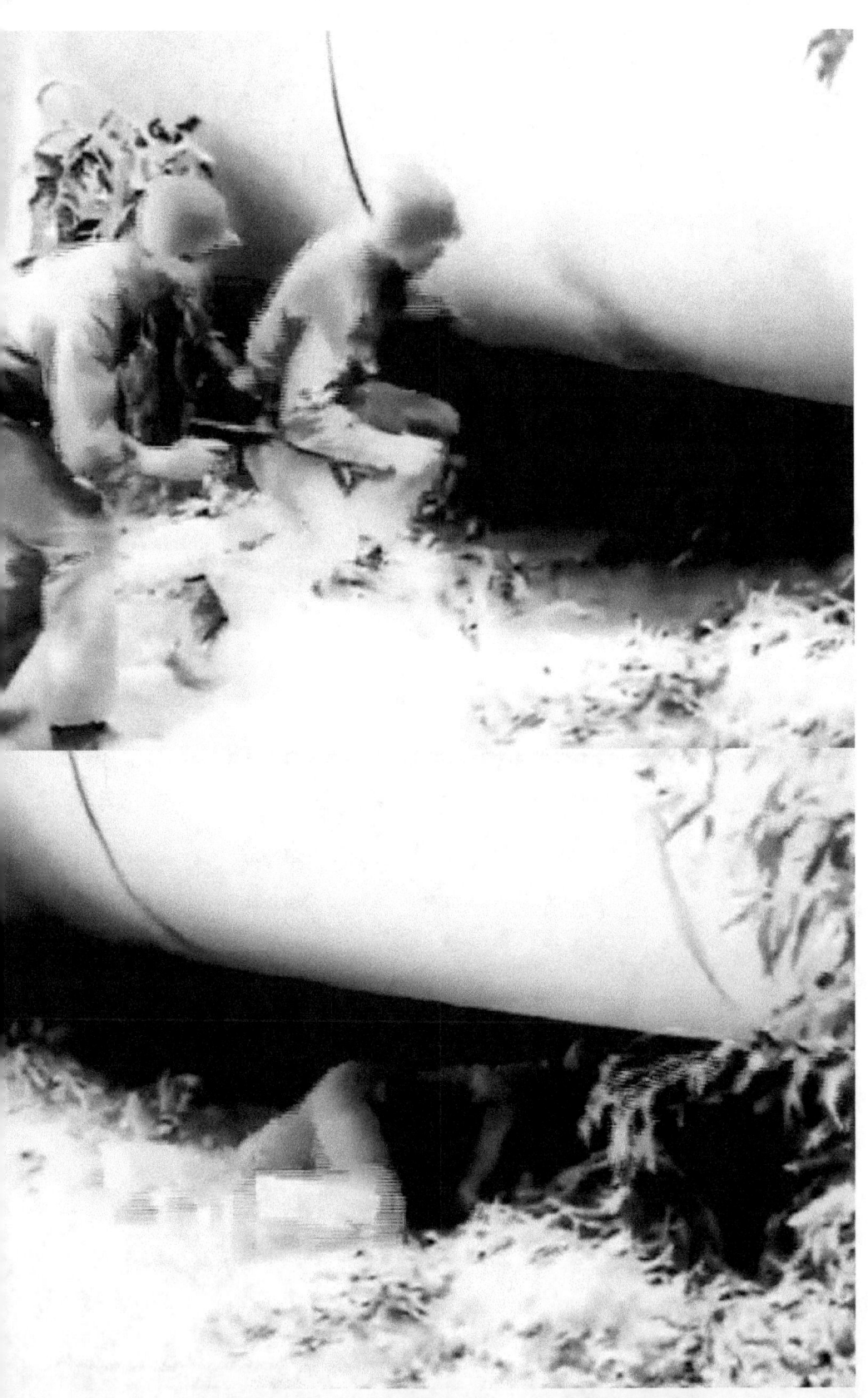

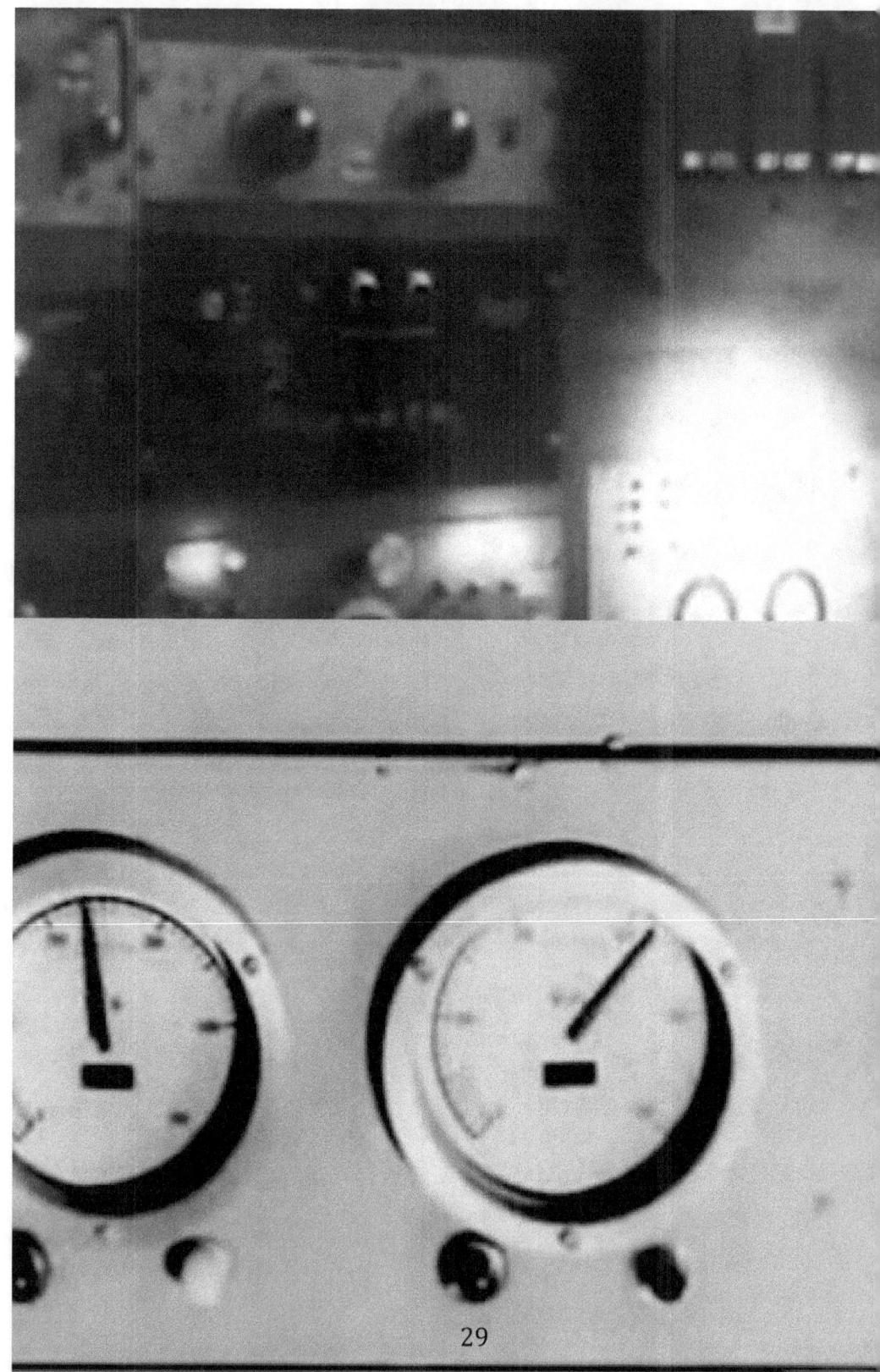

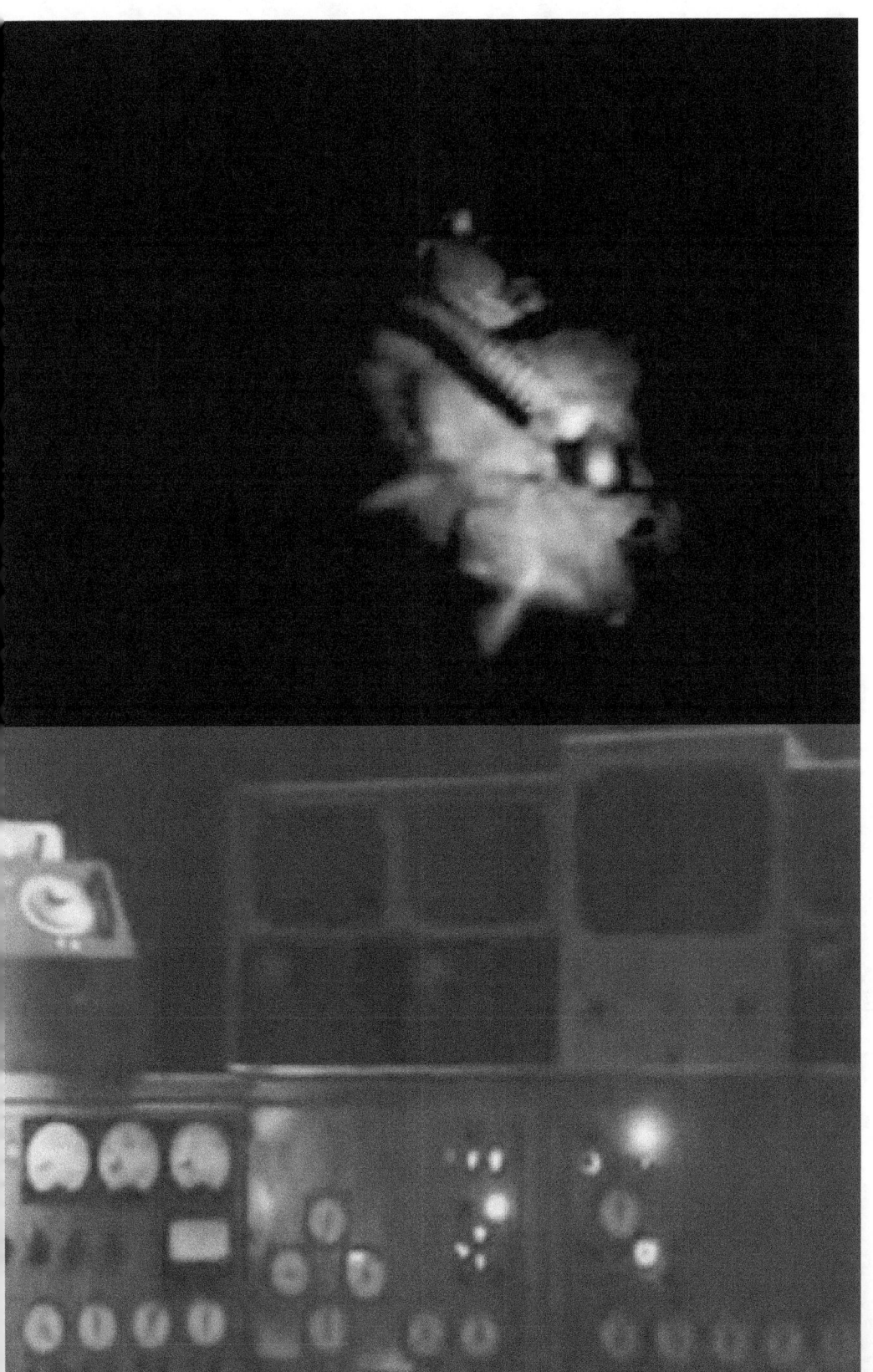

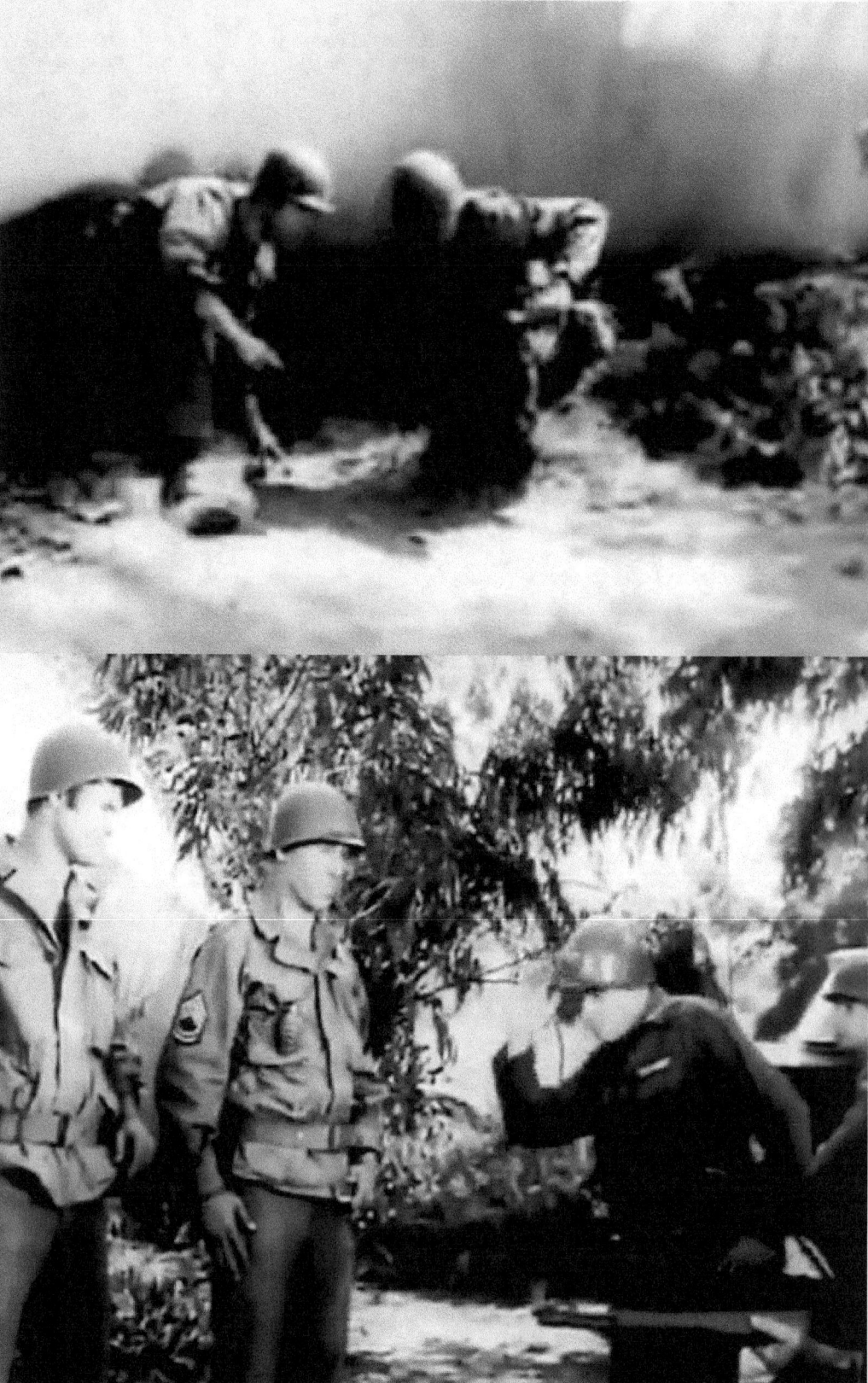

THE SERGEANT REPORTED
SEEING AN AMAZINGLY LARGE
CREATURE IN THE AFT SECTION
OF THE STRANGE CRAFT.
HE FURTHER REPORTED
THAT IT WAS SECURED BY A KIND
OF METAL HARNESS
BUT THE CREATURE COULD
STILL MOVE AROUND SOMEWHAT
AND FOR THAT REASON THEY
HAD NOT GOTTEN TOO CLOSE TO
IT. THERE WAS NO TRACE OF
EITHER BEN OR JEFF.
THE COL ORDERED CONTINUOUS
GUARD DUTY AROUND THE
SPACESHIP AND DECIDED TO SET
UP A TEMPORARY MILITARY
HEADQUARTERS AT THE
SHERIFF'S OFFICE IN TOWN.

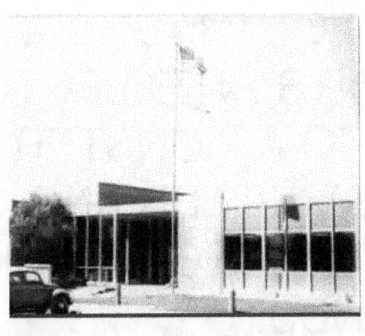

BY THE NEXT DAY COL. CALDWELL
HAD THE SITUATION WELL IN HAND
HE HAD CALLED WASHINGTON AND
RECEIVED HIS ORDERS FROM THE
HIGHEST POSSIBLE AUTHORITY. HE
WAS TO MAINTAIN TIGHT SECURITY
AND AWAIT THE ARRIVAL OF A DR.
BRADFORD WHO HAD BEEN ON
ASSIGNMENT AT THE JODRELL
RADIO BANK OBSERVATORY IN
ENGLAND. UPON ARRIVAL,
BRADFORD WAS TO TAKE
COMPLETE CHARGE OF THE
SITUATION. HE WAS THE WORLDS
LEADING AUTHORITY ON SPACE
EMISSIONS AND HAD WORKED OUT
A SERIES OF SYSTEMS THAT MIGHT
LEAD TO COMMUNICATION WITH
OTHER FORMS OF LIFE WHEN, AS,
AND IF THEY WERE CONTACTED.
MARTIN WAS OUTRAGED AT THE
GOVERNMENTS INTELLECTUAL
APPROACH TO A MONSTER THAT
HAD ALREADY KILLED AND CAUSED
THE DISAPPEARANCE OF HIS TWO
CLOSE FRIENDS.

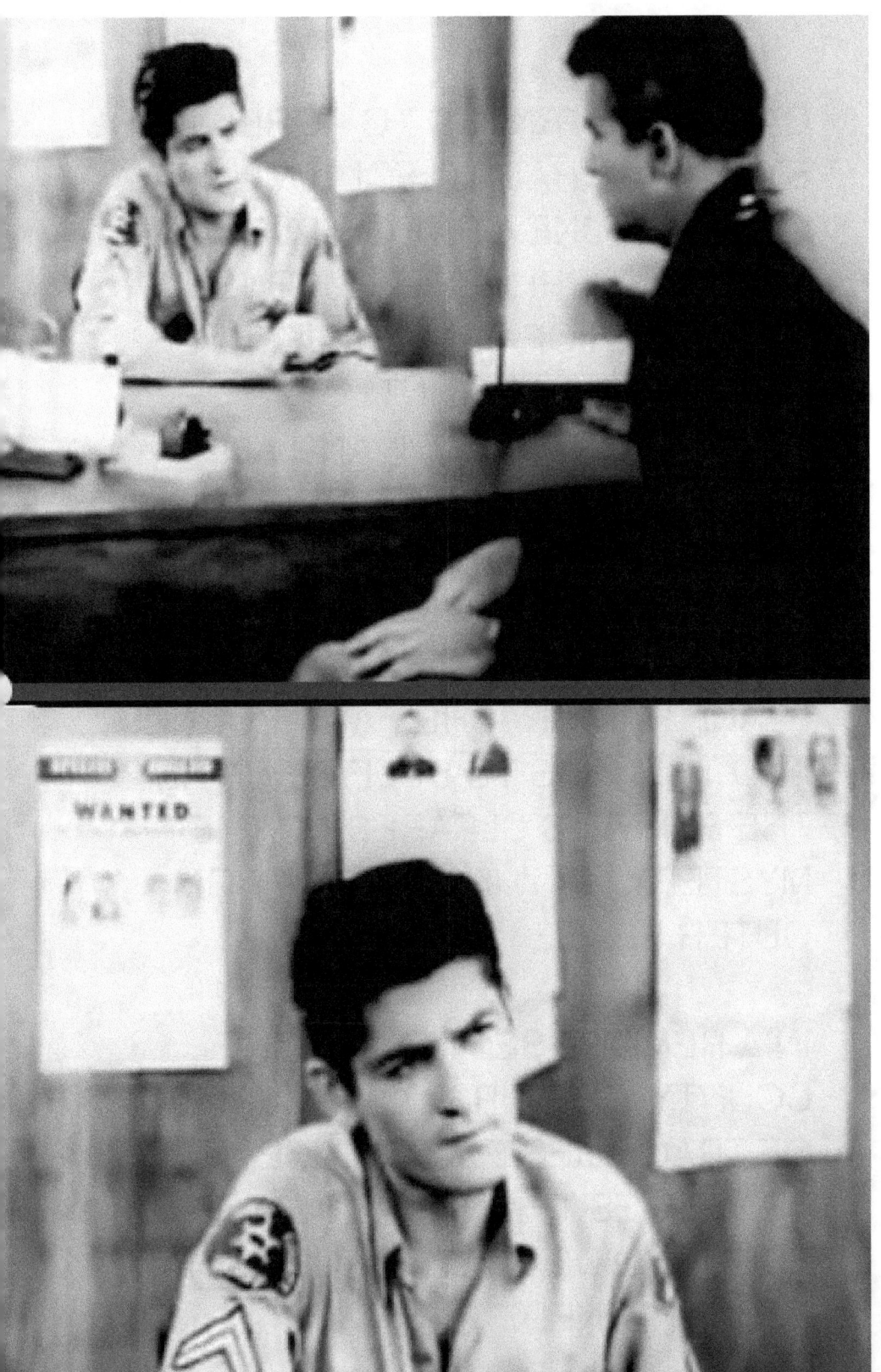

CALDWELL TENDED TO AGREE BUT
STATED HE HAD TO FOLLOW HIS
ORDERS. ONE OF THOSE ORDERS
WAS TO SUPPRESS THE NEWS OF
THE DEATH OF BEN AND JEFF.
MARTIN WAS APPOINTED
TEMPORARY SHERIFF AND ALL
NEWS FOR PUBLIC CONSUMPTION
WAS TO EMANATE FROM HIS
OFFICE. THE AIR AUTHORITY
ISSUED A COVER UP STORY THAT A
PLANE HAD CRASHED AND BURNED
AND THIS WAS TO SUFFICE UNTIL
THE EXPERTS CLEARED UP THE
MYSTERY OF THE VISITOR FROM
OUTER SPACE.

IN A REMOTE SECTION OF THE
COUNTY, THE FIRST OF A SERIES
OF TRAGEDIES TOOK PLACE,
TRAGEDIES THAT WOULD HAVE
BEEN AVOIDED IF THE PUBLIC HAD
BEEN WARNED.

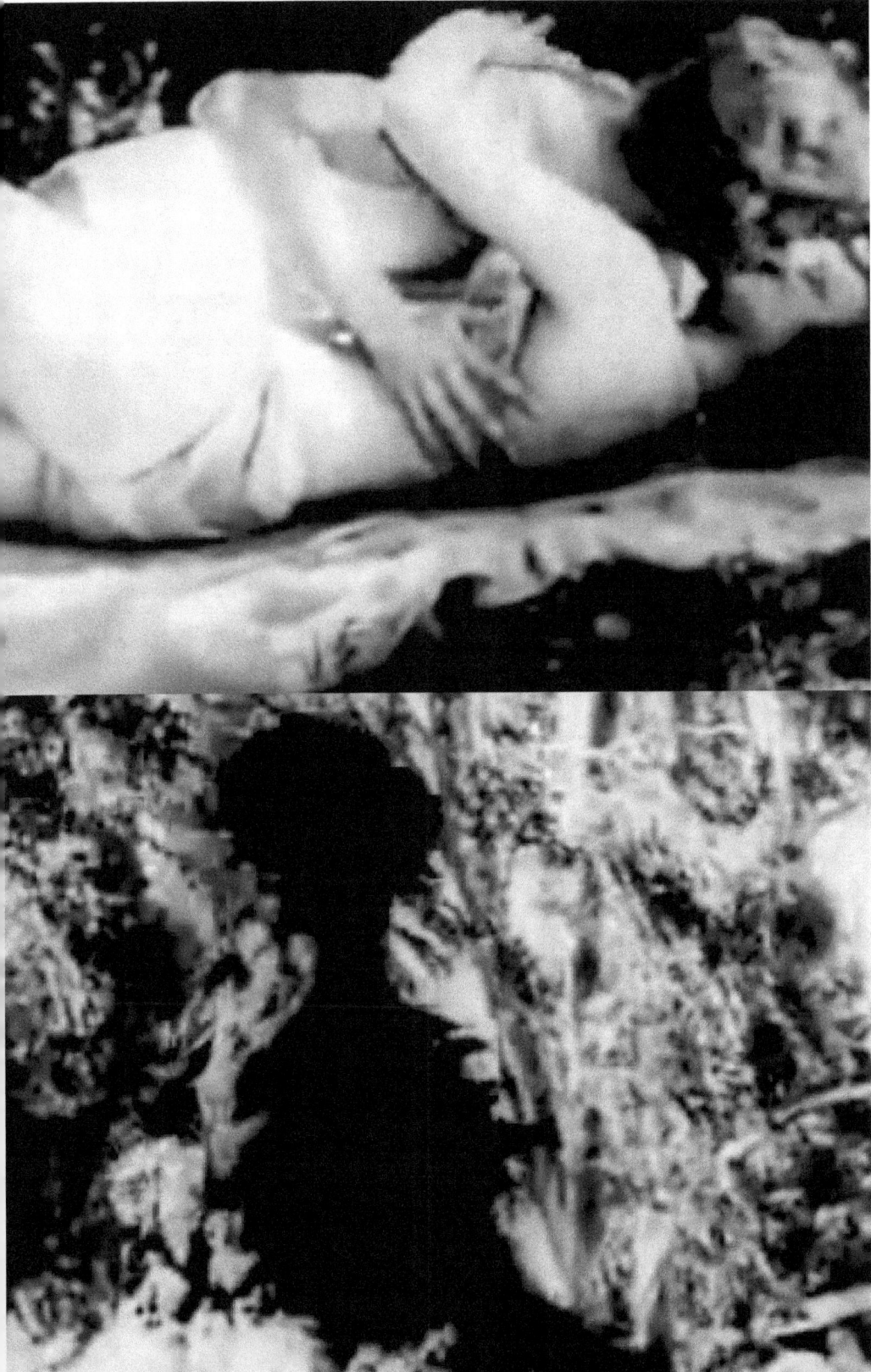

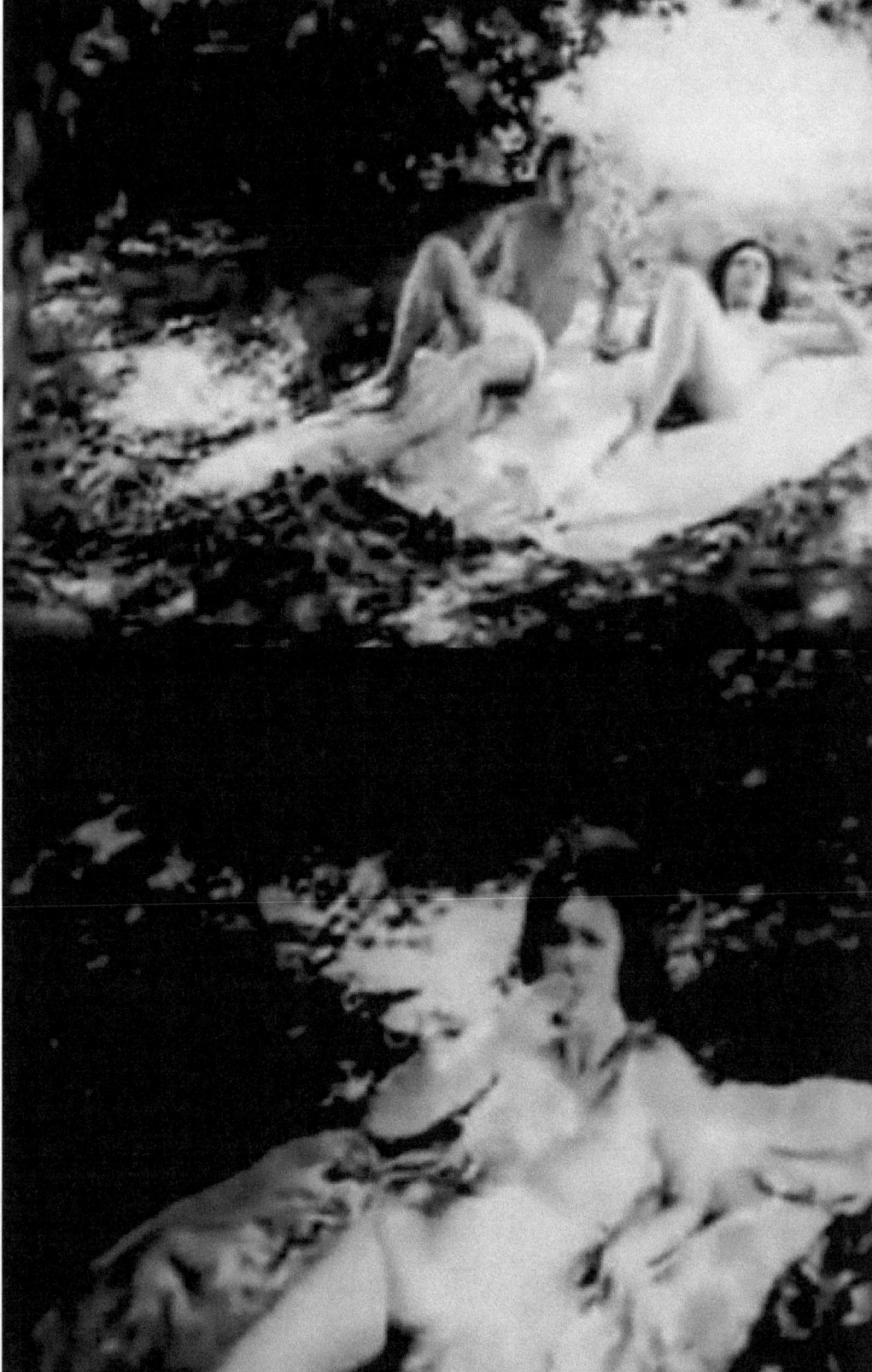

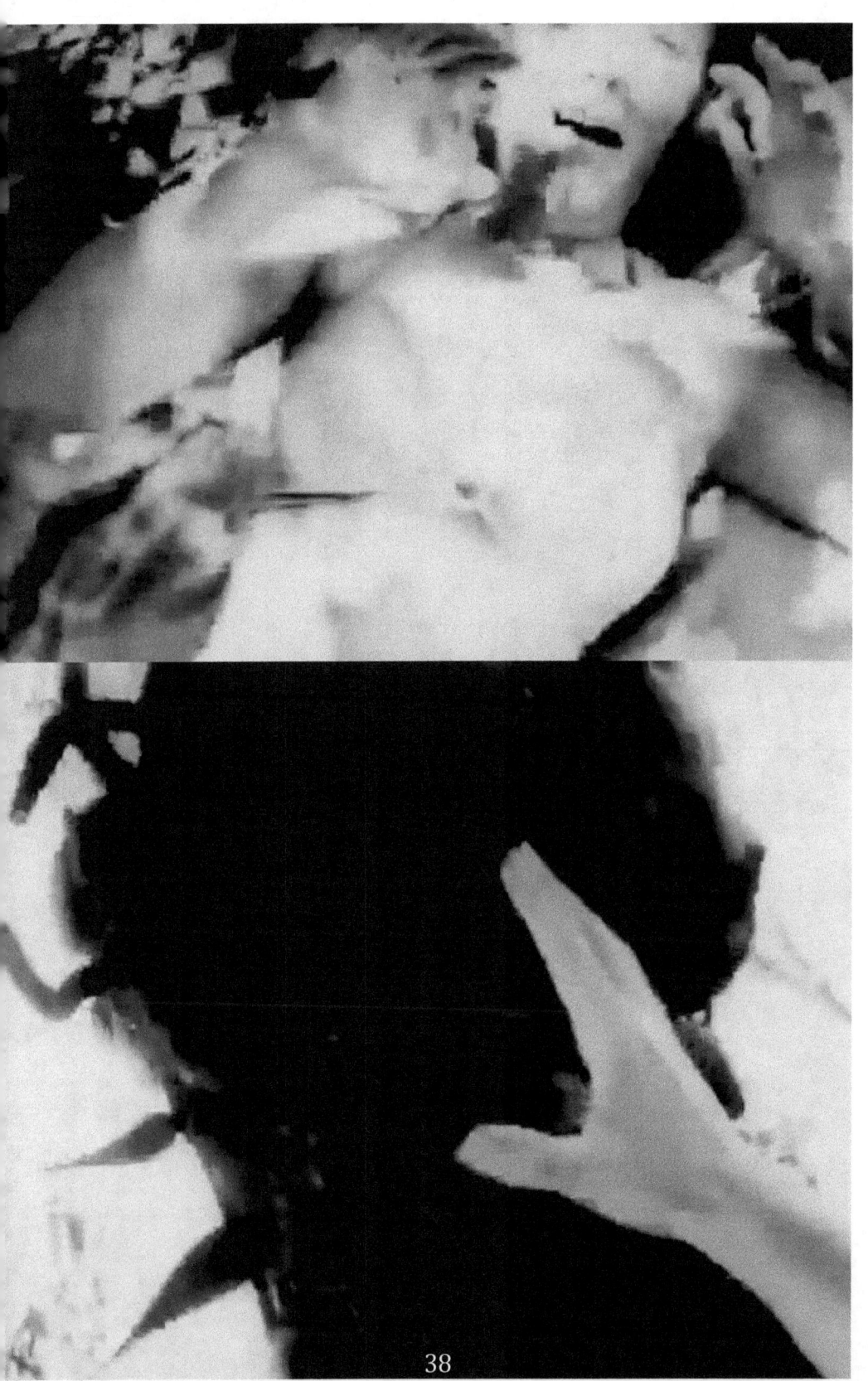

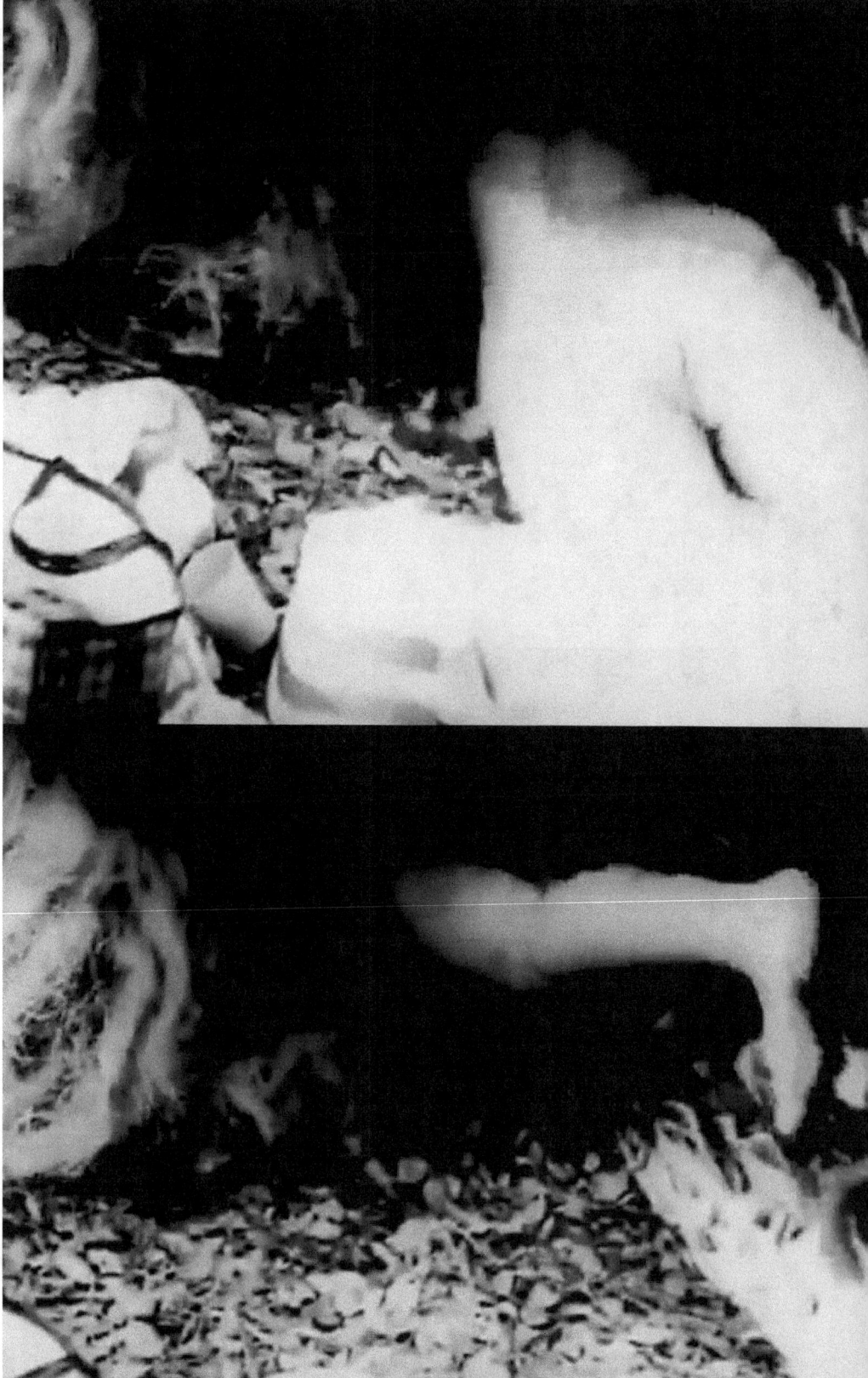

LATER THAT DAY, WHILE THEY
WERE AWAITING THE ARRIVAL OF
DR. BRADFORD, MARTIN
INSTRUCTED BARNEY, ON ADVICE
FROM COL. CALDWELL, TO PLANT IN
THE LOCAL PAPERS THE NEWS
THAT BEN AND JEFF HAD TAKEN
OFF ON A FISHING TRIP TO BRITISH
COLUMBIA.
THE COL. HAD IMPRESSED THE
BEREAVED FAMILIES WITH THE
NECESSITY OF MAINTAINING
SECRECY AND THESE BRAVE
RELATIVES HAD AGREED.

DESPITE BRETT'S INQUIRIES ABOUT
WHAT MARTIN HAD SEEN IN THE
SPACECRAFT, HE AVOIDED
SPECIFIC DETAILS FOR FEAR OF
DISTURBING HER MORE THAN SHE
WAS. IF THE TRUTH WERE KNOWN,
MARTIN WAS MORE THAN A LITTLE
DISTURBED HIMSELF.

SHERIFF BEN, RANGER JEFF PETERS R&R FISH EXPEDITION TO B.C

(ANGEL COUNTY) Sheriff Ben and County Ranger Jeff Peters have decided its time take their long planned extended fishing trip to British Columbia. "Jeff and I have some chilly ones coming to us and we're 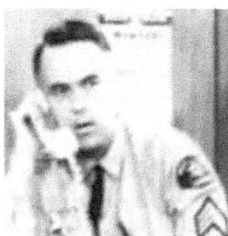 going to stay long enough to bring home a load of lunkers, Sheriff Ben said. Ben's nephew Senior Deputy Martin Gordon will take the helm of law enforcement duties in quiet peaceful Angel County during Sheriff Ben's absence and will be assisted by Junior Deputy Barney to the extent Barney's pompadour (+3") is not disturbed. Barney is still dating all the girls in town and is said to resent Martin's wife Brett for inhibiting the extent of his "pal arounds" with Acting Temporary Sheriff Martin. Residents of Angel County should avoid campfires, fishing, hanging laundry, lizard chasing, or "make-out" sessions during Ranger Jeff Peter's absence and to consider alternative indoor recreational activities such as the Afternoon Shindig (Mon-Fri 1-4 P.M.) at the Community Dance Hall. According to an unnamed source, rumors that Ranger Jeff's hat is missing are unfounded and false Story cont. p. 2

SHORTLY THEREAFTER DR. BRADFORD
ARRIVED. HE WAS A MUCH YOUNGER MAN
THAN ONE WOULD IMAGINE HIM TO BE.

–MARTIN I'D LIKE YOU TO MEET DR.
BRADFORD
–I'VE HEARD A LOT ABOUT YOU FROM THE
COL.
–NOTHING BAD I TRUST
–MARTIN AND HIS WIFE WERE IN THE
ORIGINAL PARTY THAT FOUND THE FALLEN
CRAFT.
–I'M SORRY ABOUT YOUR UNCLE.
TOUGH BREAK.
I HOPE YOU'RE FEELING BETTER
–YES A FEW HOURS OF SLEEP DID A WORLD
OF GOOD
BRADFORD THANKED THE COL FOR HIS
ASSISTANCE AND THEN ASKED TO SPEAK TO
MARTIN. BRADFORD QUESTIONED MARTIN
ABOUT EVERYTHING THAT HAD TRANSPIRED.
MARTIN DID HIS BEST TO RECALL
EVERYTHING IN PRECISE DETAIL, BUT REALLY
DIDN'T HAVE MUCH FOR HIM. THE TWO
SOLDIERS THAT HAD ENTERED THE ROCKET
EARLIER HAD BEEN SUMMONED AND
BRADFORD HOPED TO LEARN MORE FROM
THEM. THE DR. HIMSELF WOULD NOT ENTER
THE ROCKET UNTIL THE ARRIVAL OF CERTAIN
EQUIPMENT. FROM HIS DISCUSSION IT WAS
APPARENT THE DR. CONSIDERED THE
SITUATION A MAGNIFICENT OPPORTUNITY
FOR MANKIND. HE FELT THAT IF HE COULD

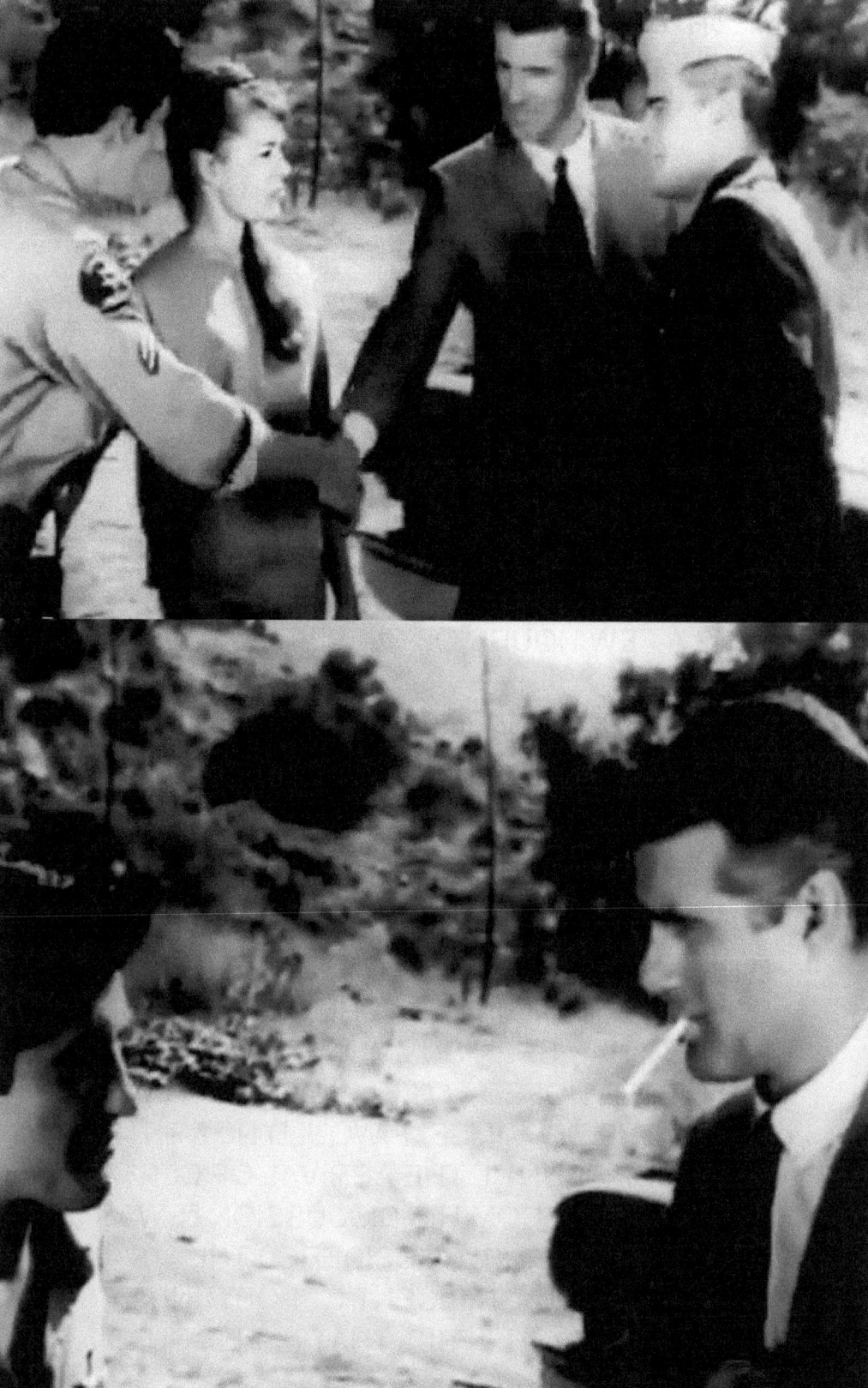

MIGHT BE POSSIBLE TO
ADVANCE HUMAN KNOWLEDGE
BY YEARS OR EVEN
CENTURIES. THE SPACESHIP
ALONE SIGNALED AN
INTELLECTUAL DEVELOPMENT
FAR IN ADVANCE OF ANYTHING
ON EARTH. WHEN MARTIN
ASKED HIM HOW HE INTENDED
TO PROTECT HIMSELF FROM
THE CREATURE, BRADFORD
SAID NOT TO WORRY. HE
HADN'T COME HERE TO BE
VICTIMIZED BY EITHER HIS OWN
OR THE CREATURE'S FEAR.

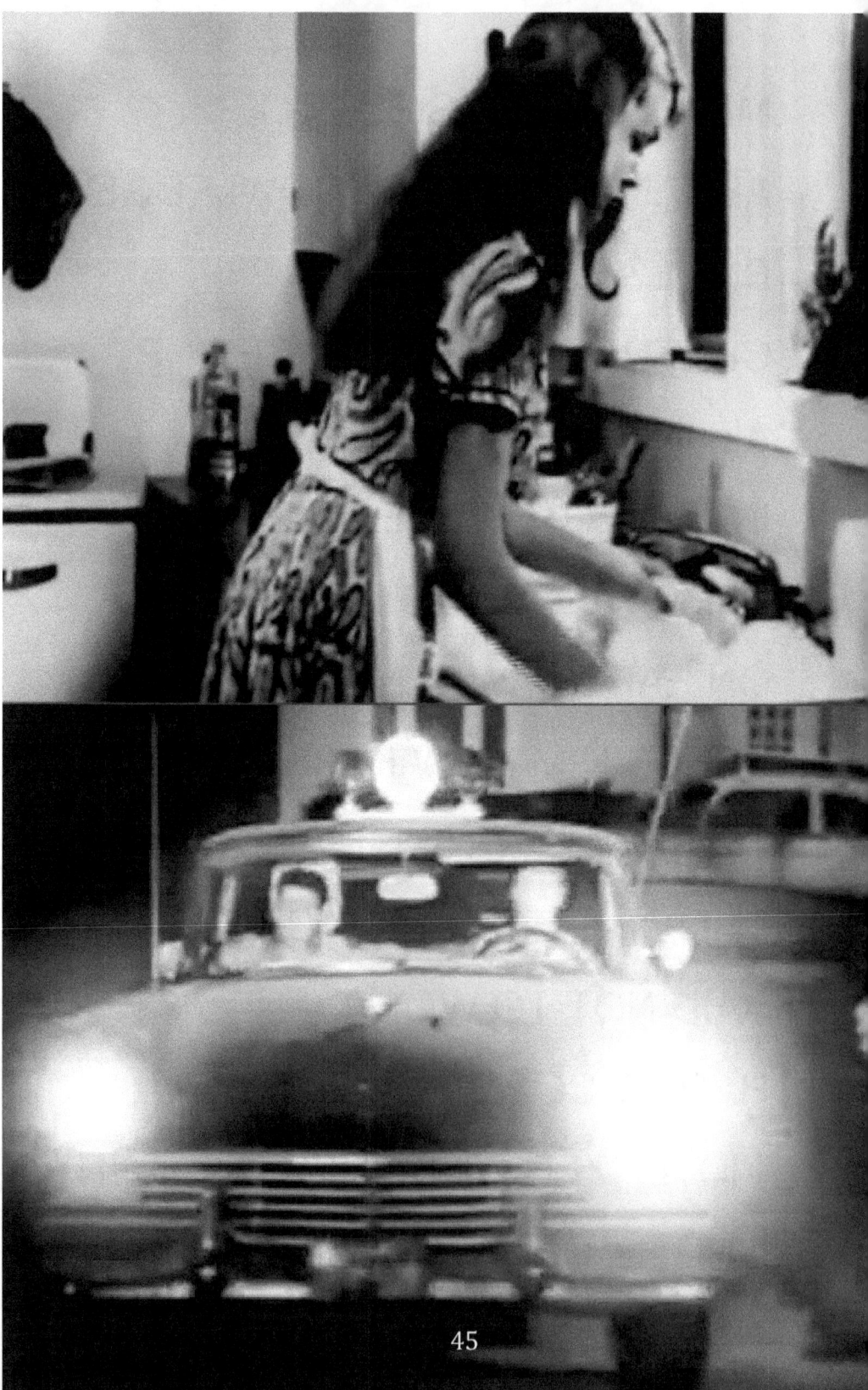

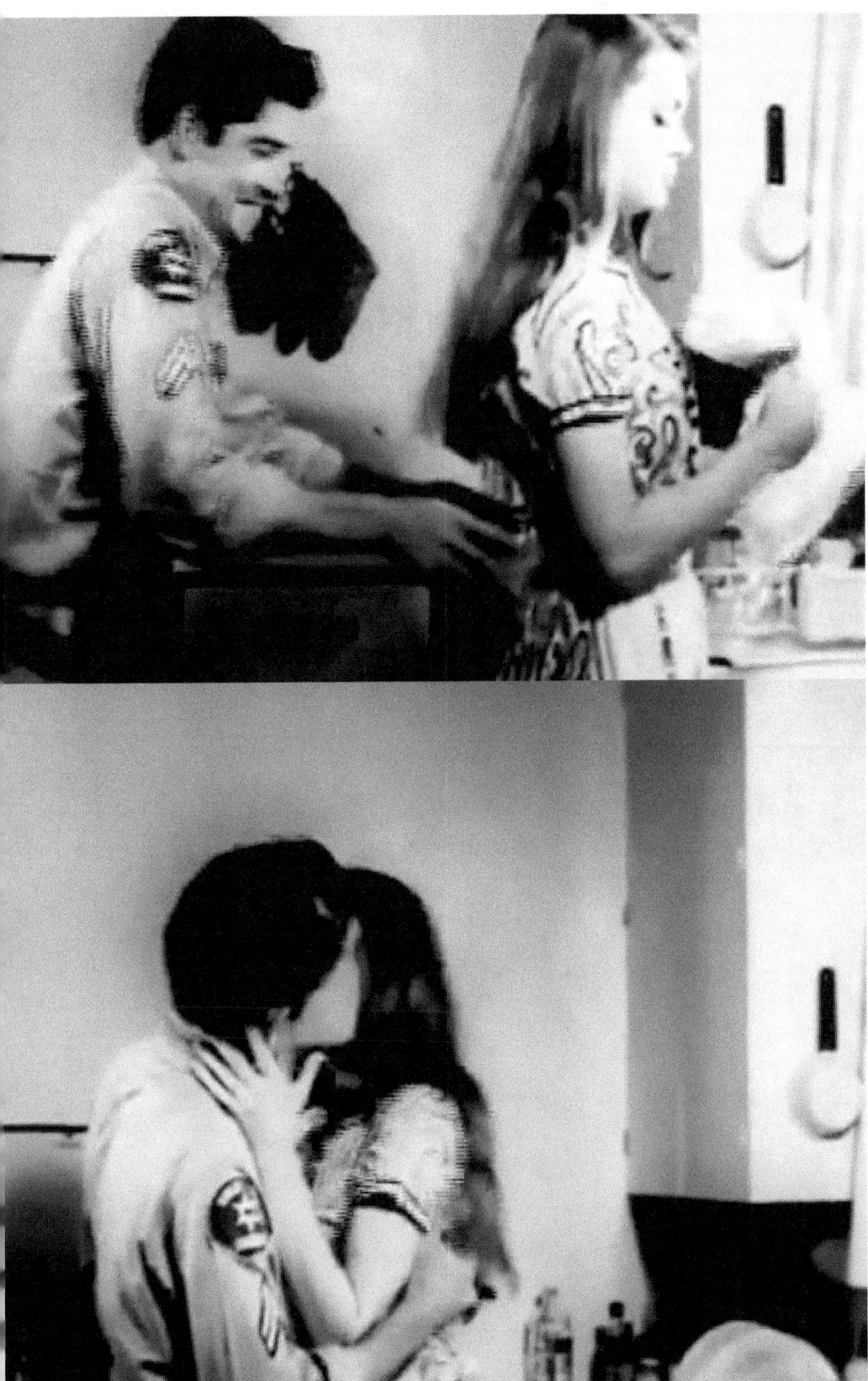

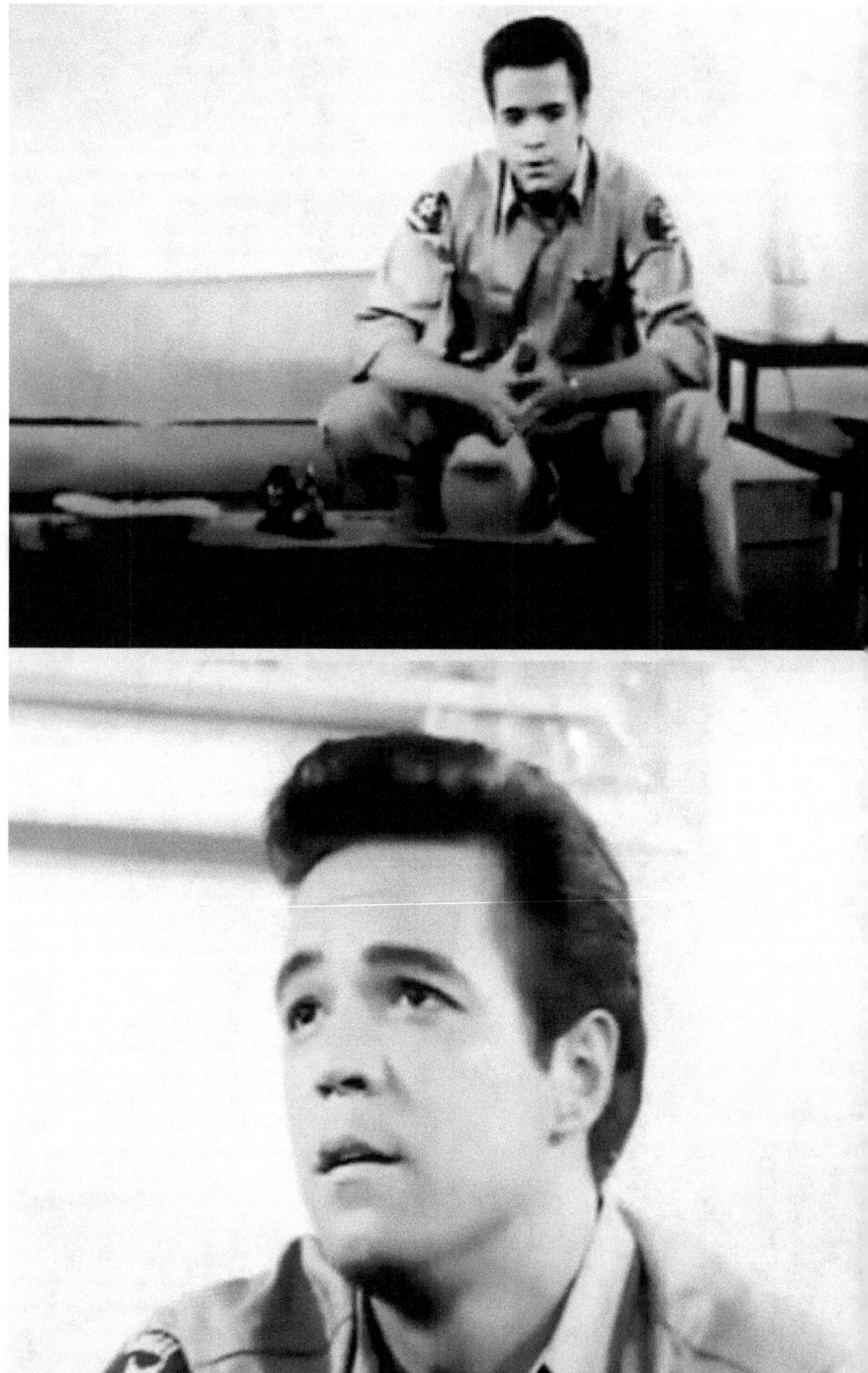

-OH HI BARNEY, WE'LL BE RIGHT OUT.

-THATS ALL RIGHT JUST TAKE YOUR TIME.

-I DIDN'T KNW WE HAD COMPANY, LOOK AT ME I'M A MESS.

-DON'T BE IMPOLITE, GO GET THE DRINKS

-NOW YOU'RE TALKING HONEY

-WHAT DO YOU HAVE BARNEY?

-HOW ABOUT A BOURBON AND SEVEN.

-COMING UP.

-WOULD YOU GET THE SEVEN HONEY.

-BARNEY YOU SHOULD TRY MARRIAGE. IT WOULD DO WONDERS FOR YOU.

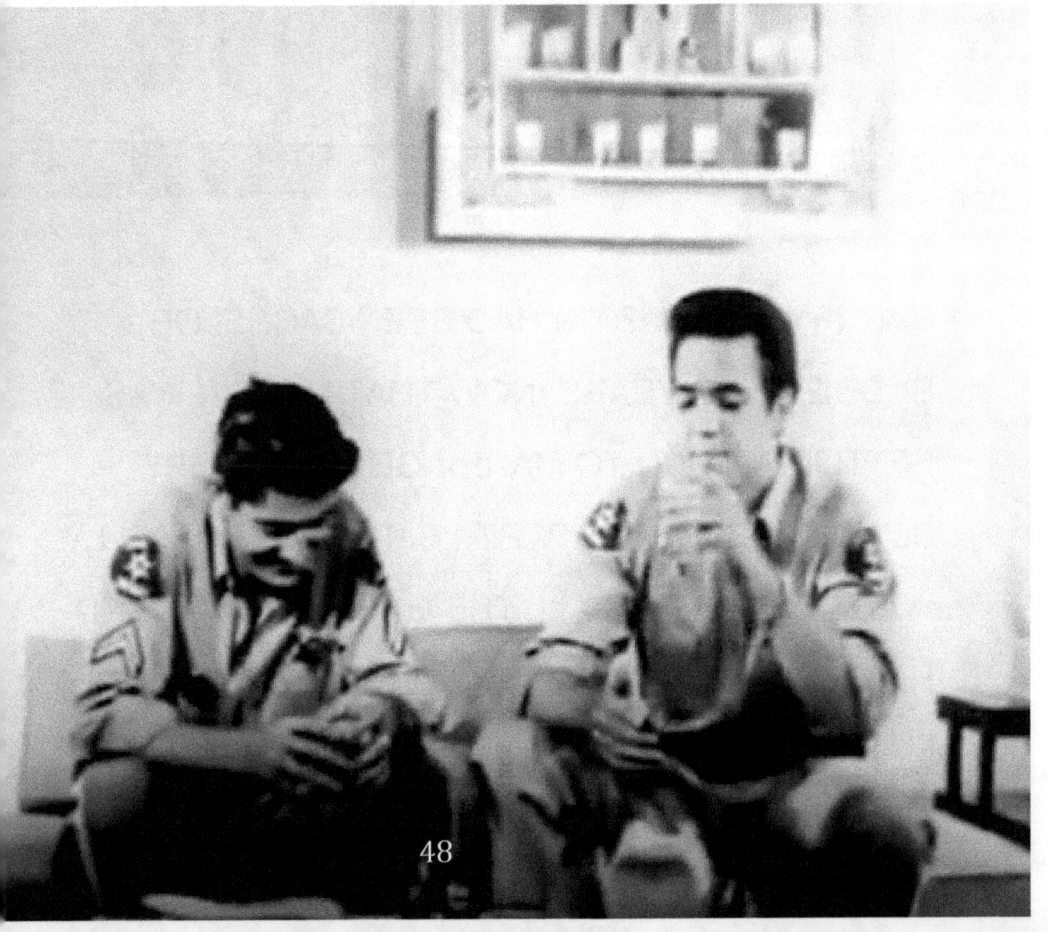

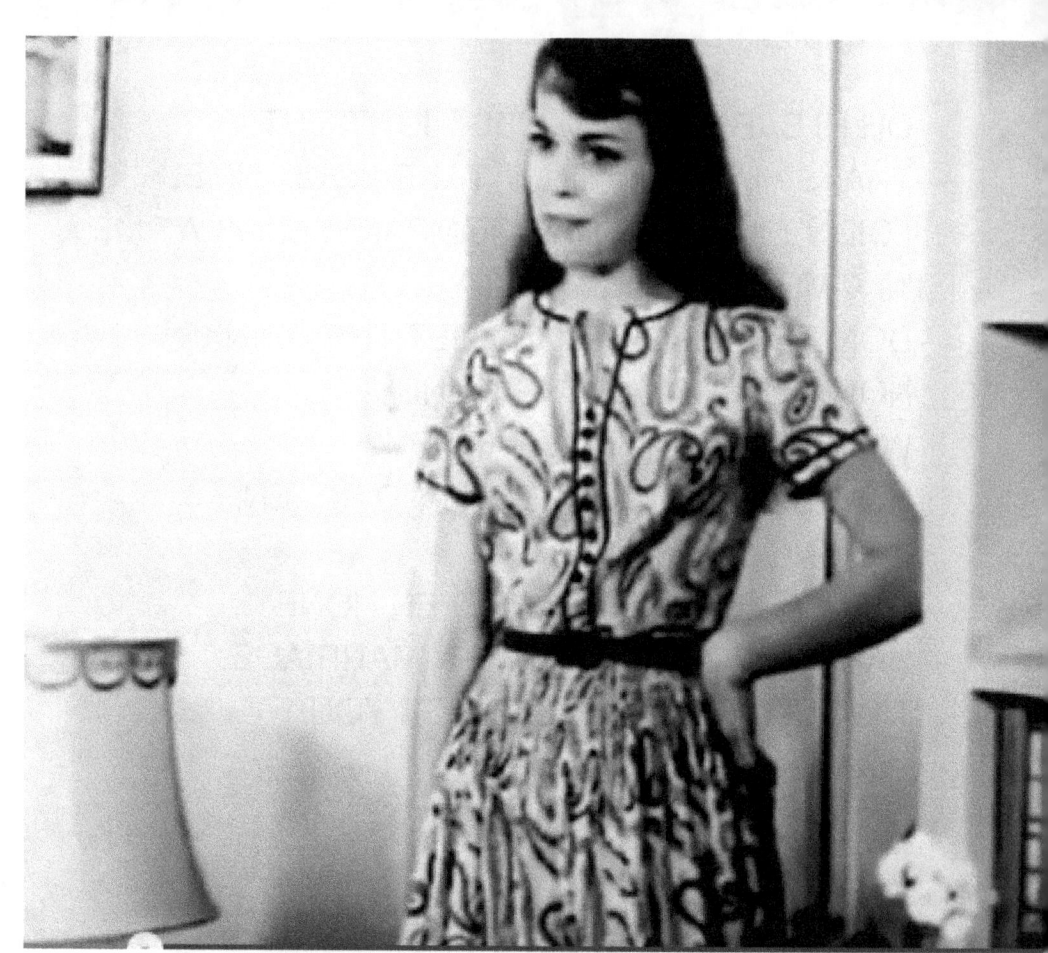

BARNEY AND MARTIN HAD BEEN BACHELOR
BUDDIES FOR YEARS. NOW THAT MARTIN WAS
SETTLING DOWN TO MARRIAGE, THEY WERE
SLOWLY DRIFTING APART. BARNEY, NATURALLY,
WAS STILL DATING ALL THE GIRLS IN TOWN AND
HE COULDN'T UNDERSTAND WHY BRETT AND
MARTIN DIDN'T PAL AROUND WITH HIM MORE
THAN THEY DID.

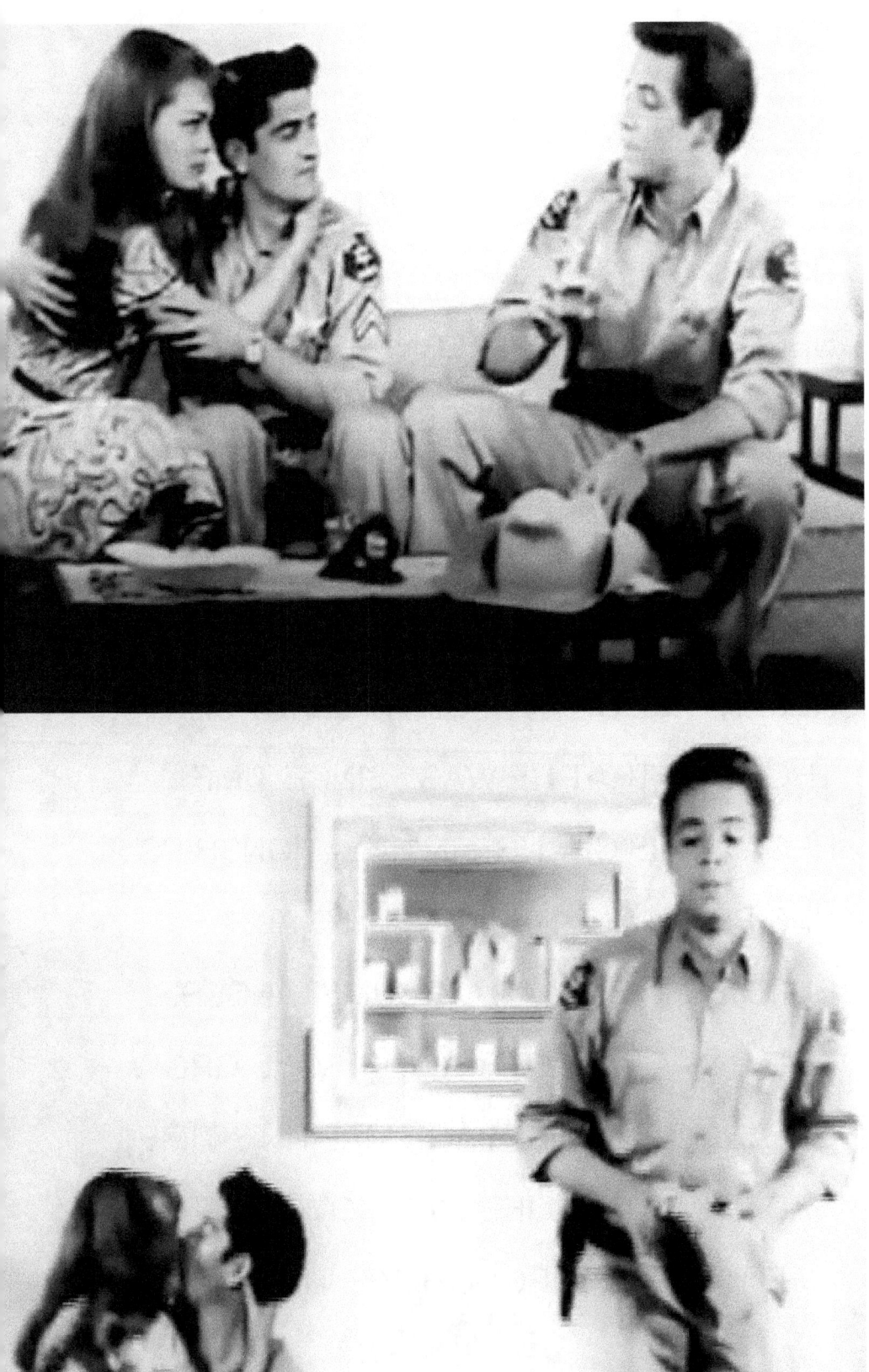

HE COULDN'T COMPREHEND THAT
MARRIED LIFE BROUGHT WITH IT NOT ONLY
NEW PROBLEMS AND DUTIES, BUT THE
NECESSARY TOGETHERNESS OF HUSBAND
AND WIFE AS WELL. DESPITE BRETT'S MOST
TACTFUL CONSIDERATINS, SUCH AS
INVITING HIM OVER TO DINNER QUITE
OFTEN, BARNEY WAS GROWING
RESENTFUL OF HER, OR AT LEAST SHE
THOUGHT THAT HE WAS. SINCE TIME
BEGAN THIS CHANGE IN RELATIONSHIPS
HAS PROBABLY HAPPENED TO ALL
BUDDIES IN SIMILAR CIRCUMSTANCES.
LIFE HAS A WAY OF MAKING BOYS GROW
UP, AND WITH MARRIAGE MARTIN'S TIME
HAD COME. HIS LIFE WAS NOW BRETT'S, A
LIFE THAT HE THROUGHLY ENJOYED.

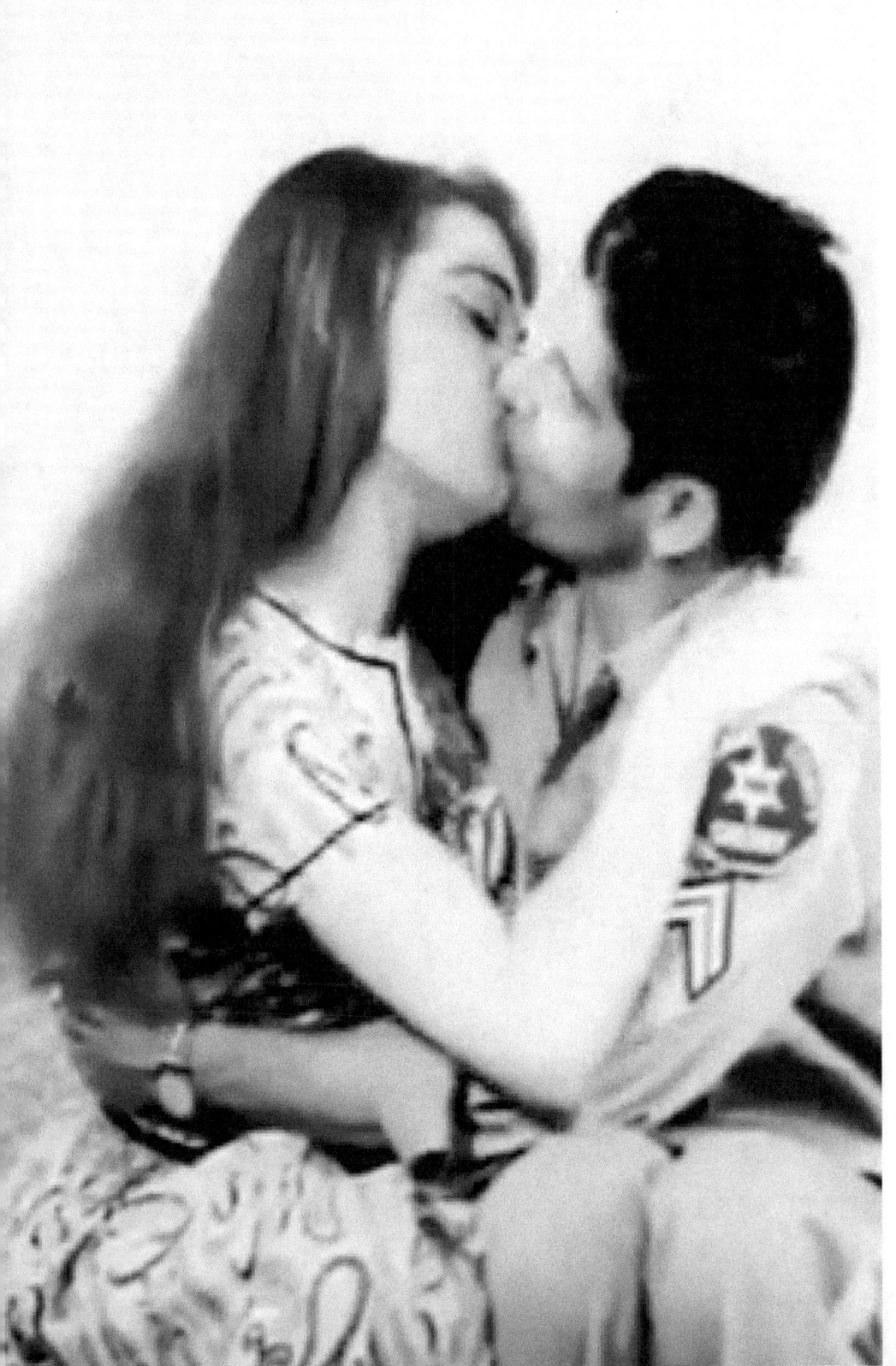

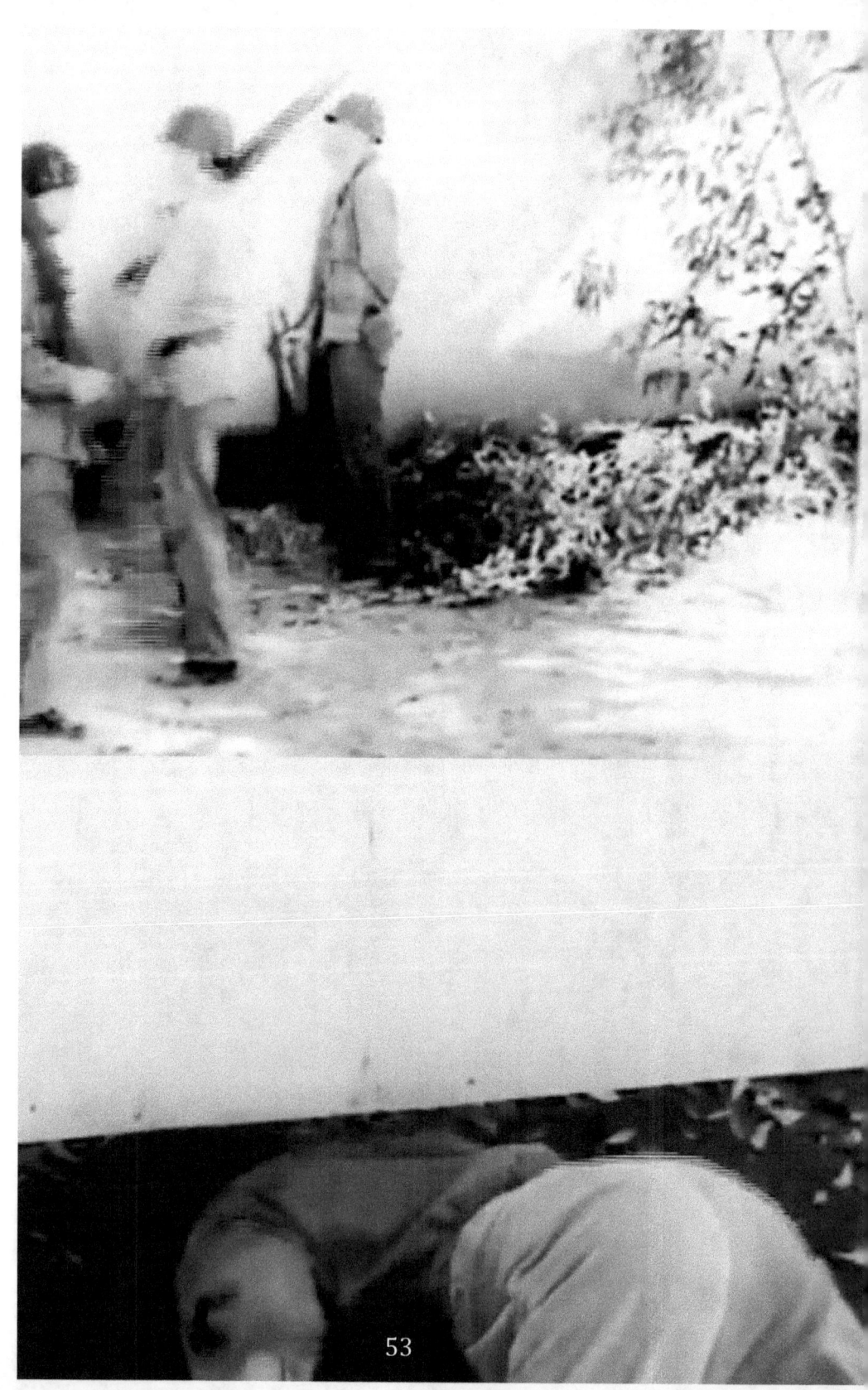

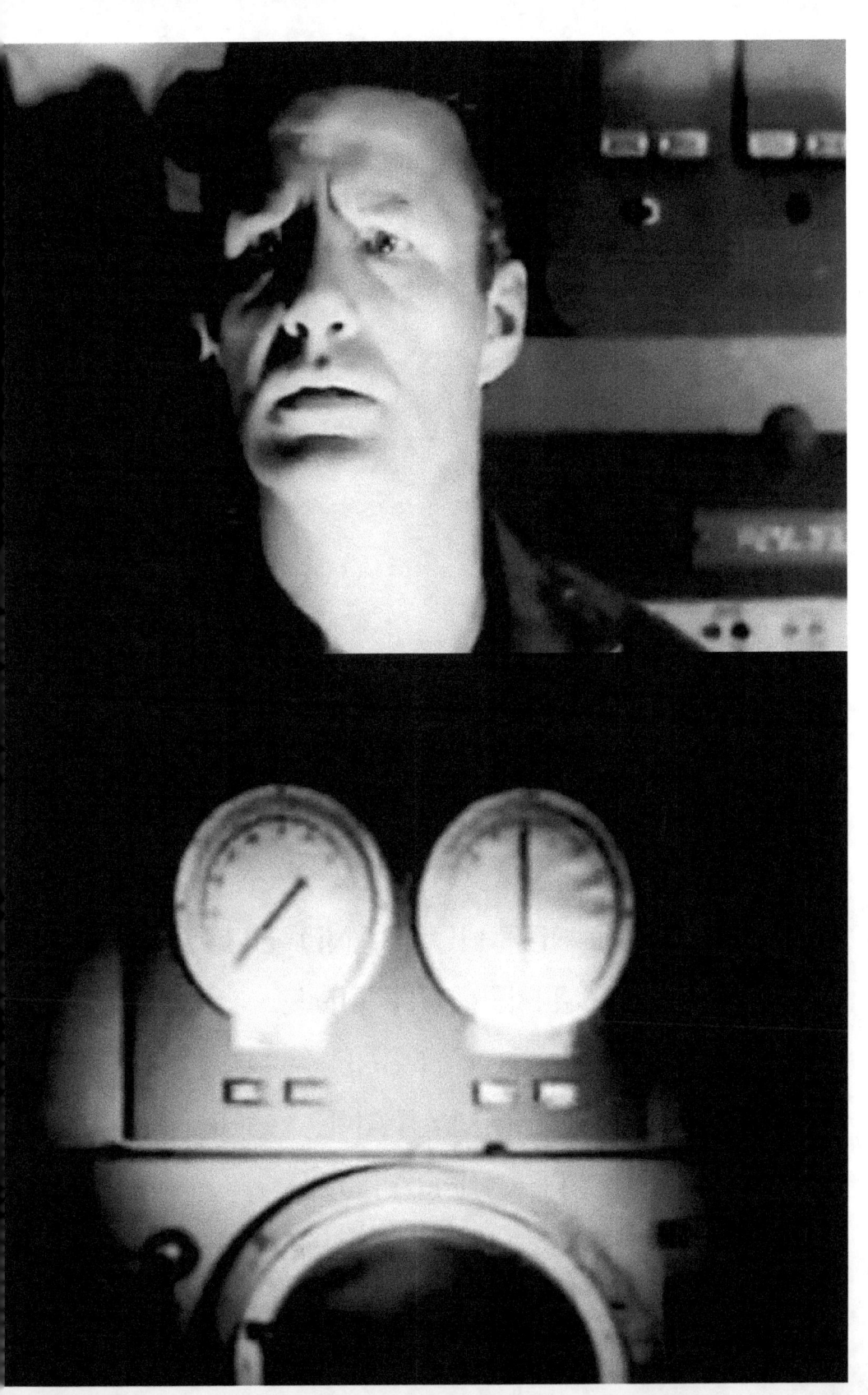

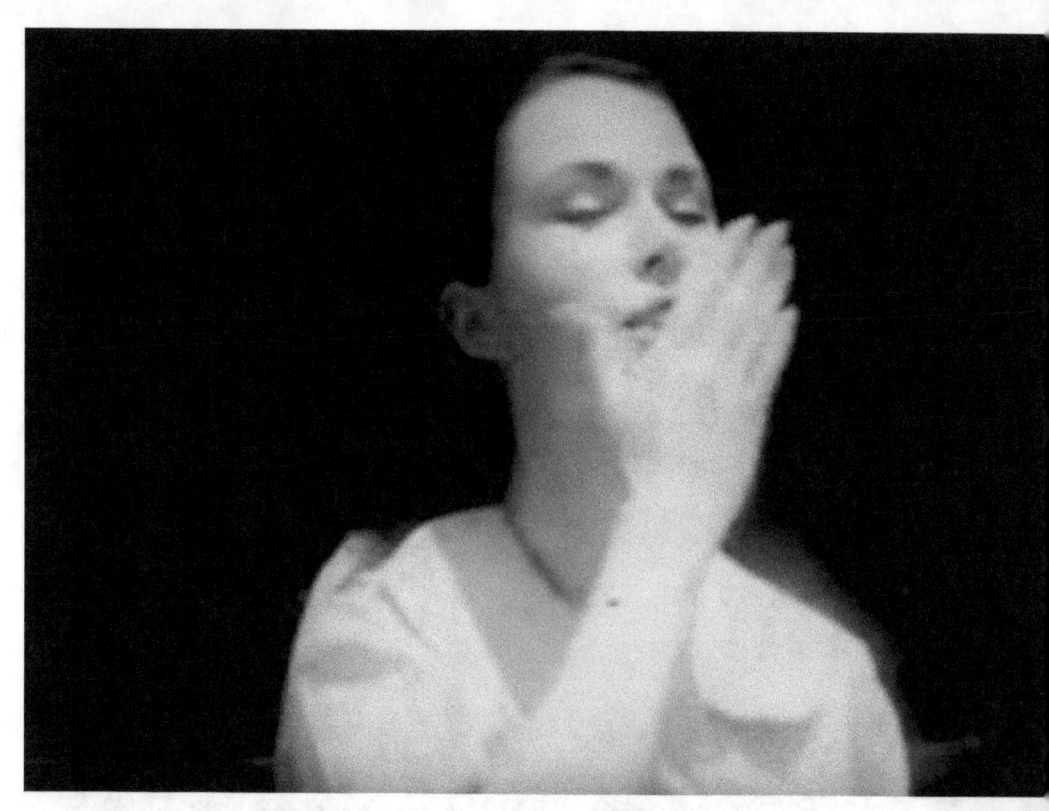

-BYE HONEY.
THE NEXT MORNING, AS USUAL
BETTY JOHNSON BLEW A GOODBYE
KISS TO HER HUSBAND, BUT FOR
THE LAST TIME
-POOR BABY
LET MOMMY TAKE YOUR
TEMPERATURE.
POOR BABY, YOU'LL FEEL BETTER
SOON.

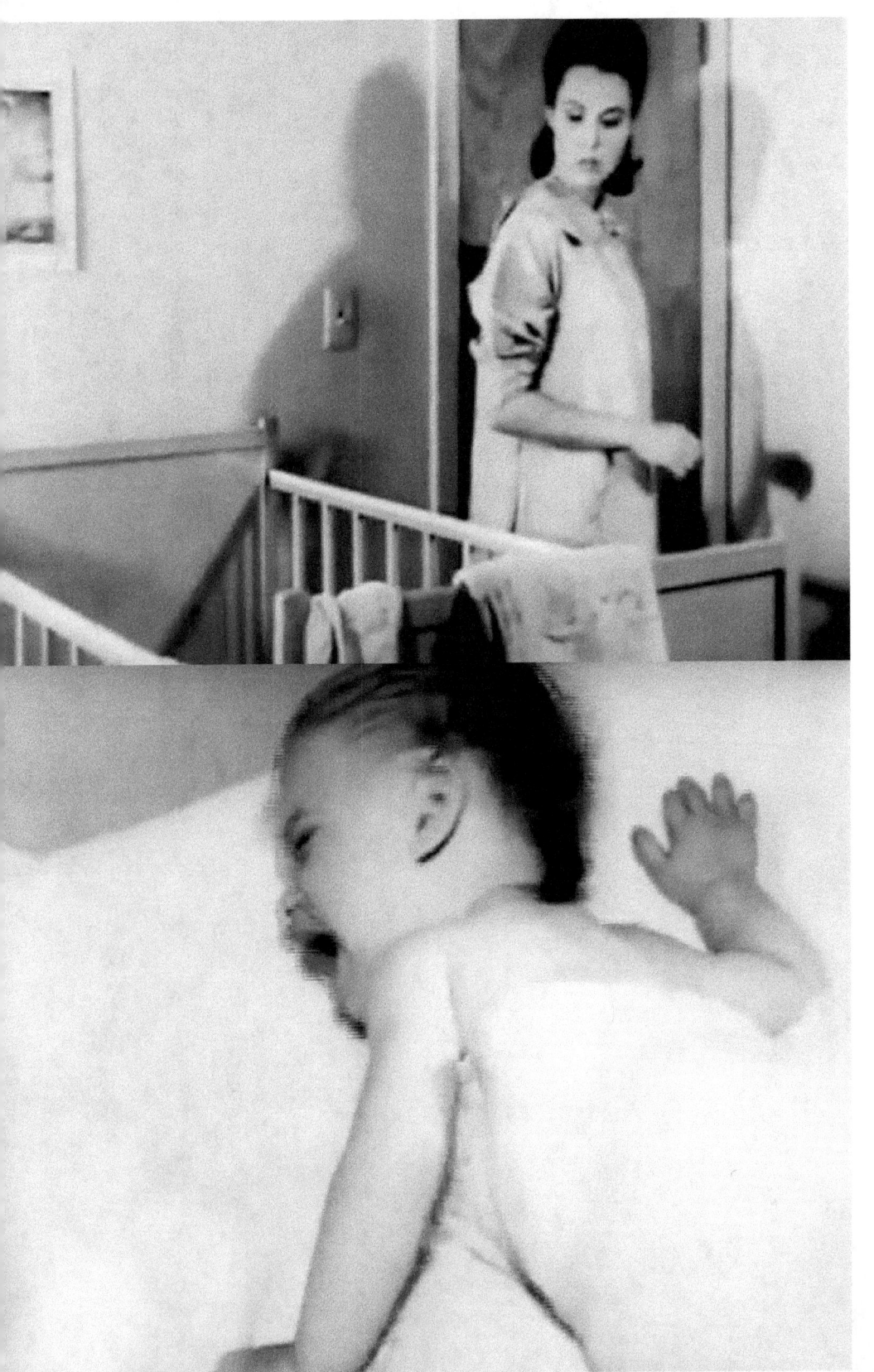

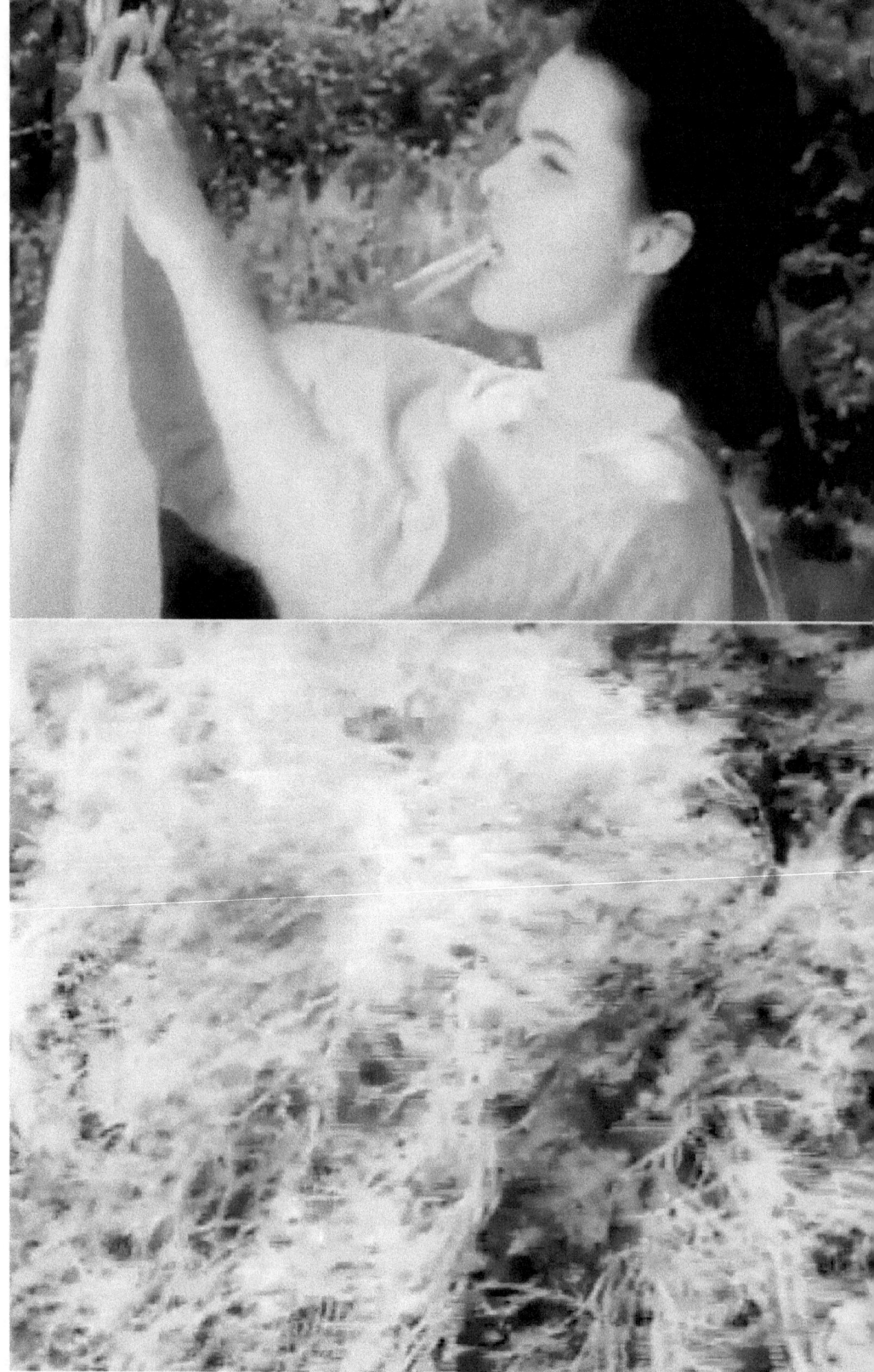

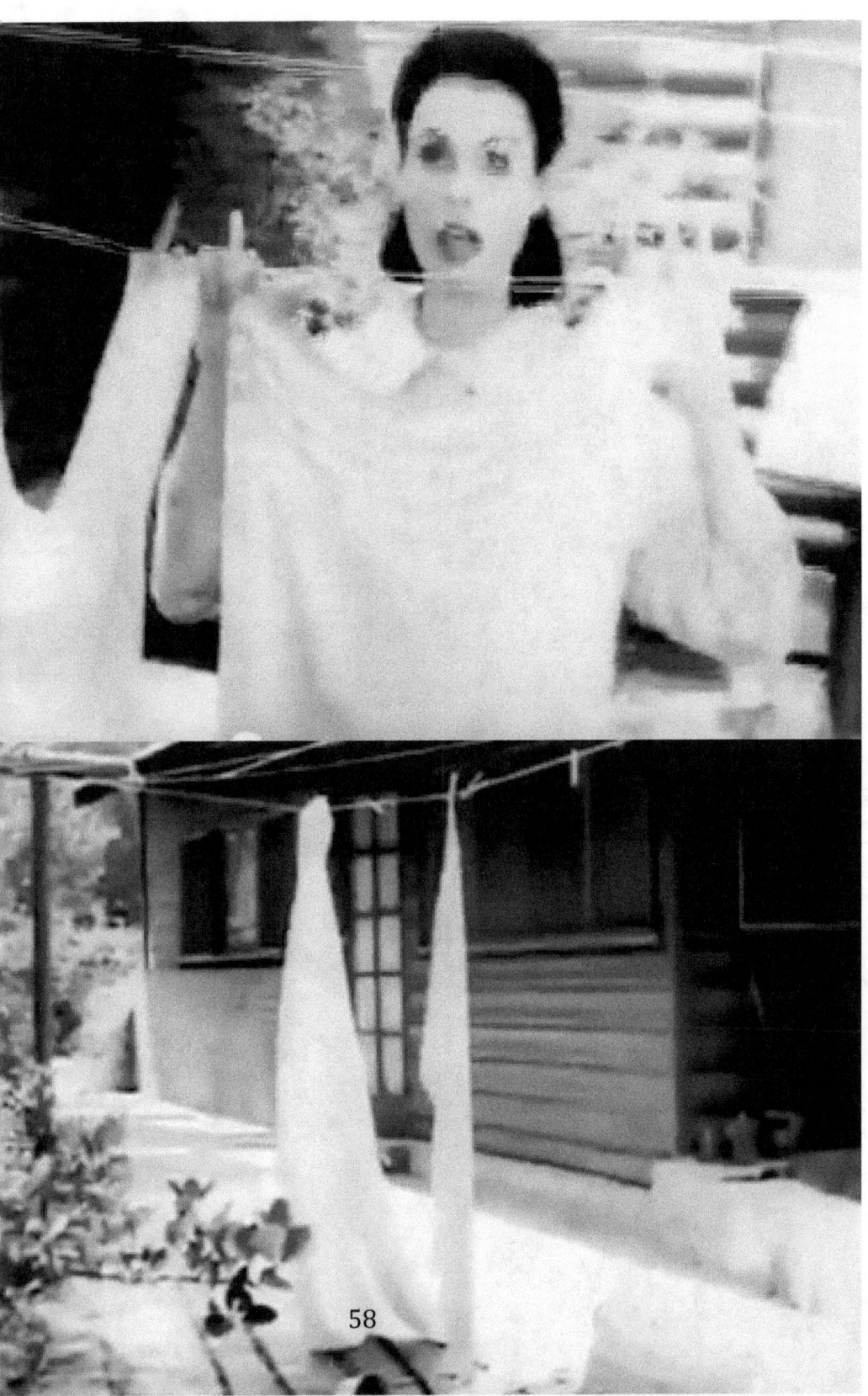

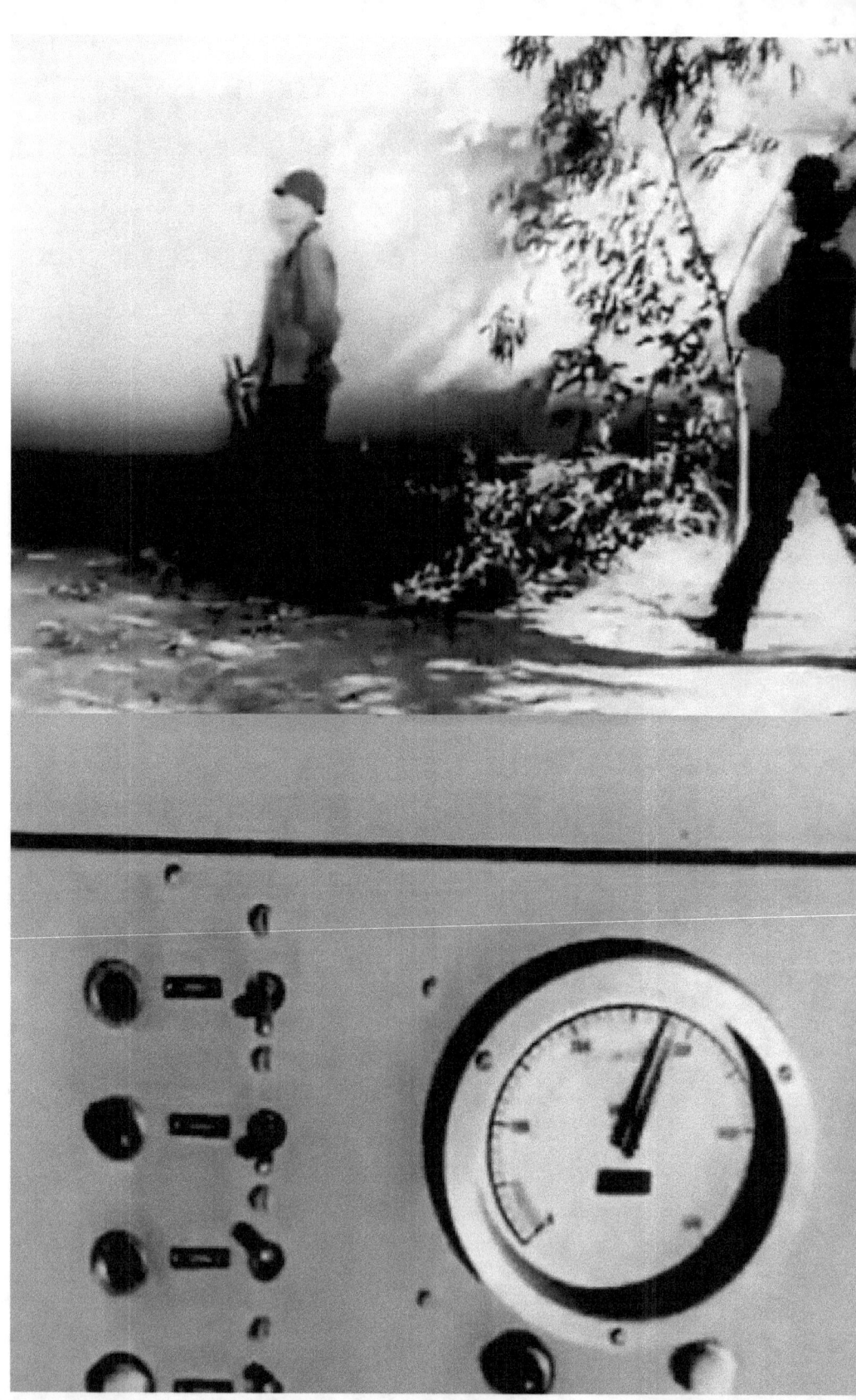

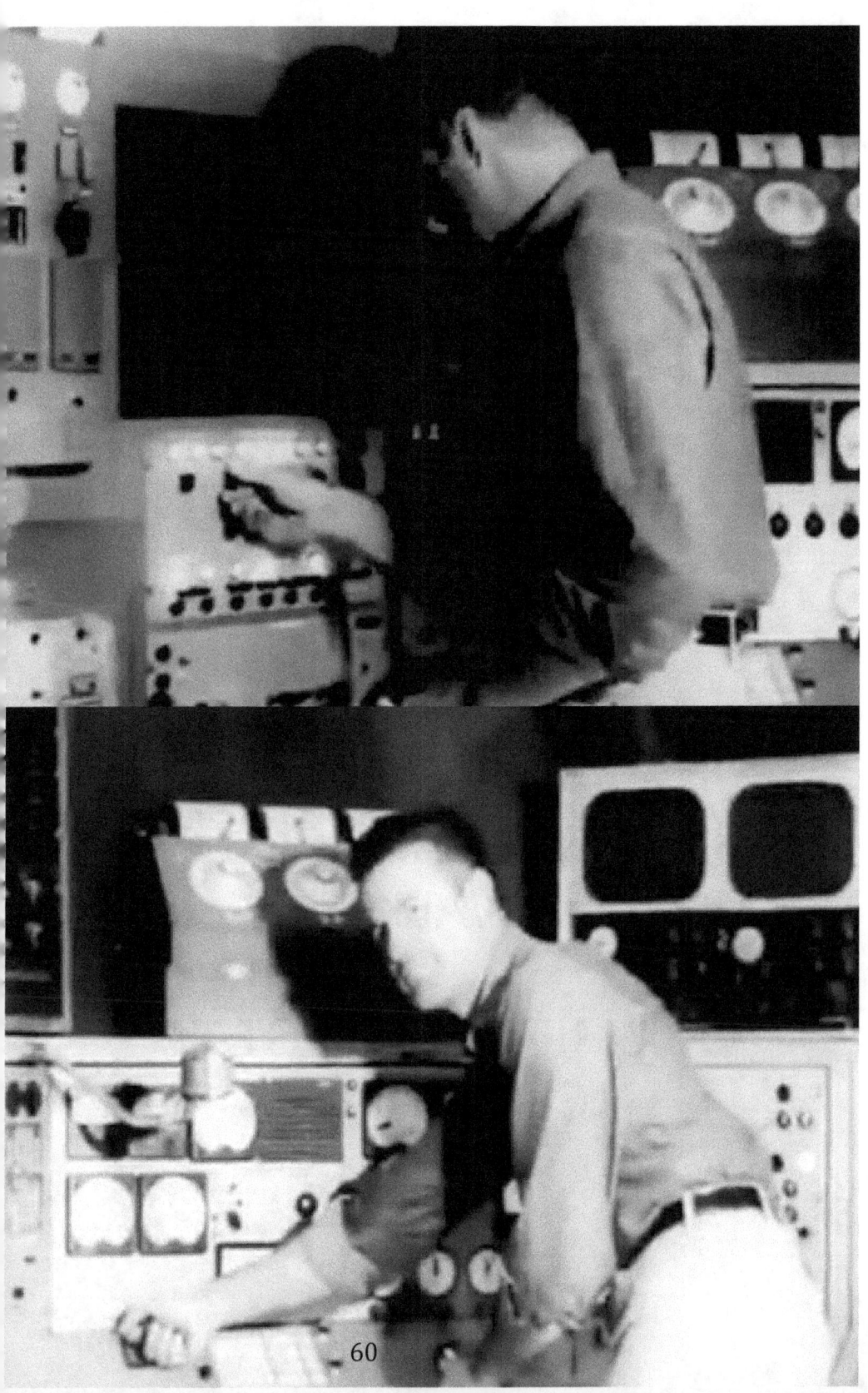

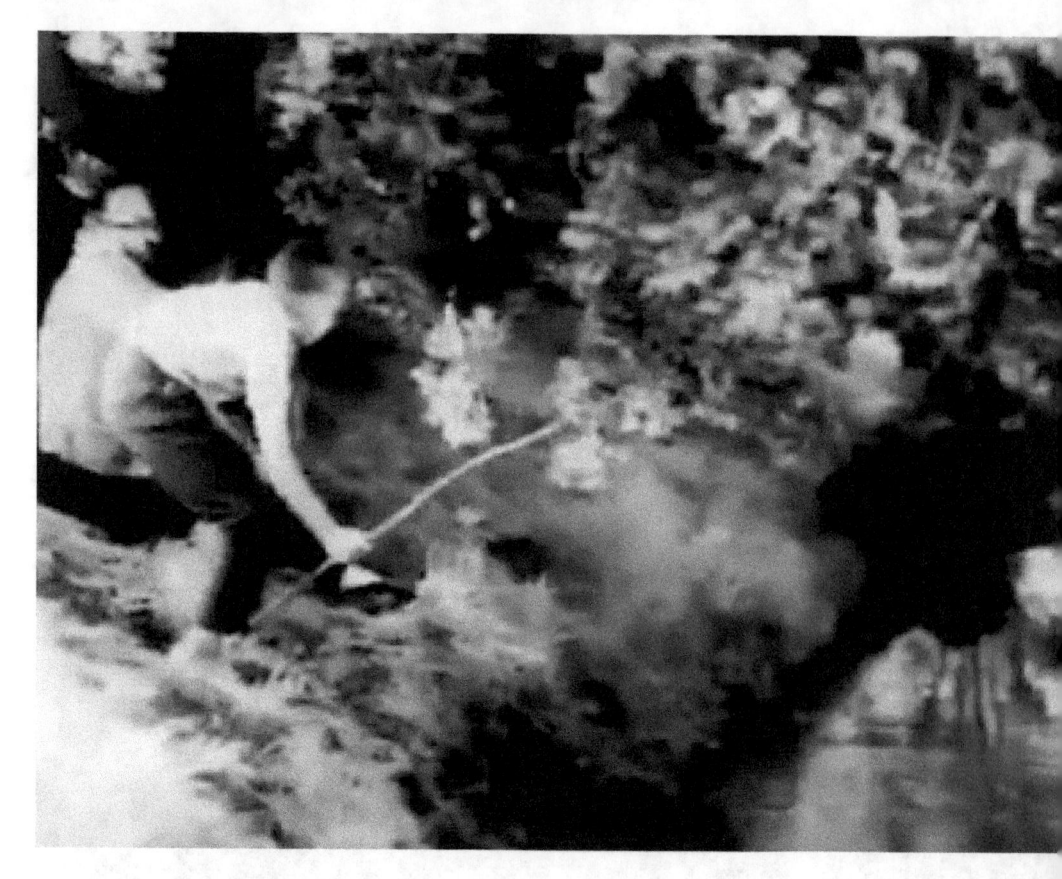

–GRANDPA CAN I GO FOR
A WALK?

–ALL RIGHT, BUT STAY
CLOSE BY.

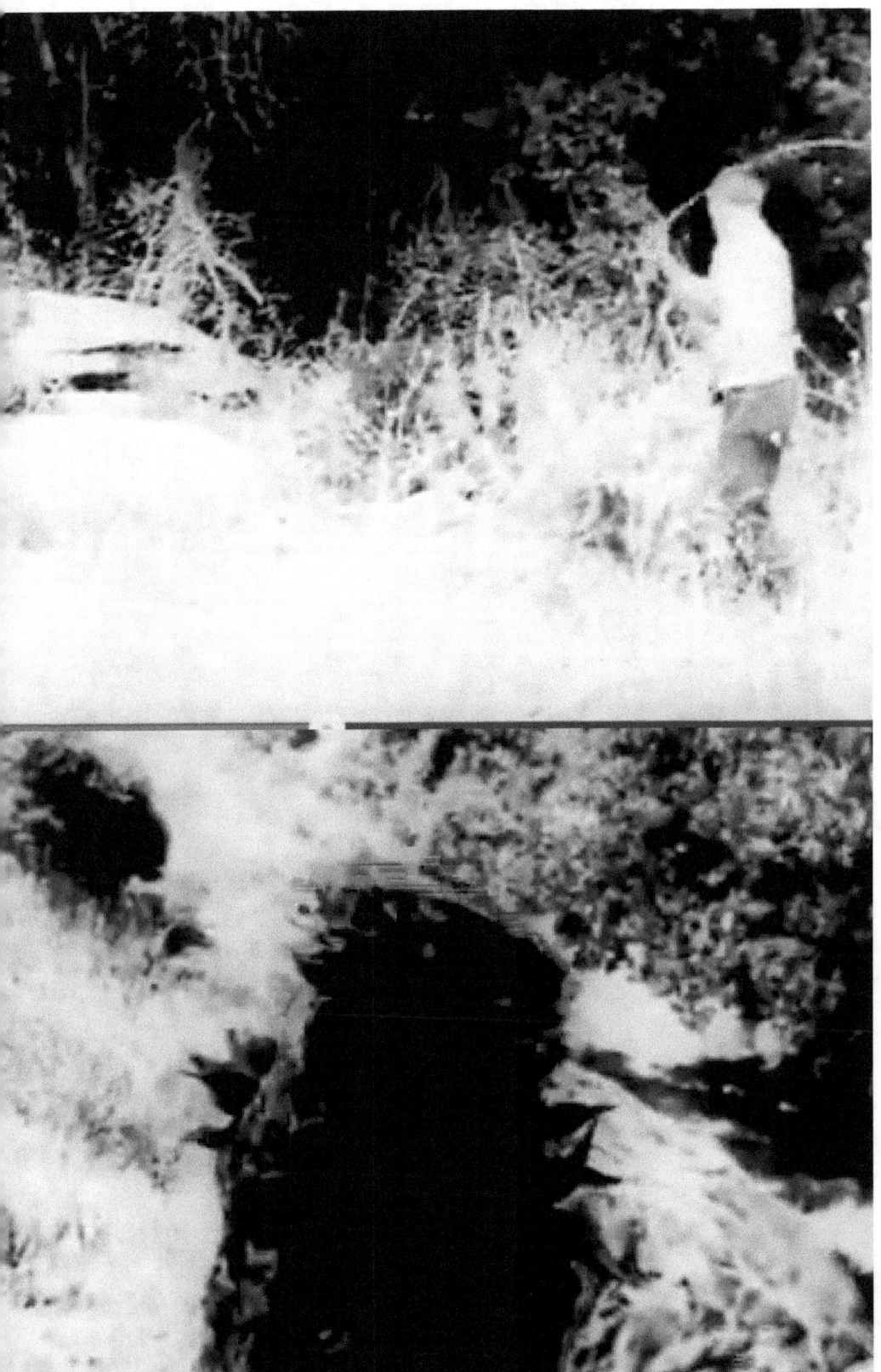

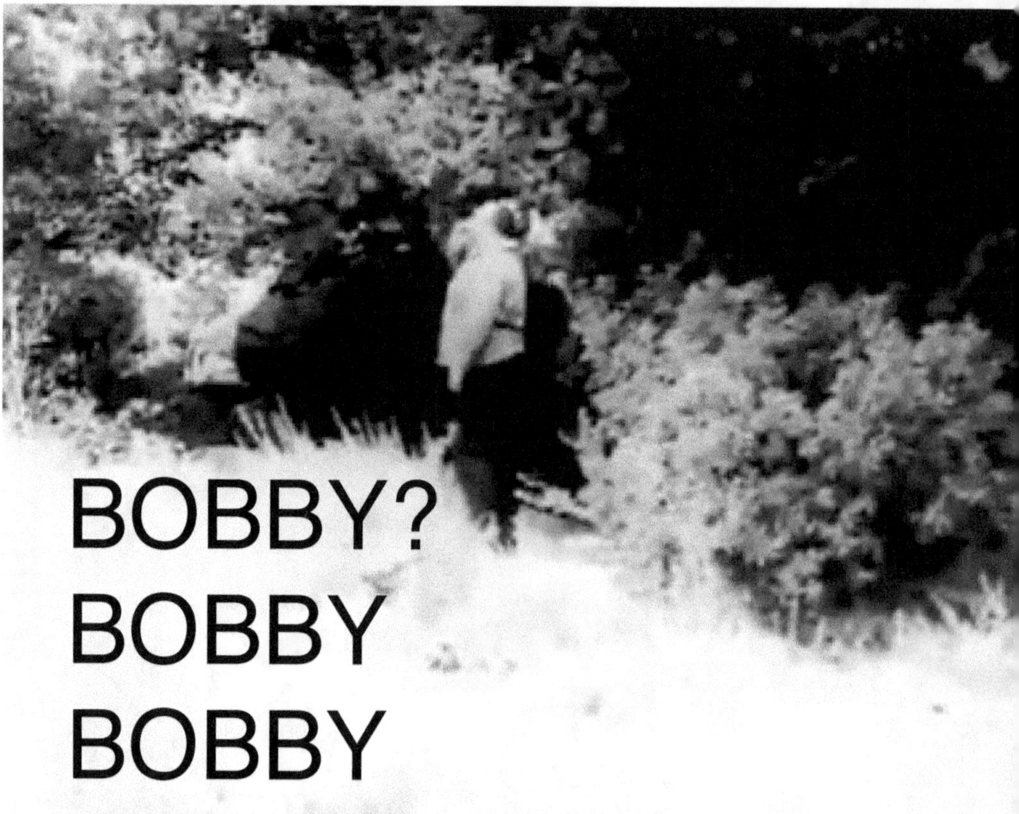

BOBBY?
BOBBY
BOBBY

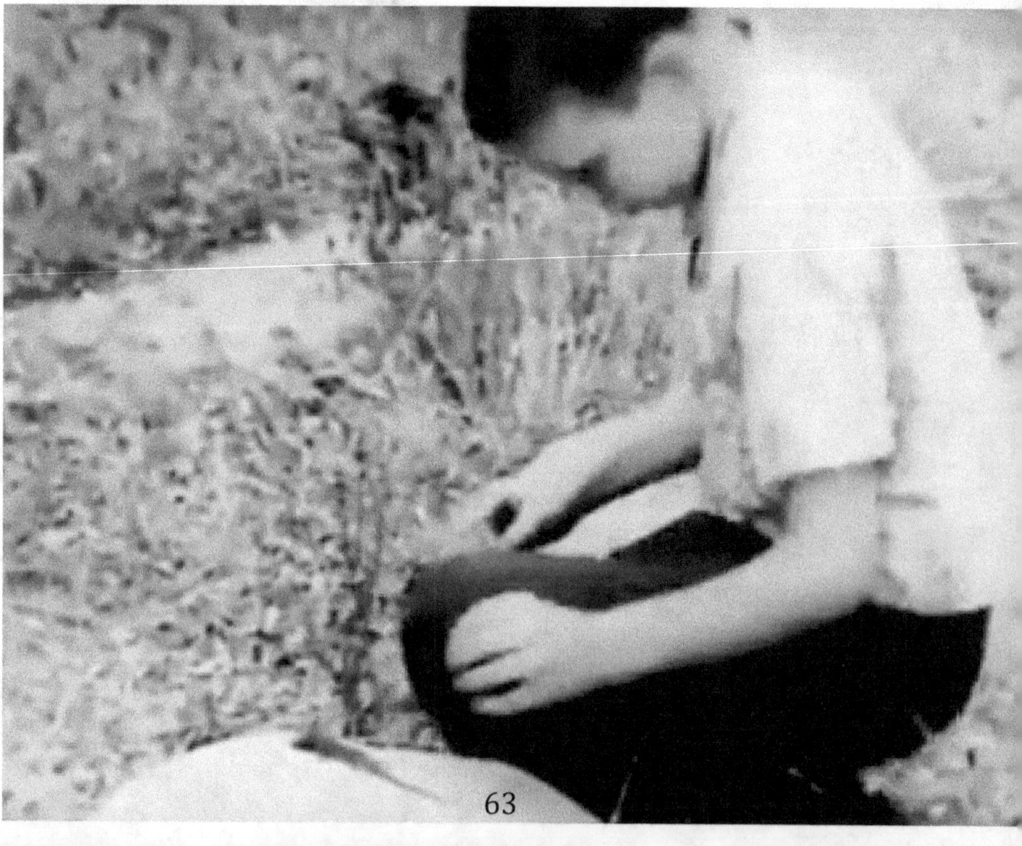

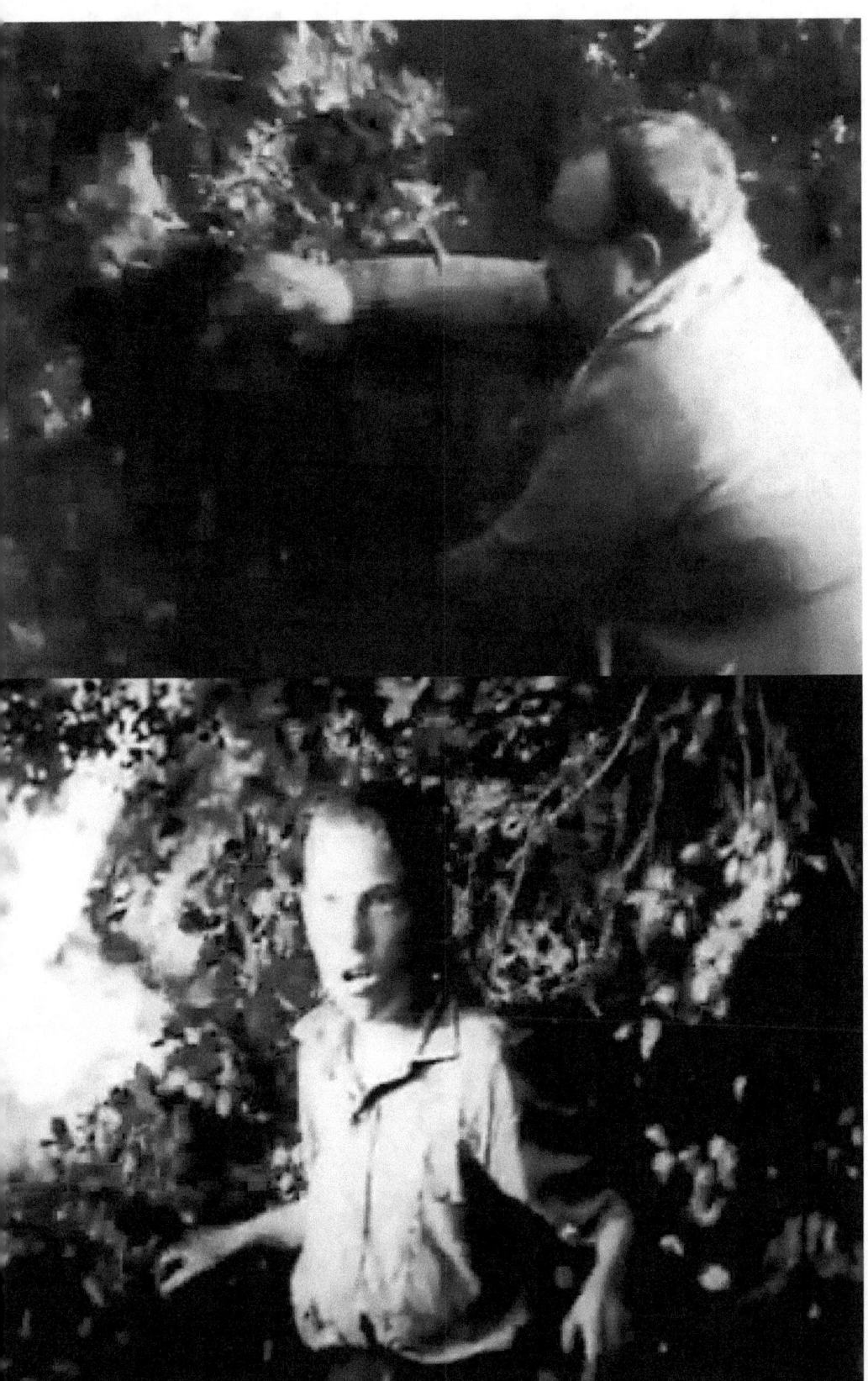

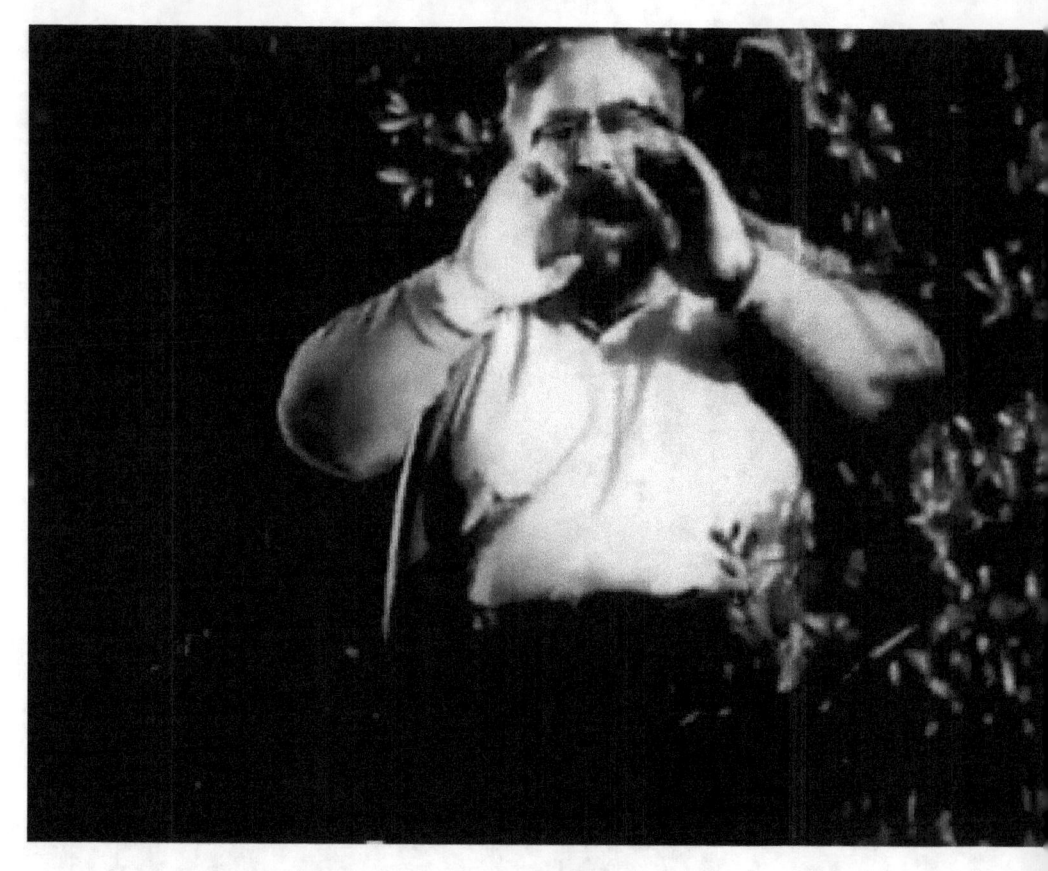

BAA-BEE!
BAA-BEE!
BOBBY...
BOBBY...

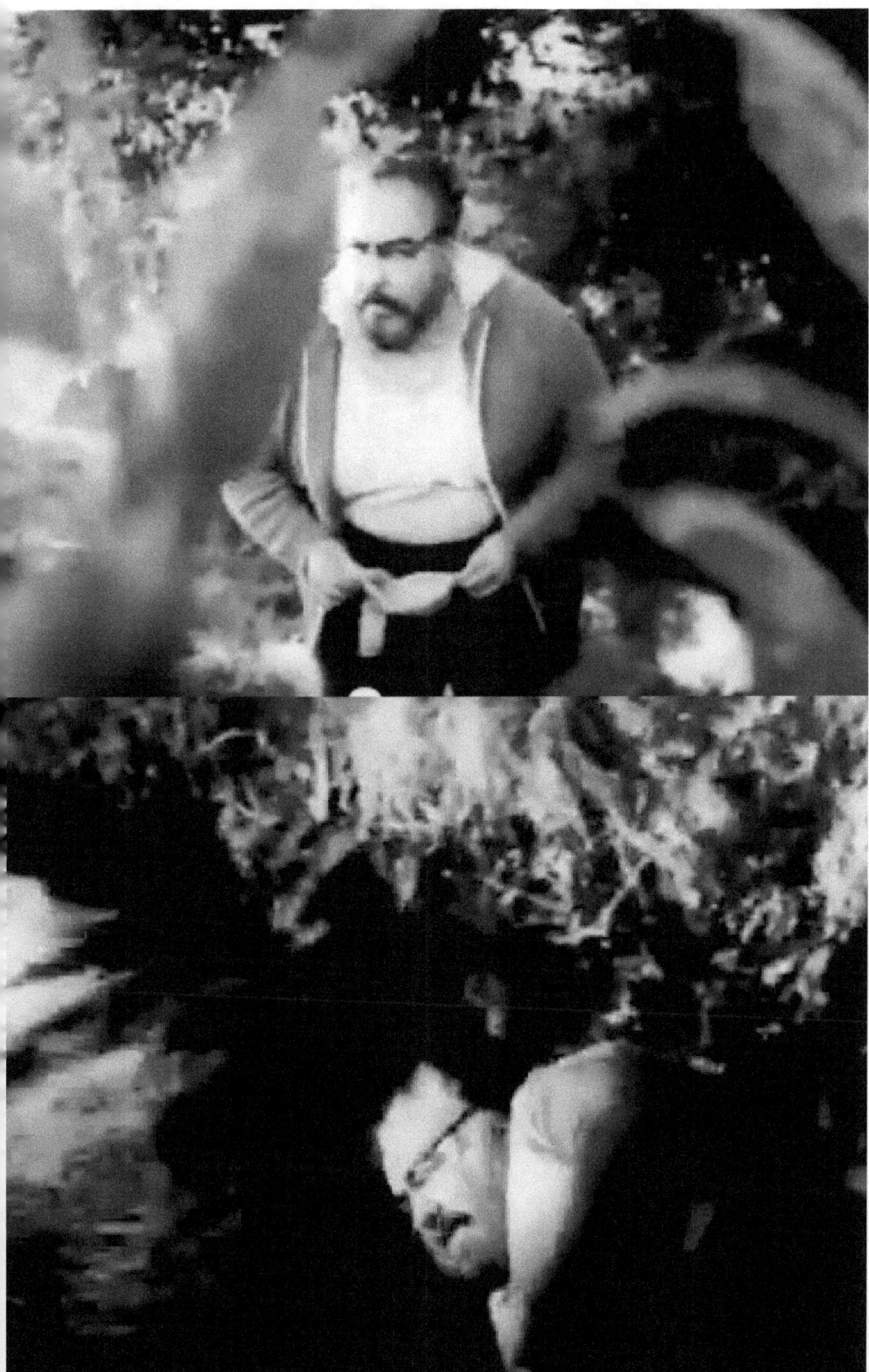

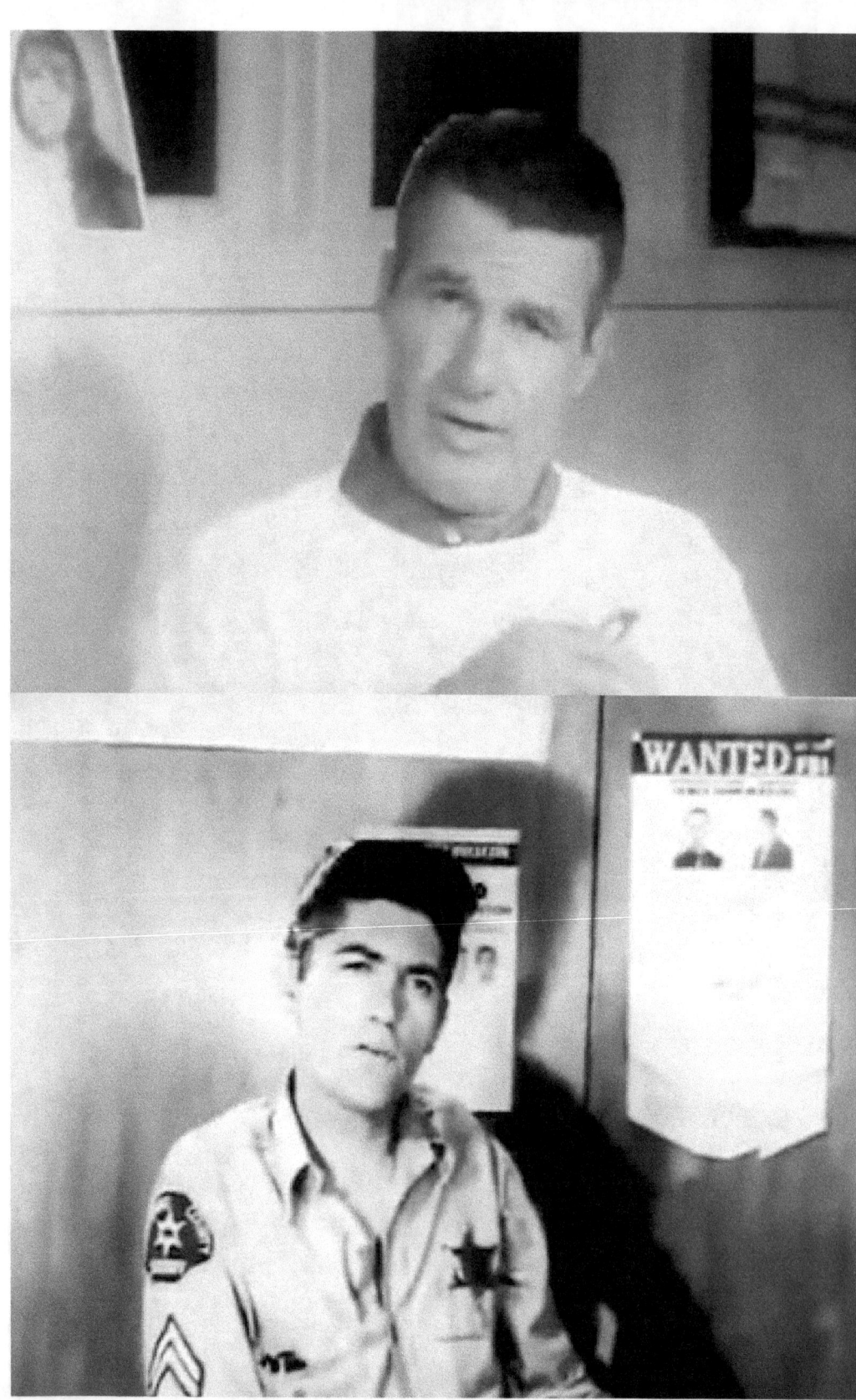

WITHIN 48 HOURS DR. BRADFORD HAD
CLOSELY EXAMINED THE SPACESHIP AND
REACHED A NUMBER OF CONCLUSIONS. HE
WAS SURE THE CREATURE HAD COME FROM
BEYOND OUR SOLAR SYSTEM BECAUSE IT
HAD ADAPTED TO OUR ENVIRONMENT SO
QUICKLY AND NO PLANET OR DEAD STAR
NEAR US HAS CONDITIONS SIMILAR TO THE
EARTH. OF SPECIAL INTEREST TO HIM WAS
THE HULL OF THE SHIP. IT WAS COMPOSED OF
AN ALLOY UNLIKE ANY THAT HUMAN SCIENCE
HAD EVER ENCOUNTERED. THE DR. HAD RUN
A NUMBER OF TESTS ON THE METAL
BUT ITS MOLECULAR STRUCTURE REMAINED
A MYSTERY. BECAUSE THERE WAS NO FOOD
ON BOARD, BRADFORD ASSUMED THE
CREATURE HAD BEEN IN A STATE OF
SUSPENDED ANIMATION, PARTICULARLY
BECAUSE IT HAD SURVIVED THE TRIALS OF
RE-ENTRY AND IMPACT WITHOUT APPARENT
HARM. SO FAR HE HAD NO SUCESS WITH
COMMUNICATING WITH IT BUT HE HAD NOT
YET EXHAUSTED ALL POSSIBILITIES. ON A
MORE SUBJECTIVE BASIS, HE HAD THE
CURIOUS FEELING THAT THE CREATURE DID
NOT WANT TO COMMUNICATE WITH HIM,
PERHAPS BECAUSE HE WAS NOT WEARING A
BIKINI OR SHEER LEGGINGS. SUCH A
CONFESSION ON THE PART OF AN EMINENT
SCIENTIST MADE MARTIN FEEL QUITE
APPREHENSIVE. 68

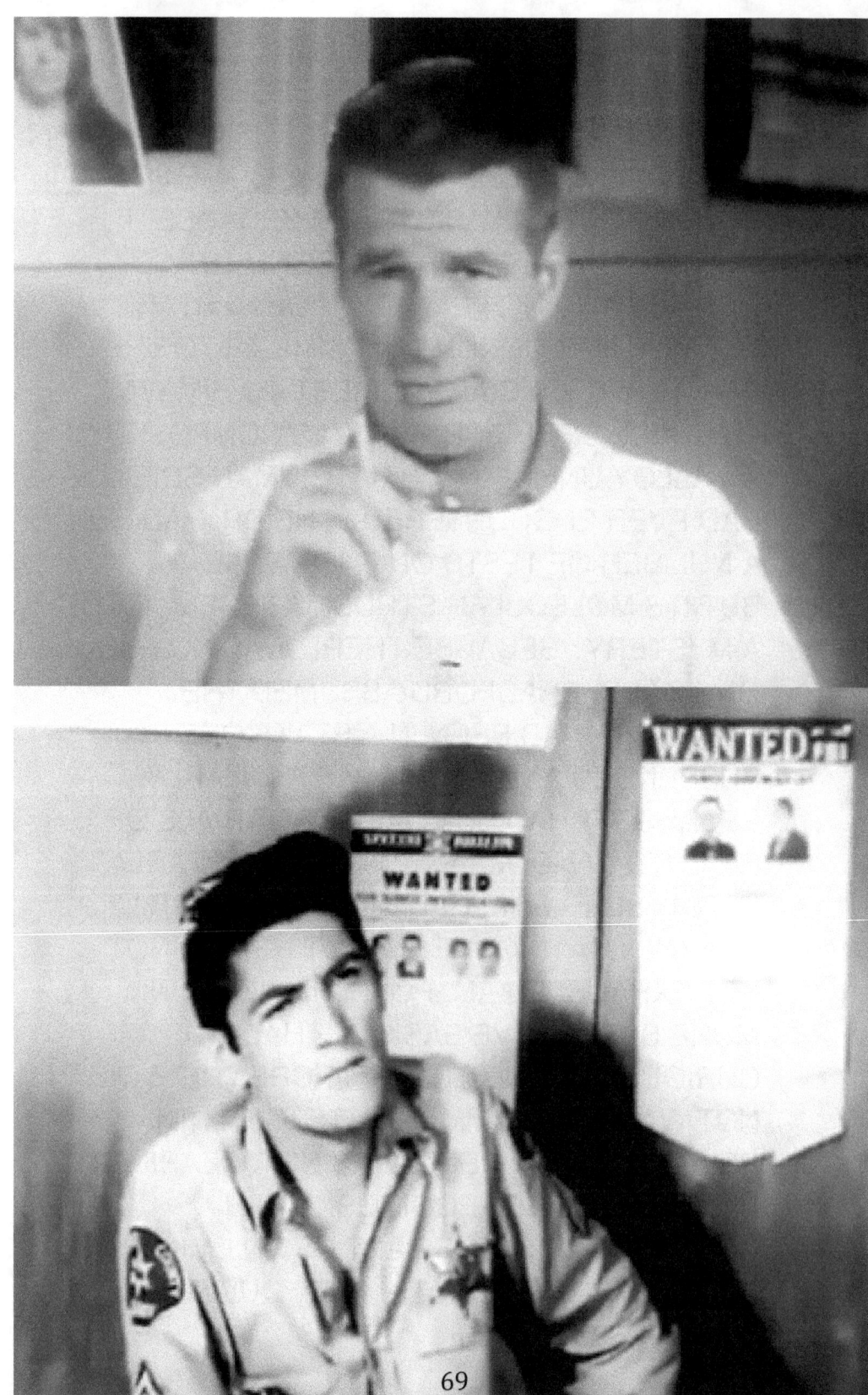

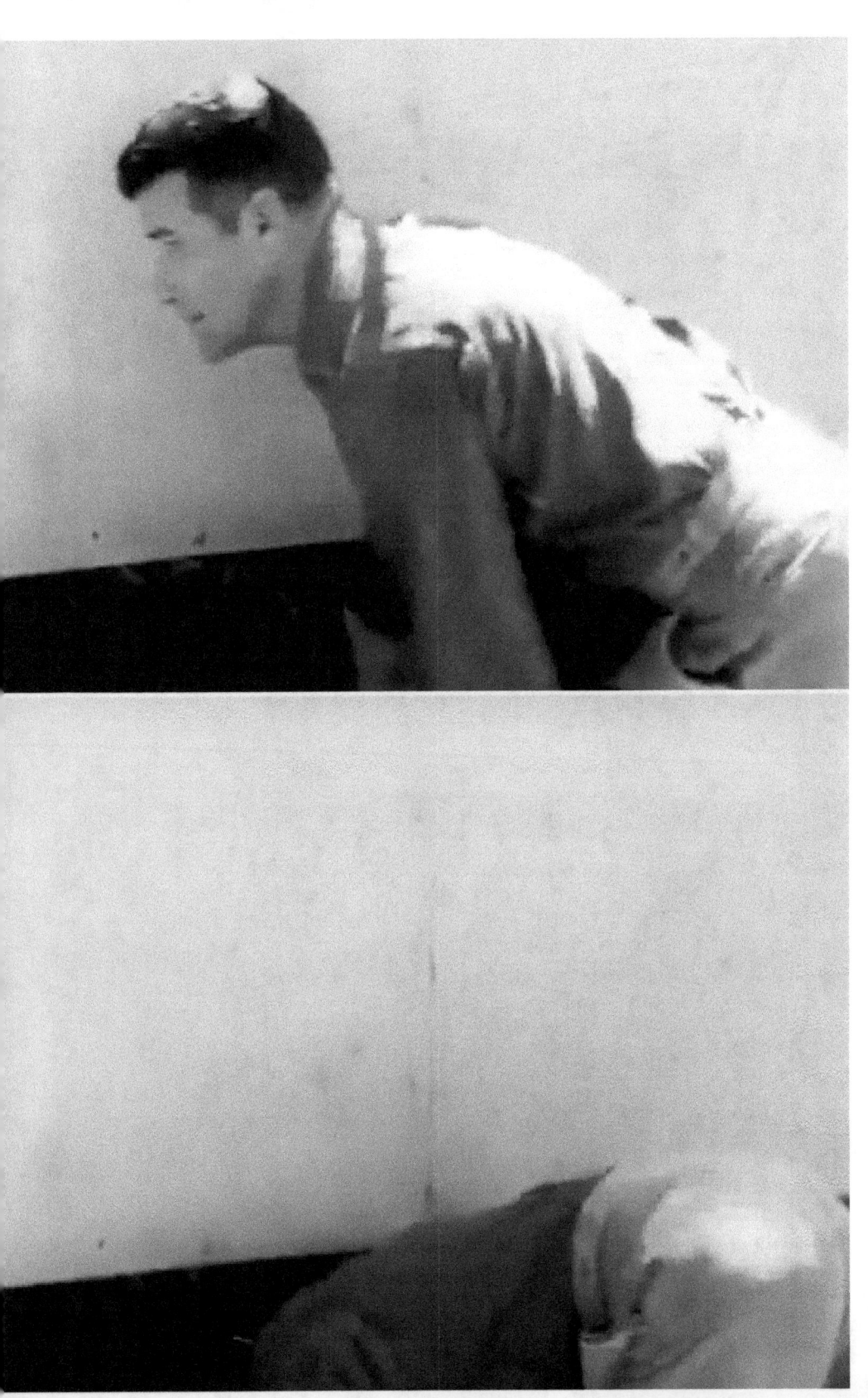

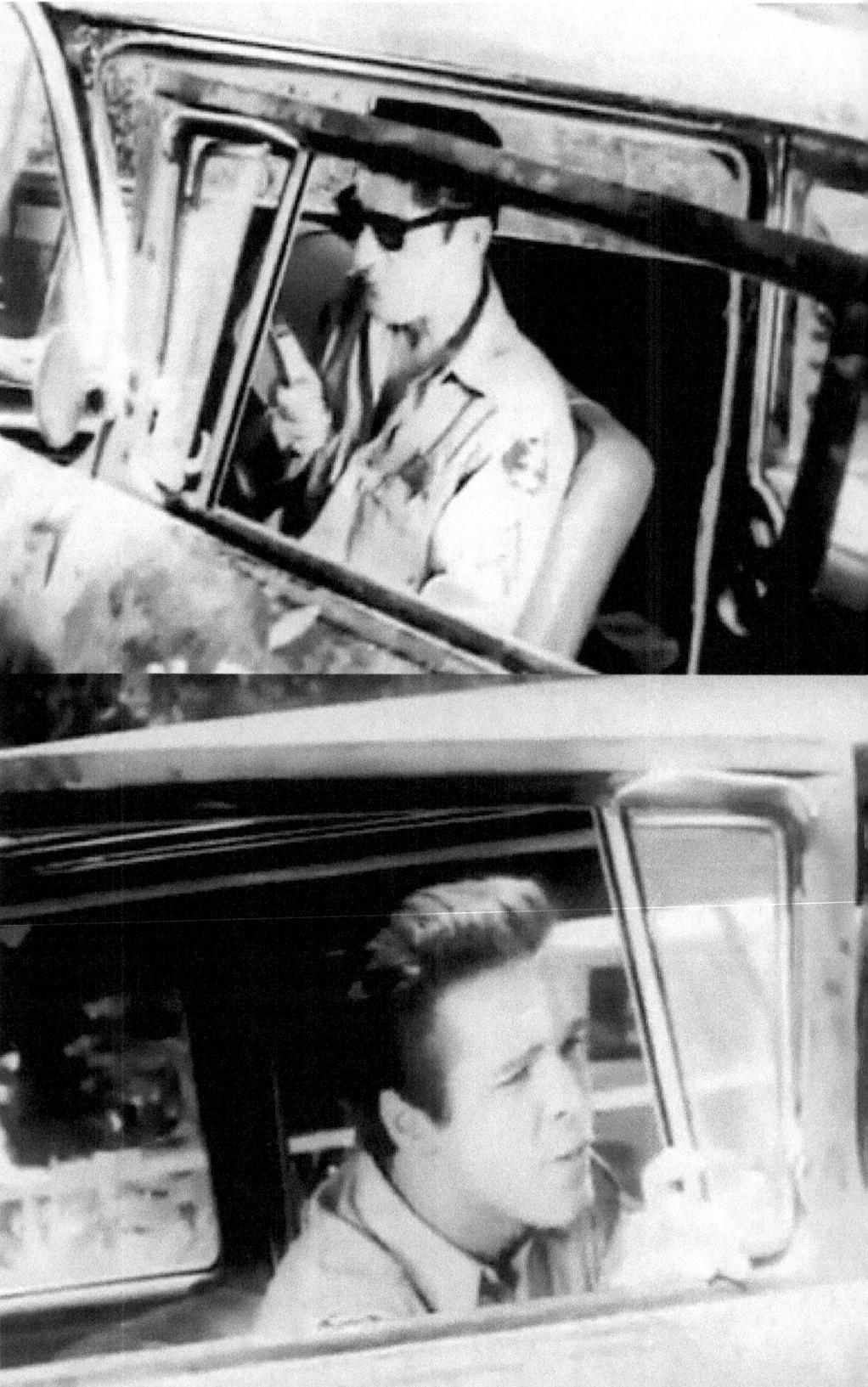

WHILE ON A ROUTINE CALL TO PICKUP INSTRUCTIONS FROM COL. CALDWELL, MARTIN RECEIVED AN URGENT MESSAGE FROM BARNEY. BARNEY WAS AT WILLOW CREEK. HE HAD RESPONDED TO A PHONE CALL BY A FRANTIC MRS. BROWN. HER HUSBAND AND GRANDSON HAD GONE FISHING AND WERE LONG OVERDUE. BARNEY WAS INSTRUCTED TO ORGANIZE A SEARCH PARTY LOCALLY AND REPORT THE RESULTS TO MARTIN. BECAUSE OF SECURITY REGULATIONS HE WAS NOT TO COME NEAR THE AREA OF THE SPACECRAFT. MARTIN SAID HE WOULD JOIN BARNEY LATER IF HE COULD.

ACTING ON A HUNCH, MARTIN DECIDED TO SEE FOR HIMELF IF THE MONSTER WAS STILL THERE. IT WAS. BRADFORD HAD INSTALLED TV CAMERAS INSIDE THE SPACESHIP AND WAS TESTING THE CREATURES REACTIONS TO SOUND, LIGHT, ELECTRICITY, COLOR AND AIR PRESSURE. WHEN MARTIN ASKED HIM IF HE HAD ANY LUCK IN COMMUNICATING WITH THE BEAST, BRADFORD CONFESSED THAT HE HADN'T BUT WOULD TRY AGAIN WHEN CERTAIN DATA WAS RETURNED TO HIM FROM COMPUTER PROCESSING. IT WAS AT THIS TIME THAT BRADFORD CAME UP WITH A FRIGHTENING THEORY, NAMELY THAT THE CREATURE MIGHT BE A PRODUCT OF ENGINEERING, THE SAME ENGINEERING THAT BUILT THE SPACESHIP. WHAT HE DIDN'T UNDERSTAND WAS WHY SOME FORM OF COMMUNICATION HAD NOT BEEN BUILT INTO

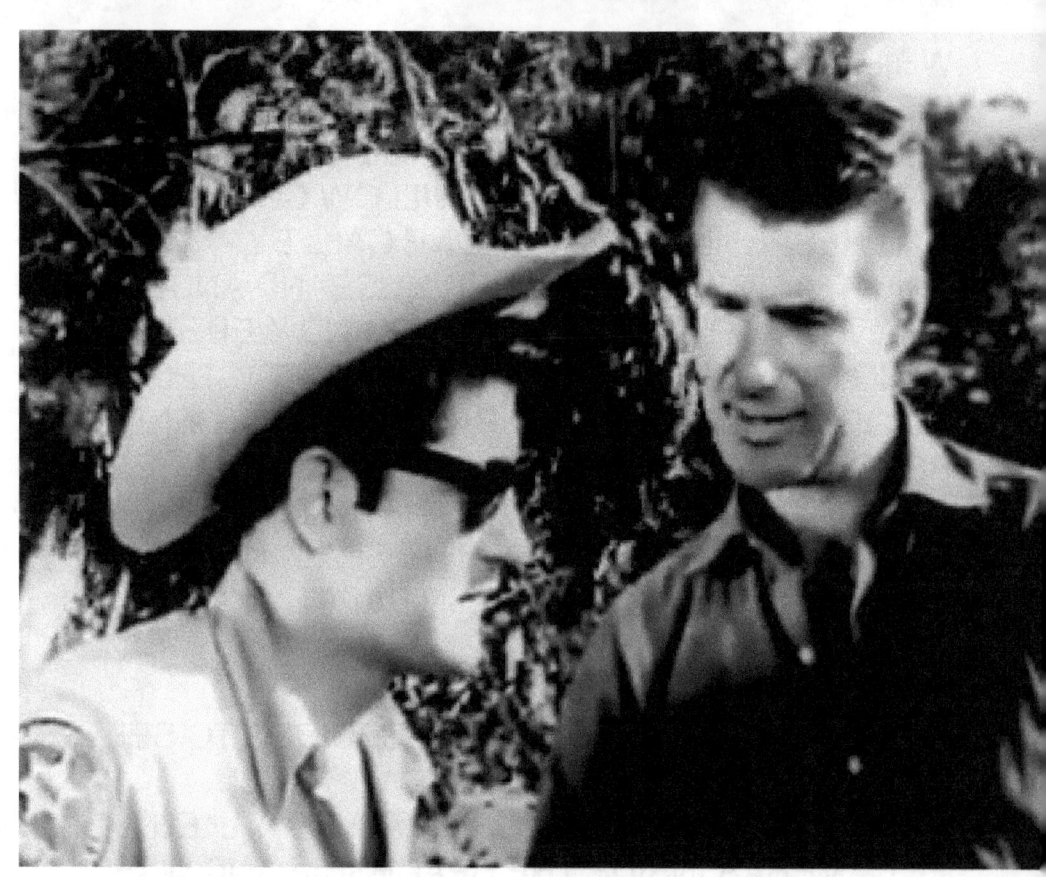

THE CREATURE. WHEN MARTIN ASKED HIM IF
THIS WEREN'T SOMETHING TO WORRY ABOUT,
BRADFORD SAID NO, IT WAS PROBABLY HIS
OWN FAILING AT NOT BEING ABLE TO
ESTABLISH COMMUNICATIONS. T SEEMED TO
MARTIN THAT IF BRADFORD'S THEORY WAS
CORRECT, HUMANITY MIGHT BE IN GRAVE
DANGER. BRADFORD DISMISSED MARTIN'S
FEAR BY POINTING OUT THAT THE CREATURE
WAS NOT EXHIBITING ANY SIGNS OF VIOLENCE
AND BESIDES IT WAS FIRMLY SECURED BY THE
HARNESS.

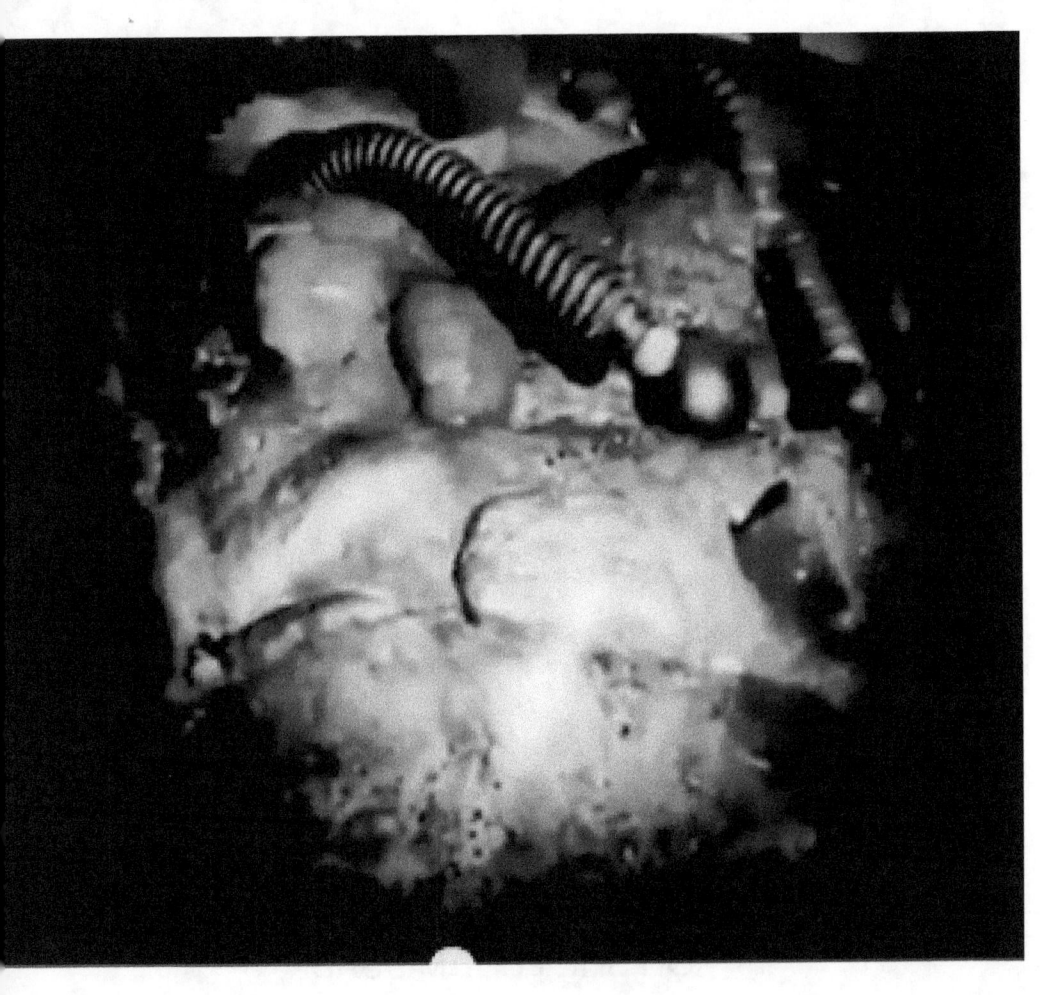

THAT AFTERNOON IN MONCRIEF

PARK A GROUP OF NEIGHBORS

GOT TOGETHER FOR A

HOOTENANY.

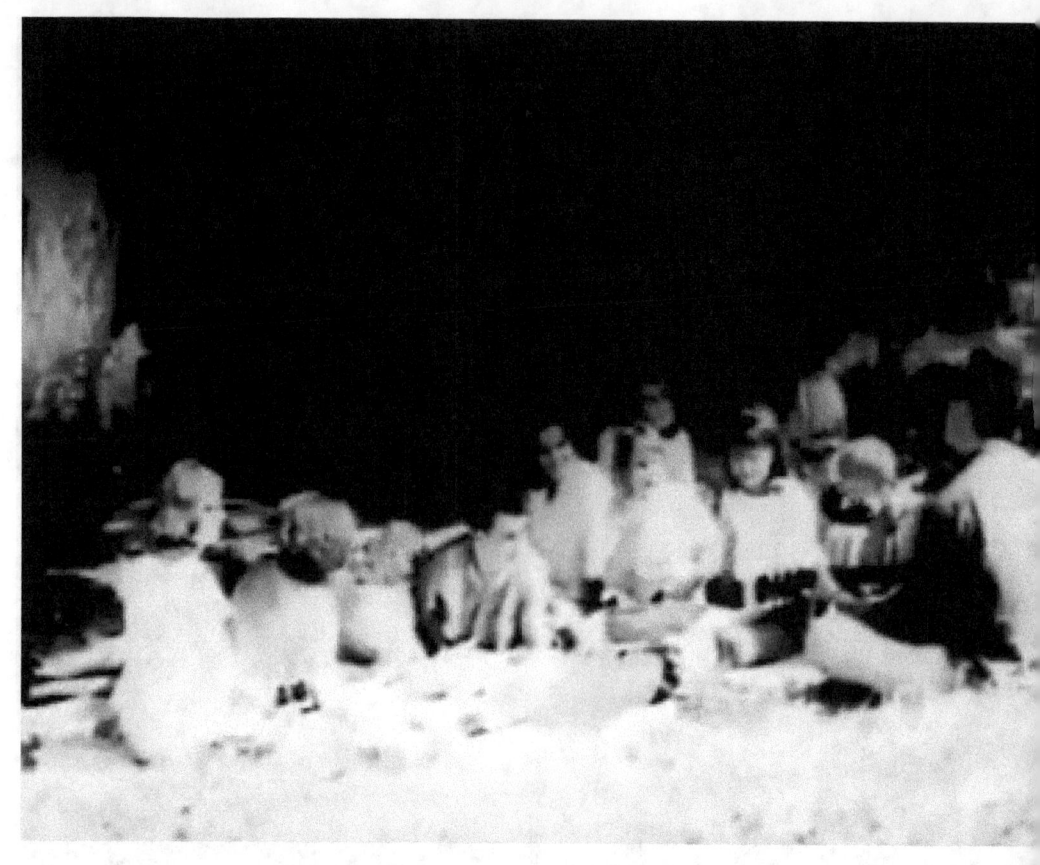

OH SHE LEFT ME SAD

BUT STILL I AM HAPPY IN FACT I AM GLAD

FOR I AM AS FREE AS THAT BIRD IN THE TREE

CAUSE SHE LEFT ME ALONE

AND COULD NOT MARRY ME

I SAID THAT I LOVED HER AND WOULD TILL I DIE

I TRIED TO FORGET HER AND I REALLY DID TRY

BUT I'LL STILL THINK OF HER TILL

THE DAY THAT I DIE

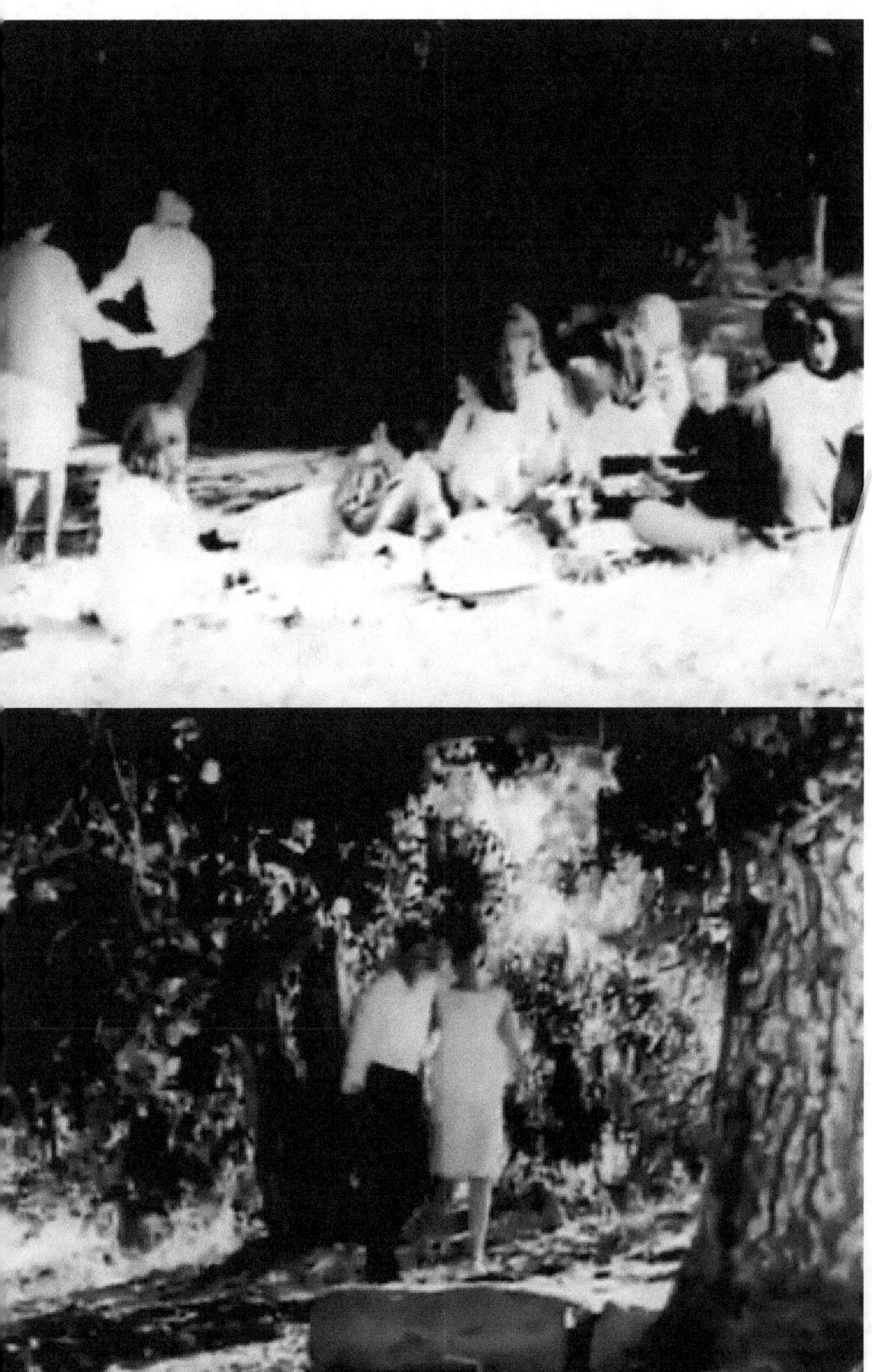

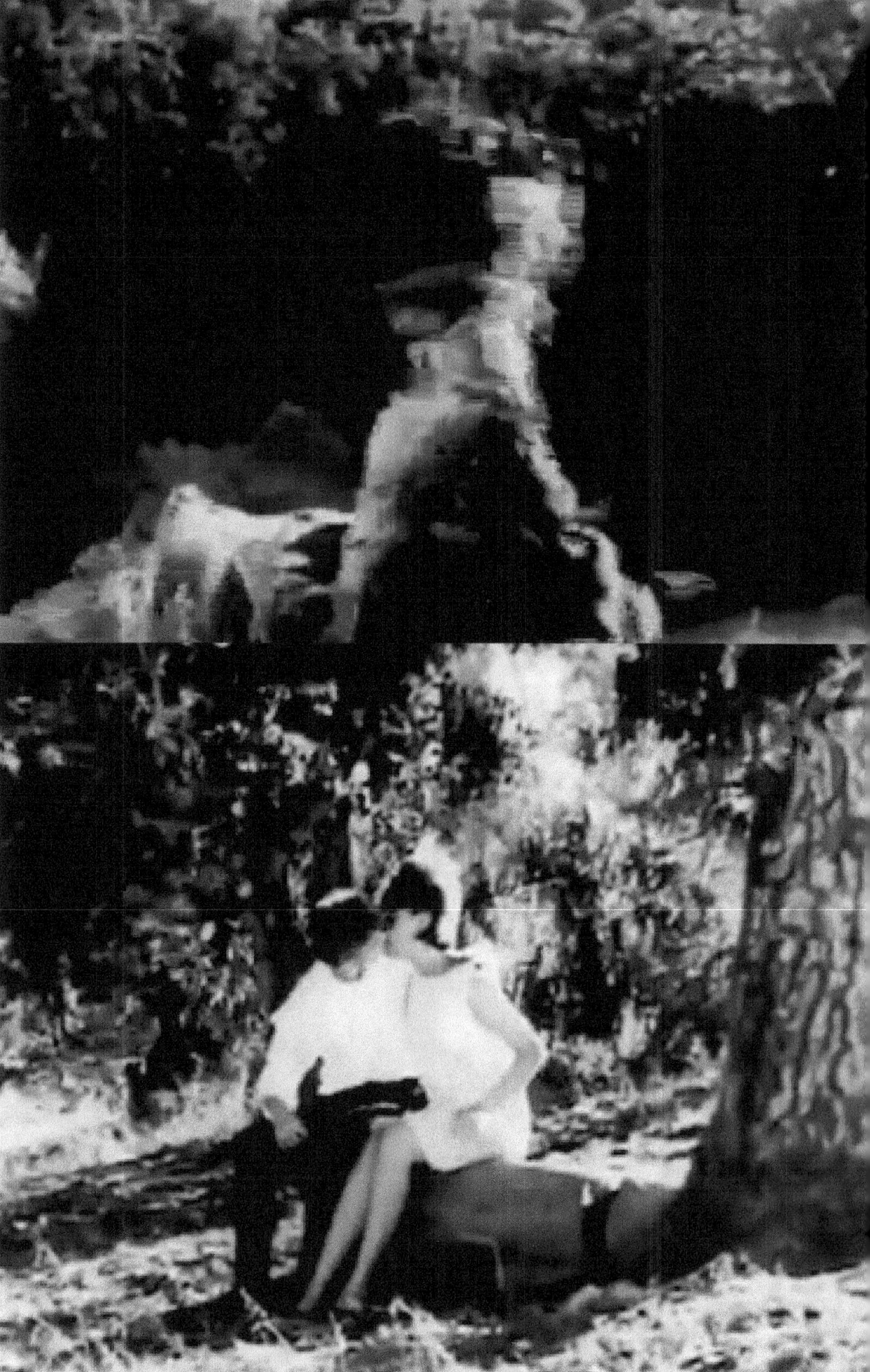

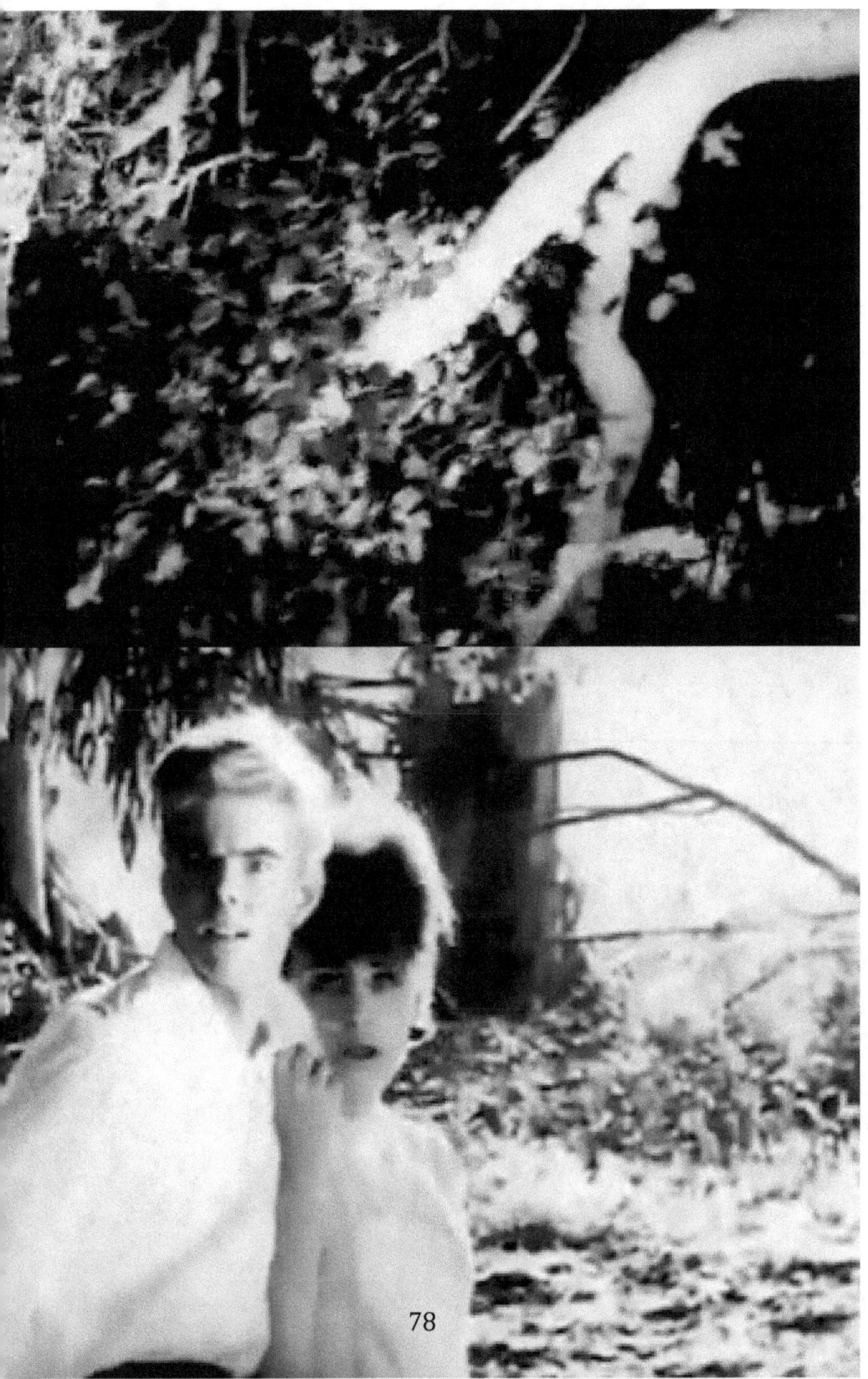

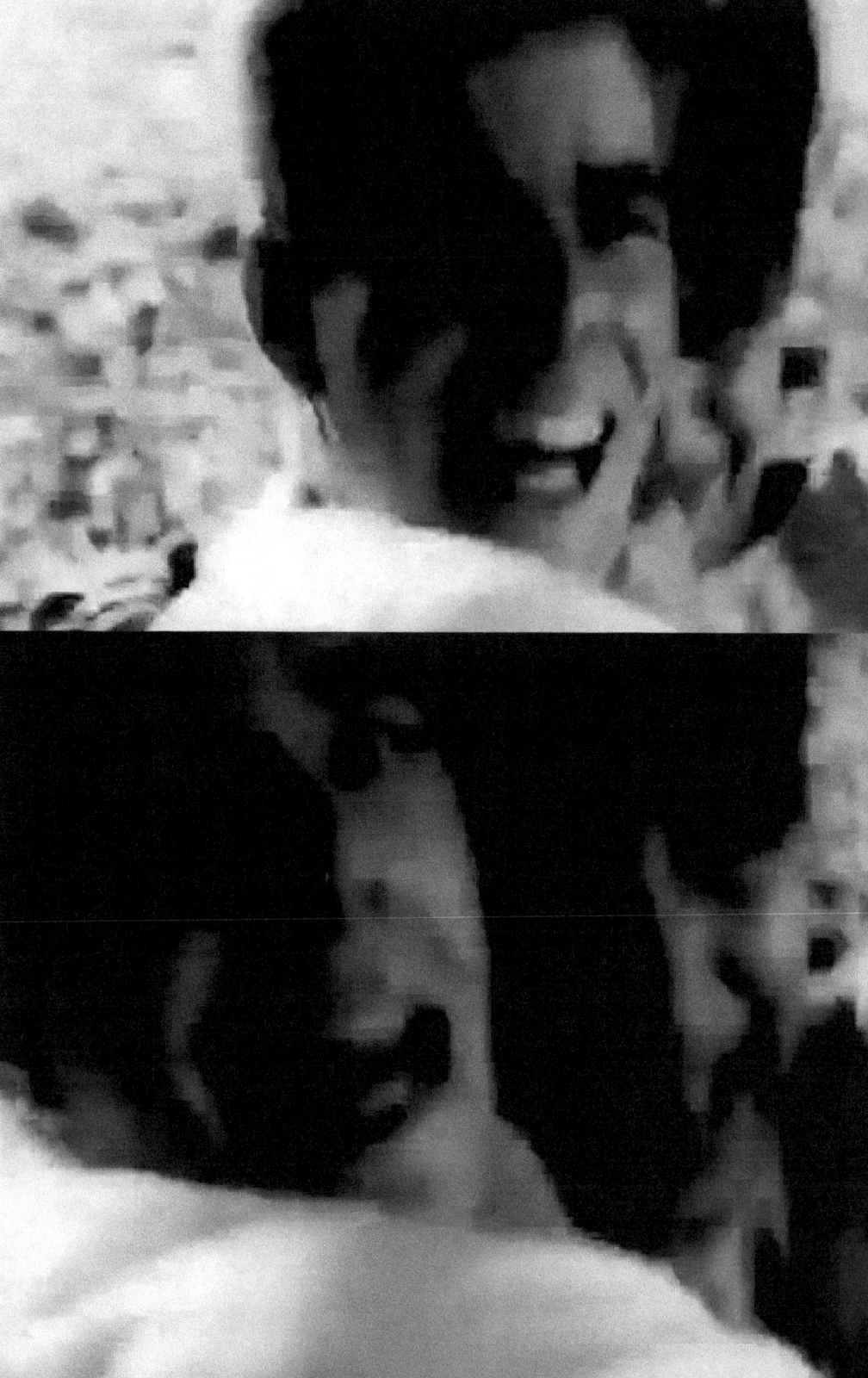

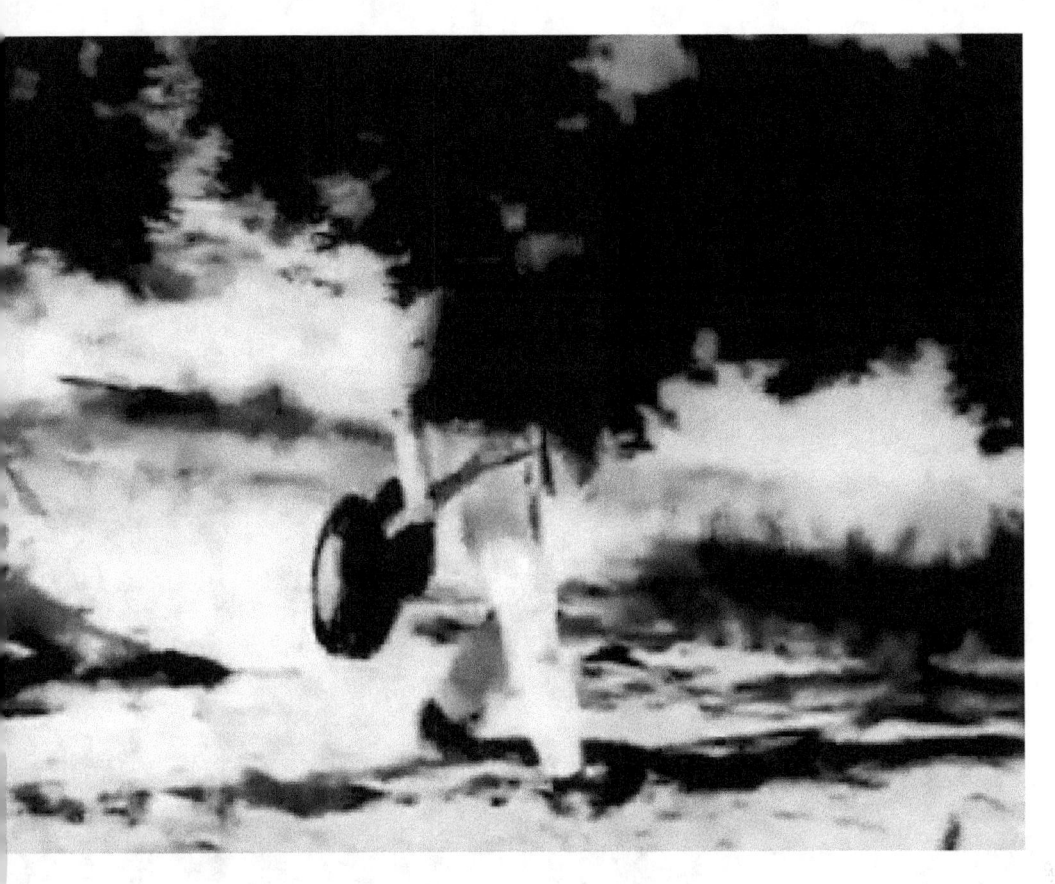

—WHAT IS IT

—YOU STAY THERE

STAY CALM

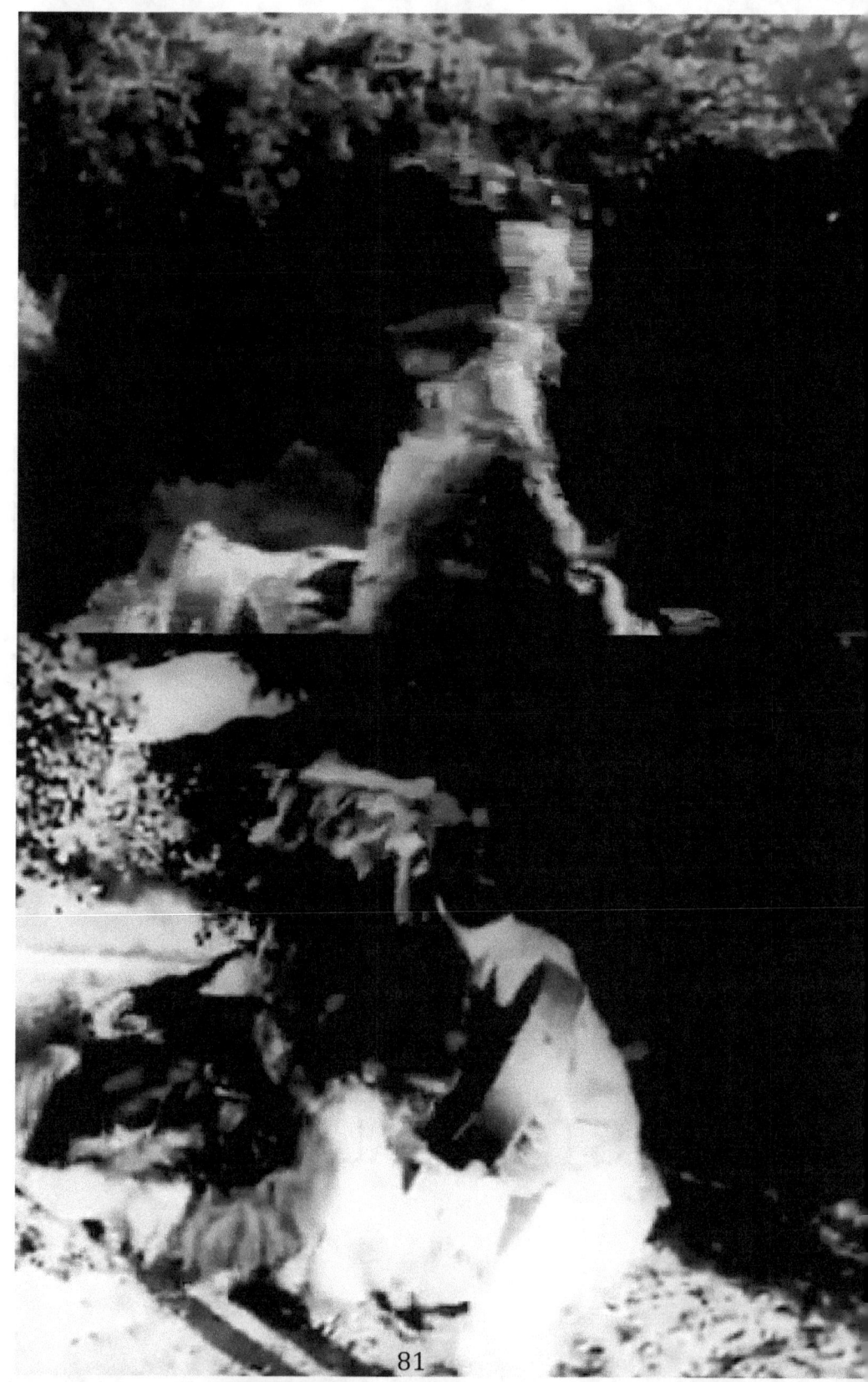

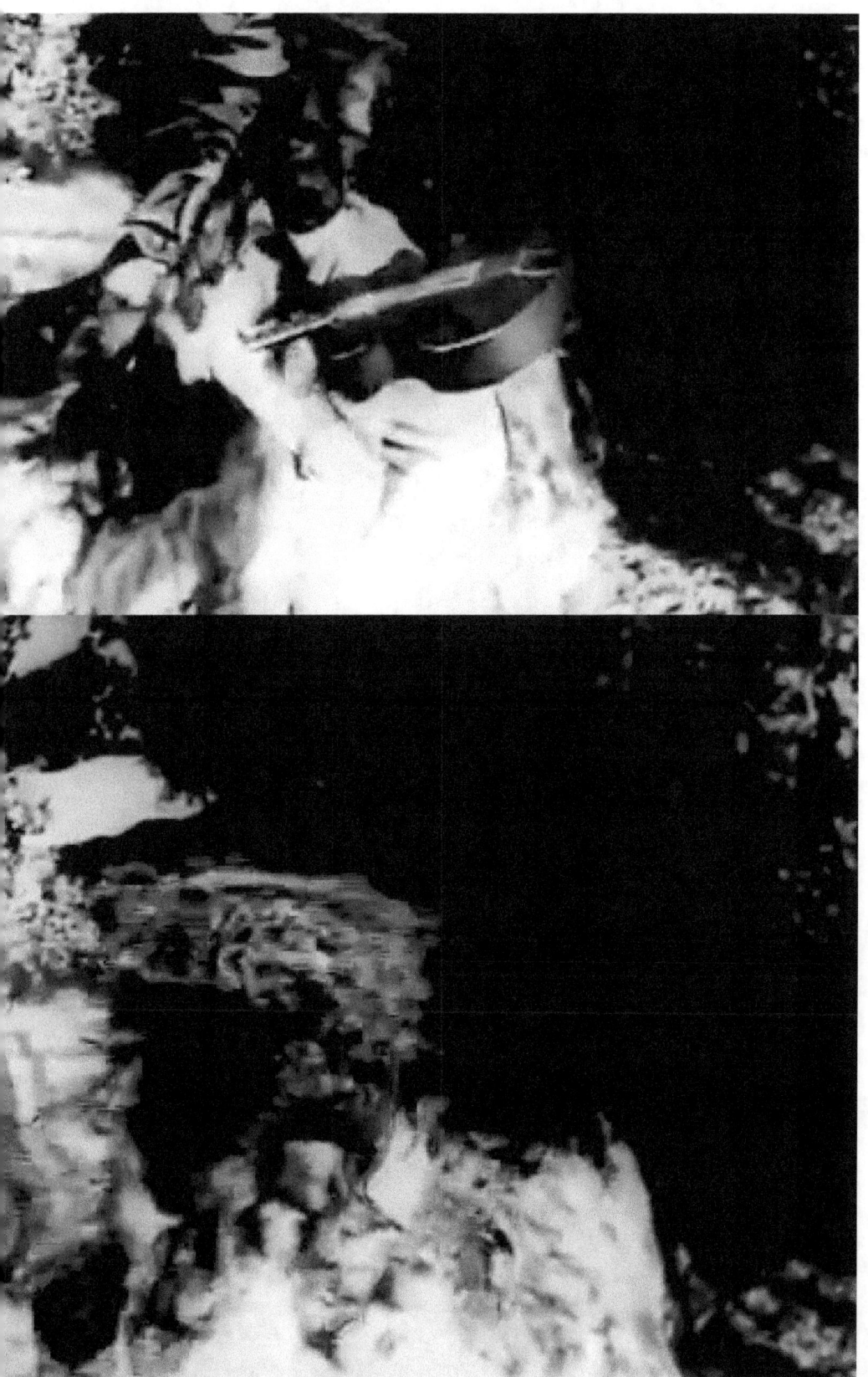

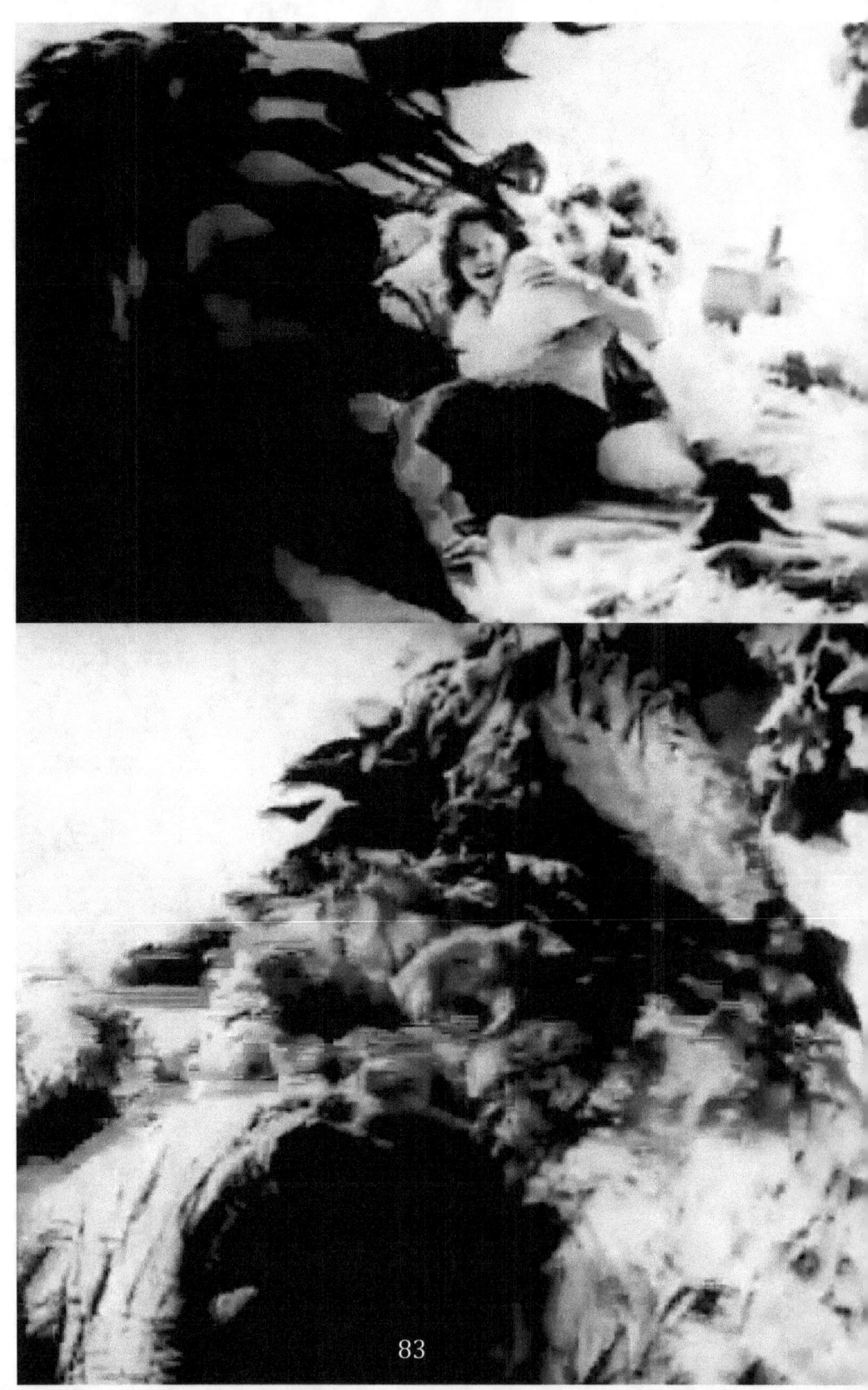

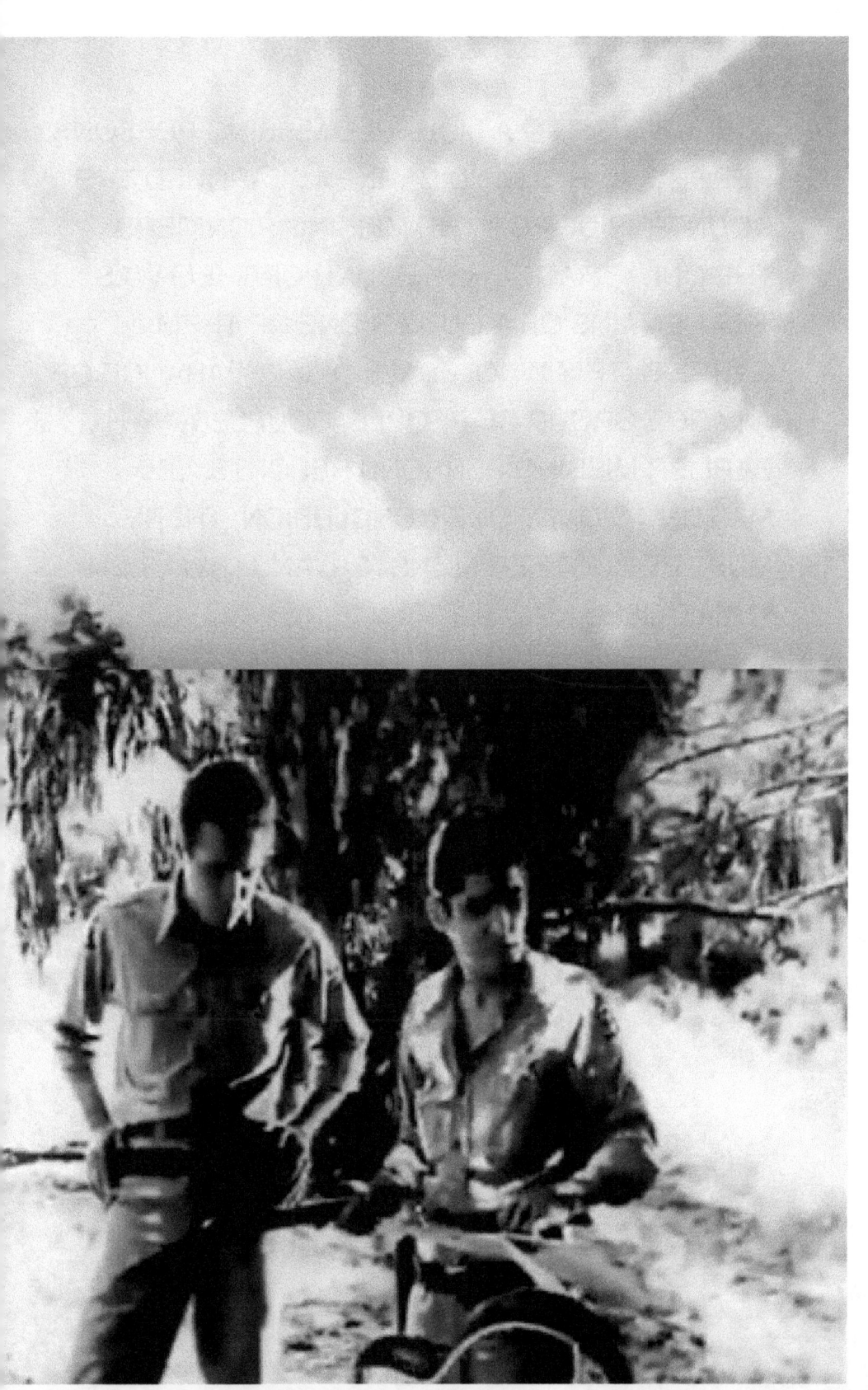

IN RESPONSE TO A MULTIPLE MISSING PERSONS
REPORT, MARTIN AND BARNEY SEARCHED THE
COUNTRYSIDE FOR THE MISSING PICNICERS.
THE ONLY TRACE THEY FOUND OF THEM WAS
THE REMAINS OF A GUITAR ONE OF THEM
CARRIED. THIS WHOLESALE DISAPPEARANCE OF
A LARGE GROUP OF PEOPLE, COUPLED WITH
EARLIER MISSING PERSONS REPORTS, LED
MARTIN TO ONLY ONE CONCLUSION: THERE
MUST BE ANOTHER MONSTER, AND IT WAS ON
THE LOOSE.

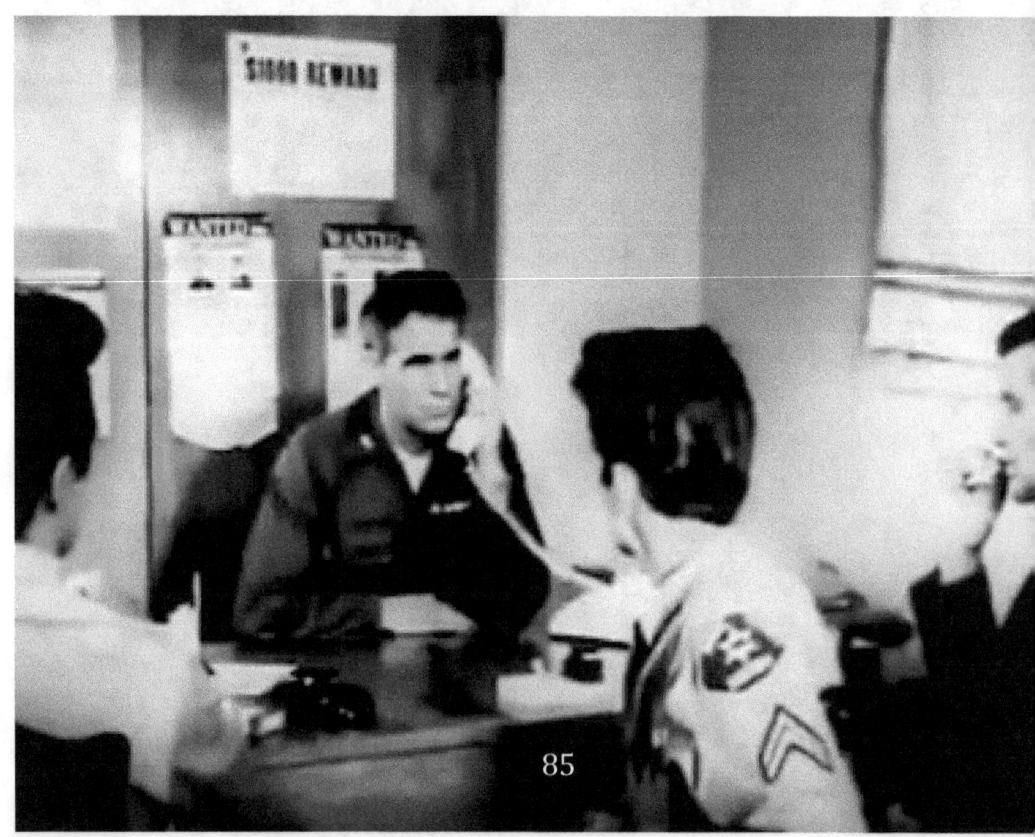

THE COL. LISTENED TO MARTIN'S THEORY
AND AFTER CONSULTING WITH BRADFORD,
DECIDED TO CALL WASHINGTON. HE WAS
TOLD TO FOLLOW HIS OWN GOOD
JUDGEMENT BUT UNDER NO CIRCUMSTANCES
WAS HE TO ALARM THE POPULACE. THE COL.
DECIDED TO ORGANIZE A COUNTYWIDE
SEARCH. MARTIN'S ASSIGNMENT WAS TO
SEARCH THE NORTH END OF THE COUNTY.
WHILE MARTIN AND BRETT WERE ENGAGED
BY THE SEARCH, THE MONSTER WAS MOVING
TOWARD THE COMMUNITY DANCE HALL

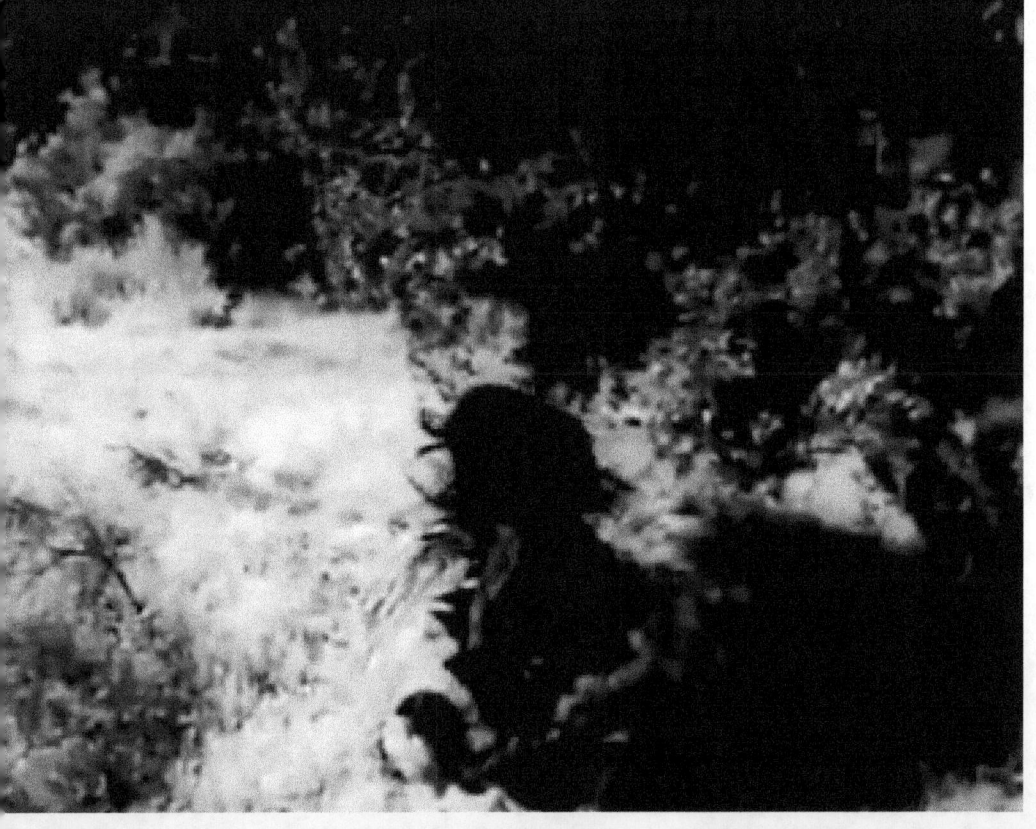

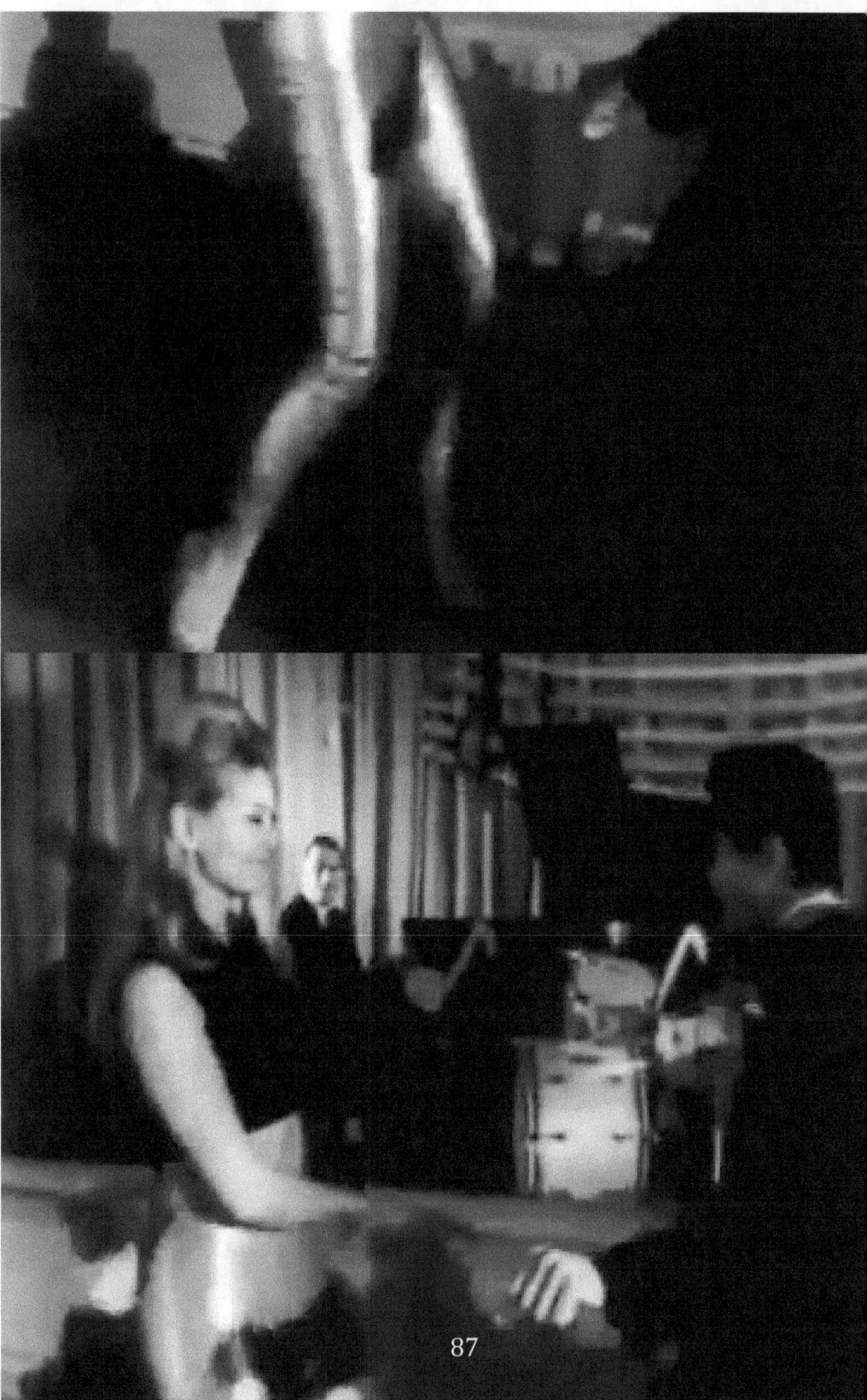

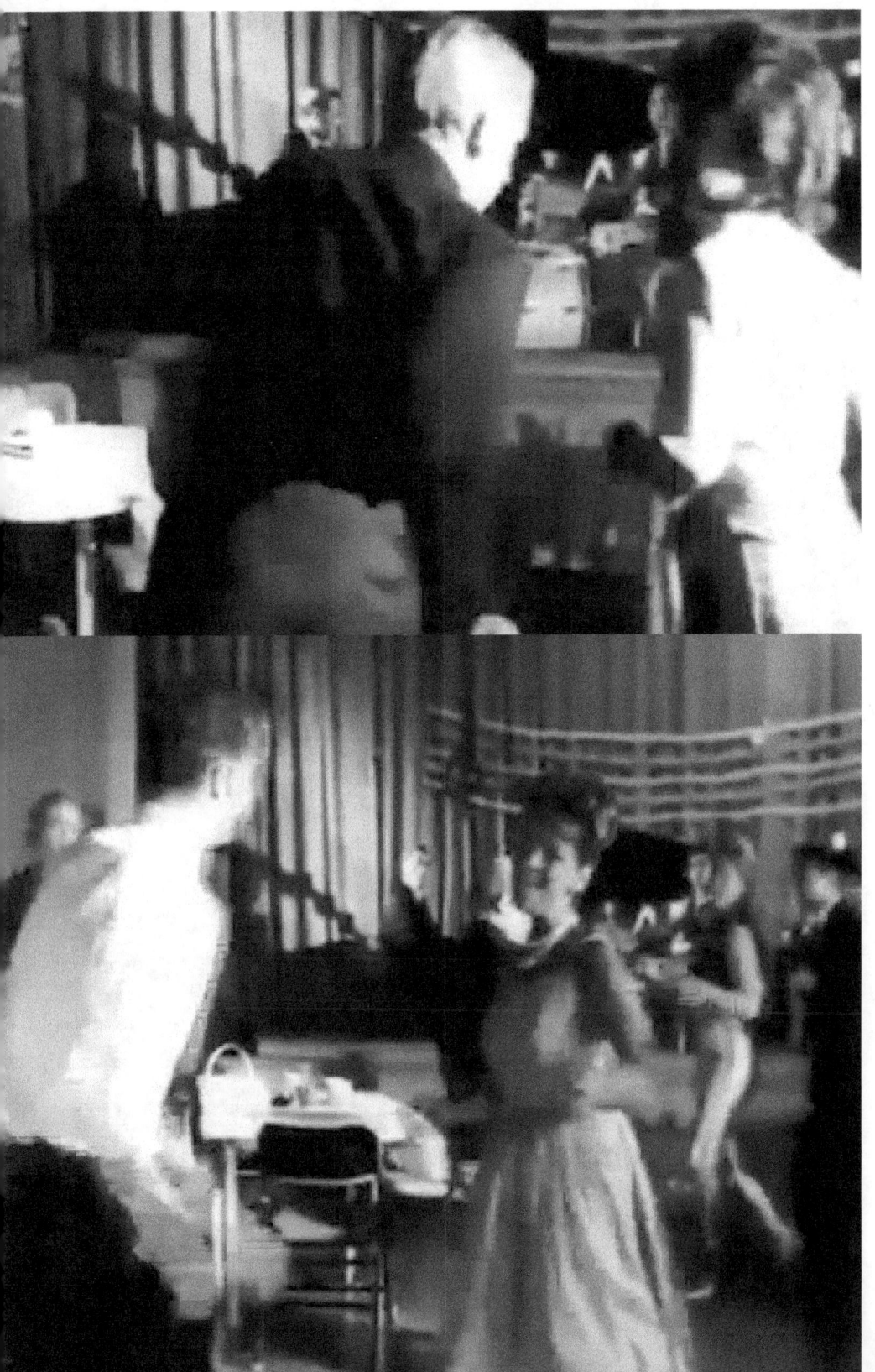

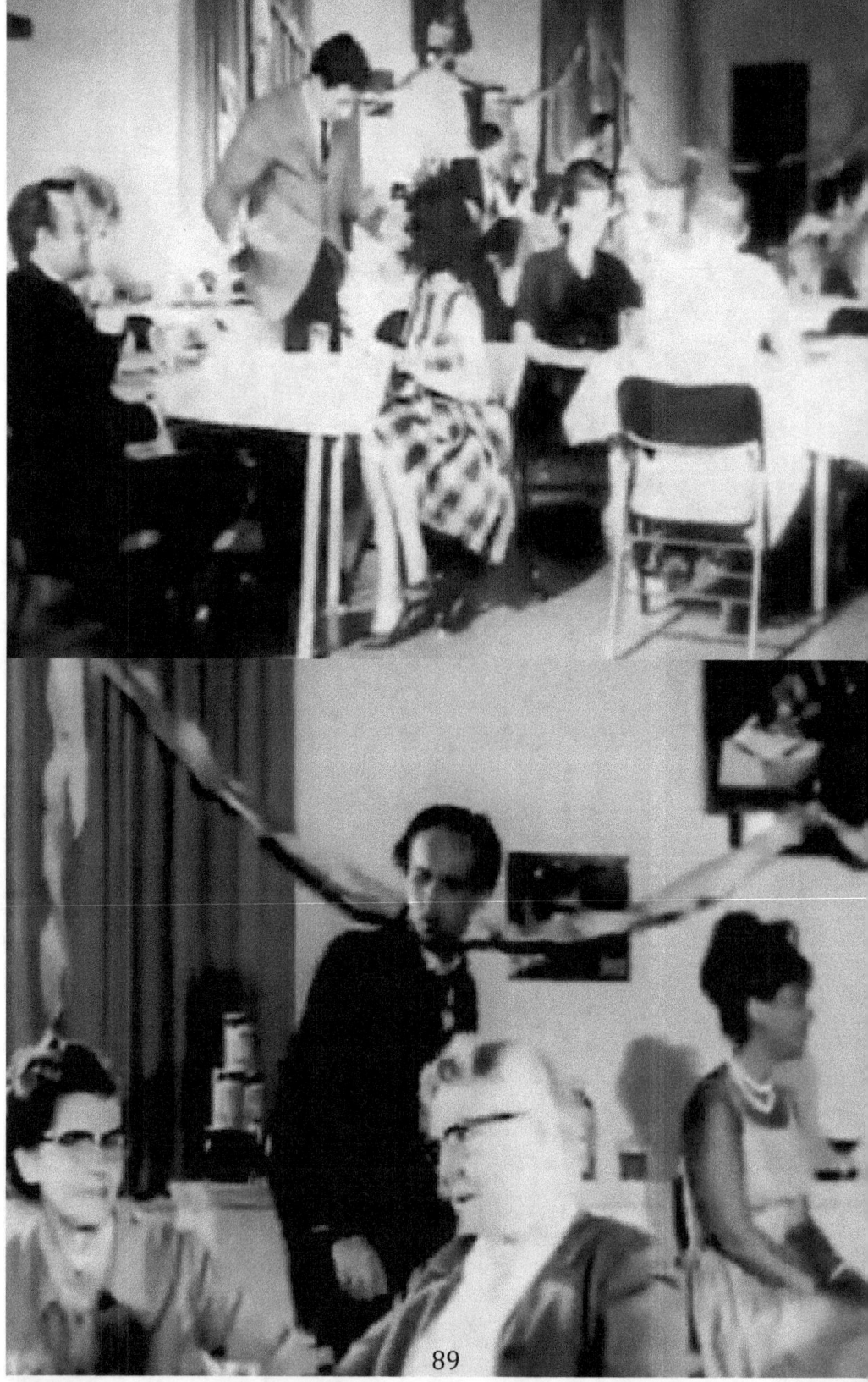

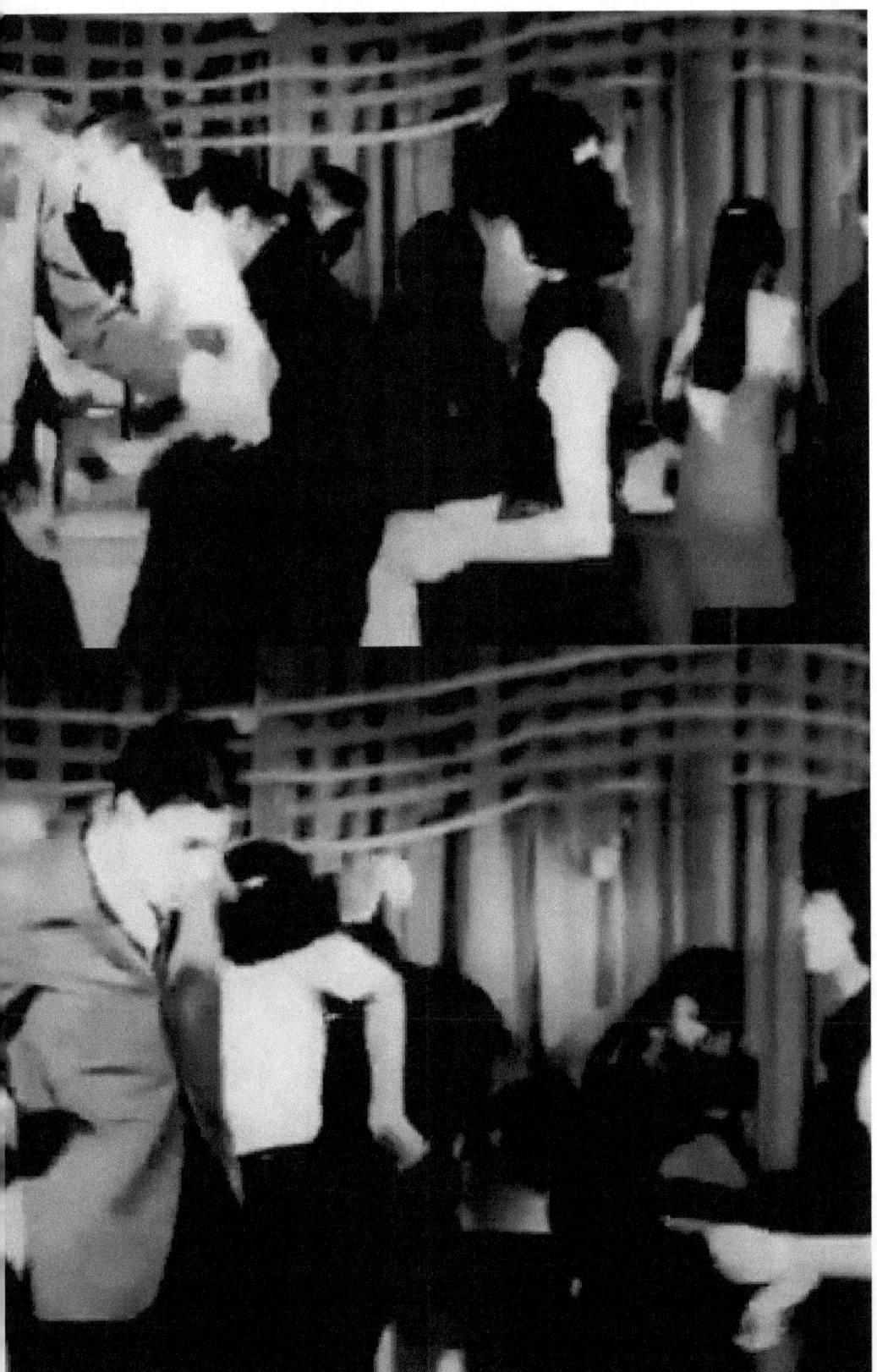

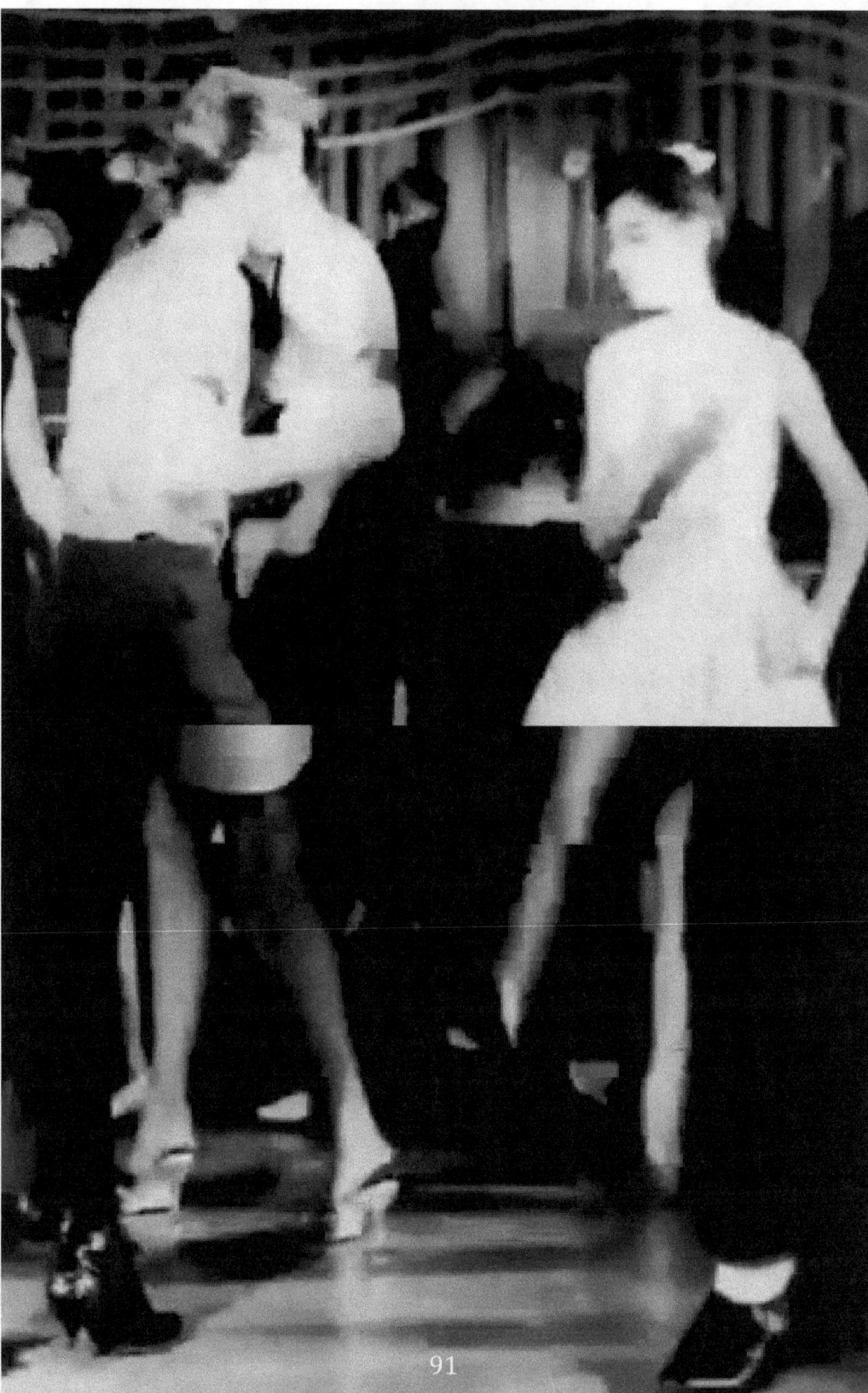

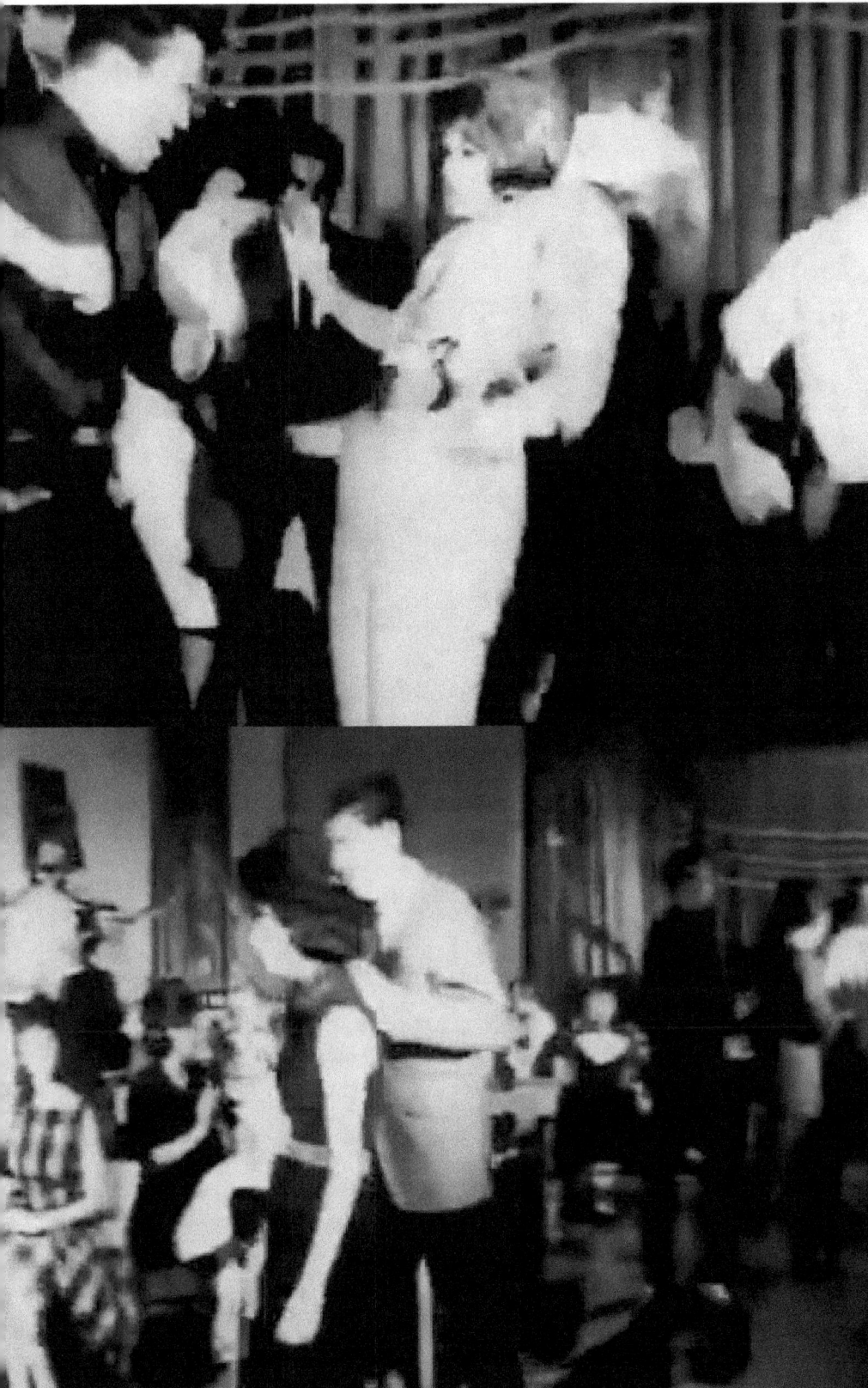

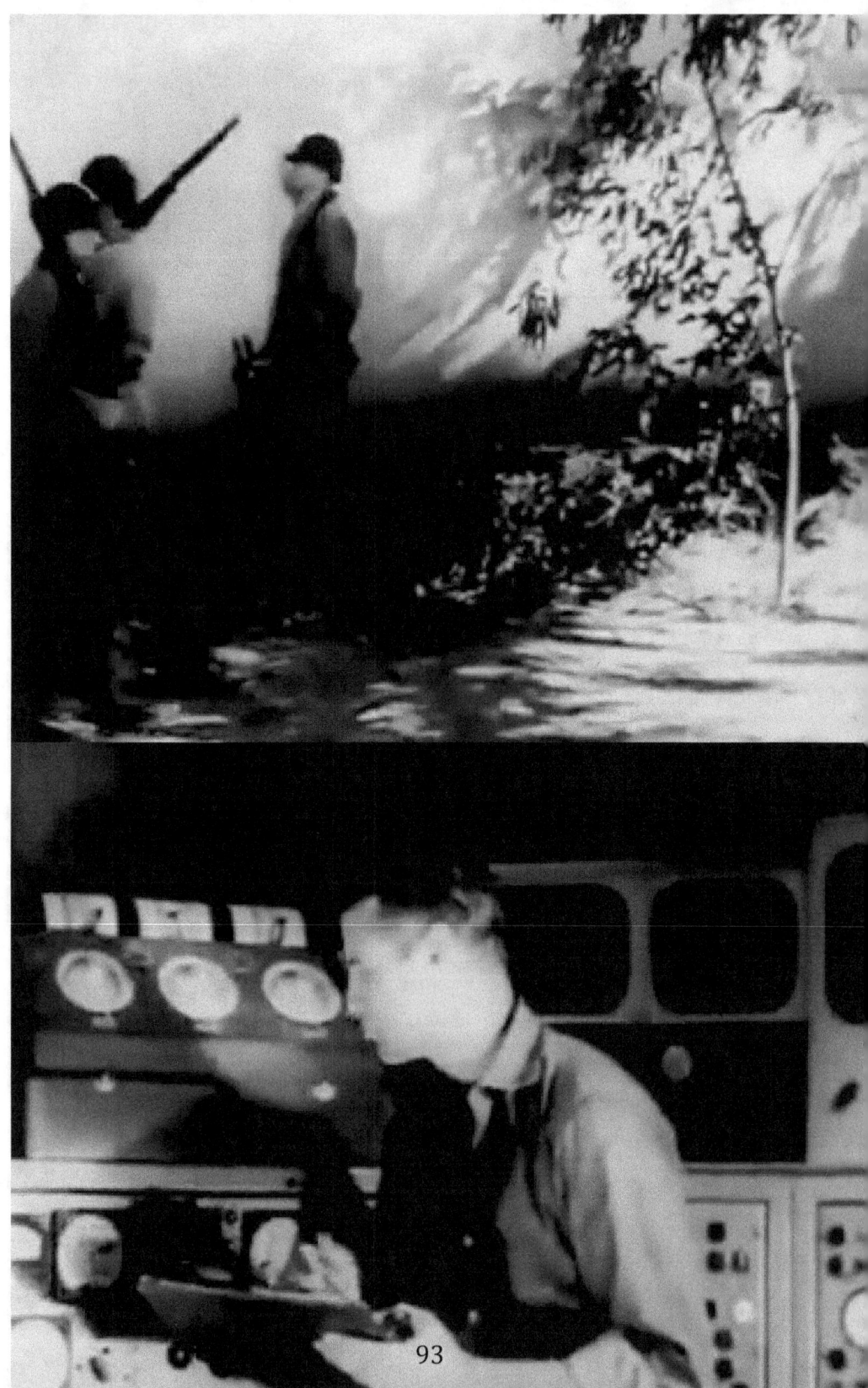

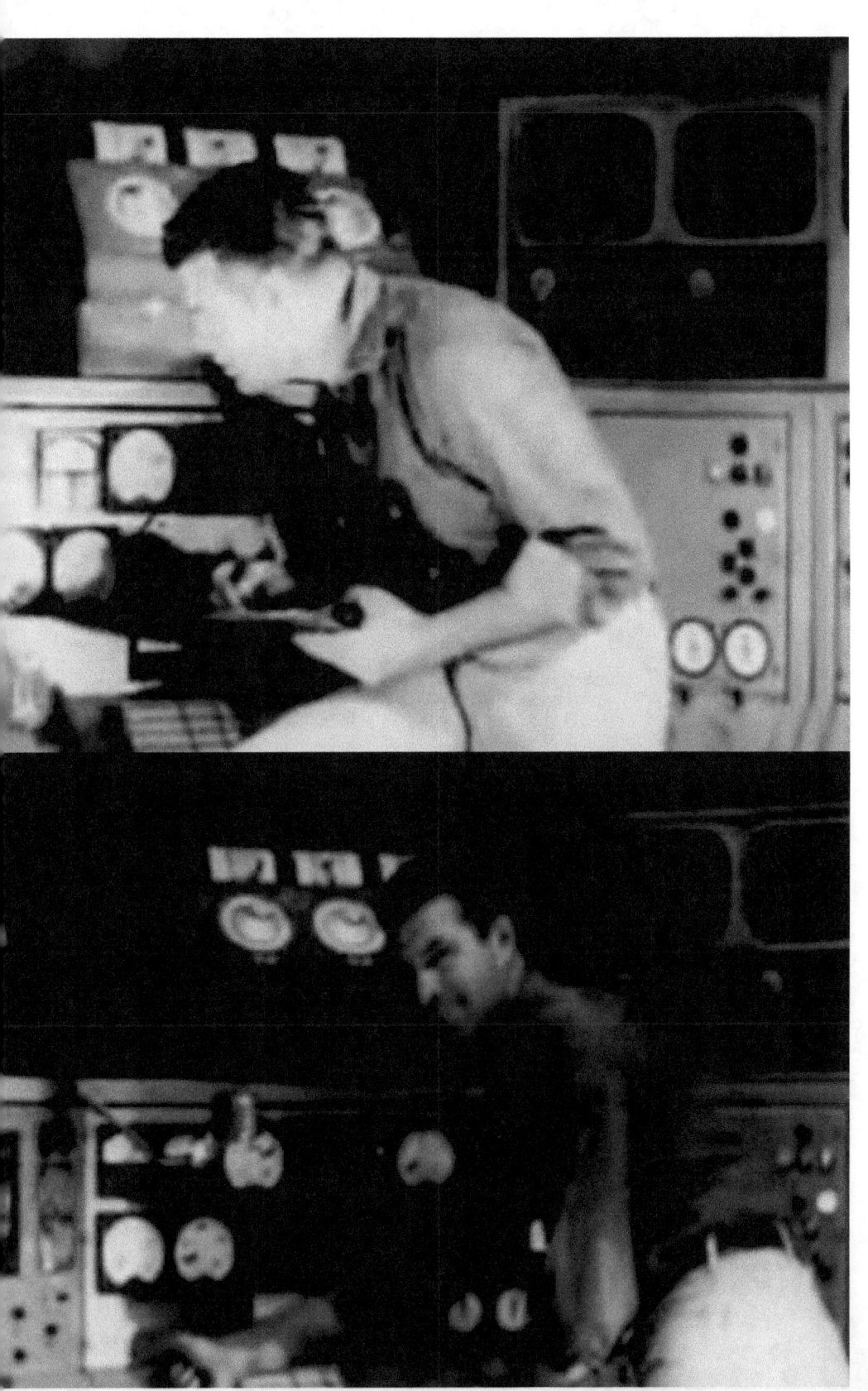

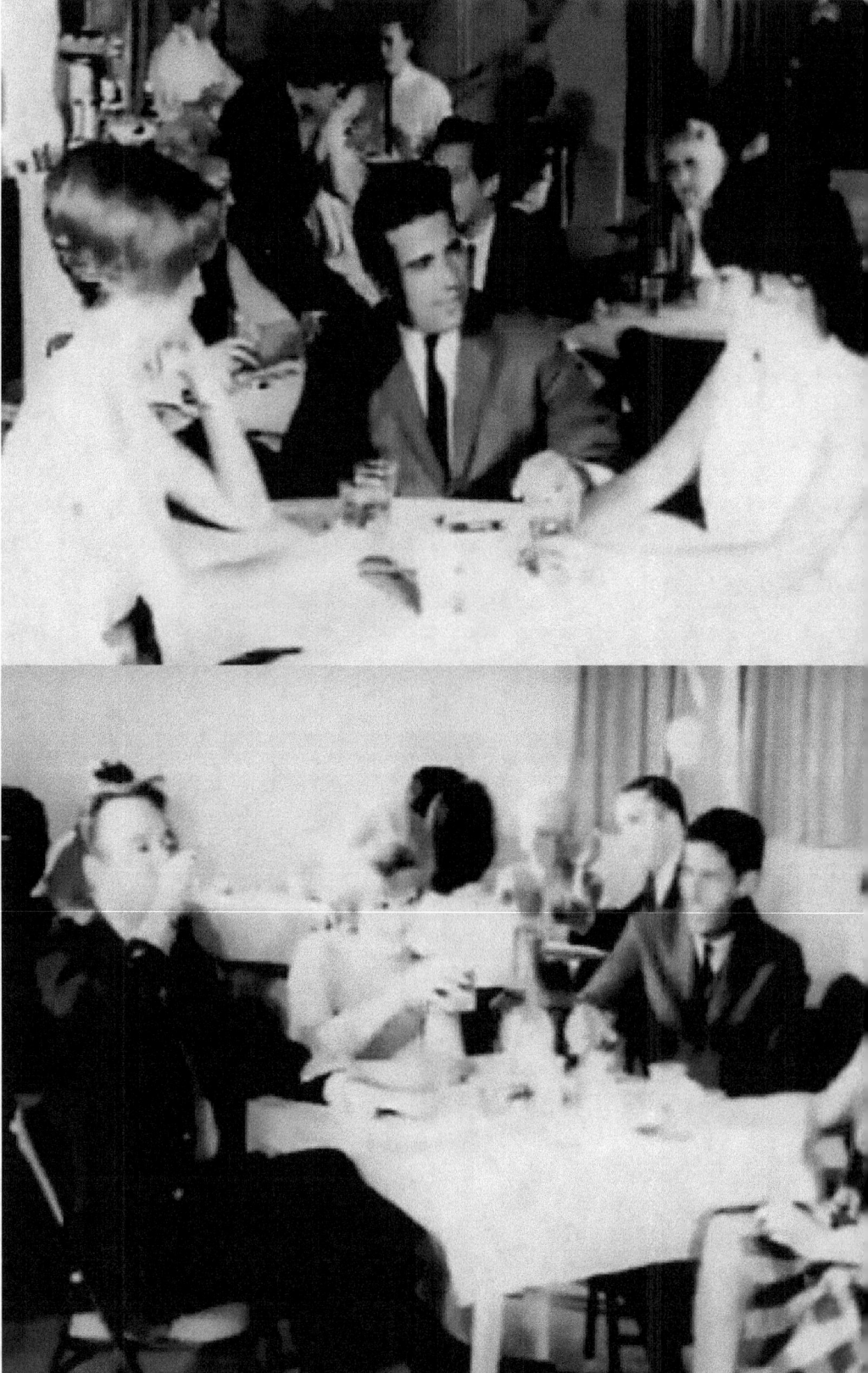

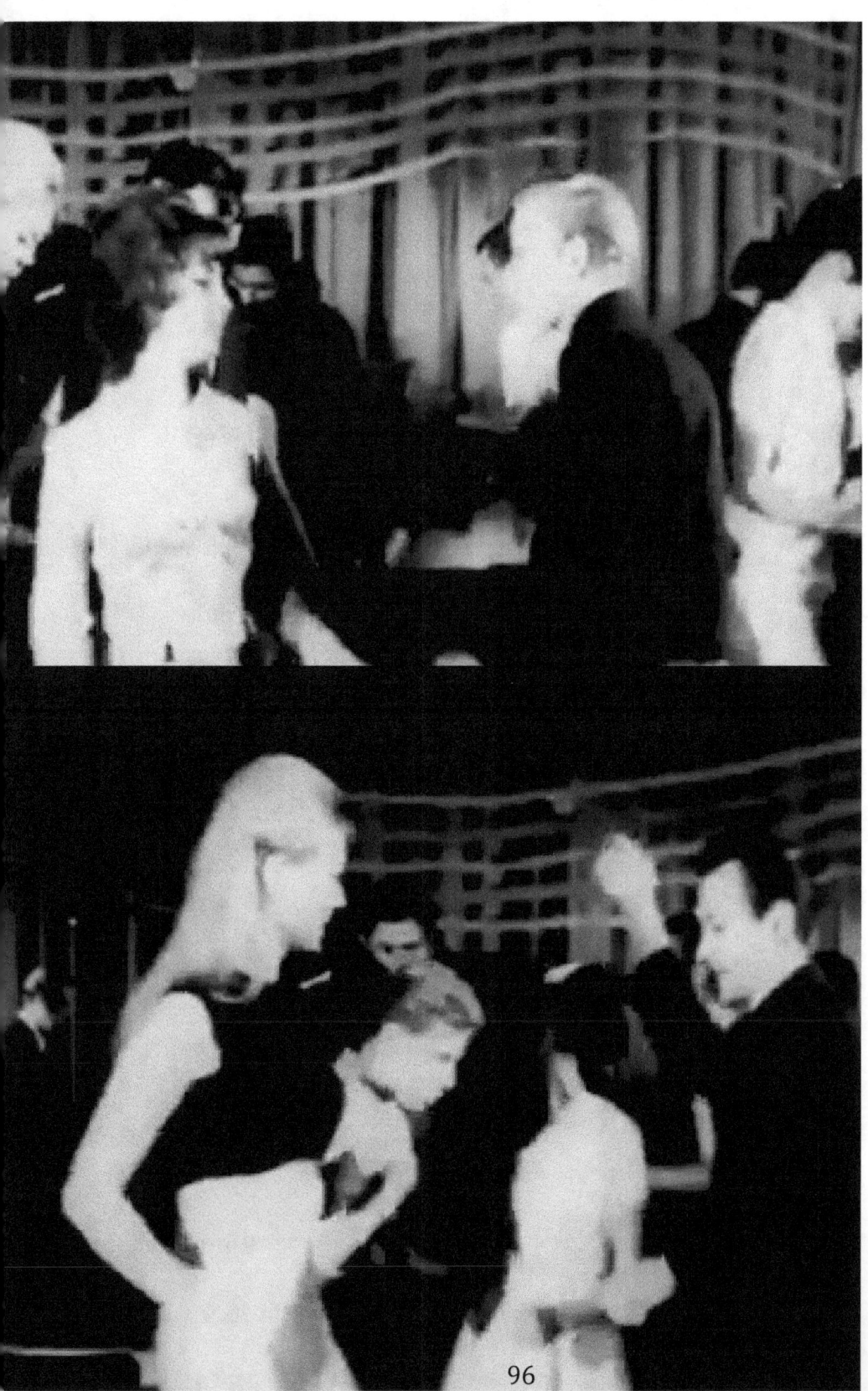

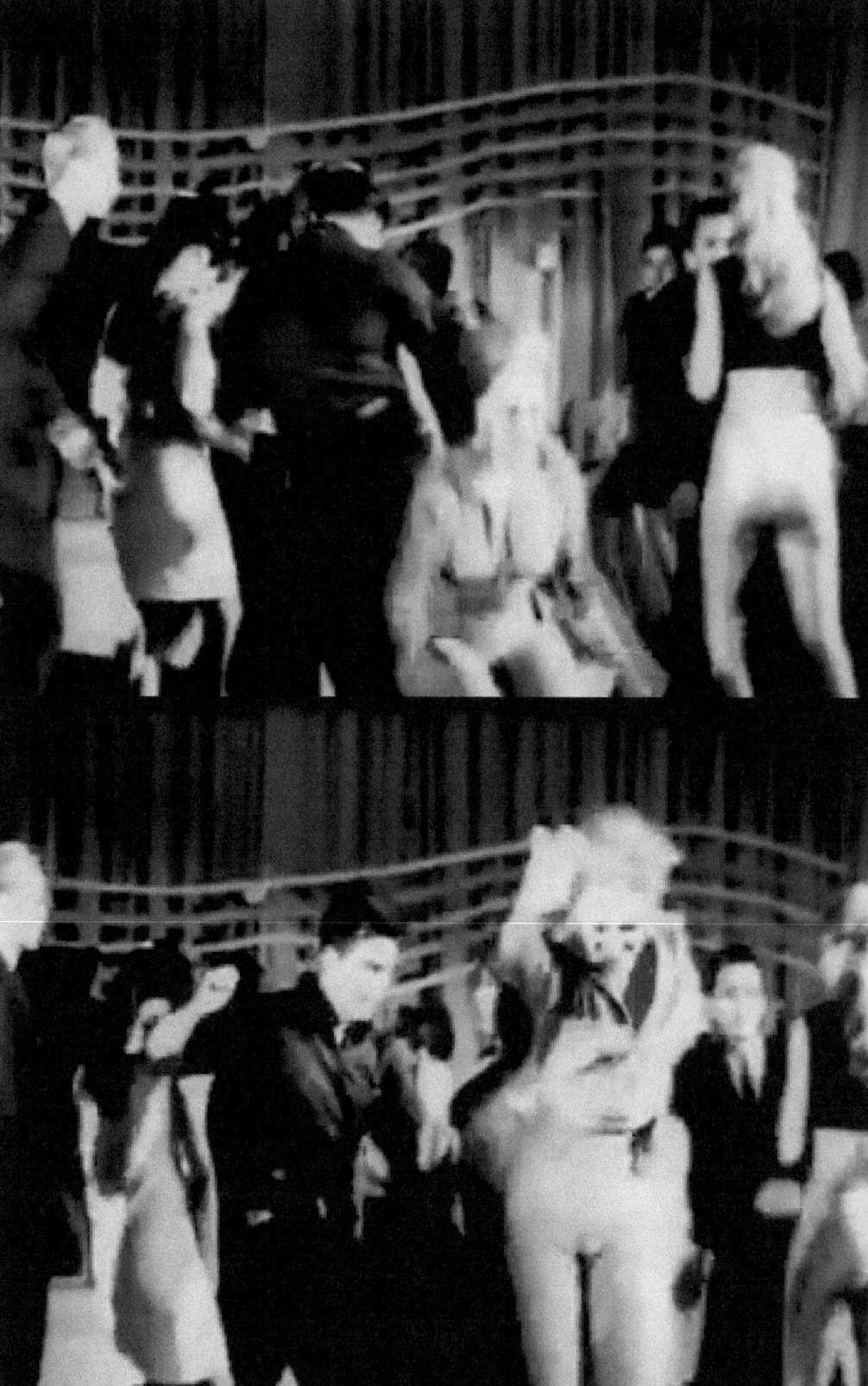

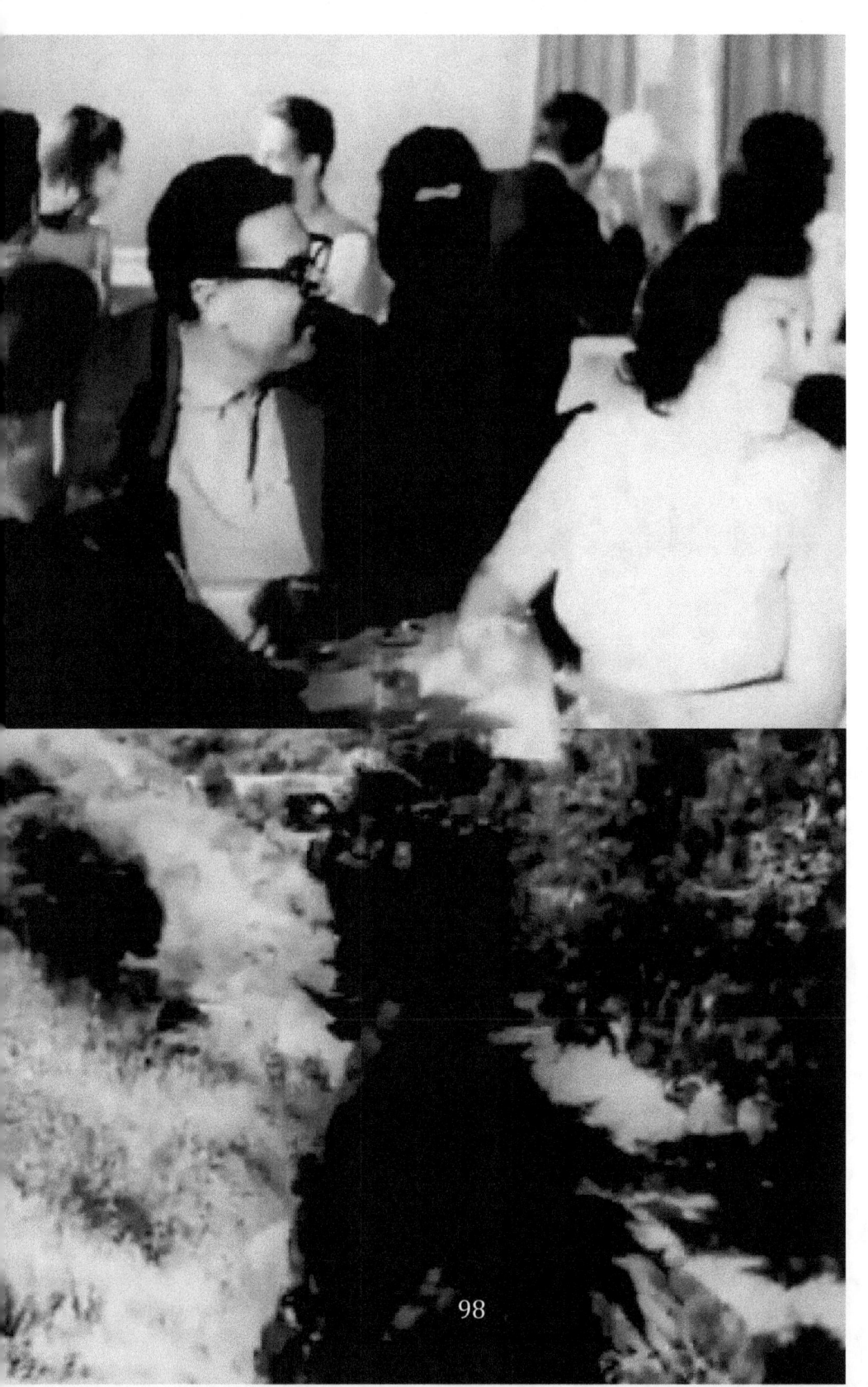

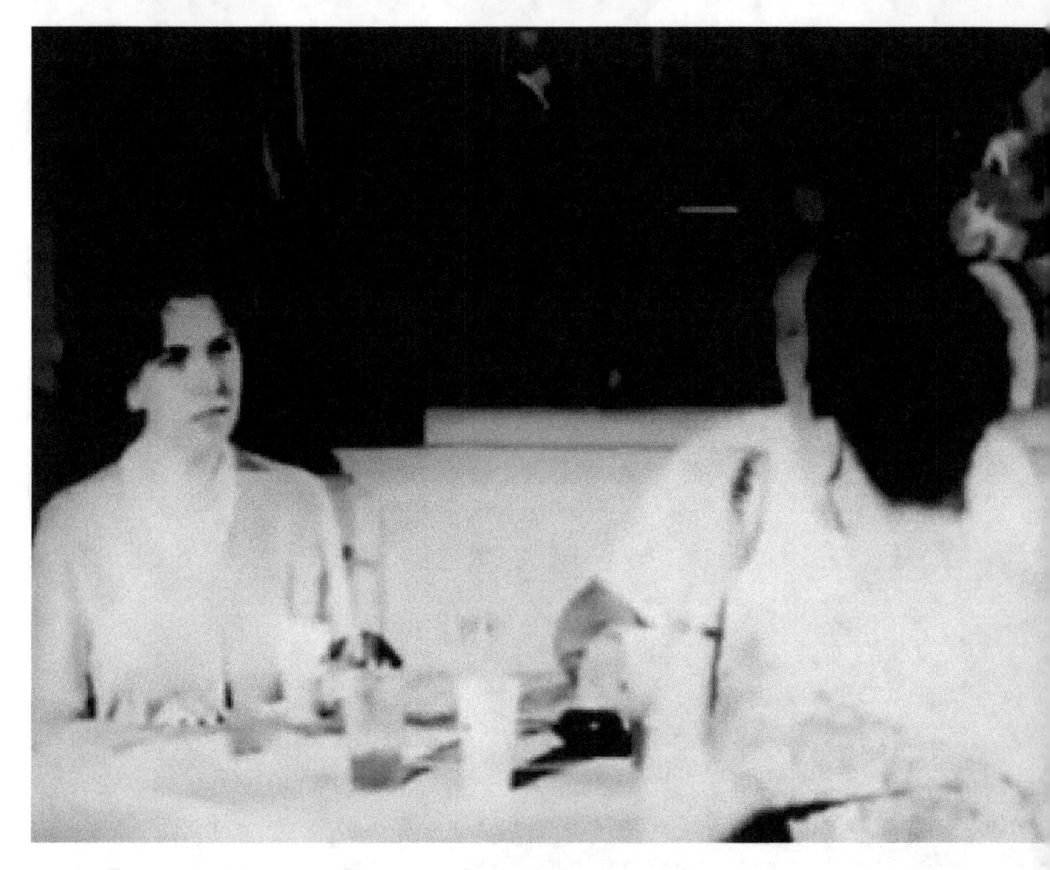

-TO HELL WITH HIM

COME ON RITA

I'VE HAD ENOUGH OF THAT GUY

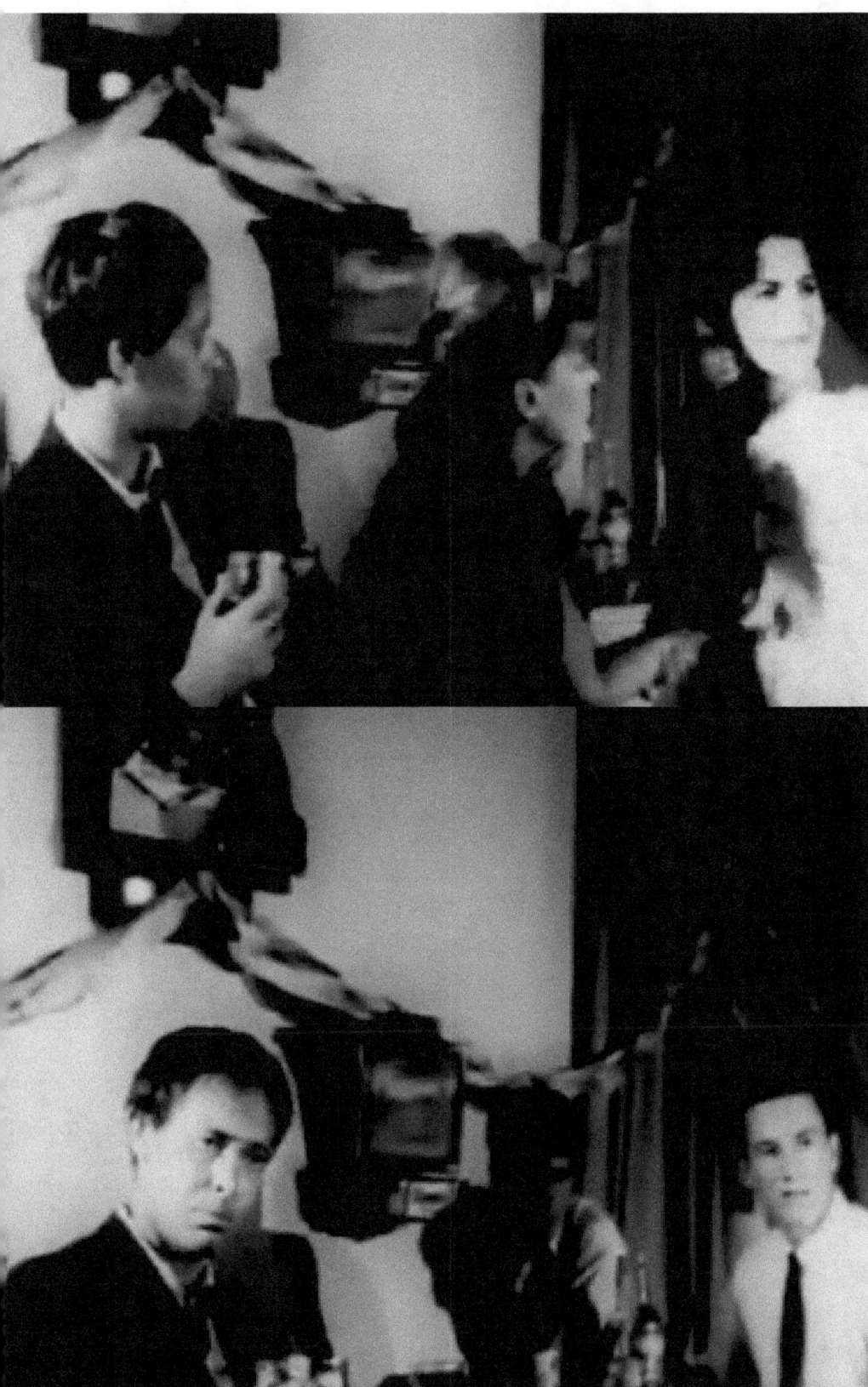

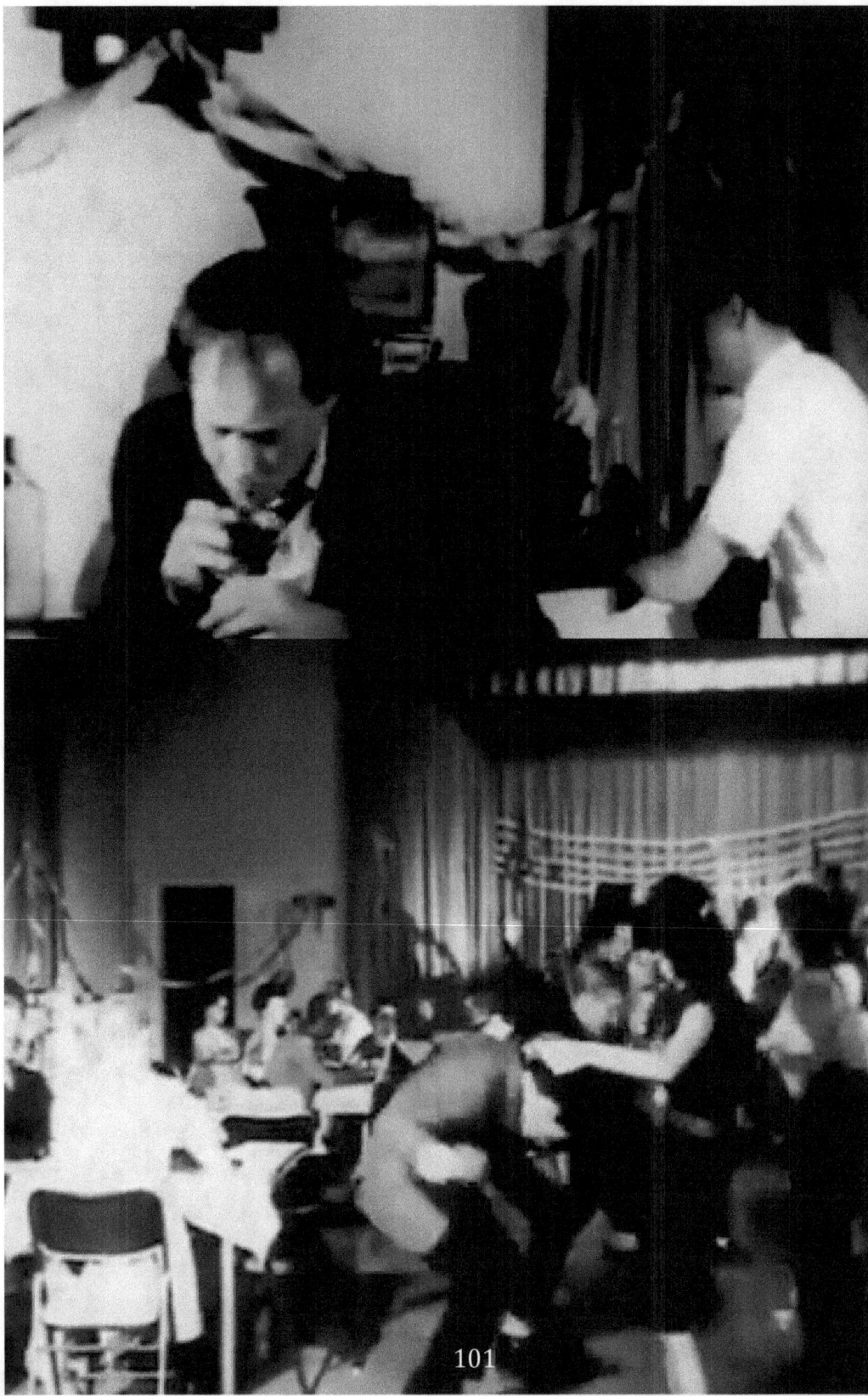

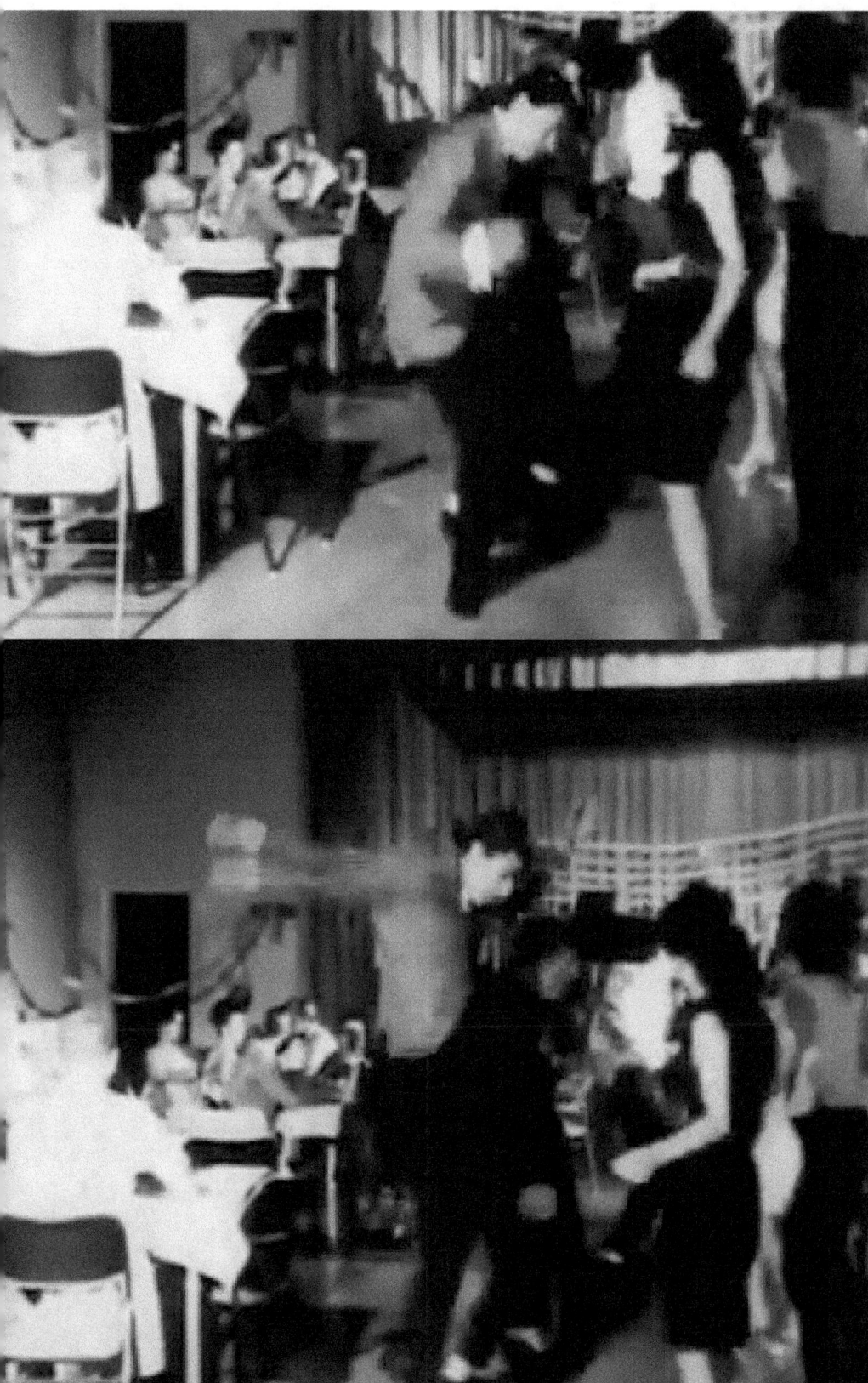

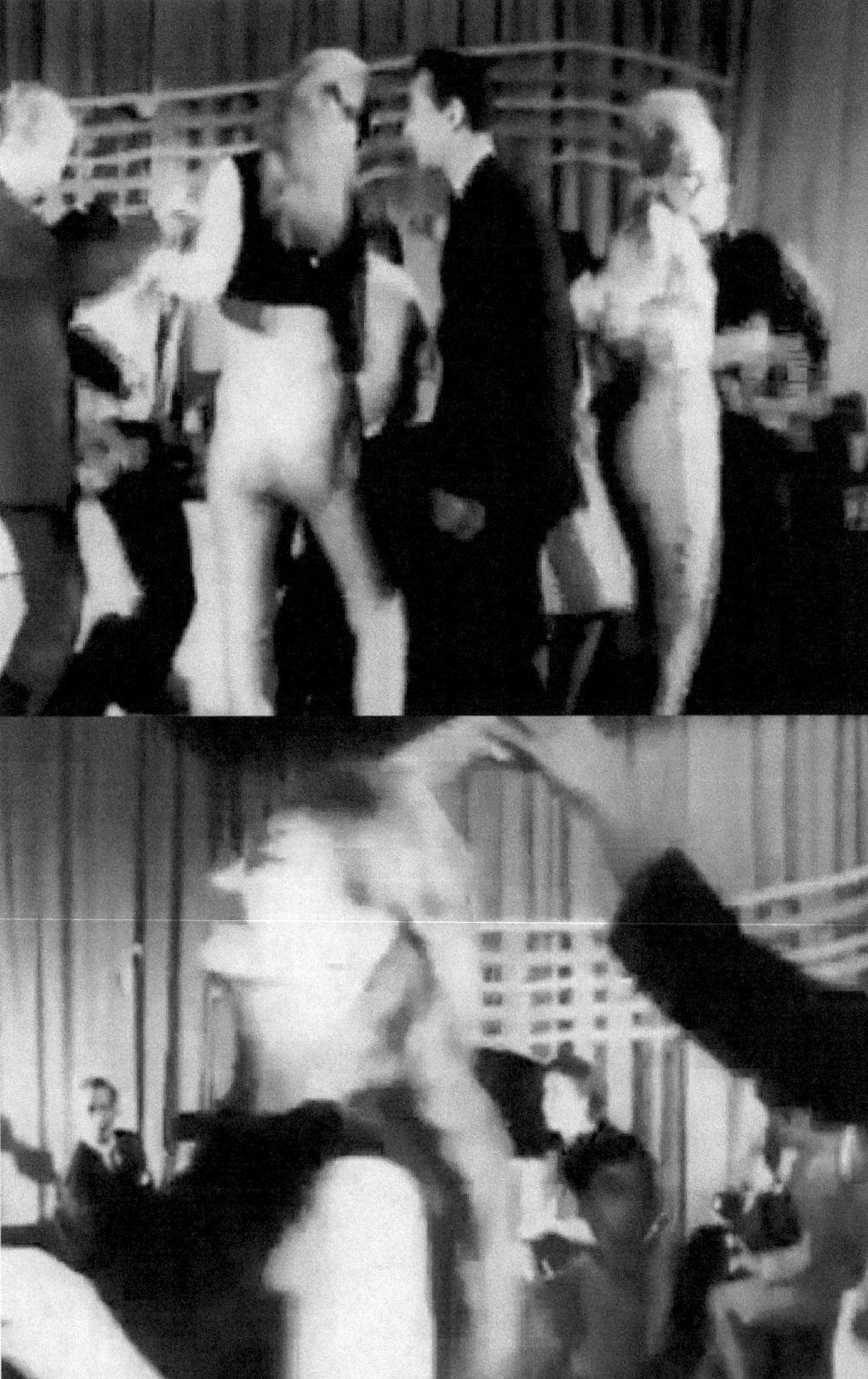

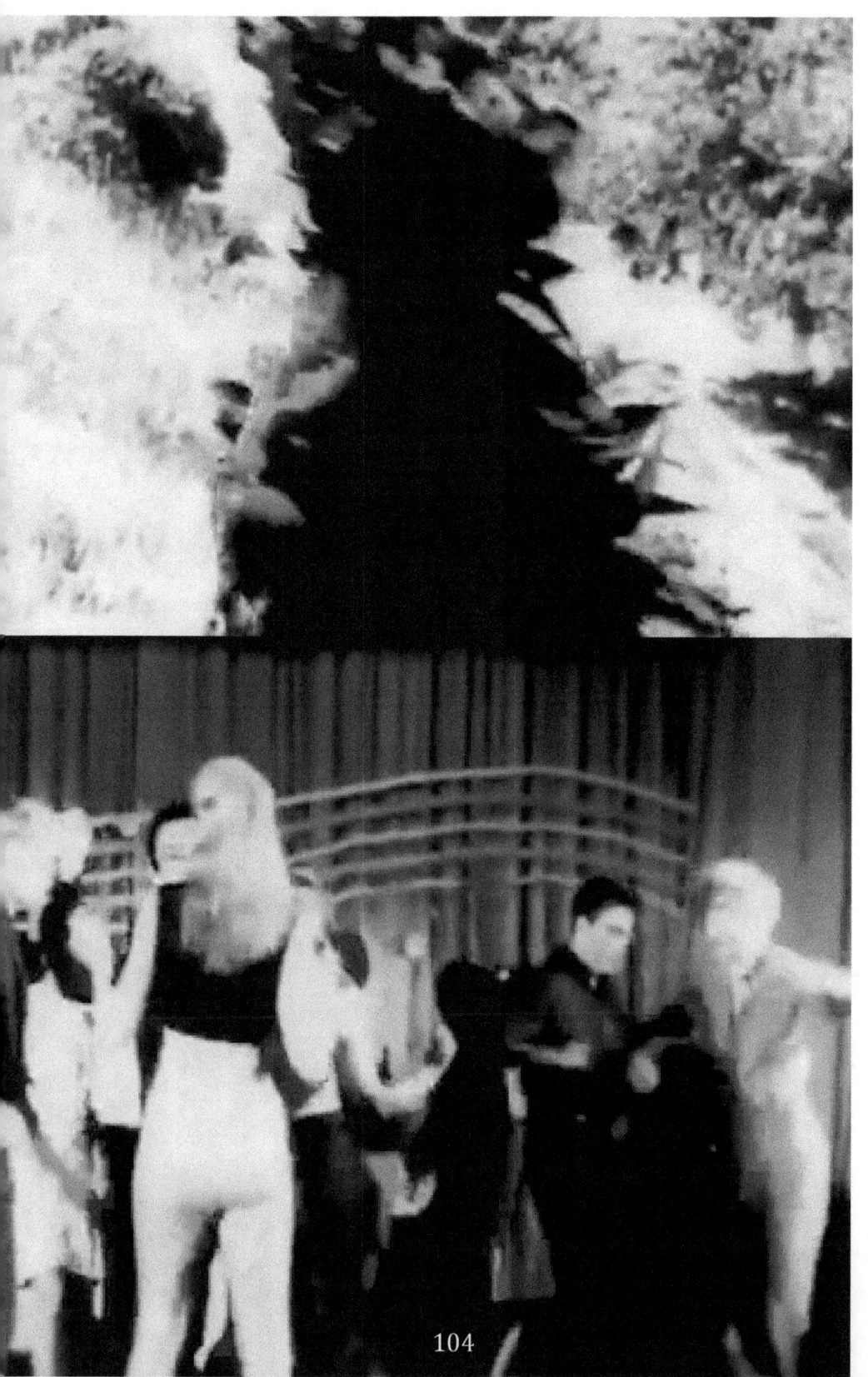

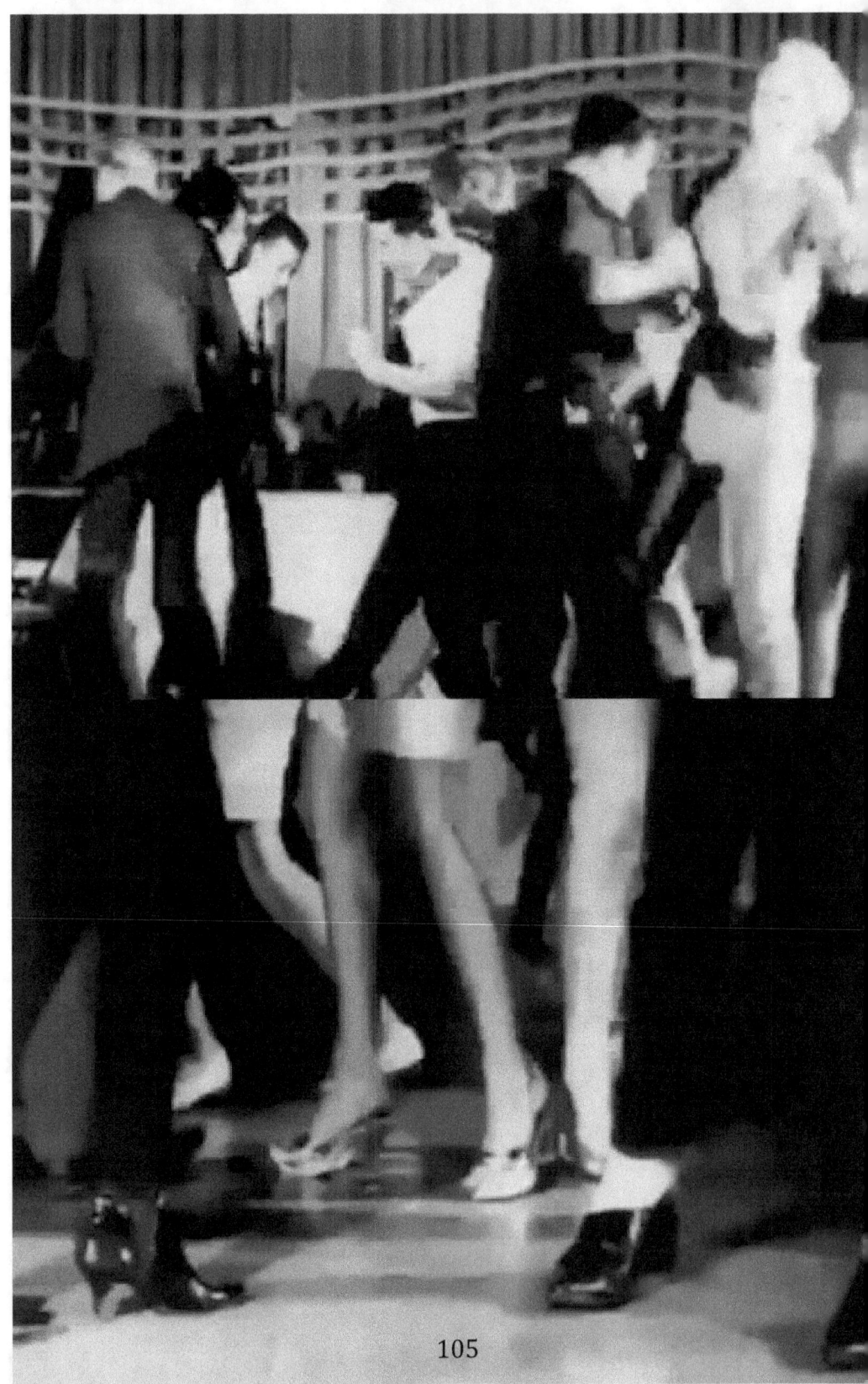

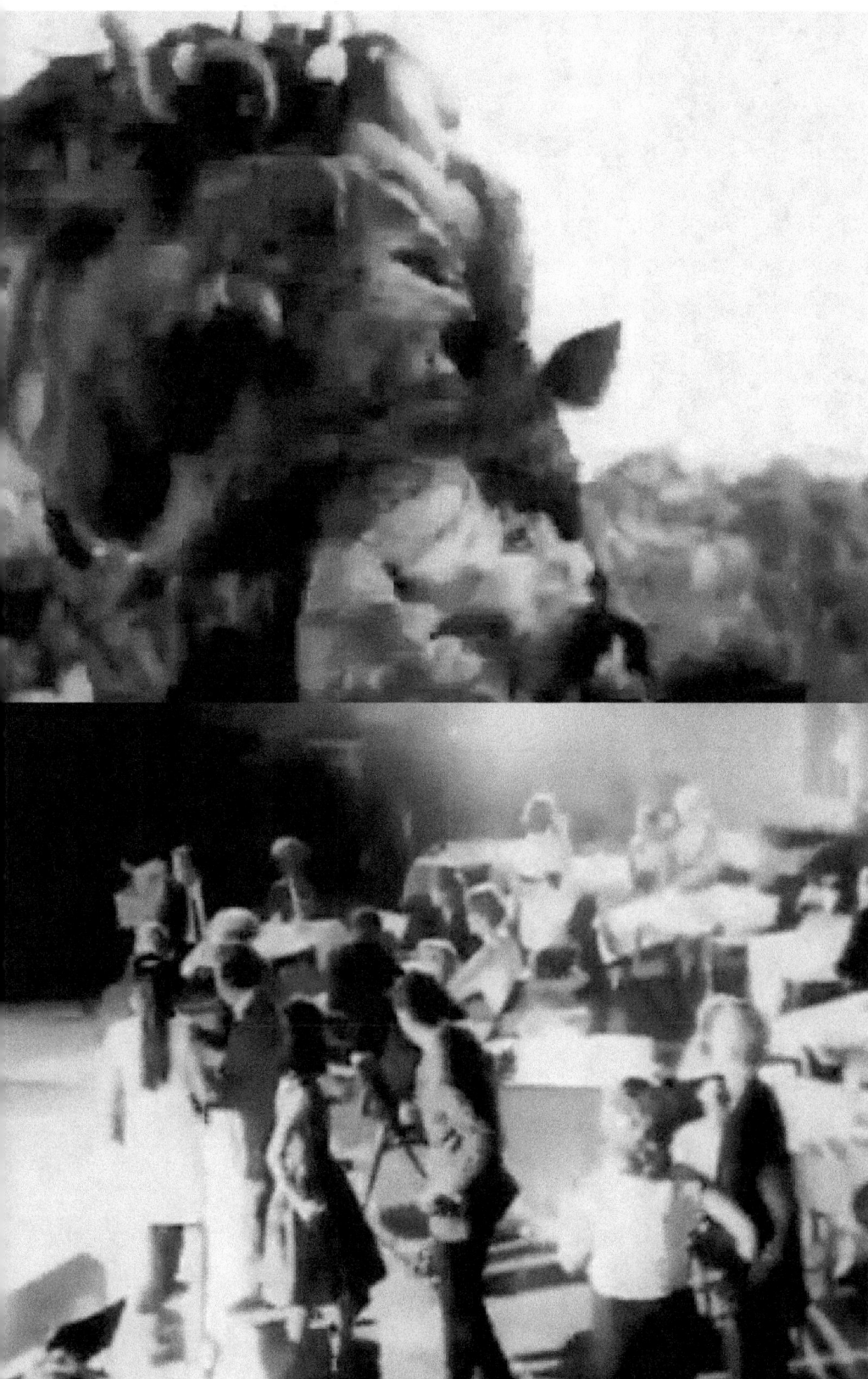

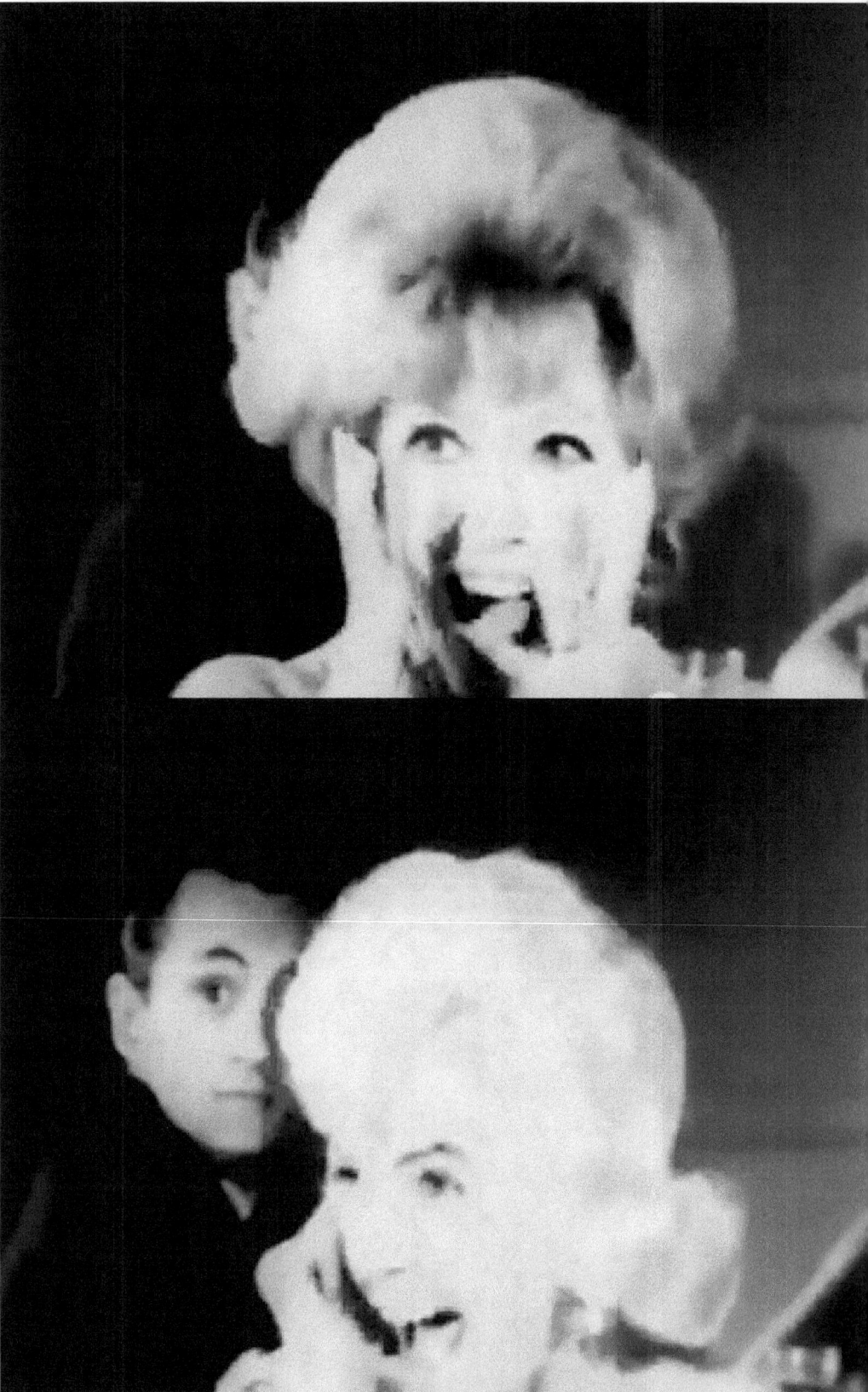

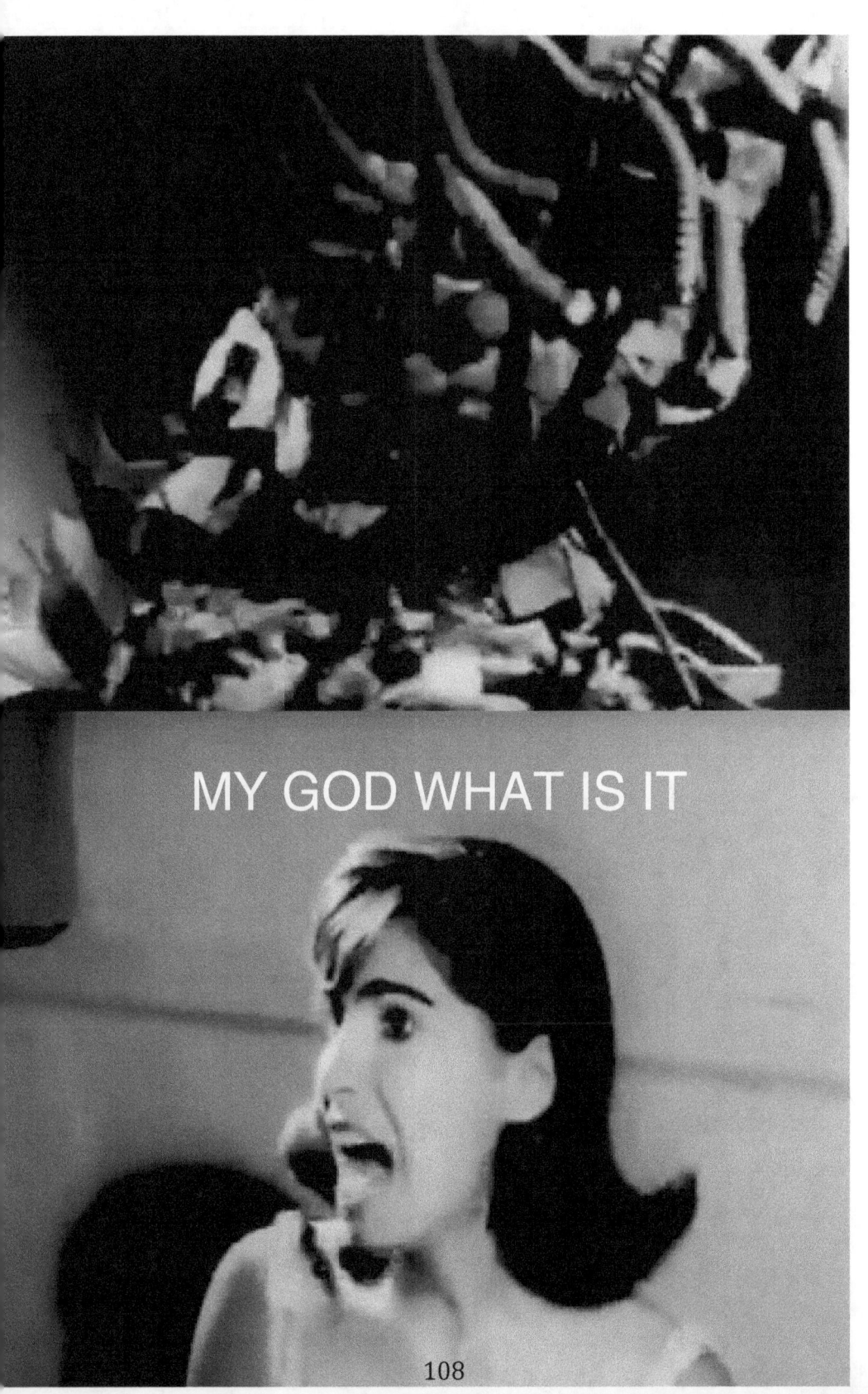

MY GOD WHAT IS IT

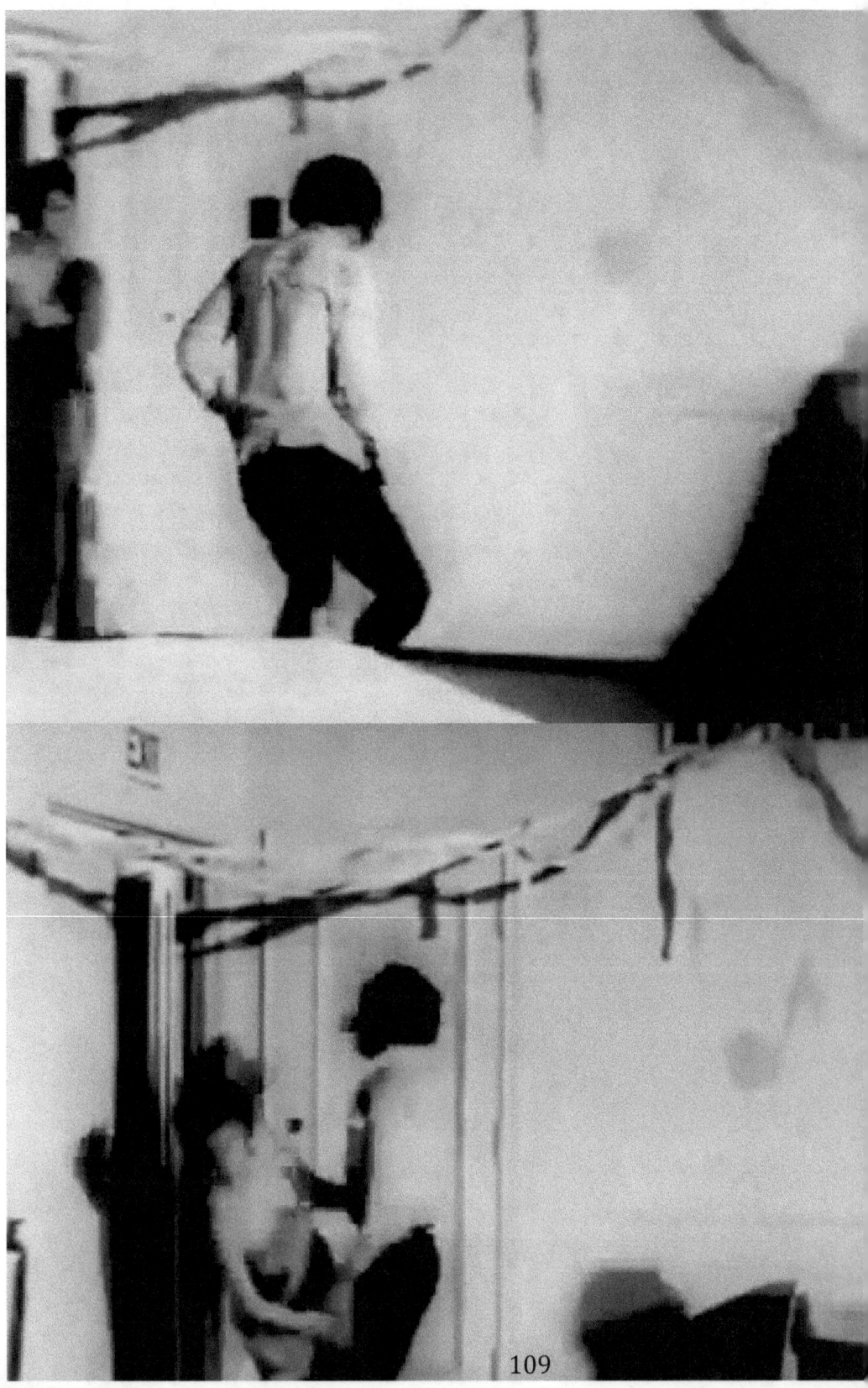

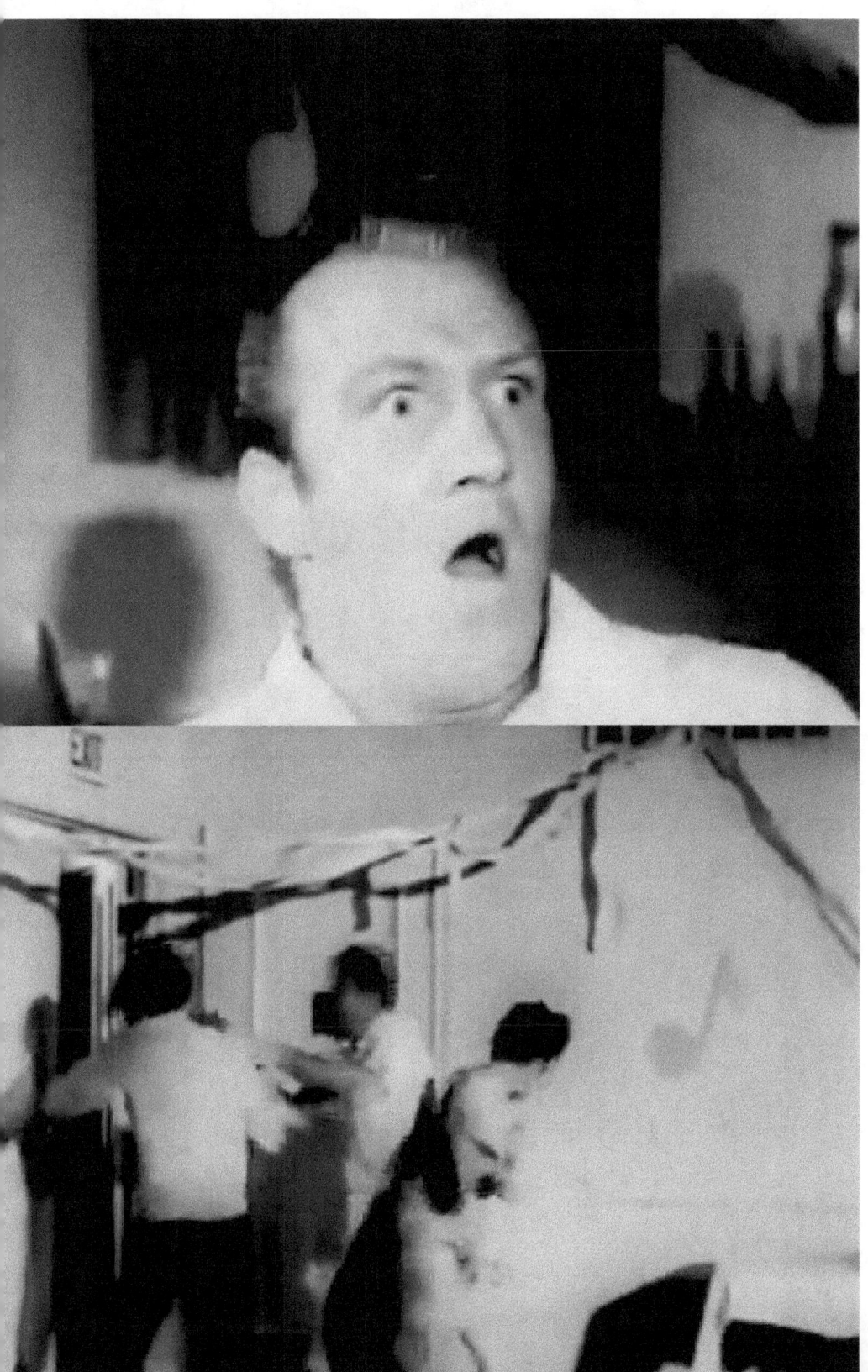

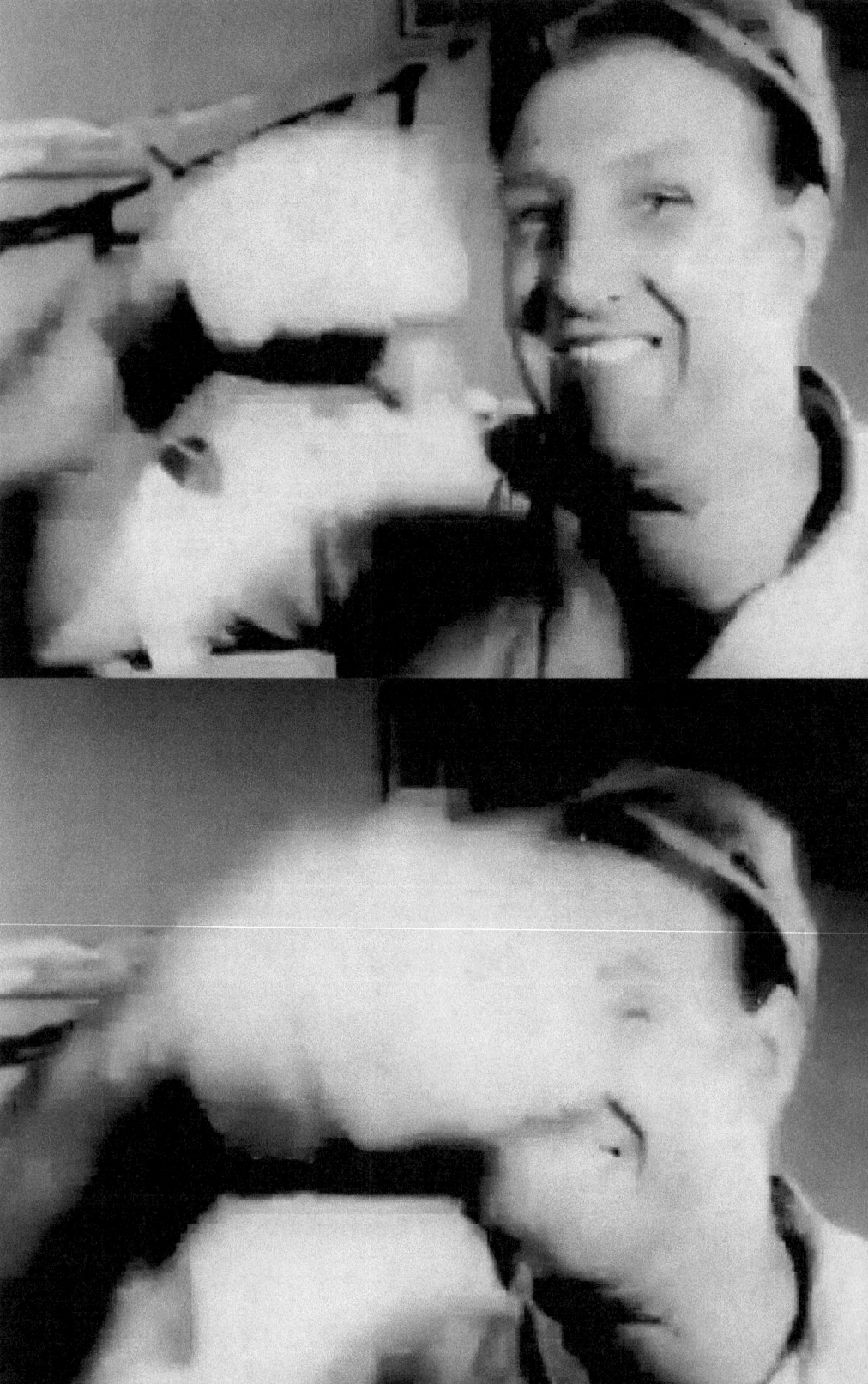

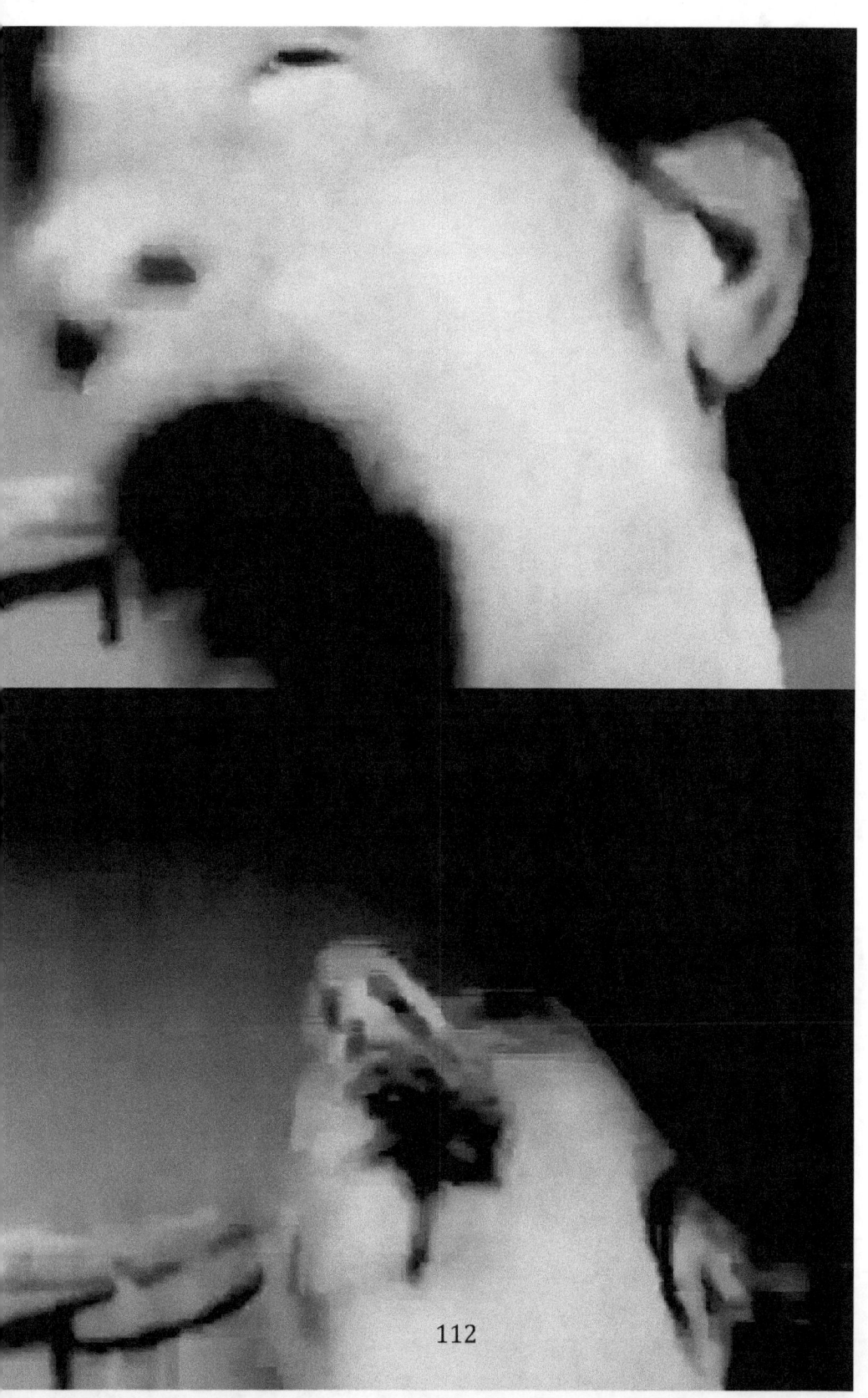

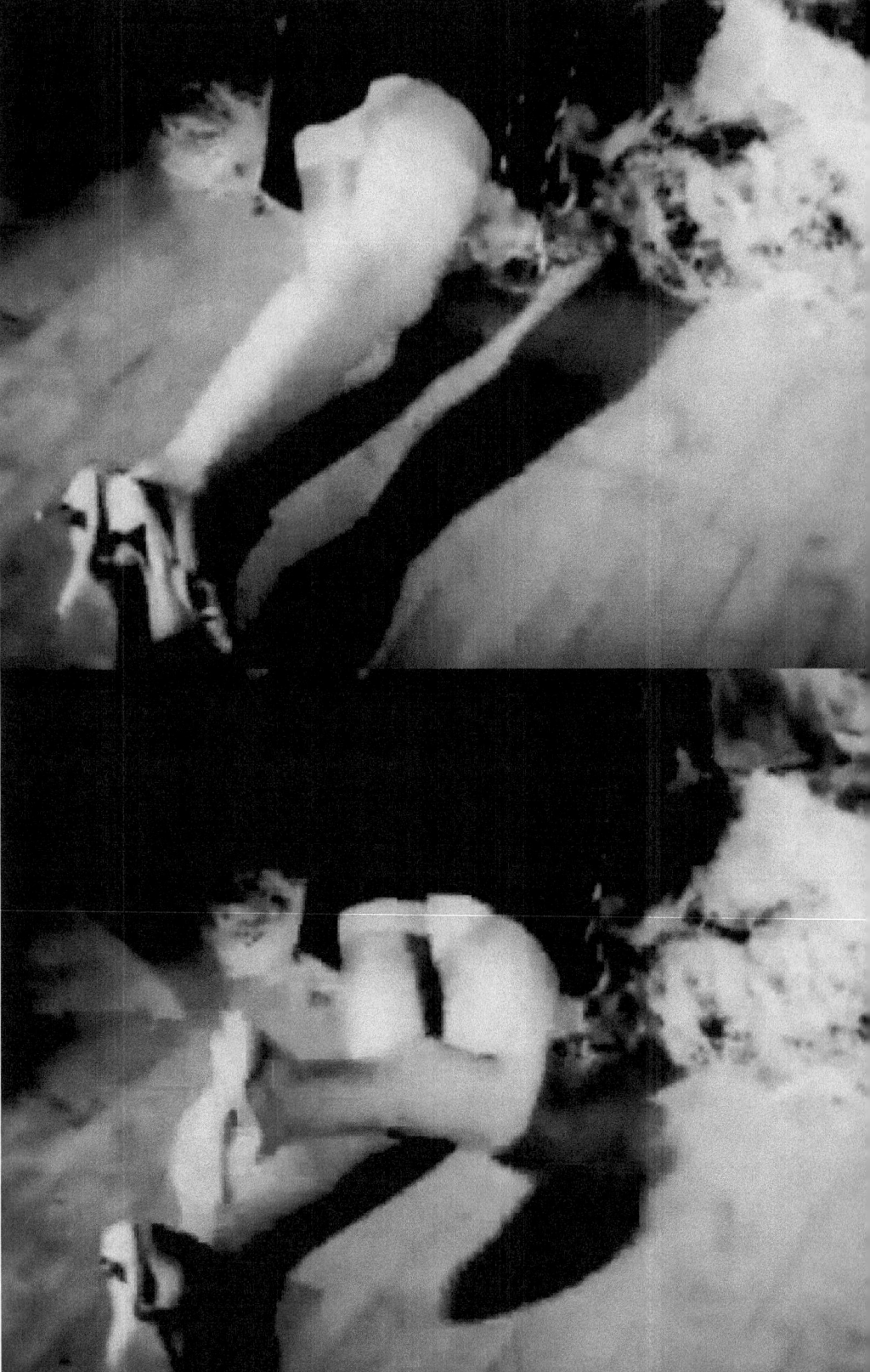

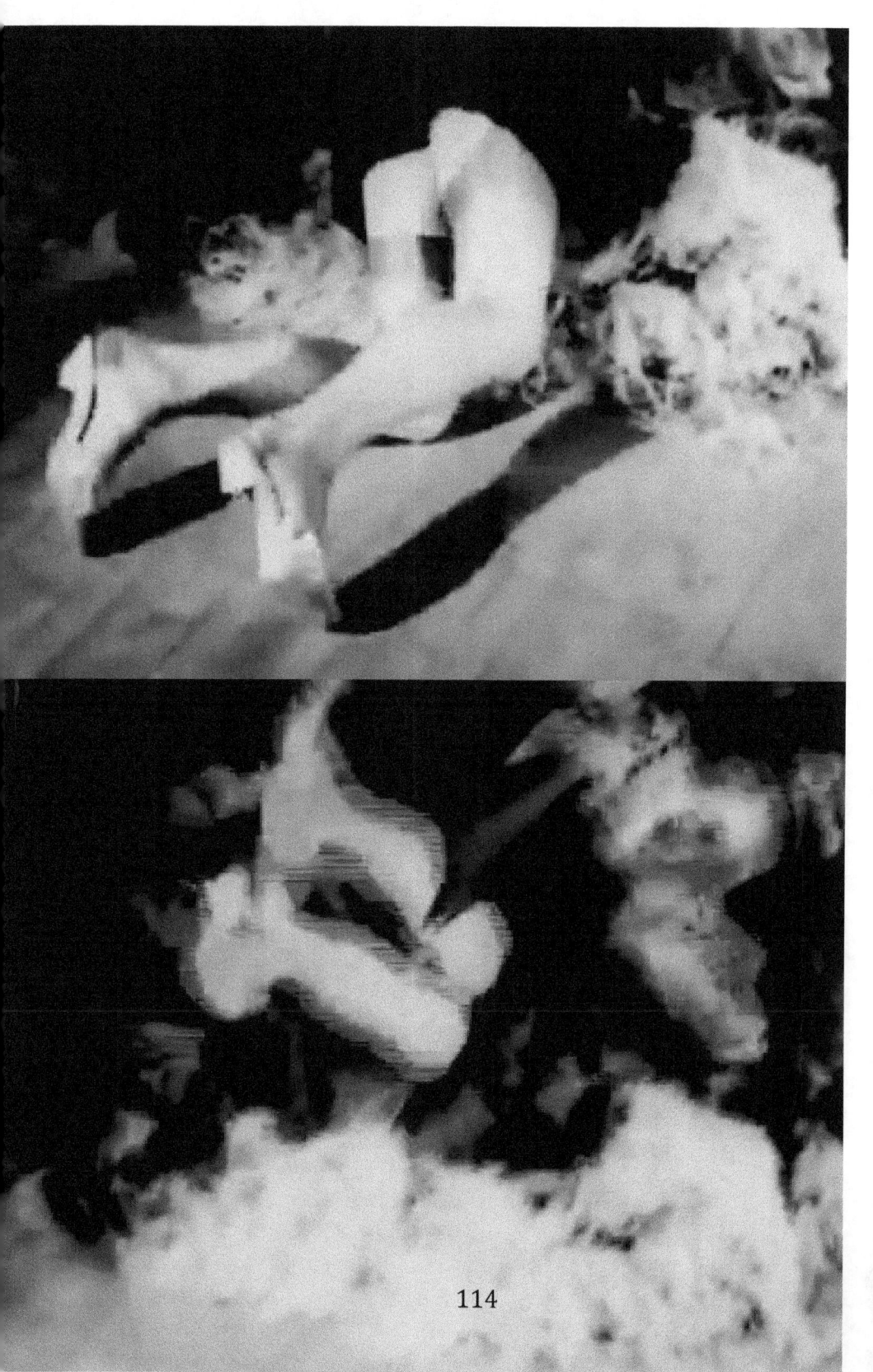

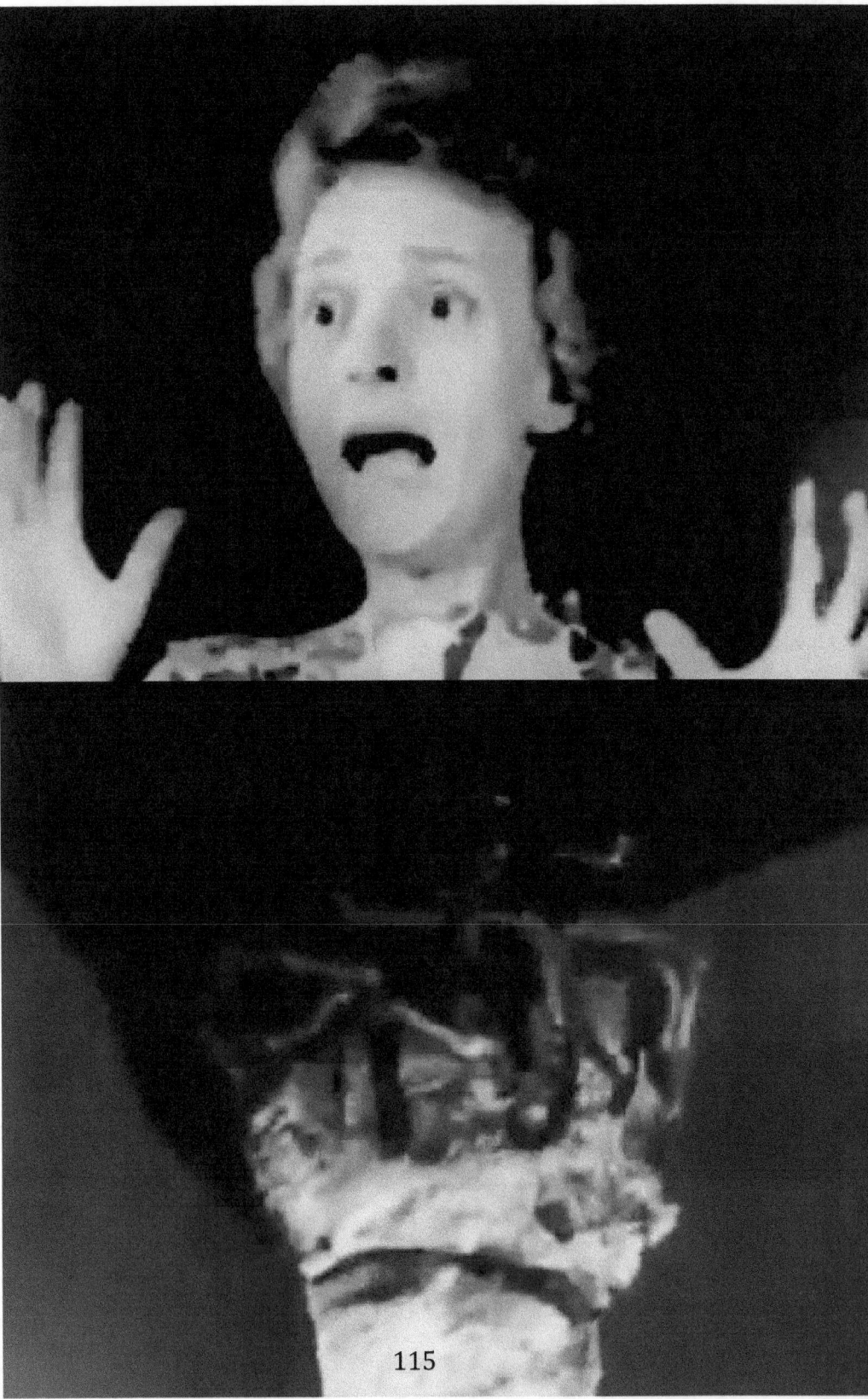

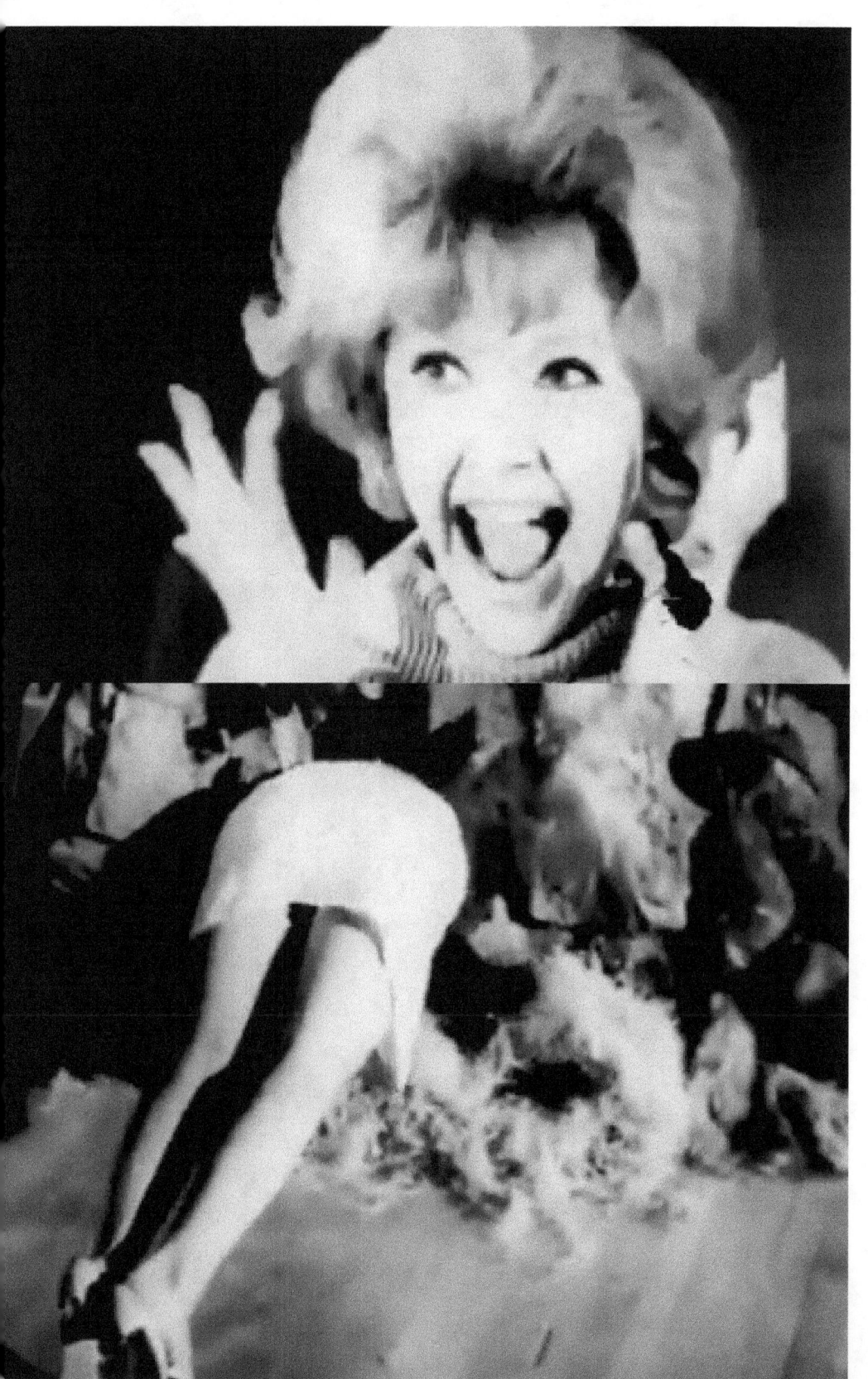

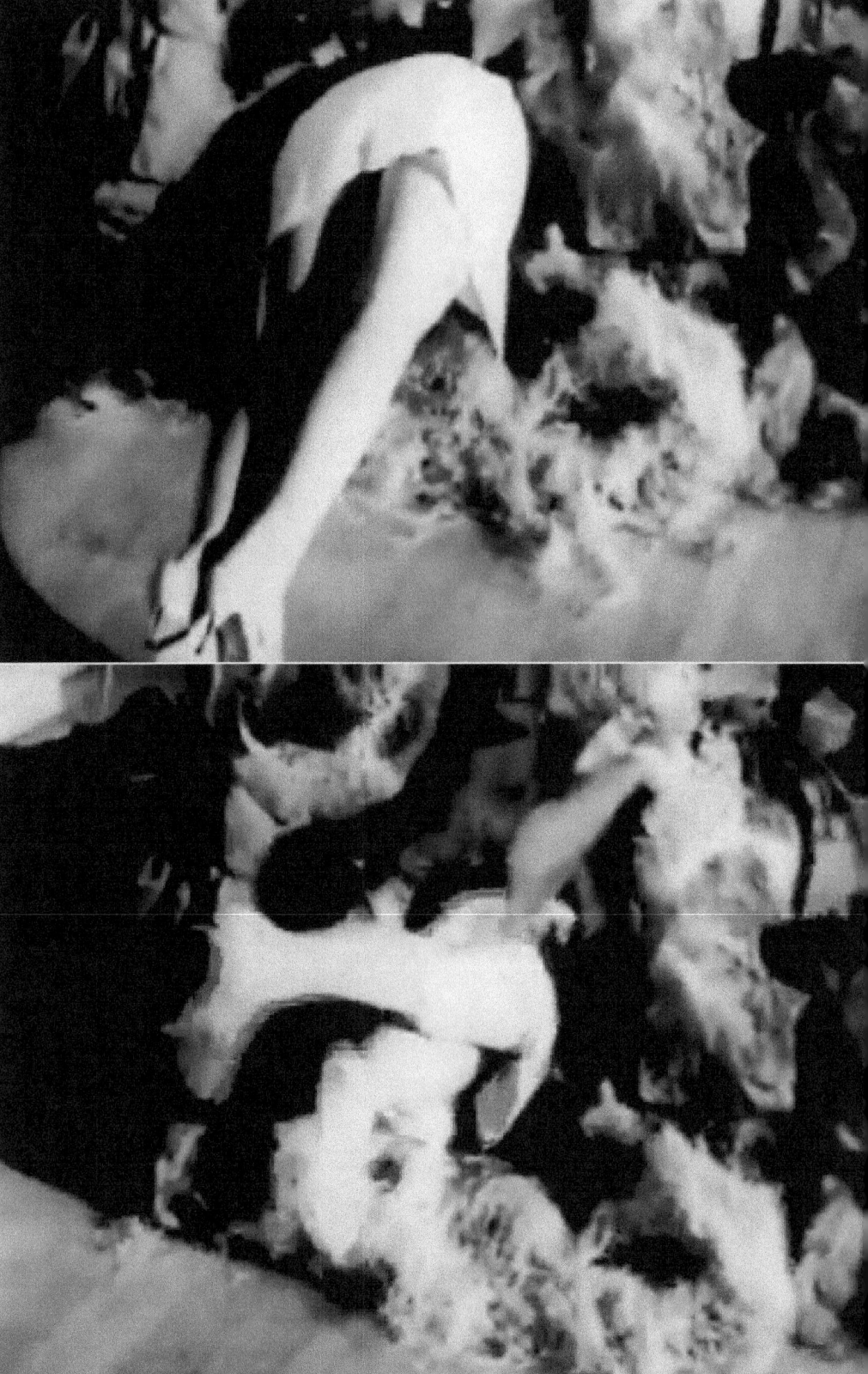

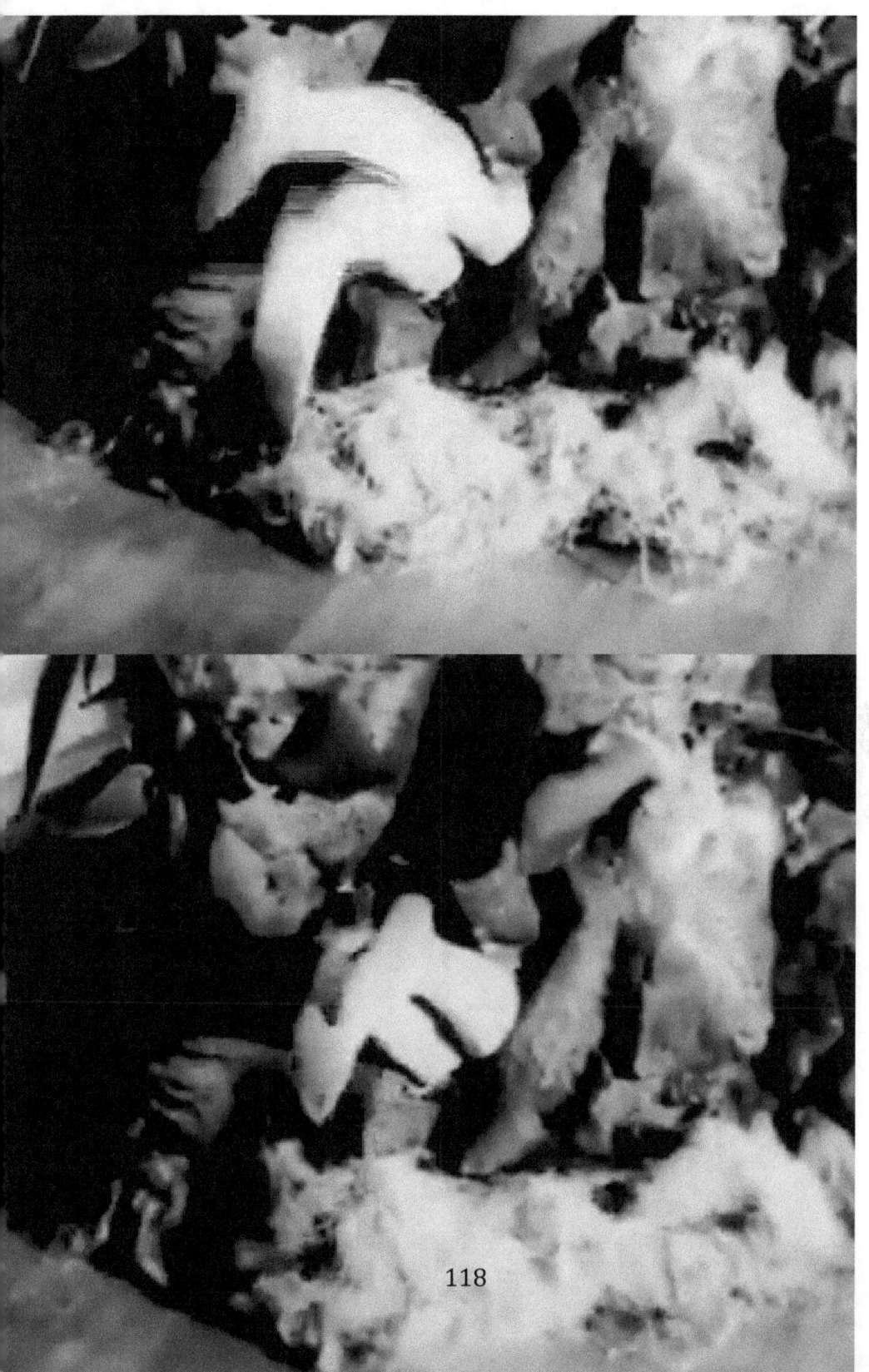

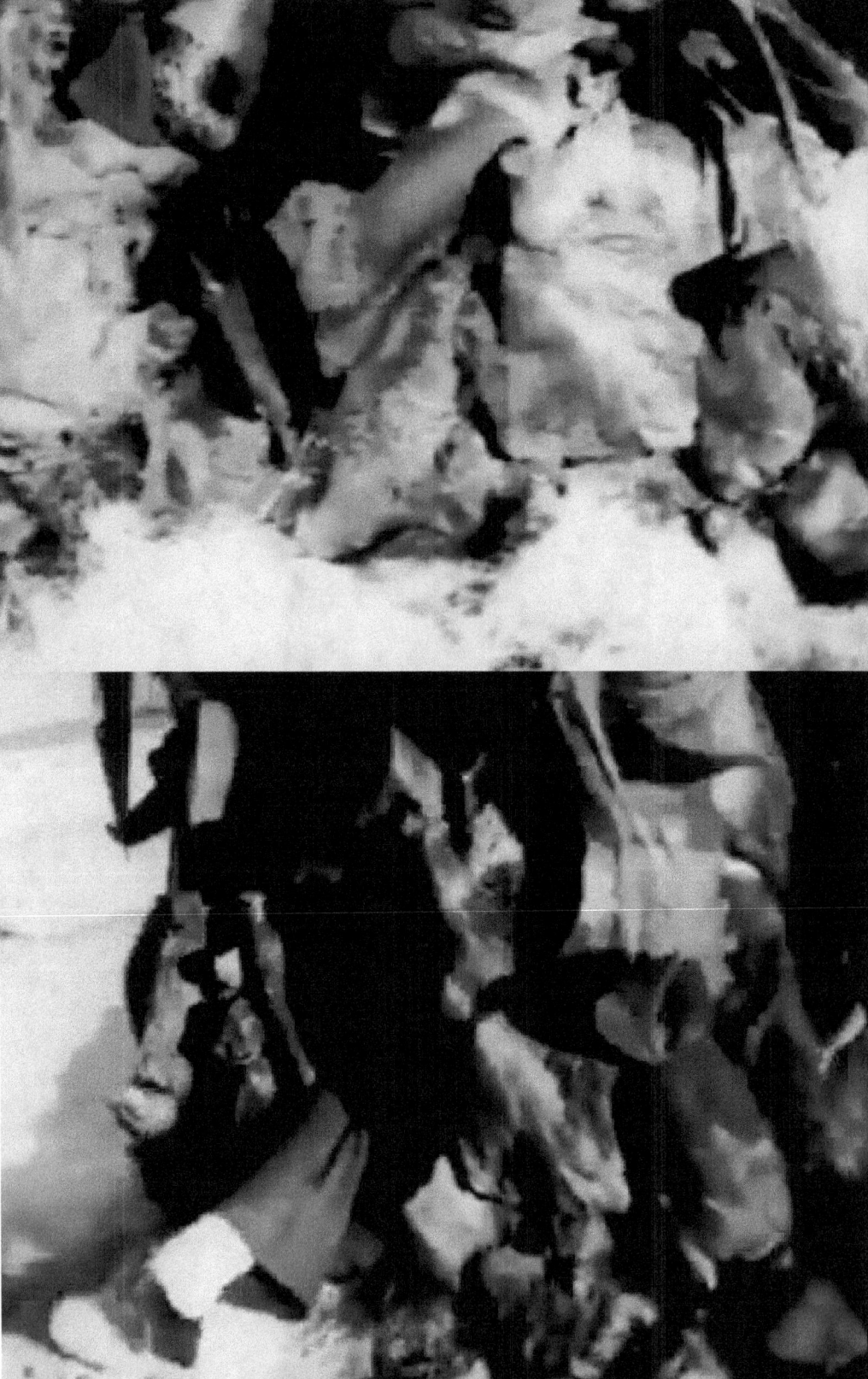

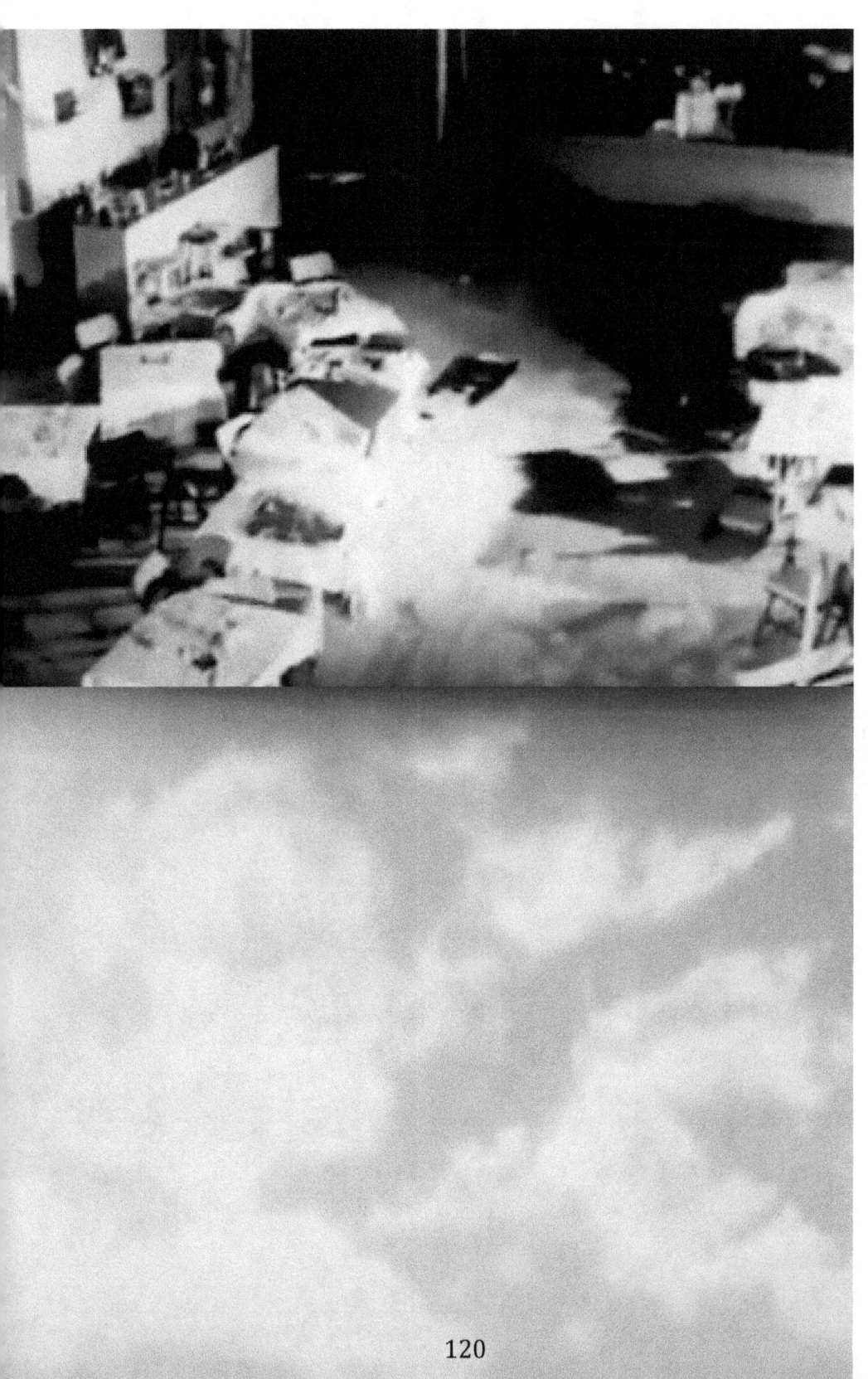

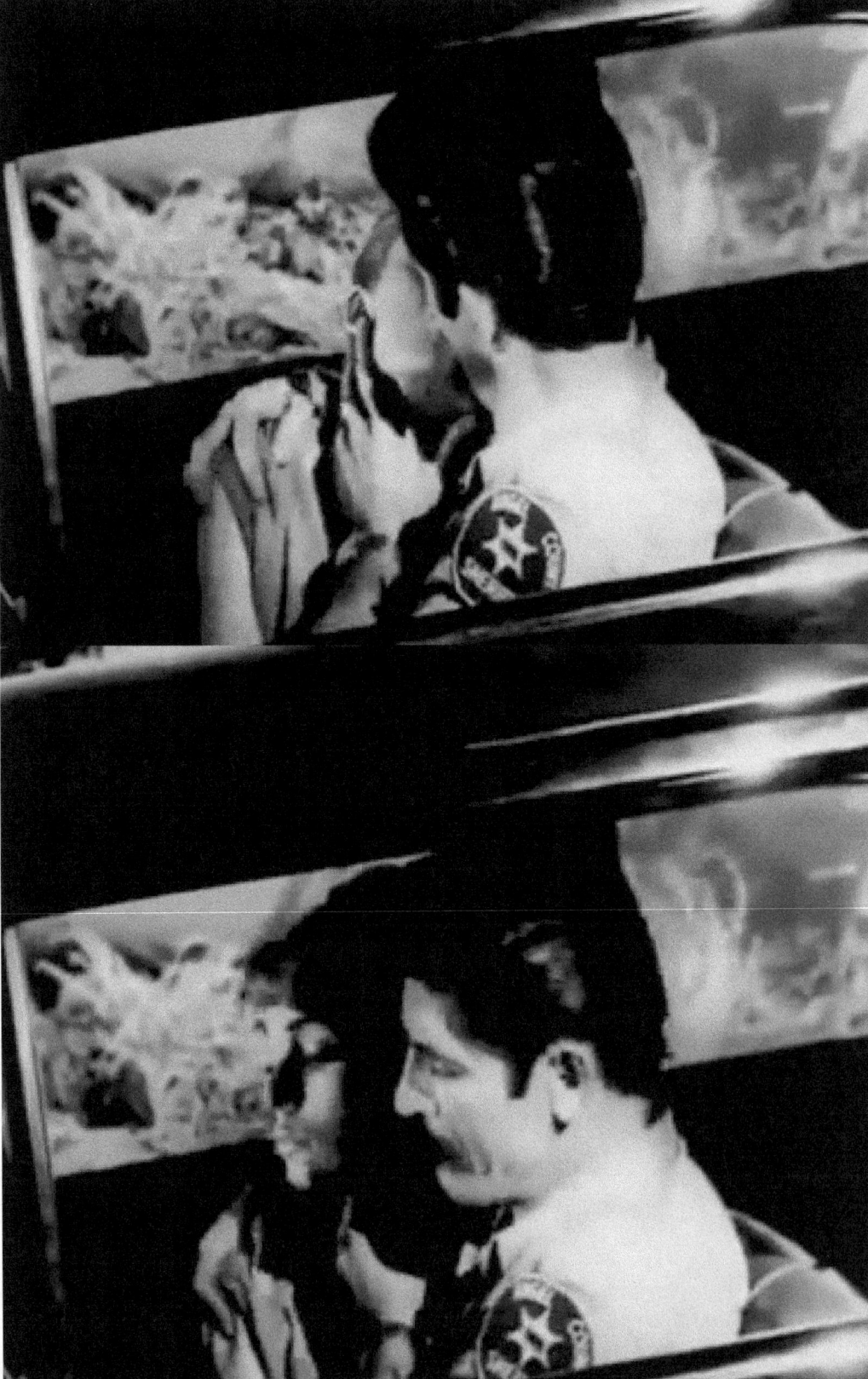

WHILE MARTIN AND BRETT
WERE TAKING A BREAK
FROM THE SEARCH,
A CALL CAME THROUGH
WHICH CONFIRMED MARTINS
THEORY. COL CALDWELL
TOLD HIM OF THE
MONSTERS ATTACK AT THE
DANCE HALL. HIS TROOPS
NOW HAD ORDERS TO
DESTROY THE MONSTER
AND HE ASKED FOR
MARTIN'S ASSISTANCE.
MARTIN SAID HE WOULD
JOIN THE COL. AS QUICKLY
AS POSSIBLE.

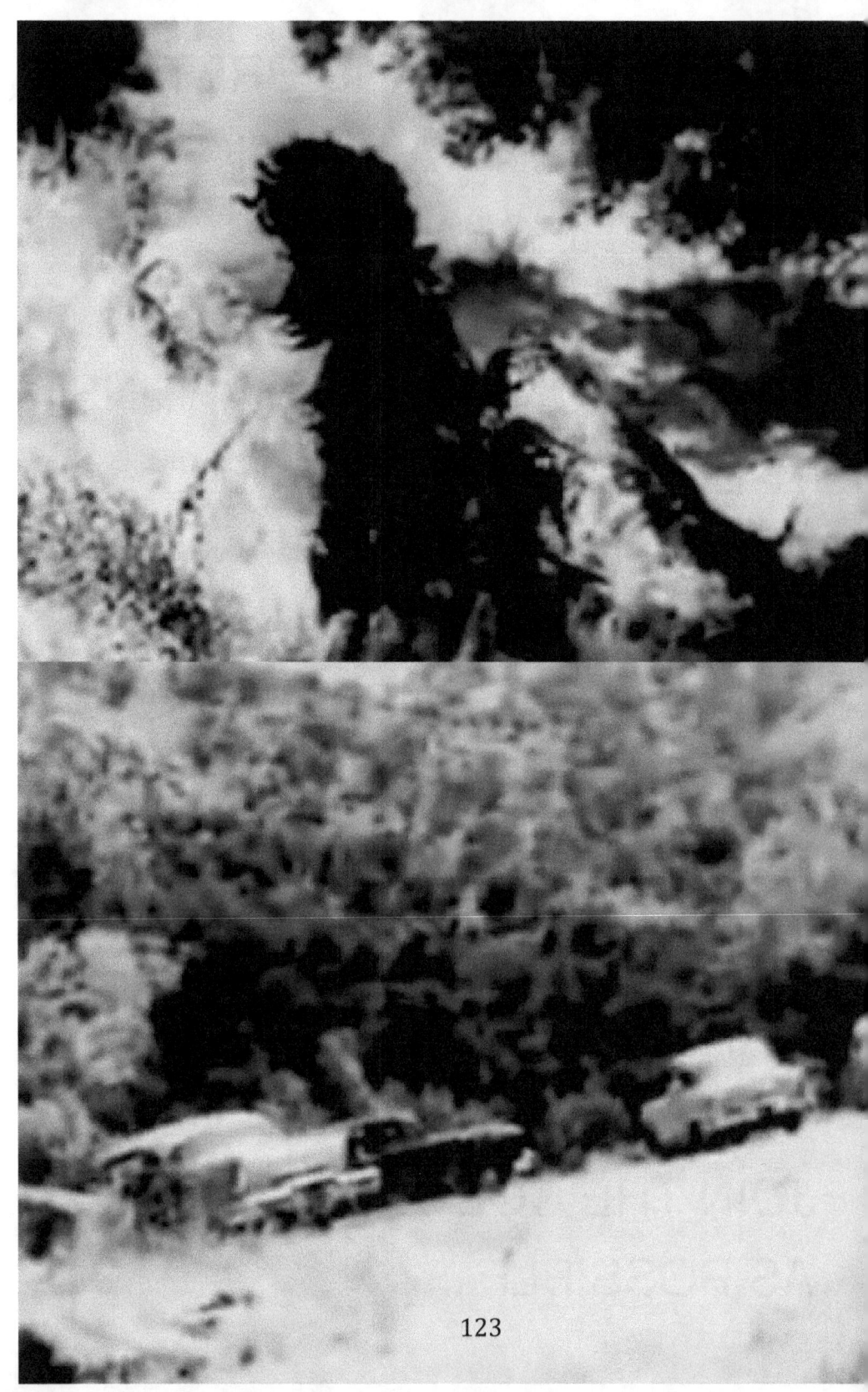

THE MONSTER NEXT APPEARED
IN LOVERS LANE.
ANYONE WHO EXPERIENCED
THAT CATASTROPHE AND
SURVIVED WOULD NEVER GO
THERE AGAIN.

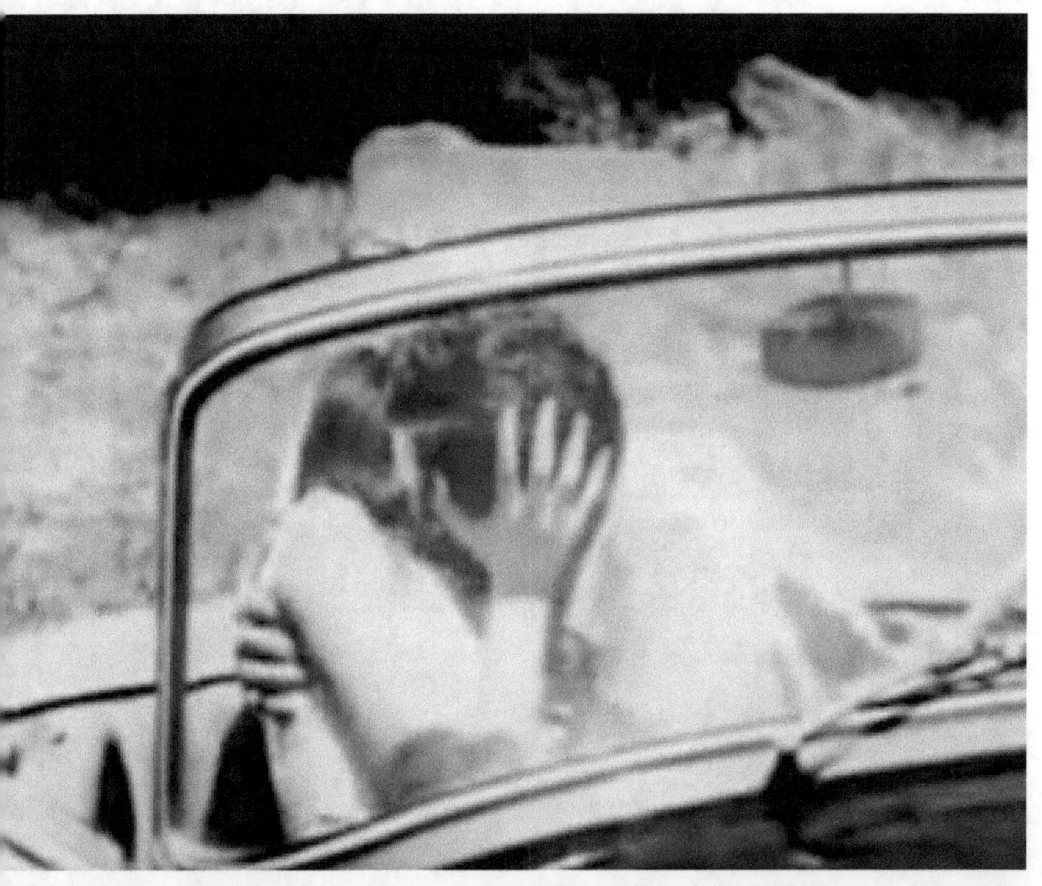

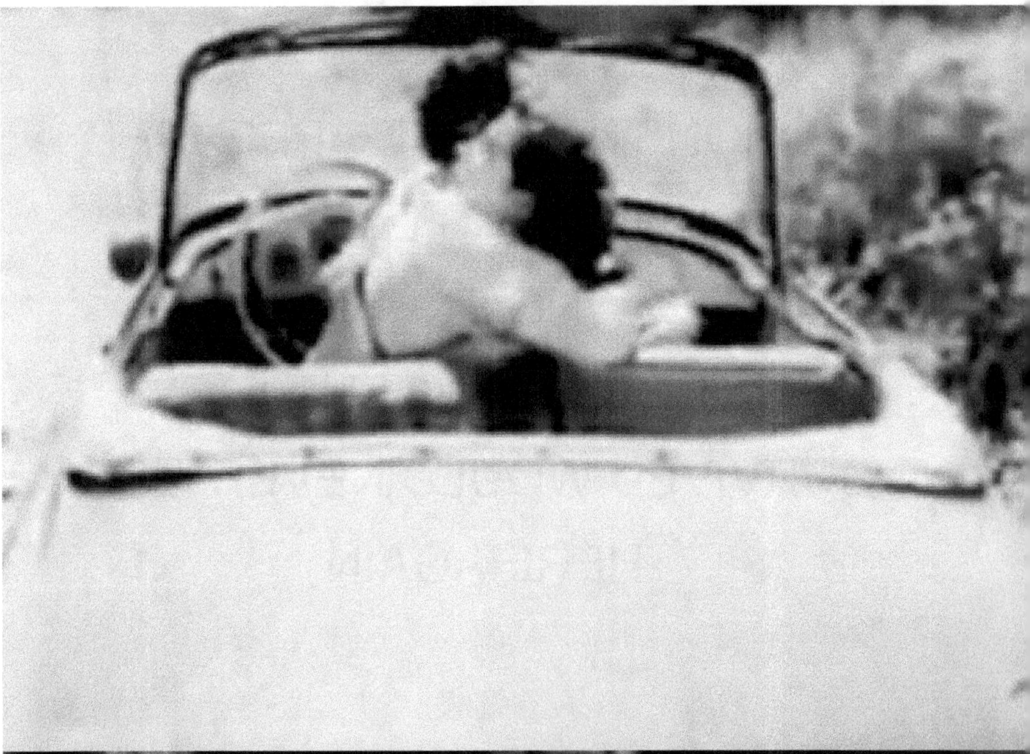

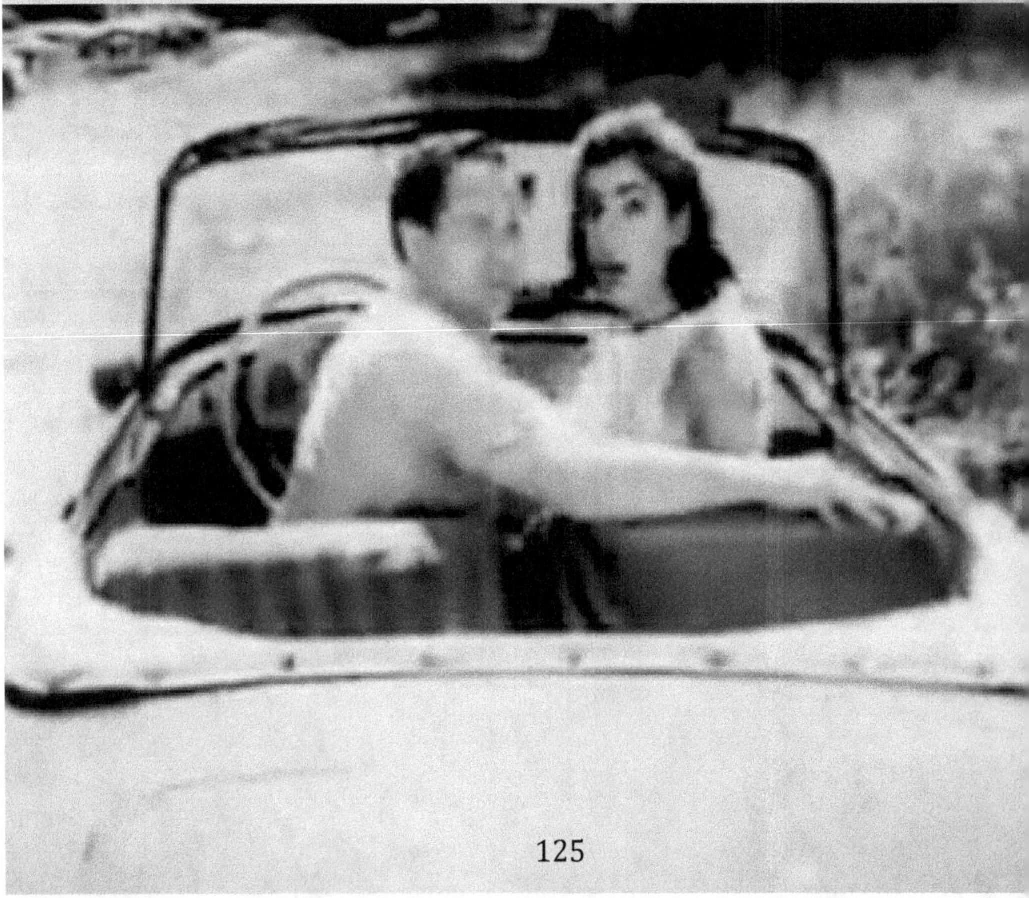

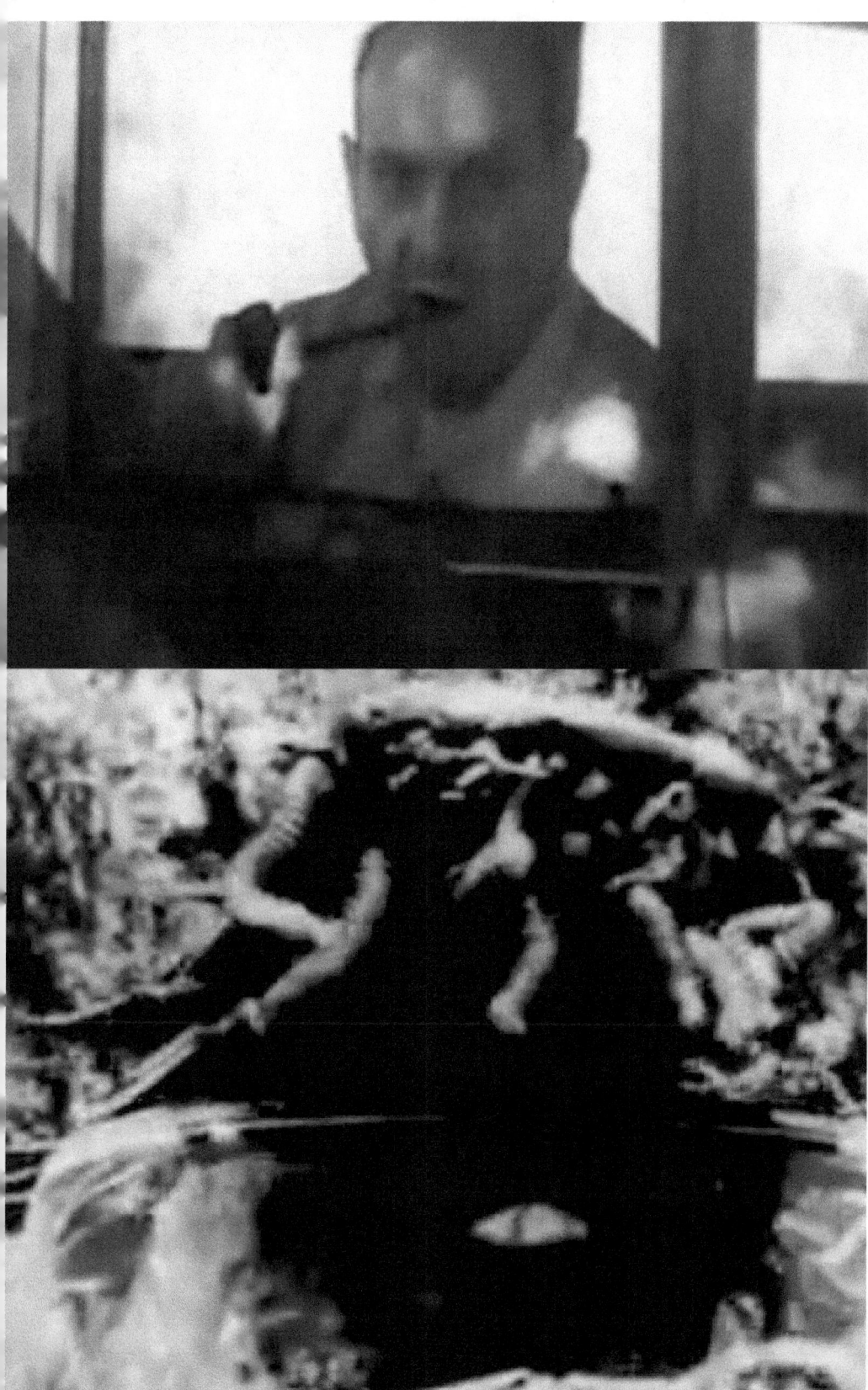

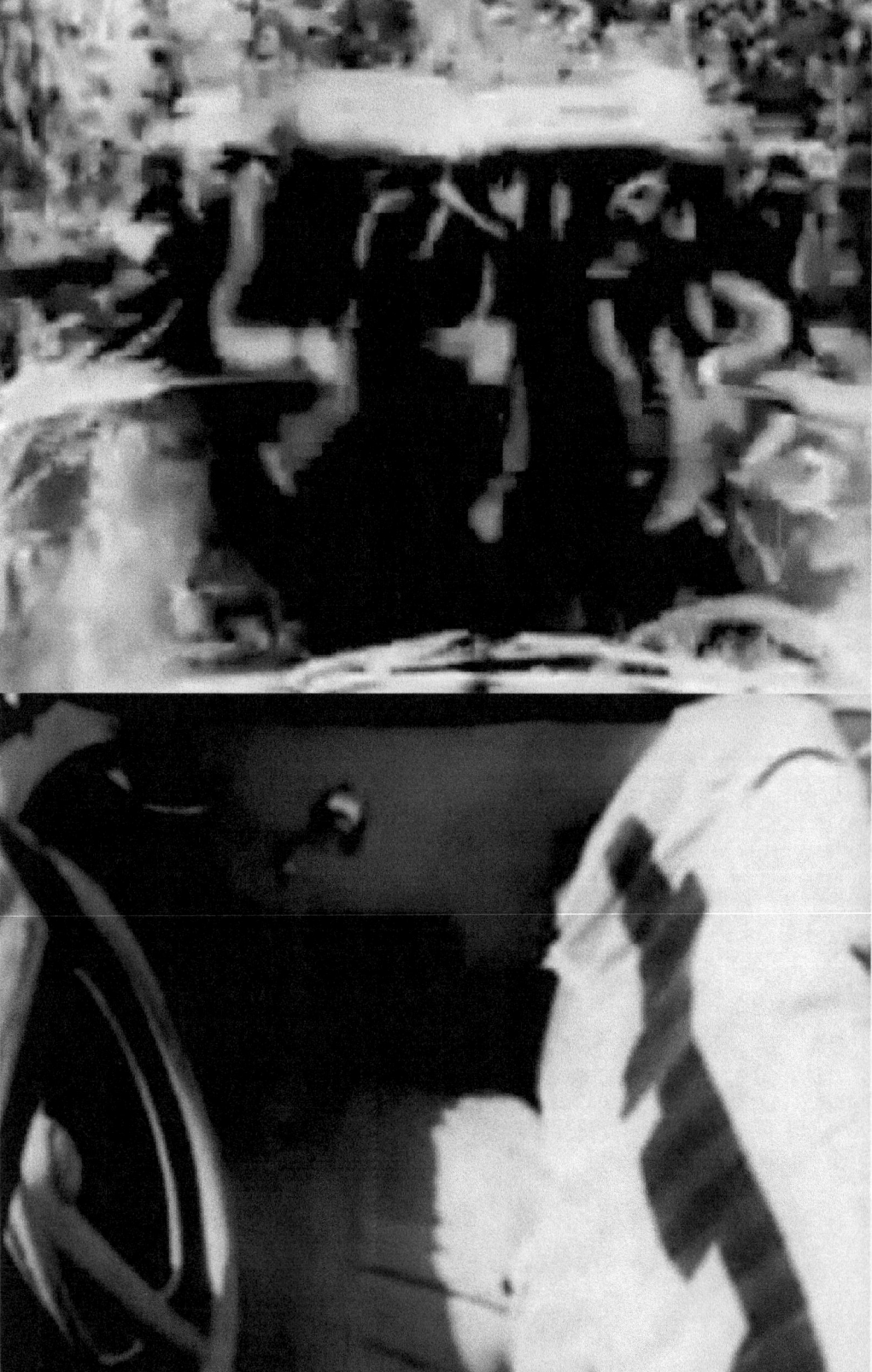

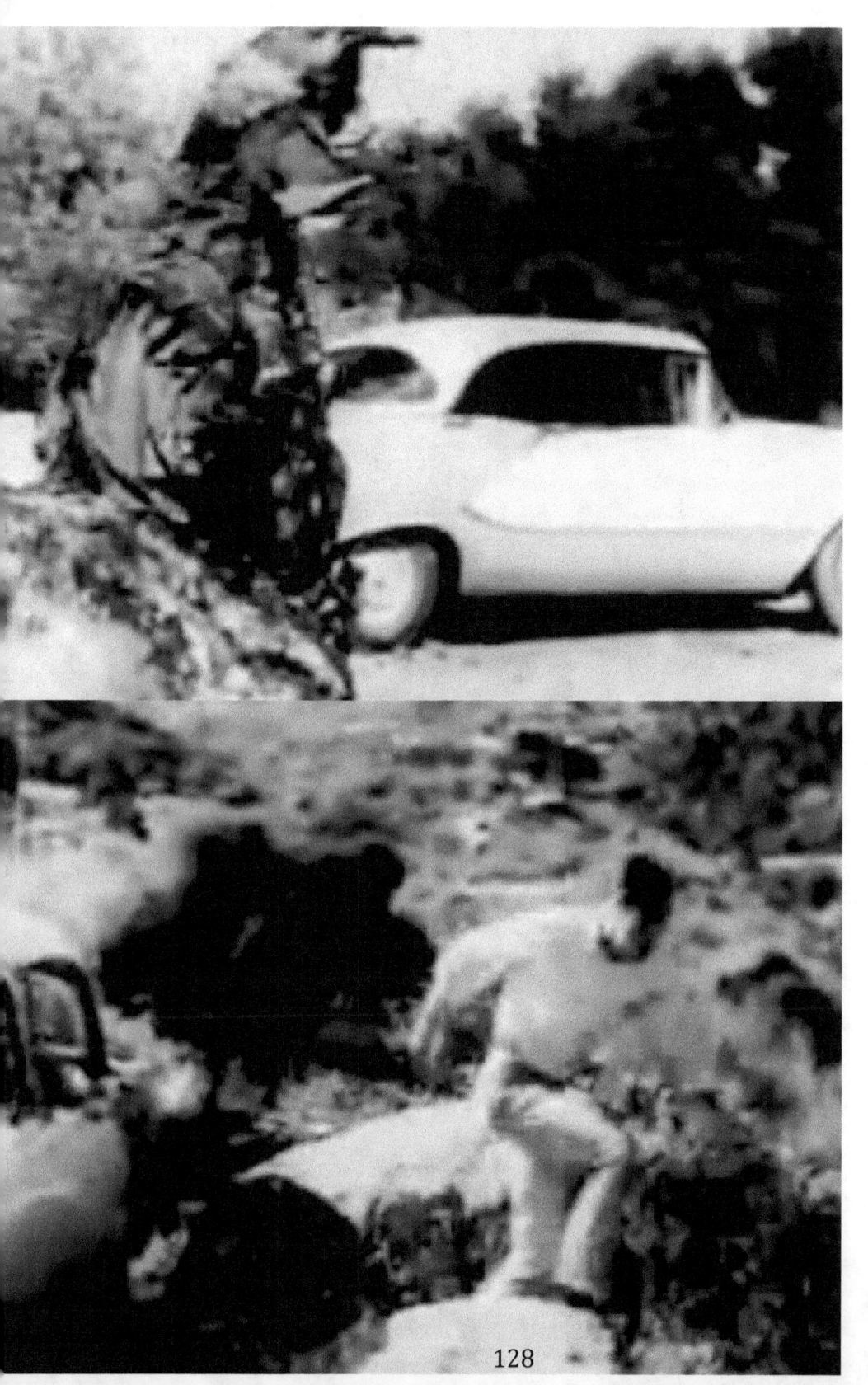

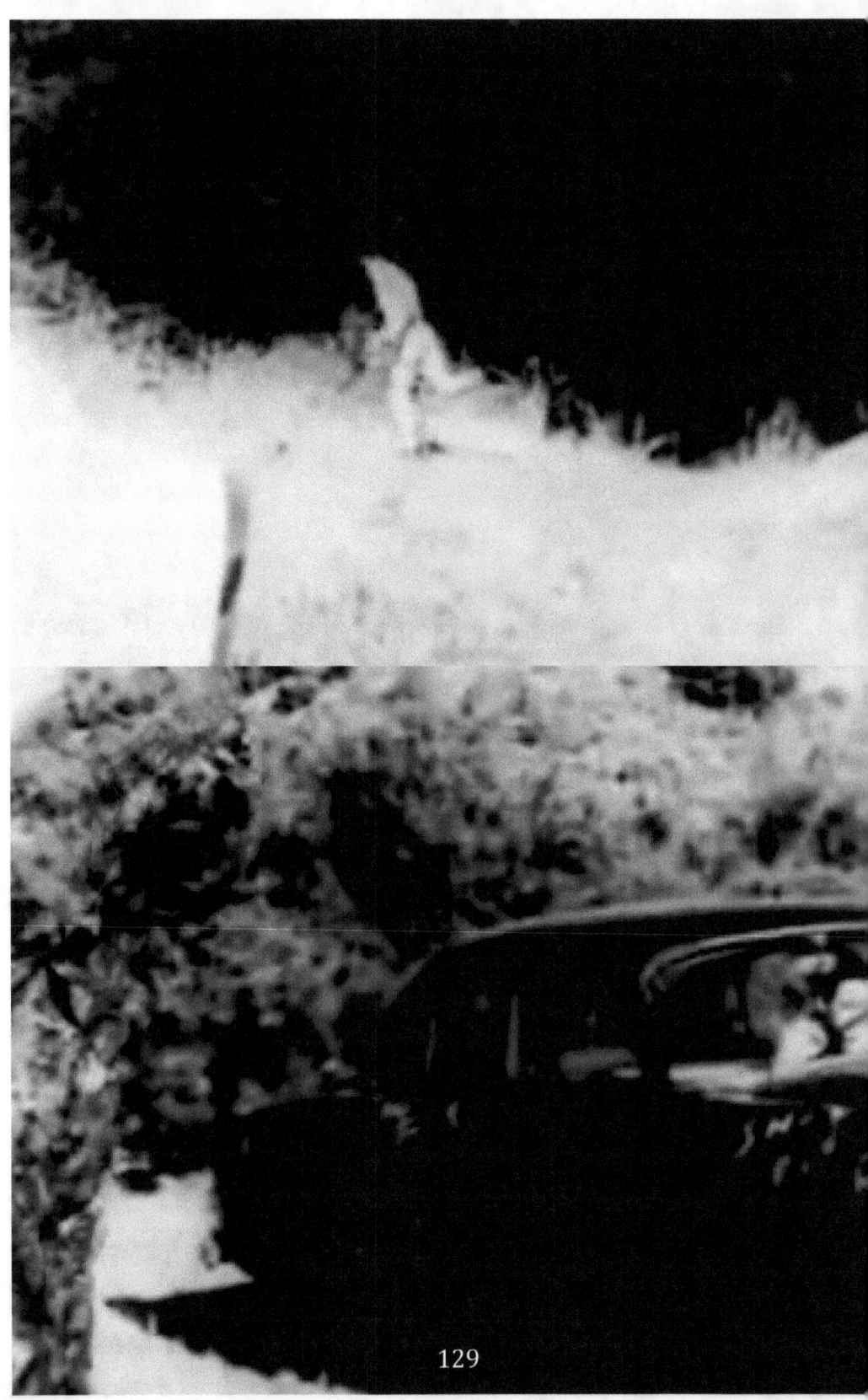

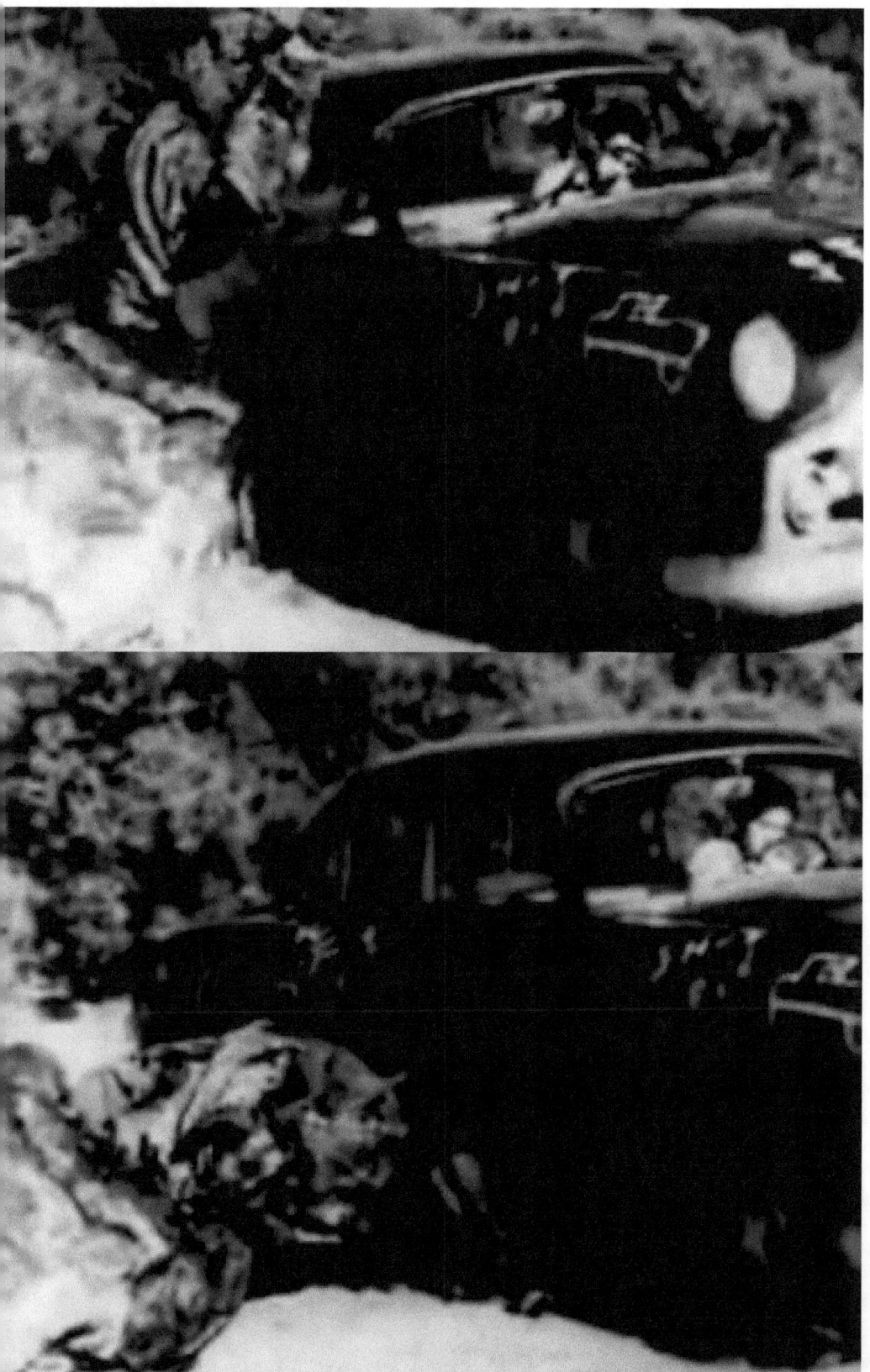

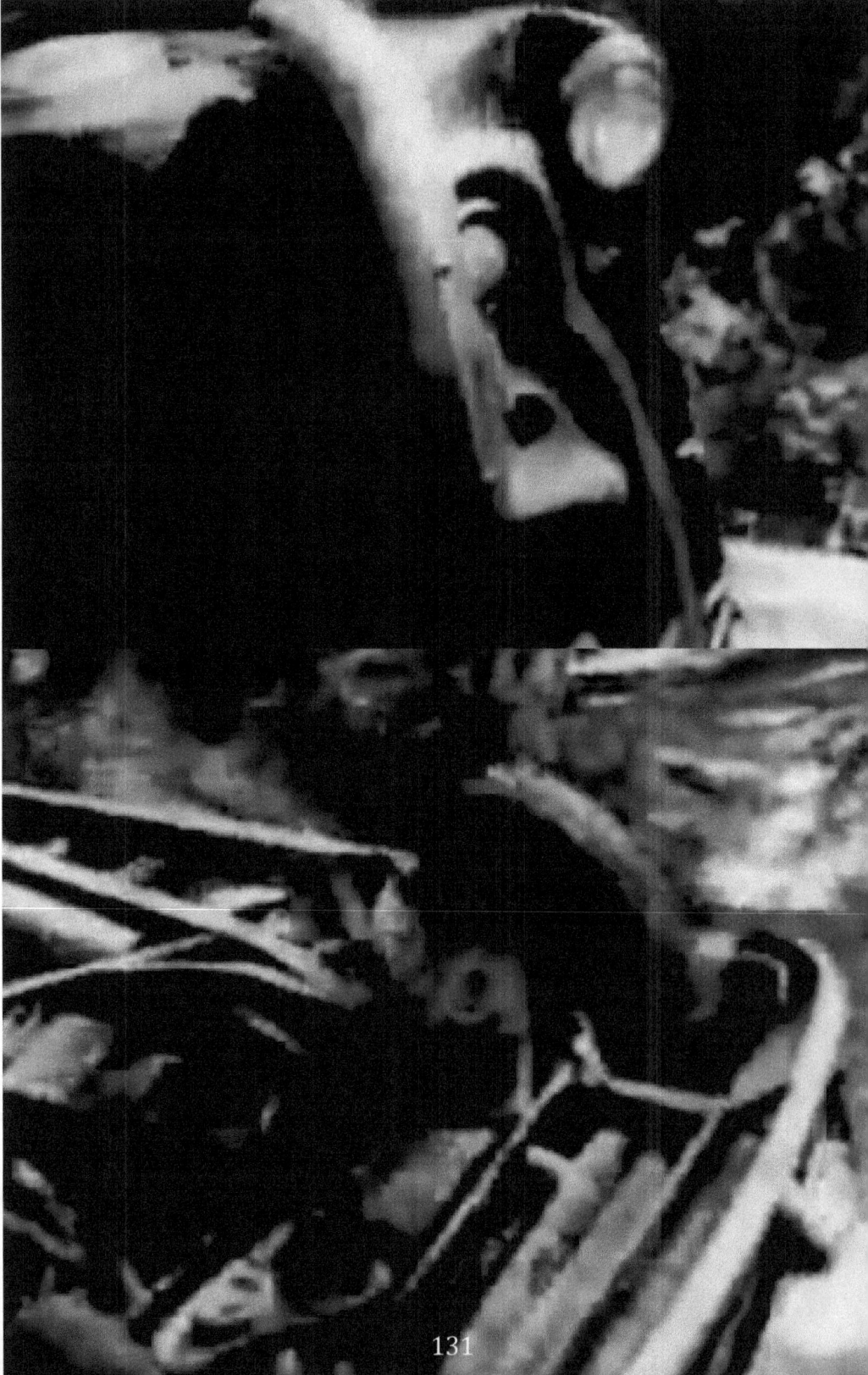

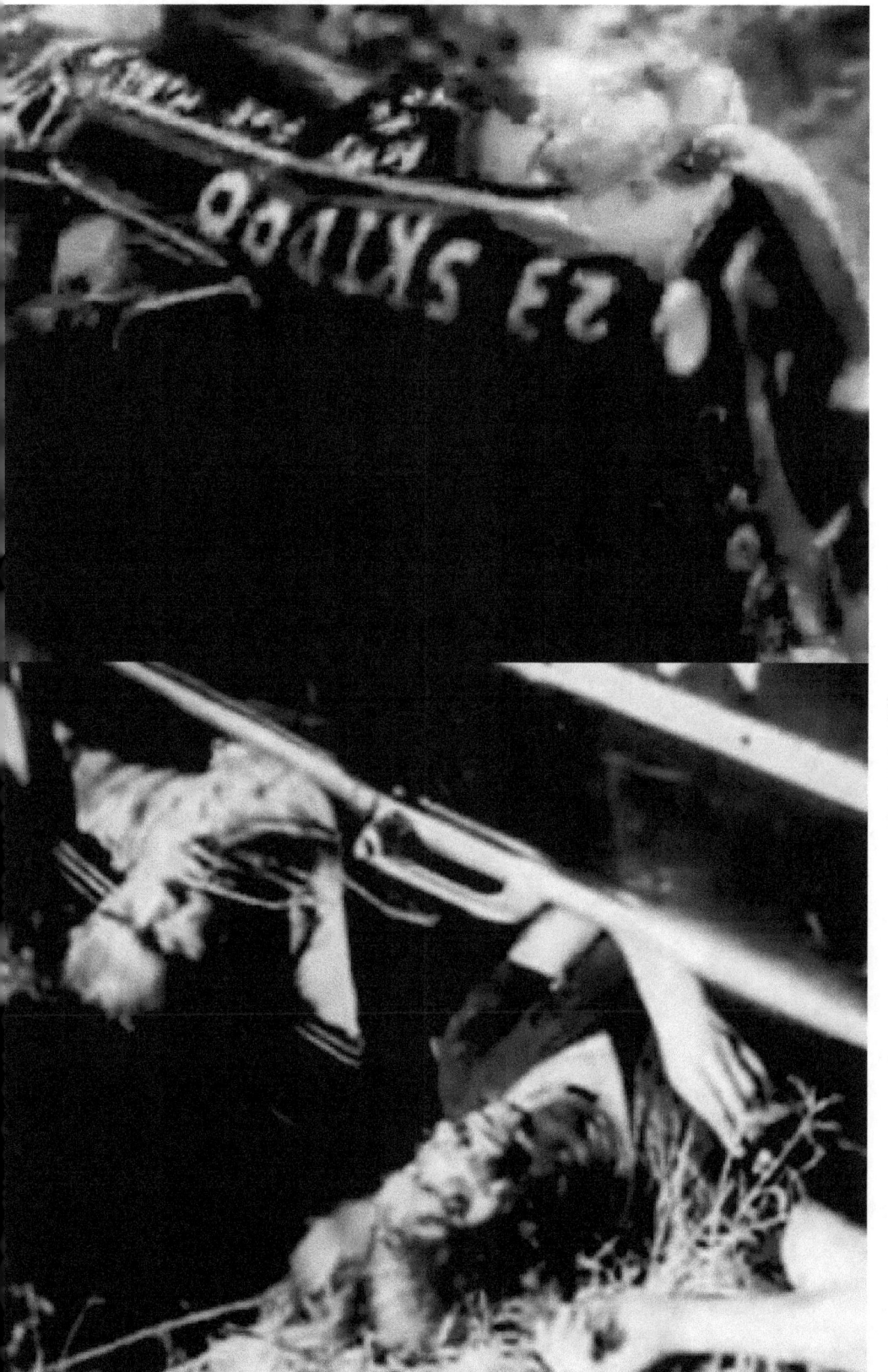

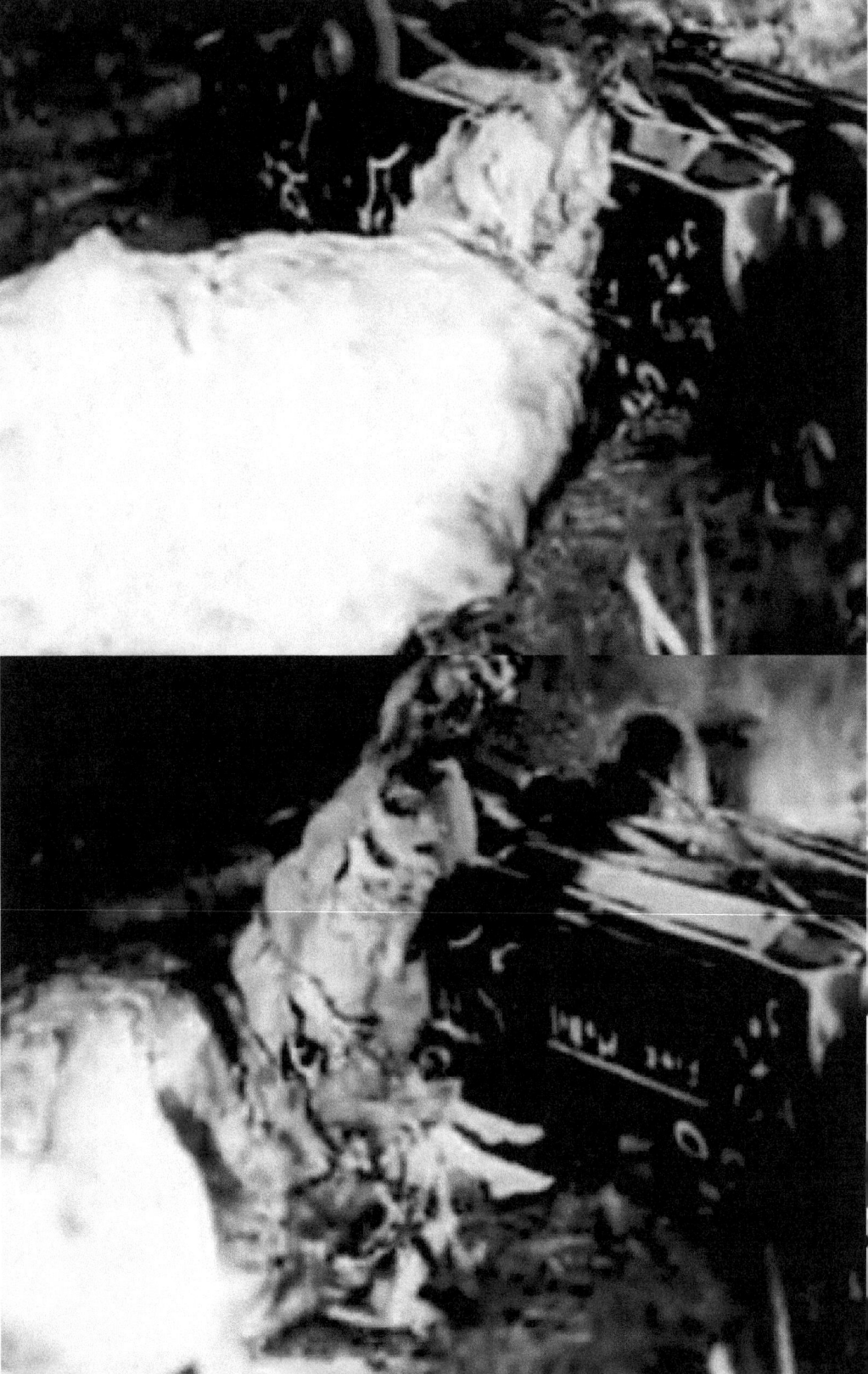

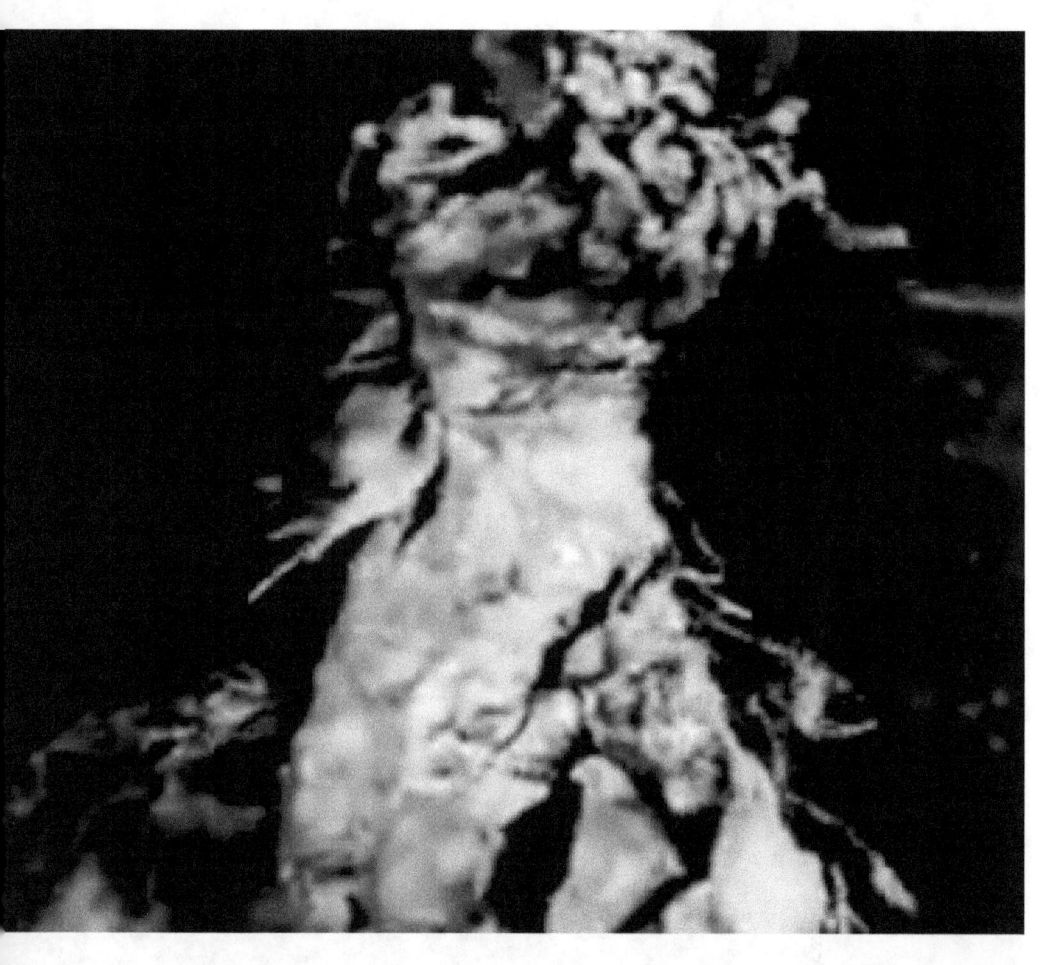

IT WAS ALMOST AN HOUR
BEFORE CALDWELL LEARNED
OF THE MONSTER'S
DEVASTATING NEW ATTACK.

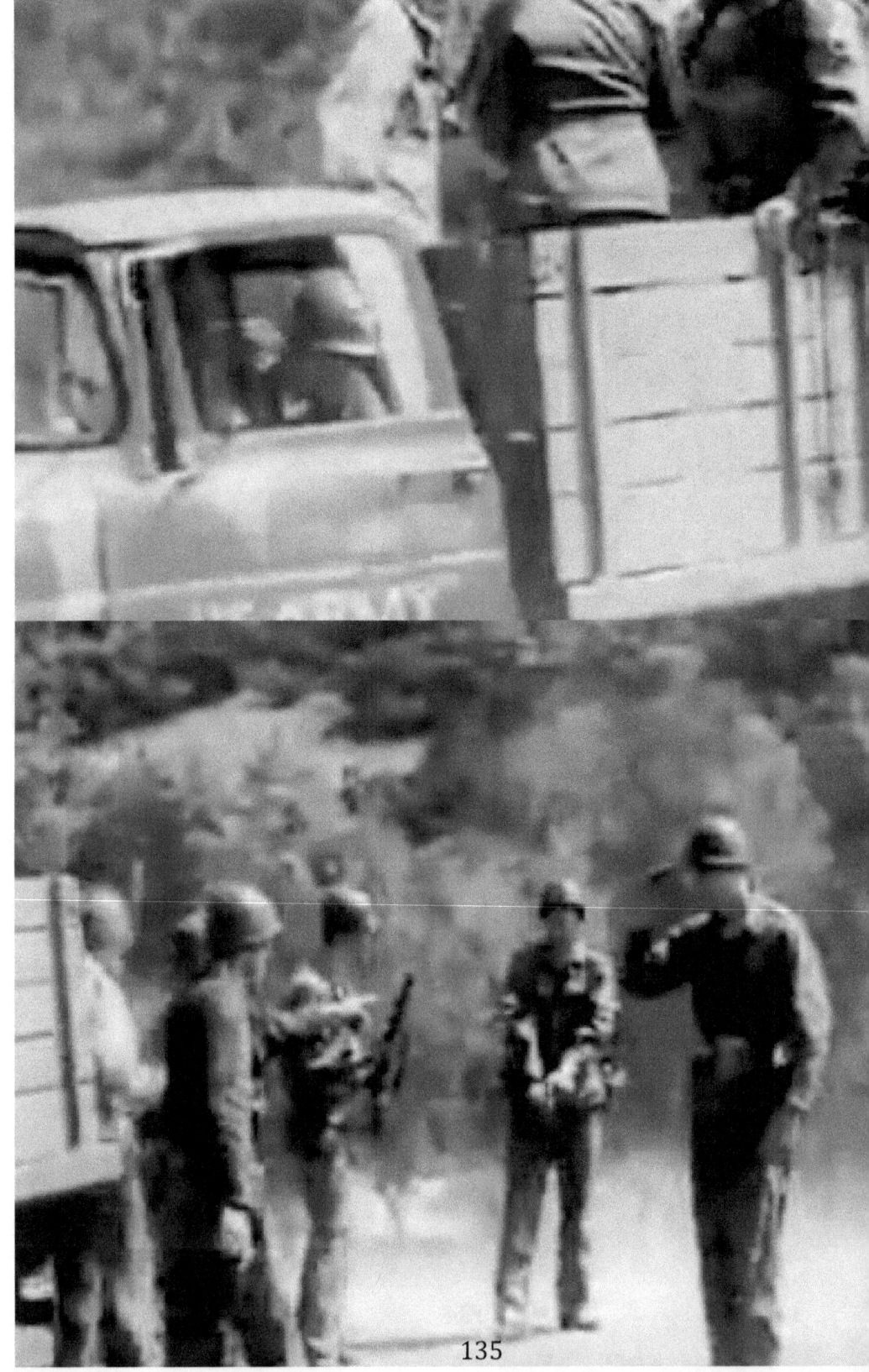

COL. CALDWELL WASTED NO
TIME ORDERING HIS MEN INTO
ACTION. IT WAS AT THIS POINT
THAT BRADFORD INTERCEDED.
HE DEMANDED THAT THE
MONSTER BE TAKEN ALIVE AT
ALL COSTS.

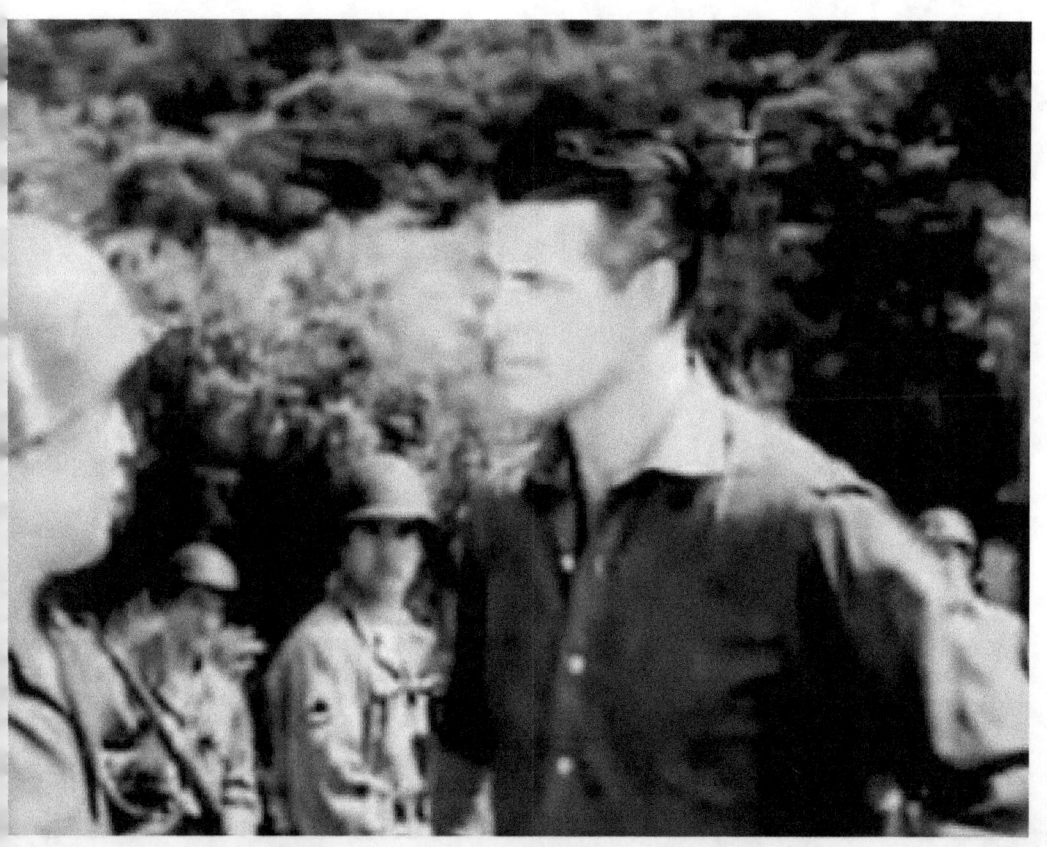

THE COL'S. PROTESTS ABOUT THE
DEAD AND MISSING MADE NO
IMPRESSION ON BRADFORD.
CALDWELL CONCEDED TO THE
POINT OF ASSURING BRADFORD
THEY WOULD NOT DESTROY THE
MONSTER IF THEY COULD AVOID IT.

-GET ON WITH IT LIEUTENANT
-MOVE IT OUT MEN

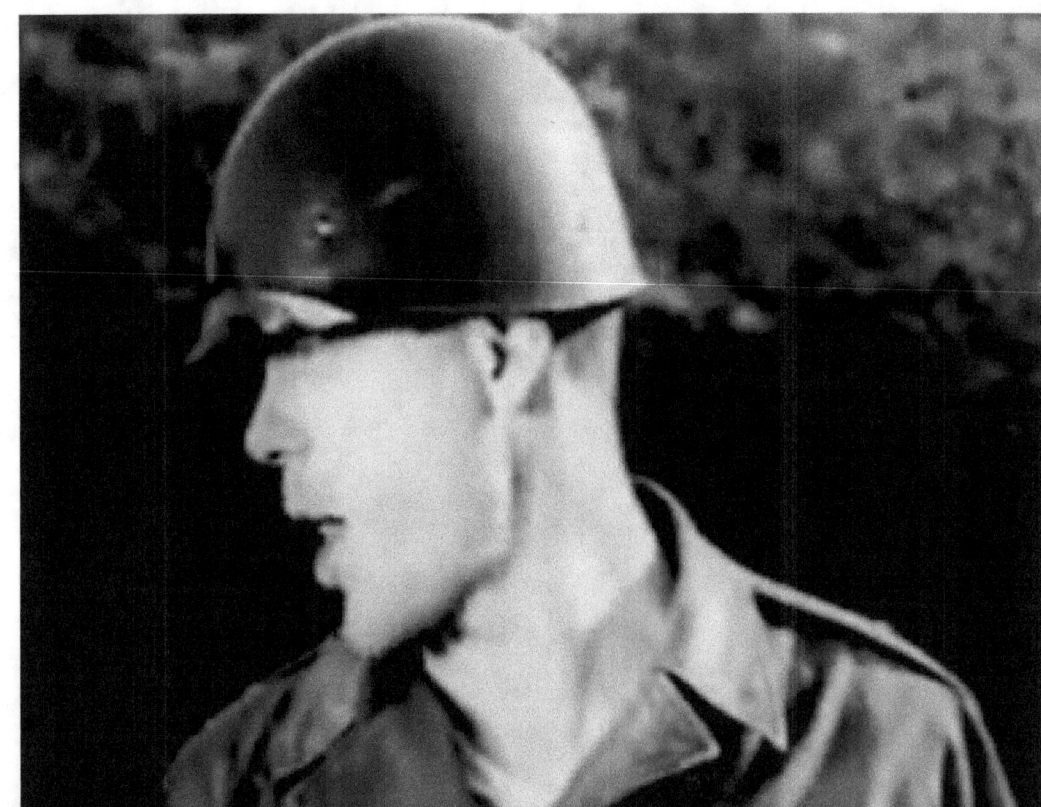

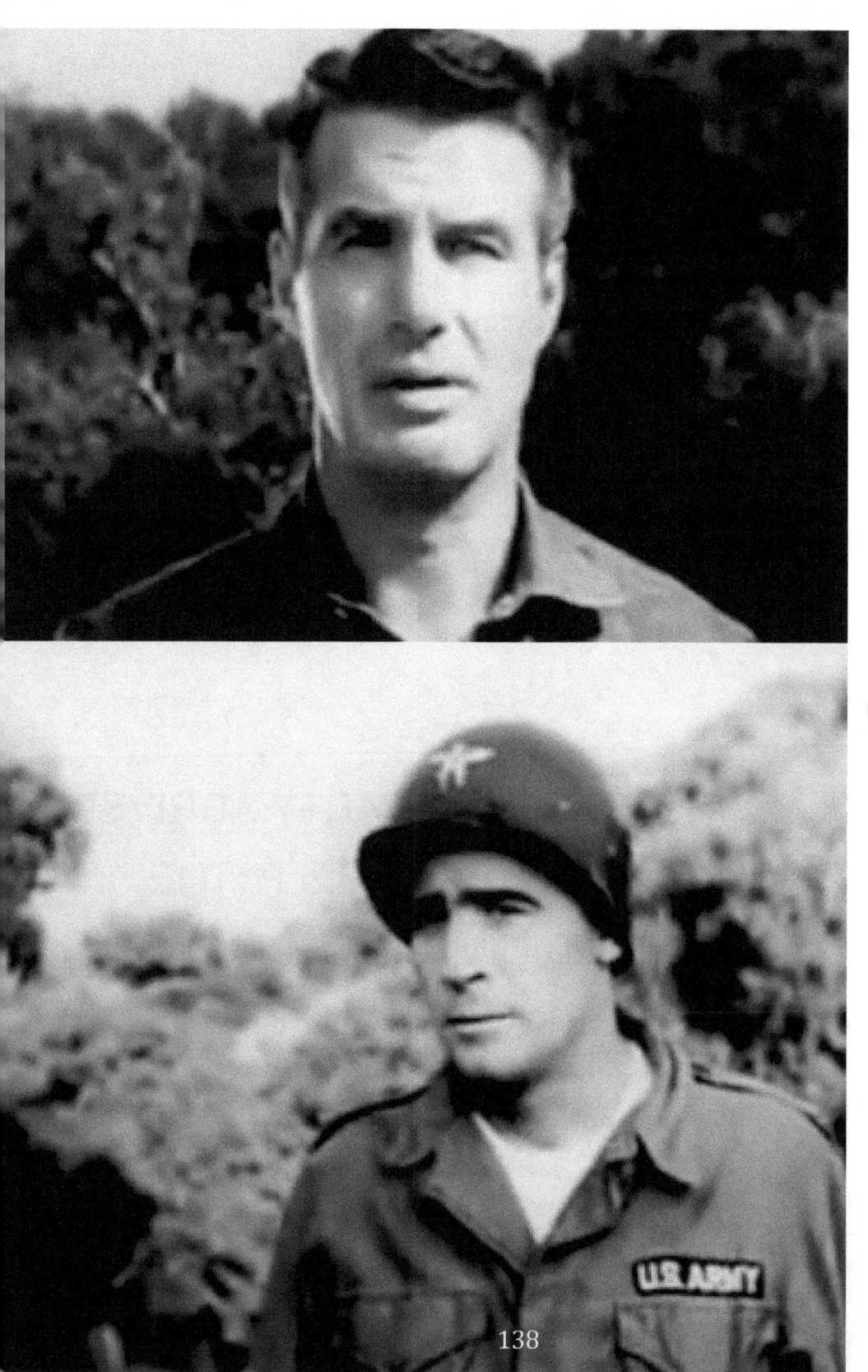

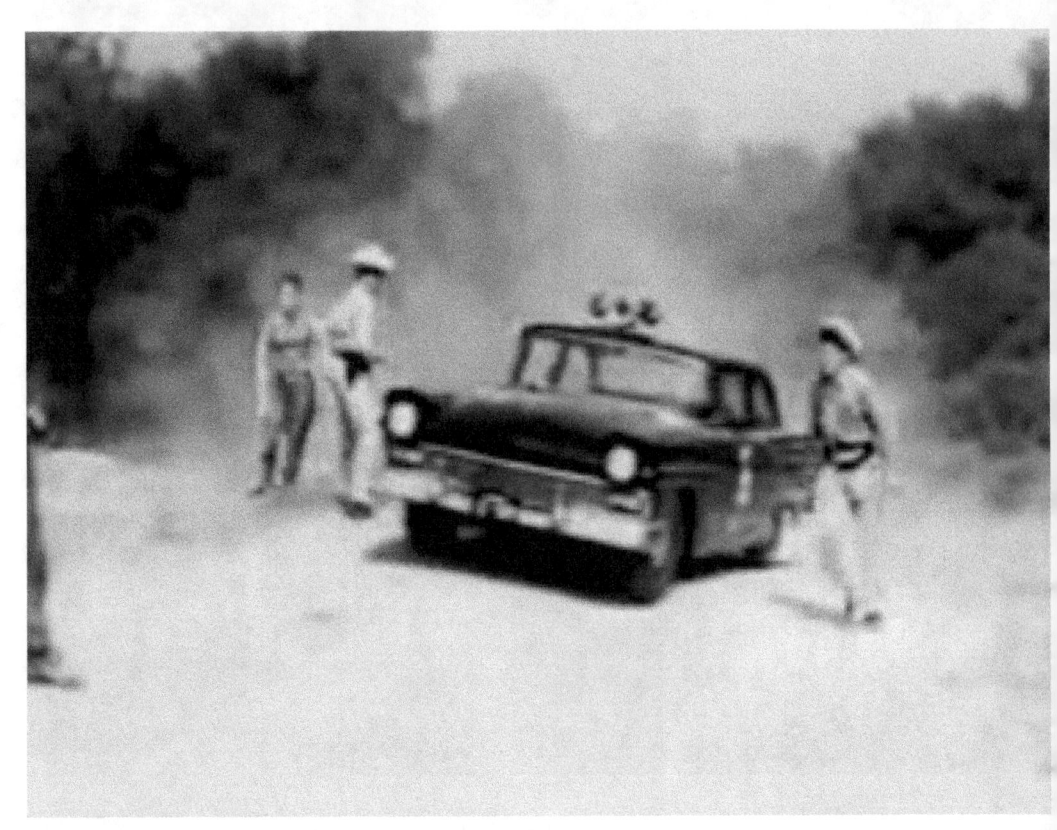

WHEN MARTINS PARTY ARRIVED
AND OFFERED TO HELP, THE
COL TOLD HIM ENOUGH LIVES
WERE BEING ENDANGERED.
THEY WERE TO BE PART OF THE
SECOND LINE OF DEFENSE, TO
BE USED ONLY IF NECESSARY.

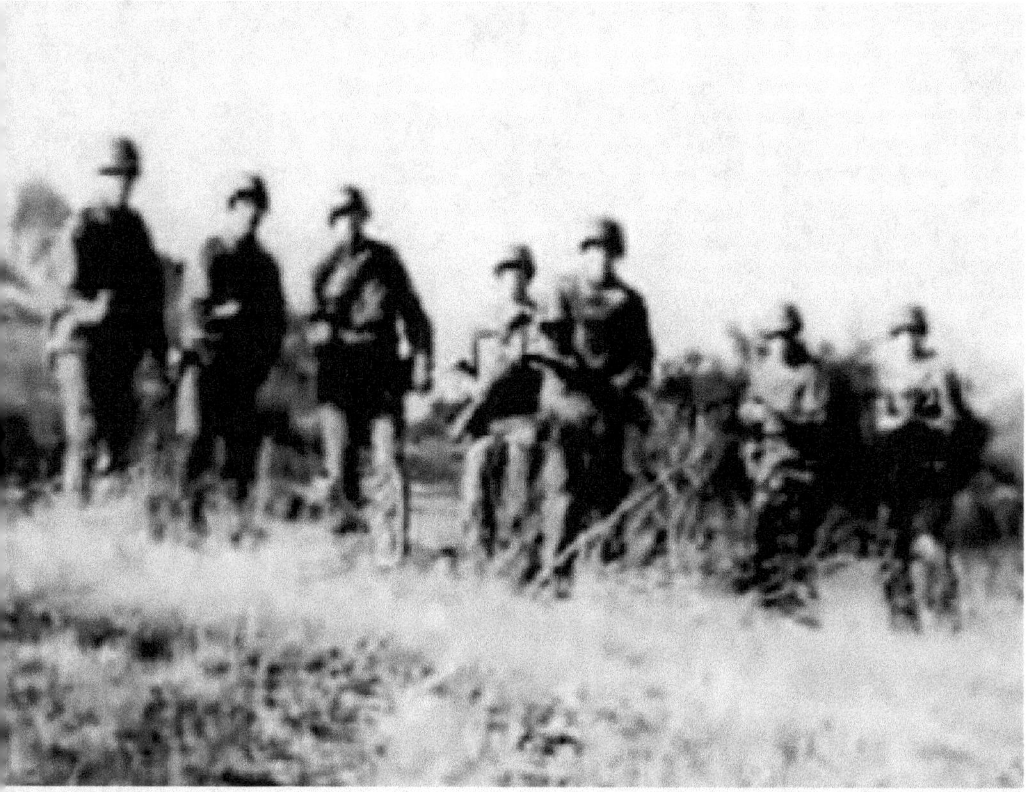

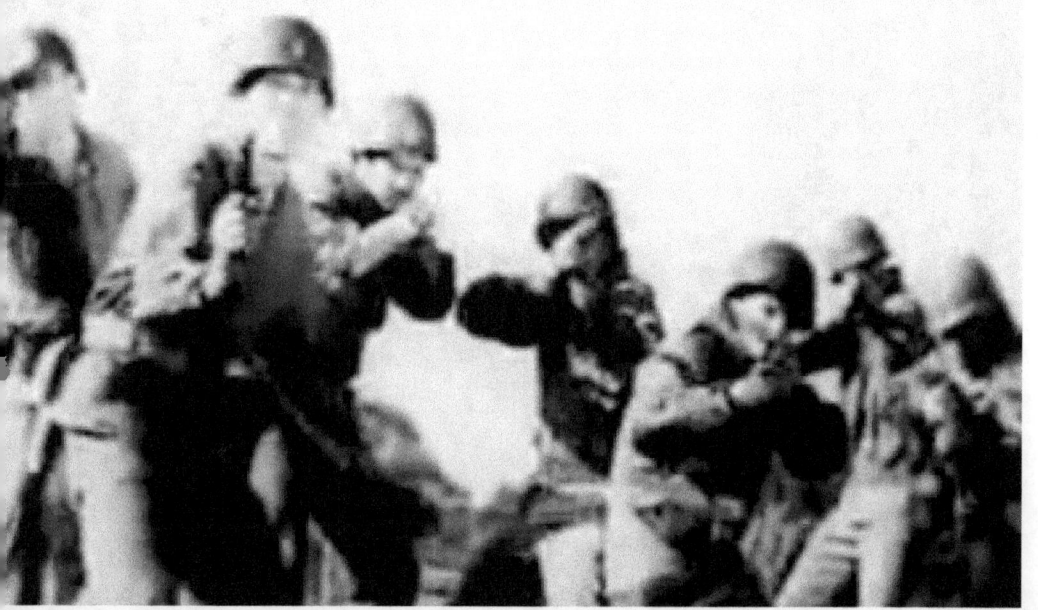

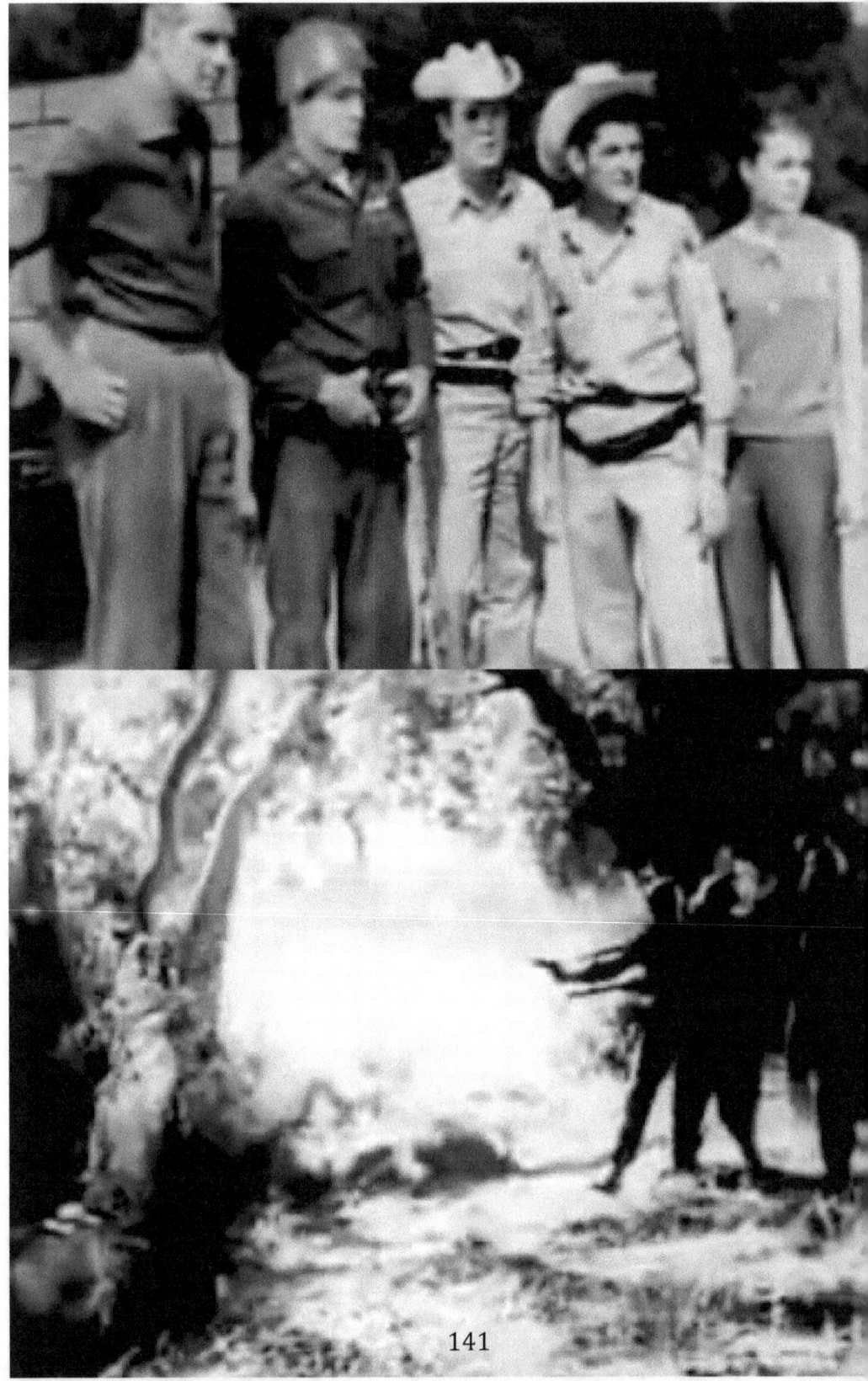

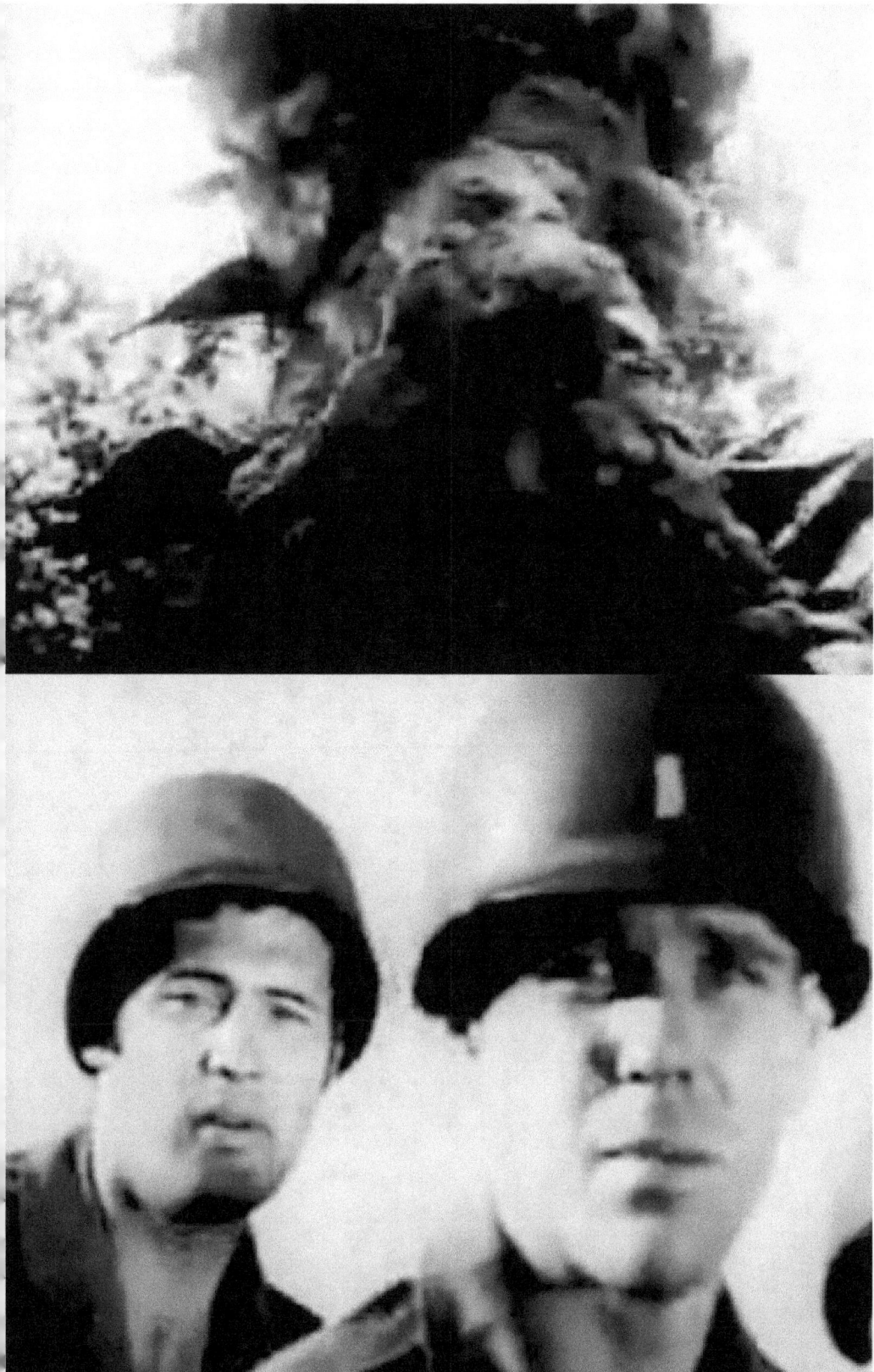

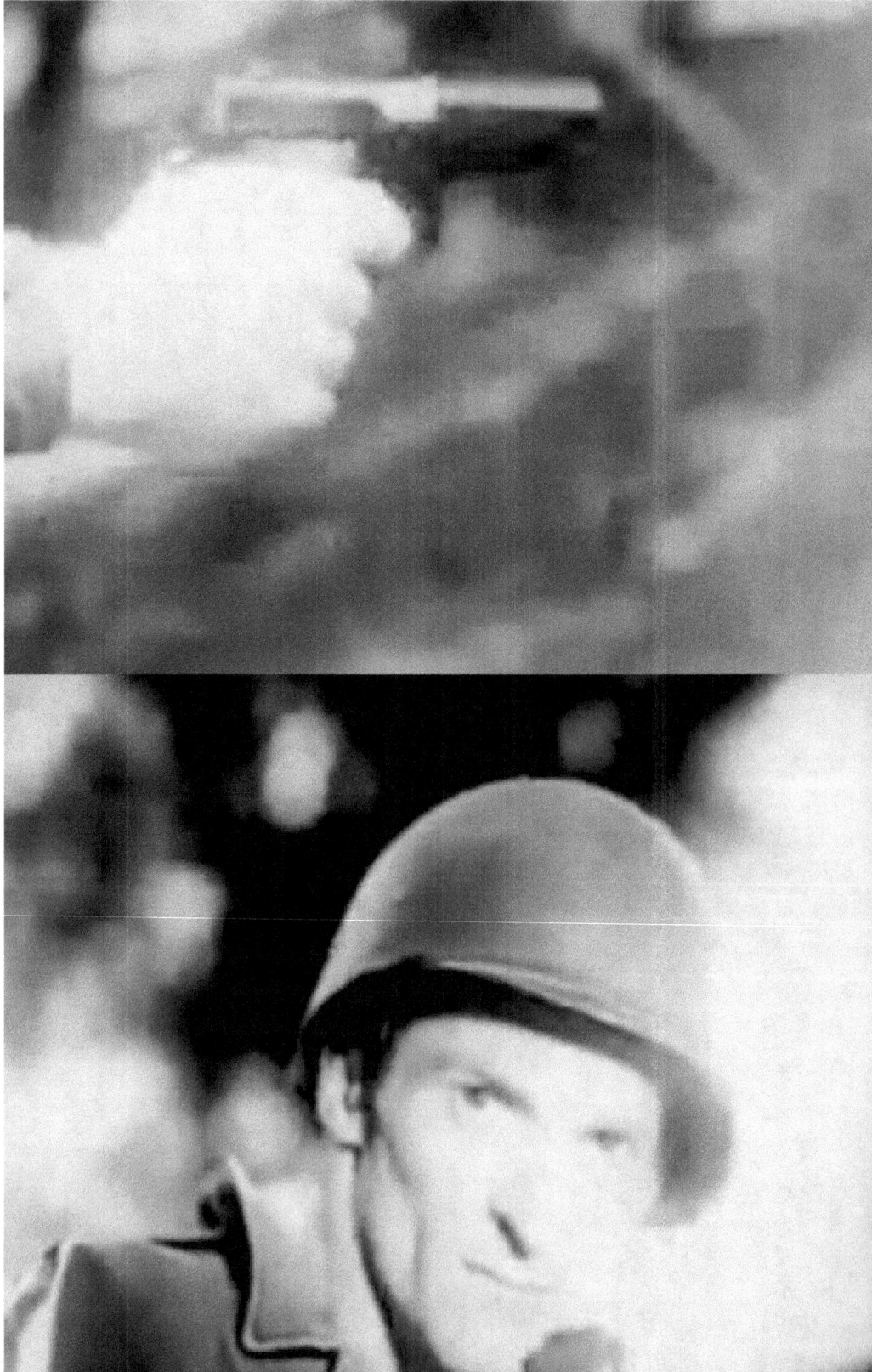

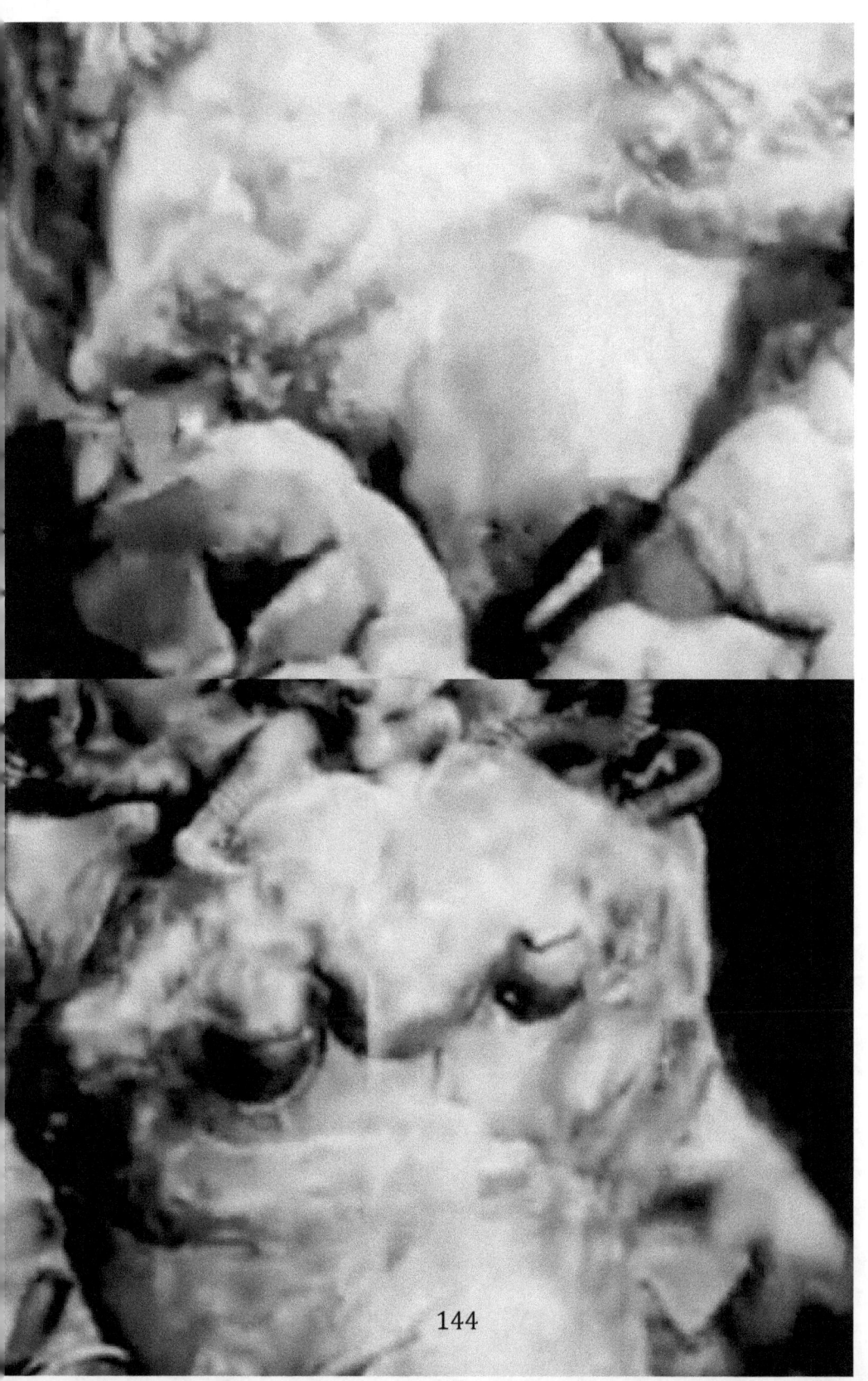

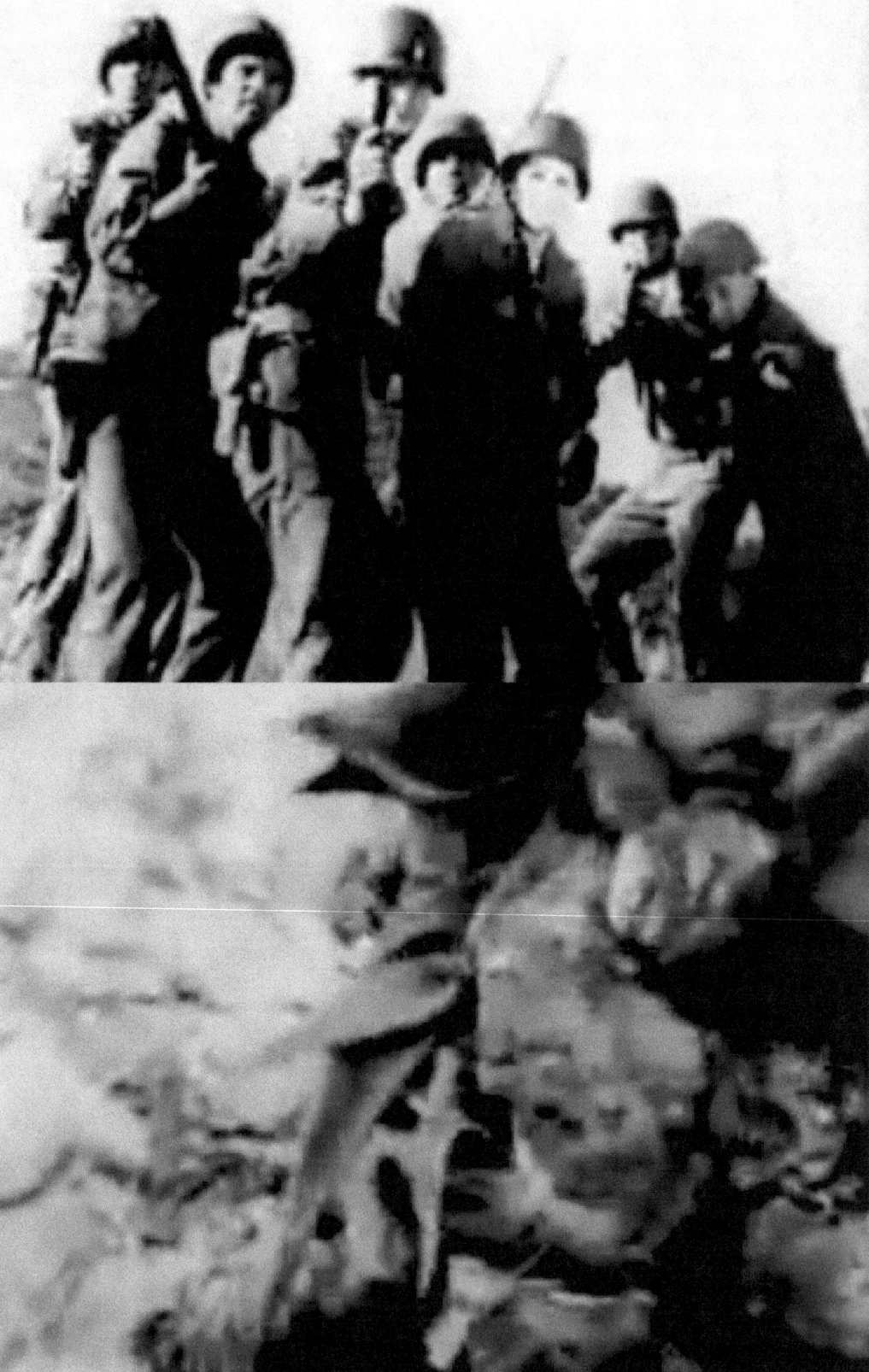

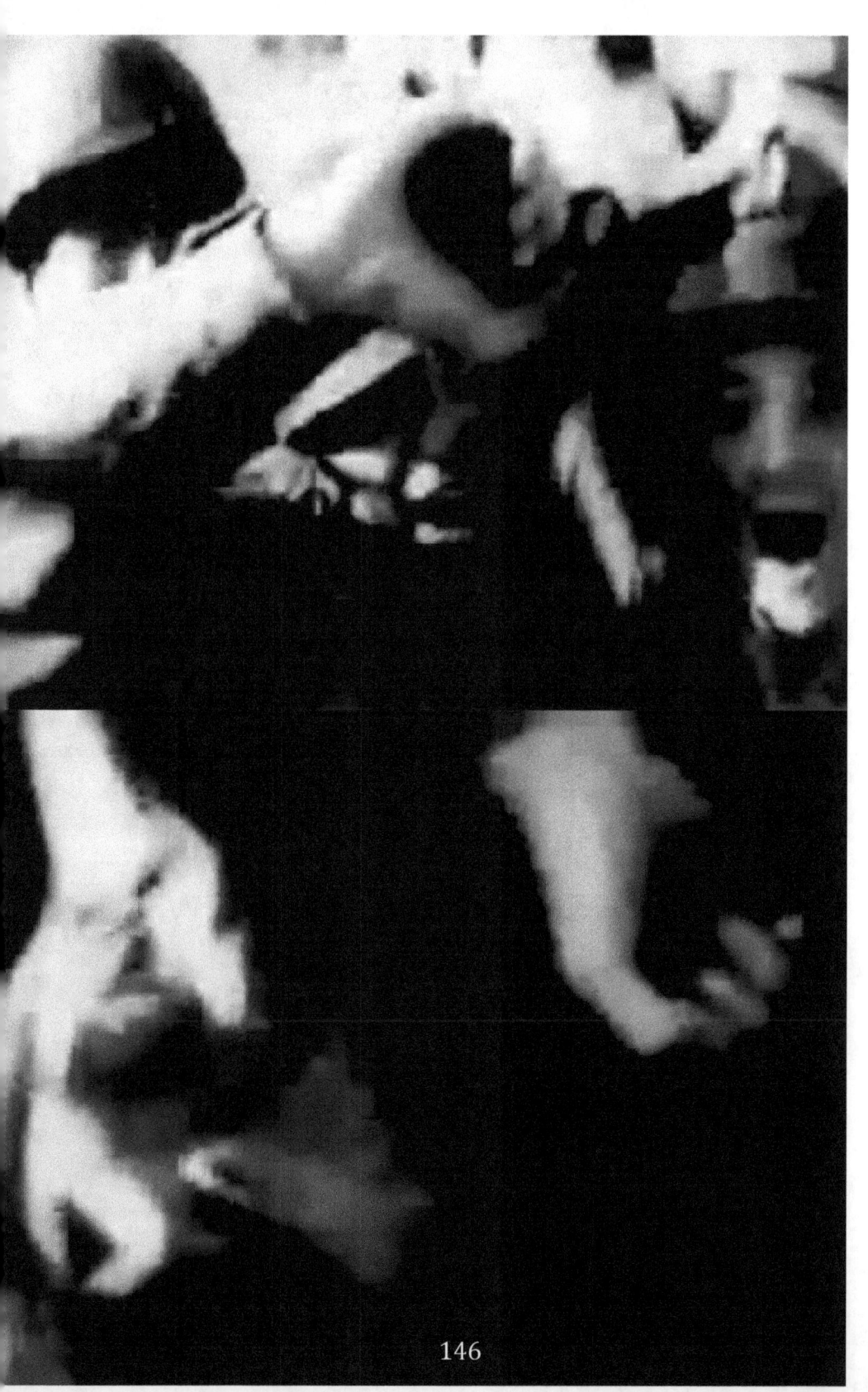

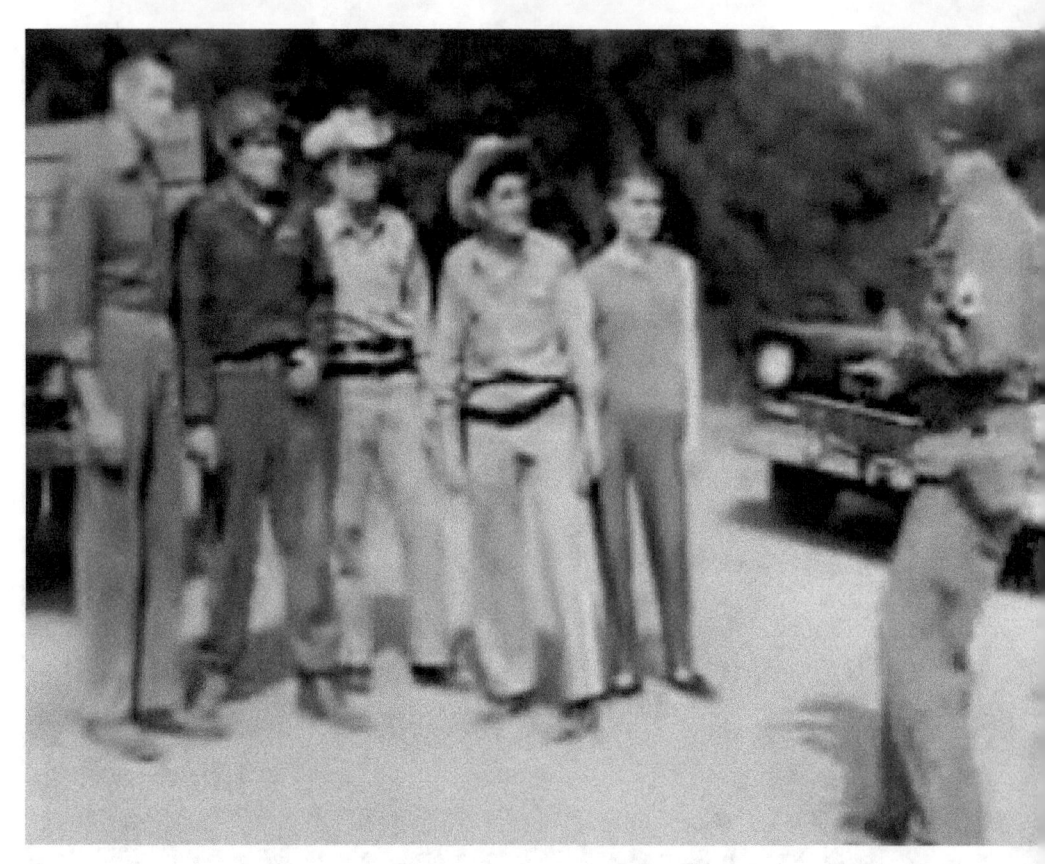

THE SERGEANT, A SHAKEN MAN,
RETURNED BABBLING ABOUT WHAT
HAD HAPPENED. CALDWELL,
REALIZING THE FULL DANGER OF
THE SITUATION, DECIDED HE HAD
ONLY ONE MEANS LEFT TO STOP
THE MONSTER: GRENADES.

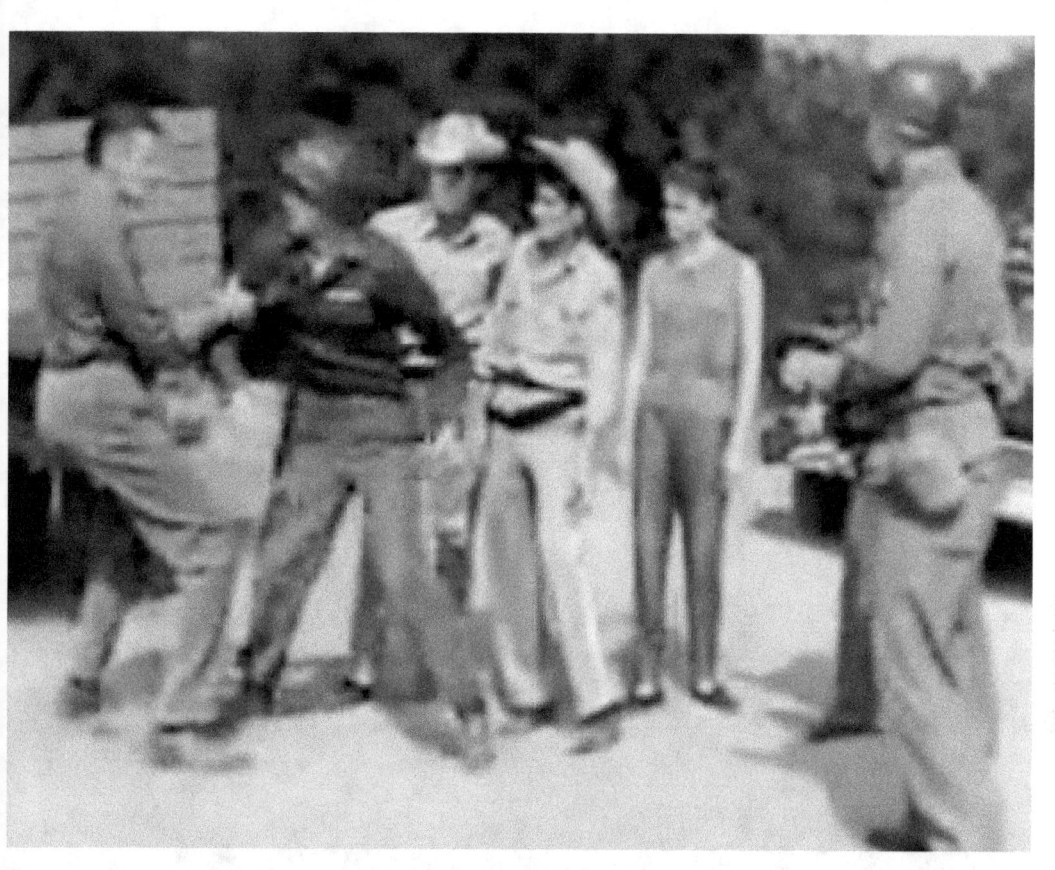

NOW BRADFORD MADE A DRASTIC
MOVE. ACTING ON HIS SUPERIOR
AUTHORITY, HE FORBADE
CALDWELL TO DESTROY THE
CREATURE. THE COL., MORE
CONCERNED WITH SAVING HUMAN
LIVES THAN ADVANCING SCIENCE,
TOLD BRADFORD TO GO TO HELL.
-GET OUT OF MY WAY

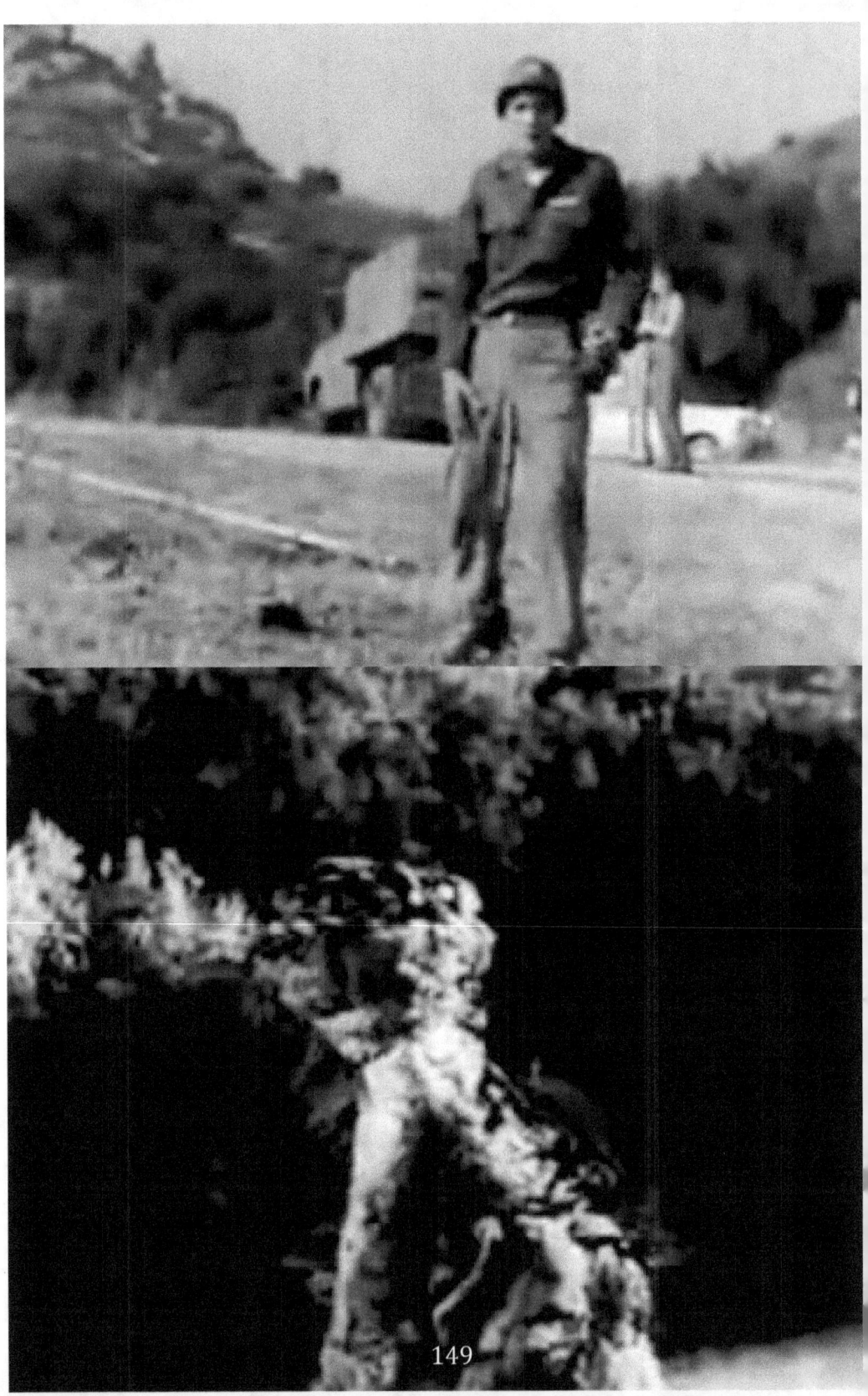

149

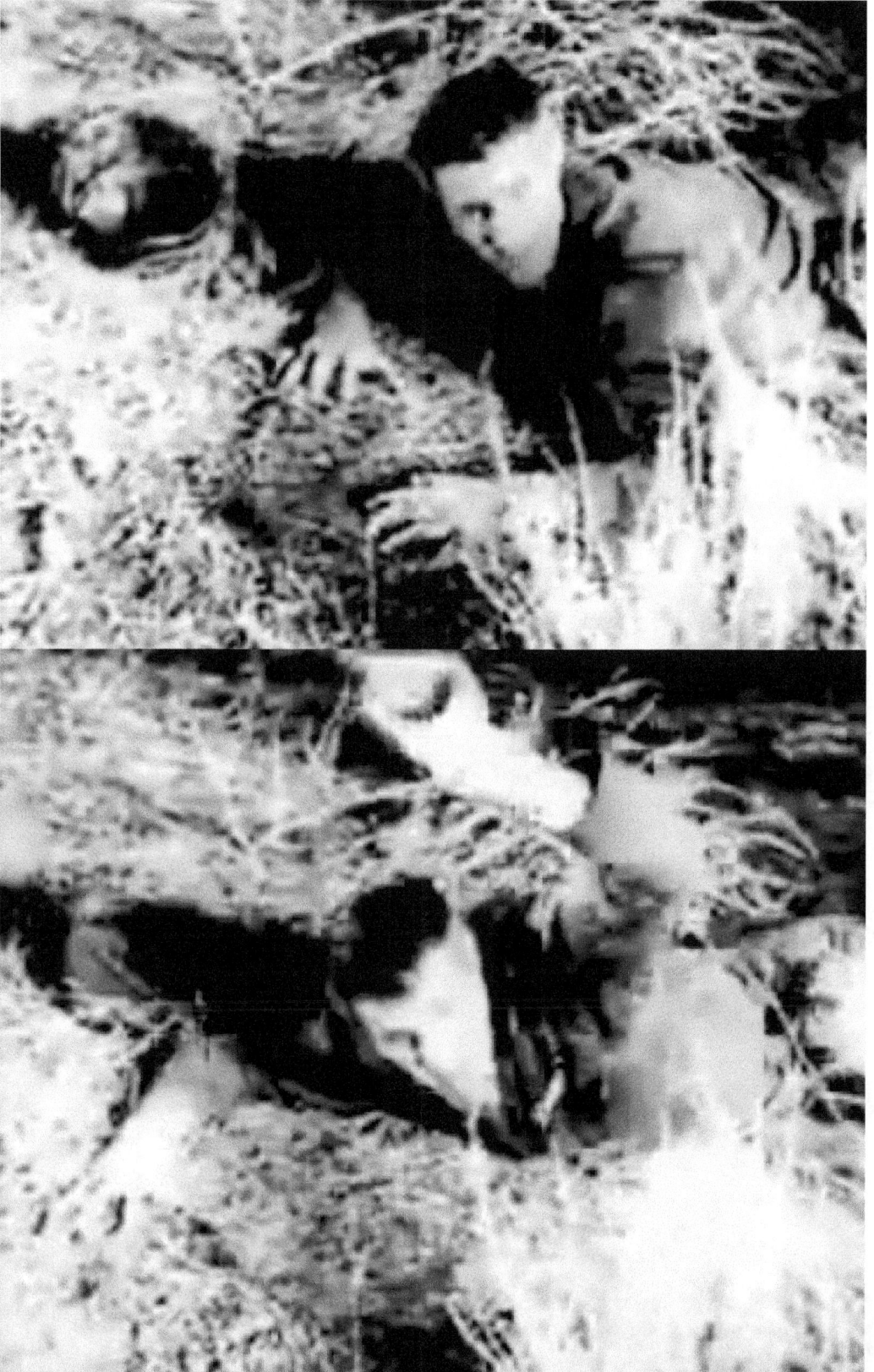

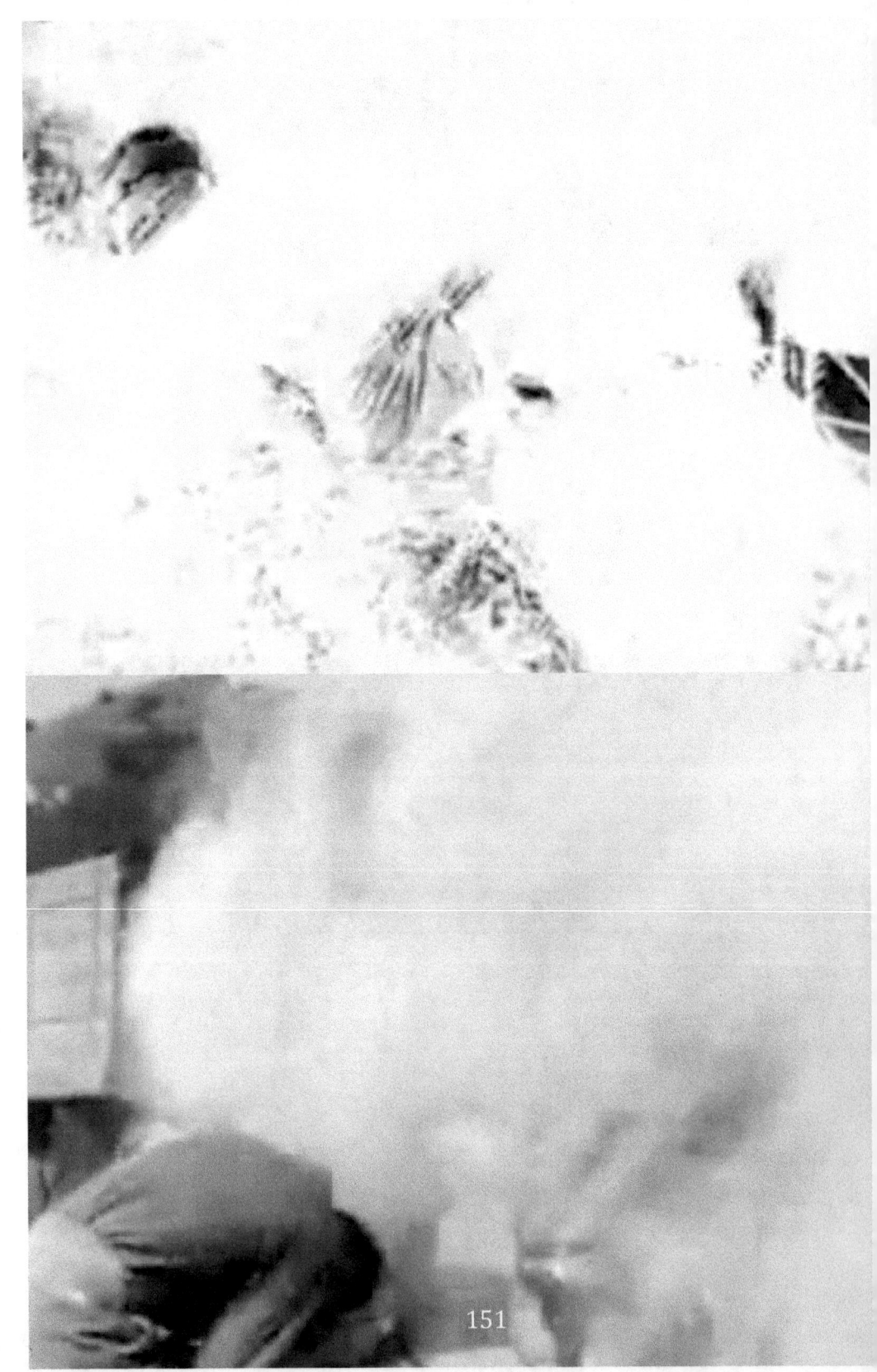

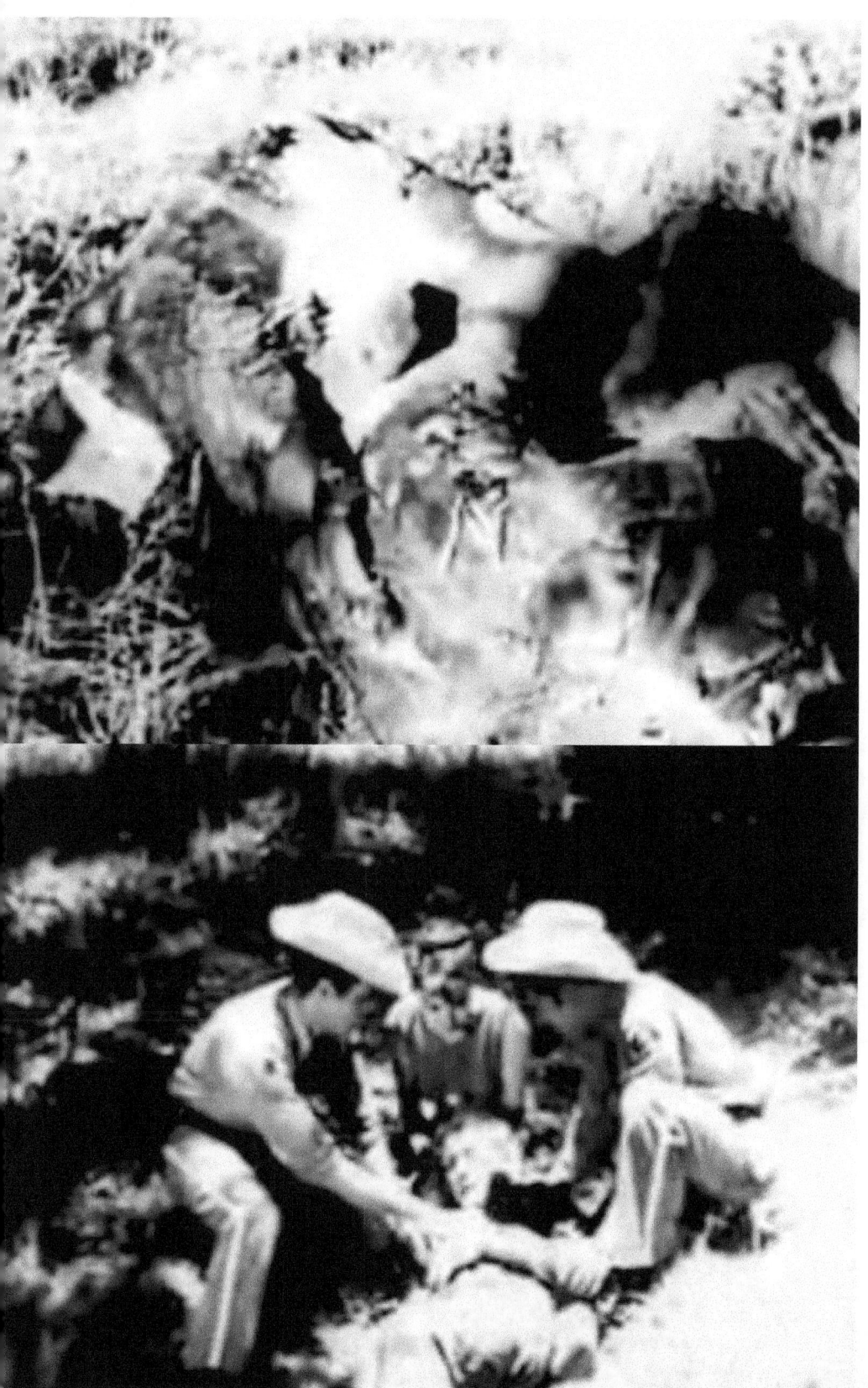

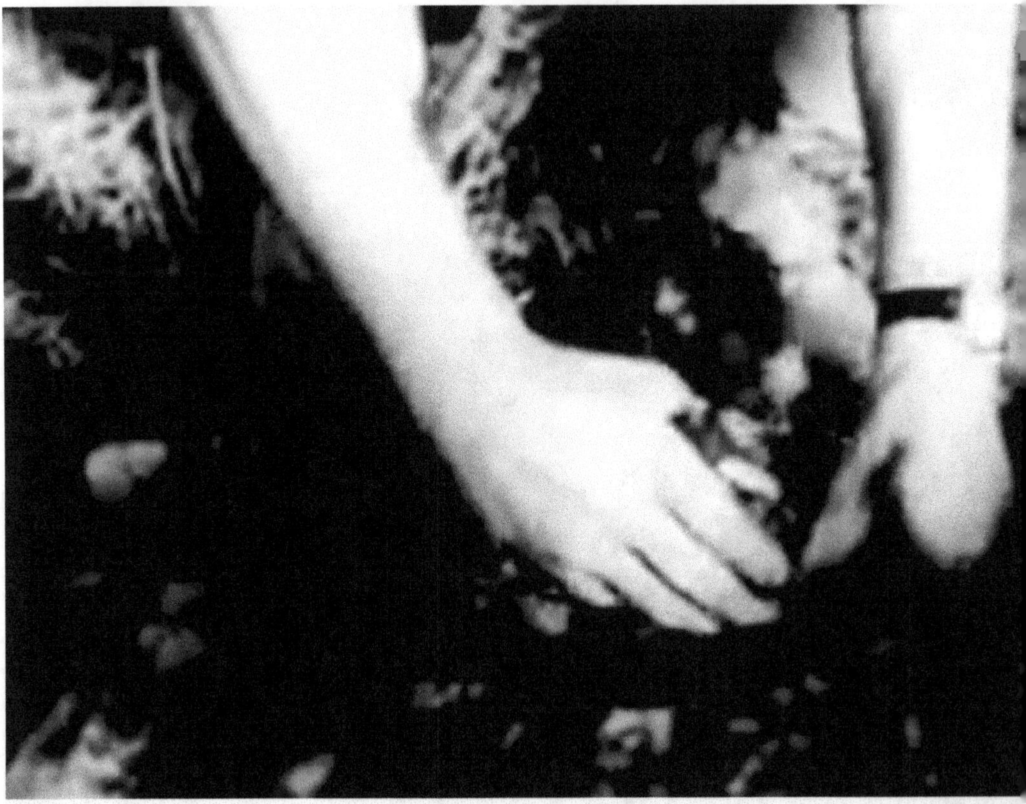
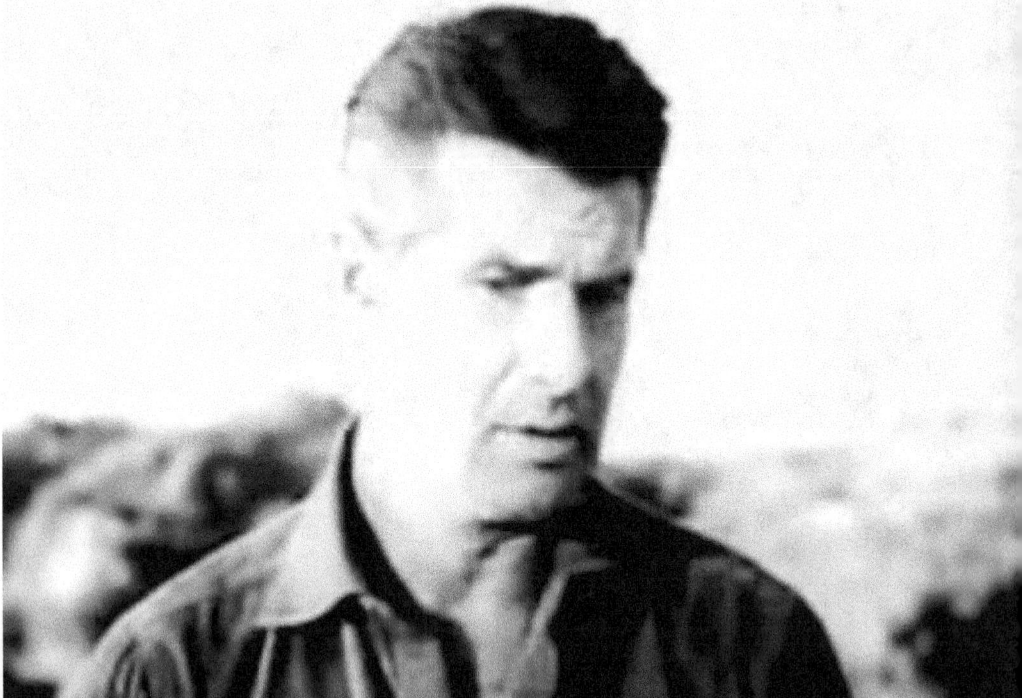

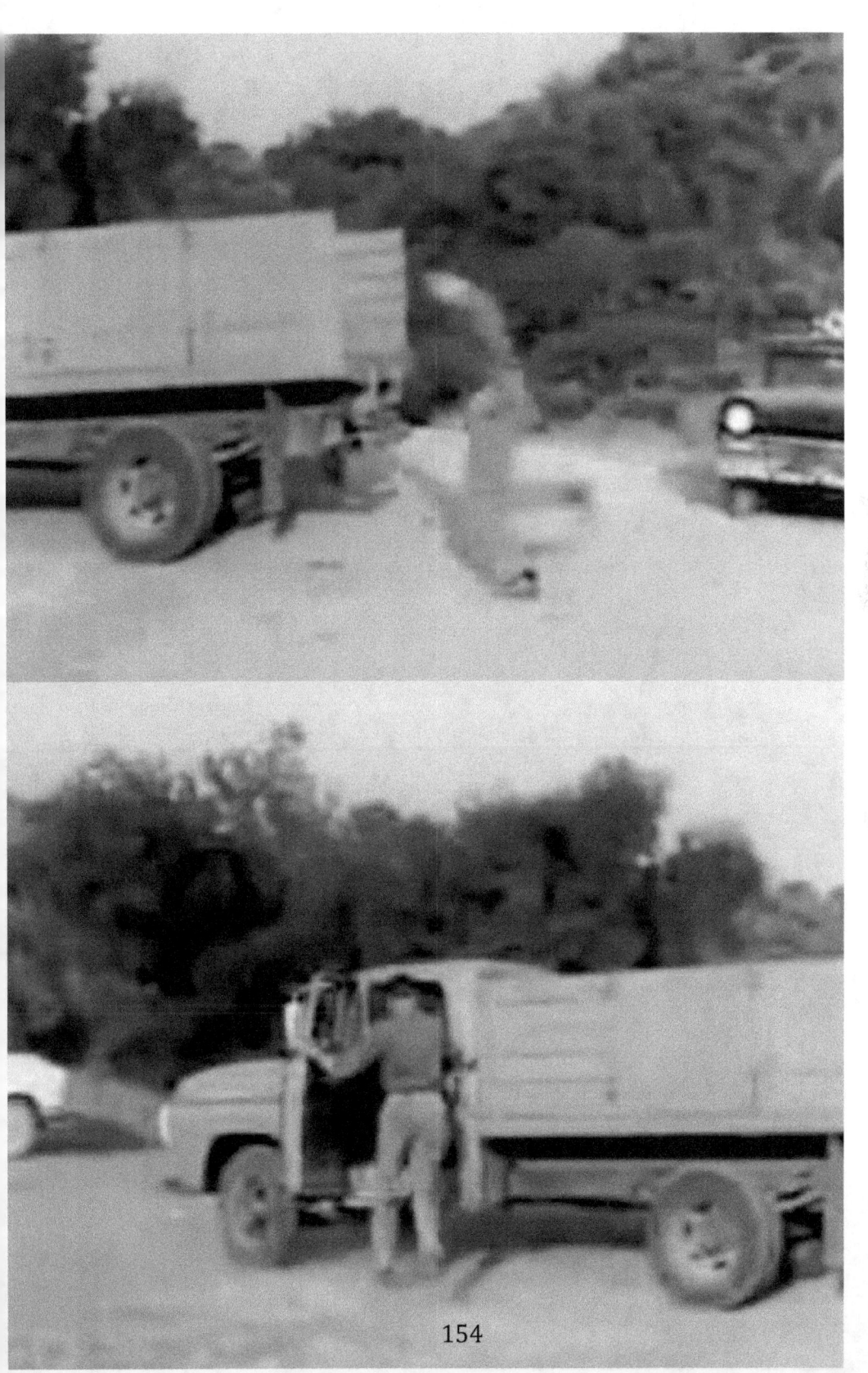

154

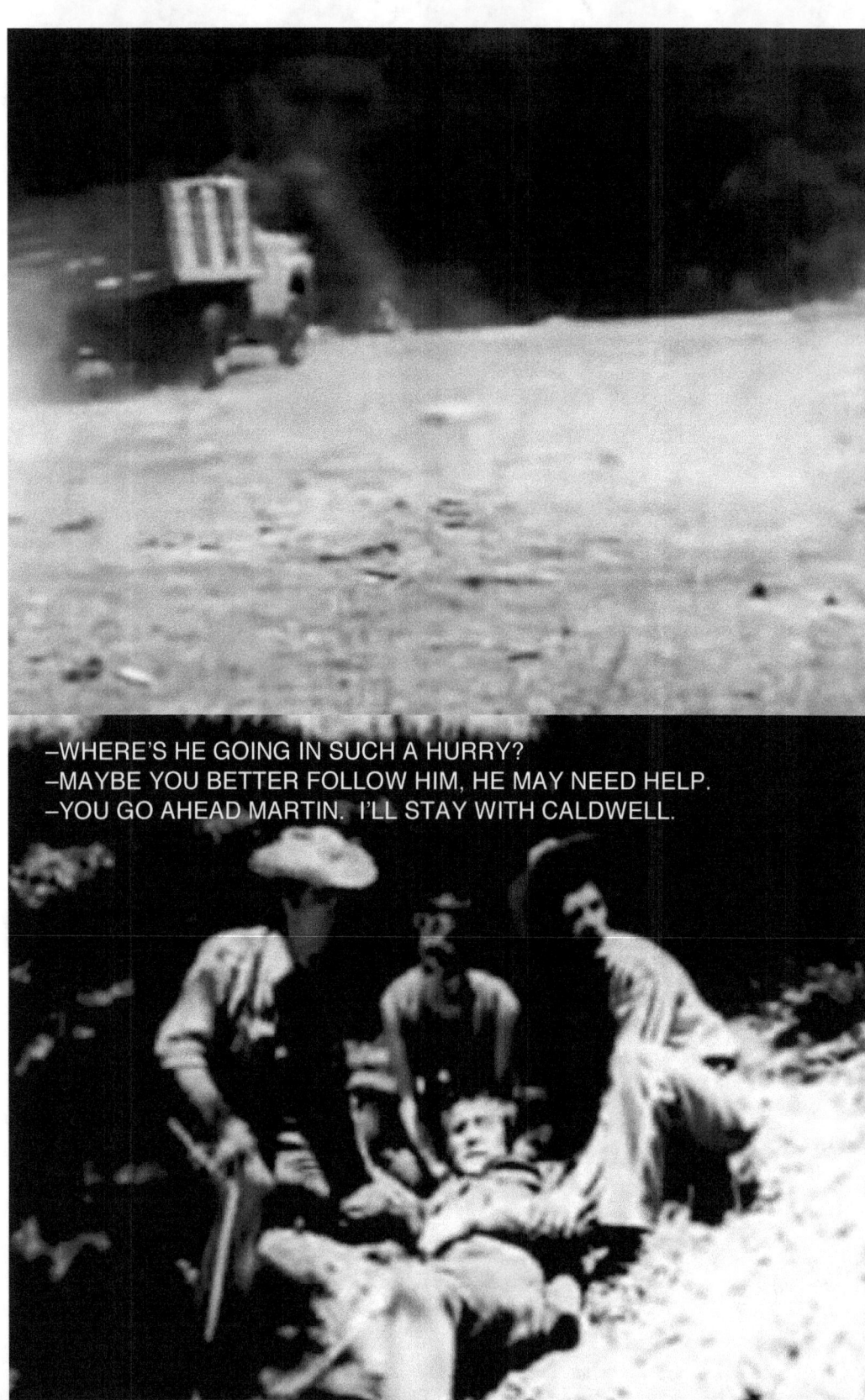

-WHERE'S HE GOING IN SUCH A HURRY?
-MAYBE YOU BETTER FOLLOW HIM, HE MAY NEED HELP.
-YOU GO AHEAD MARTIN. I'LL STAY WITH CALDWELL.

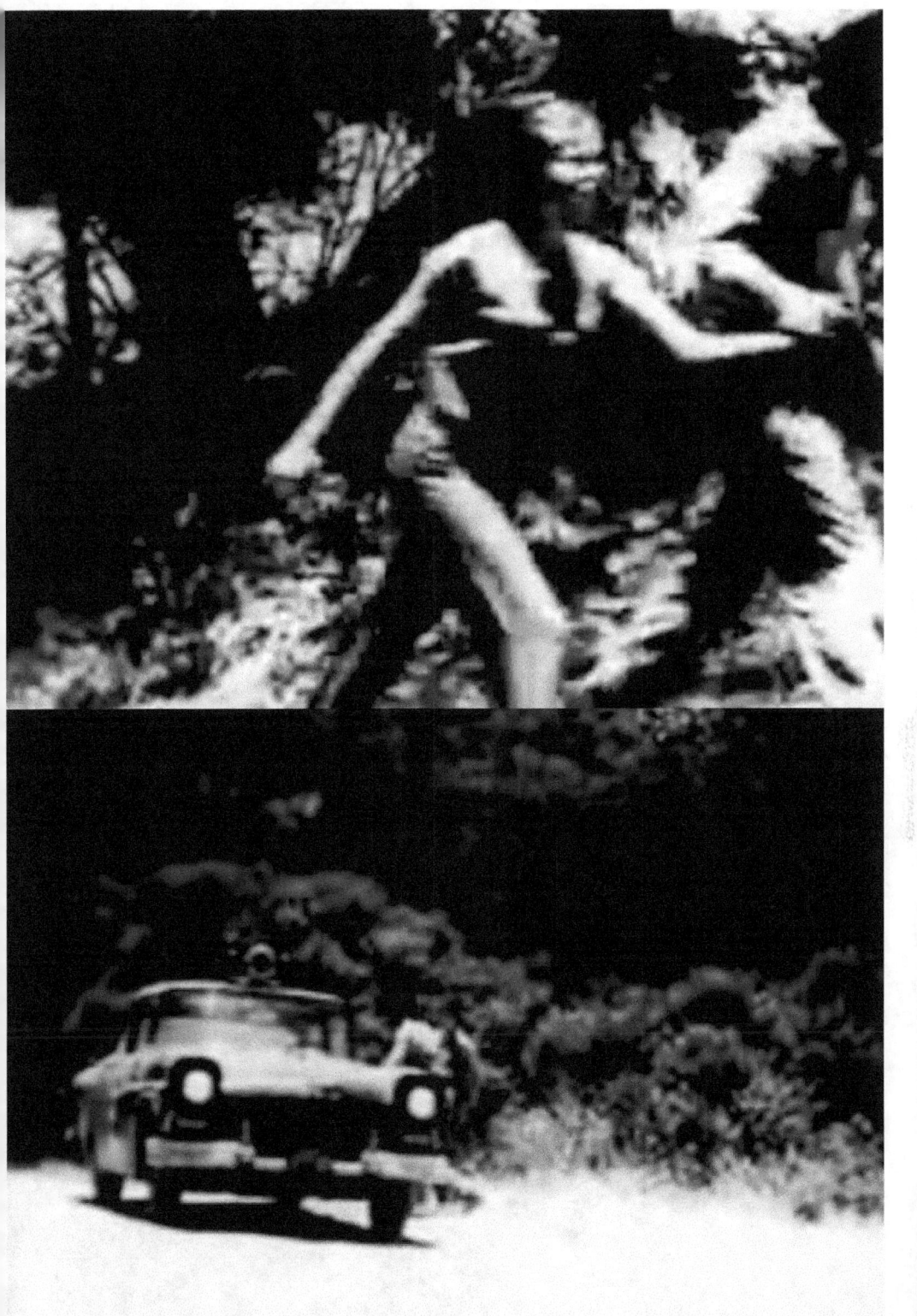

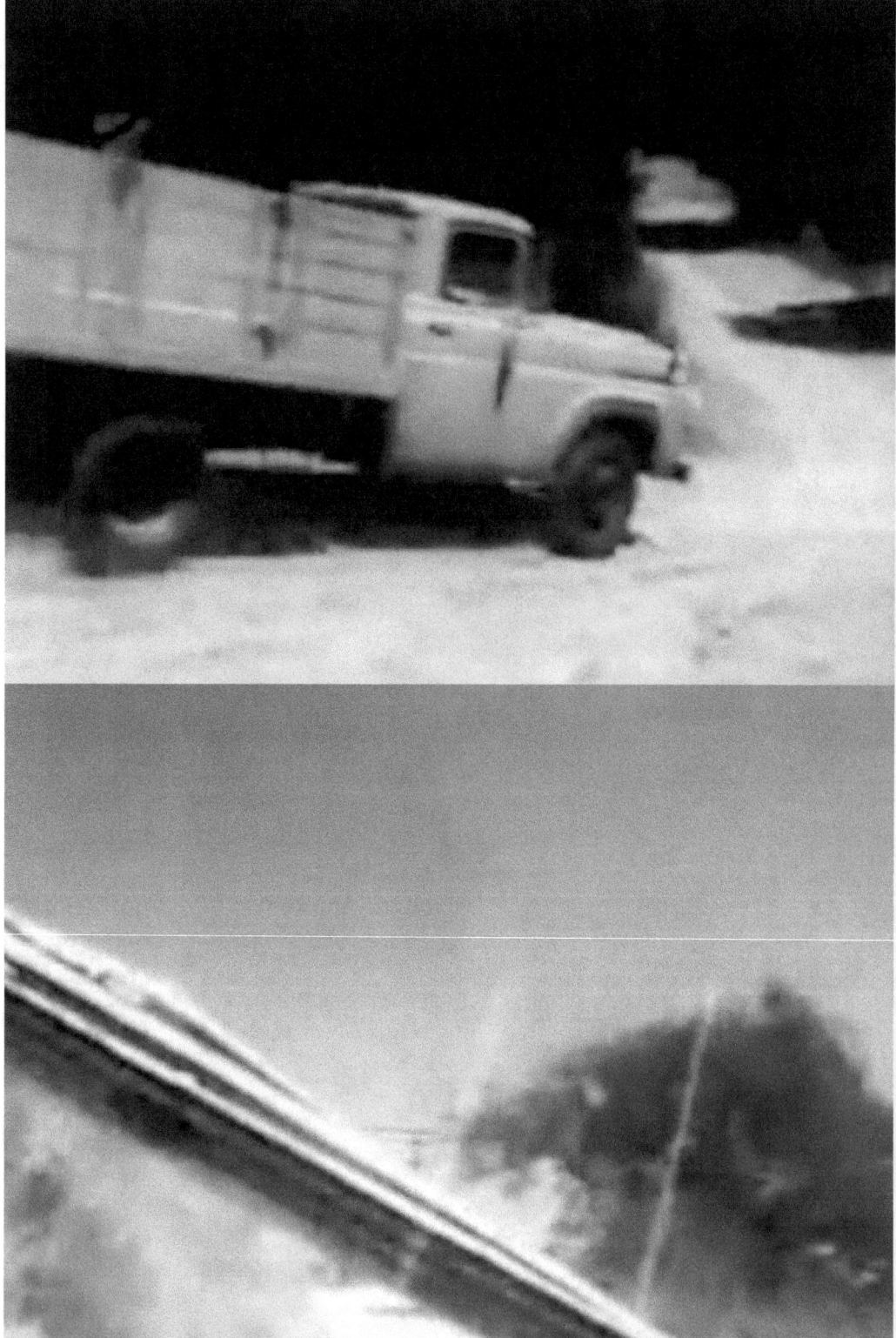

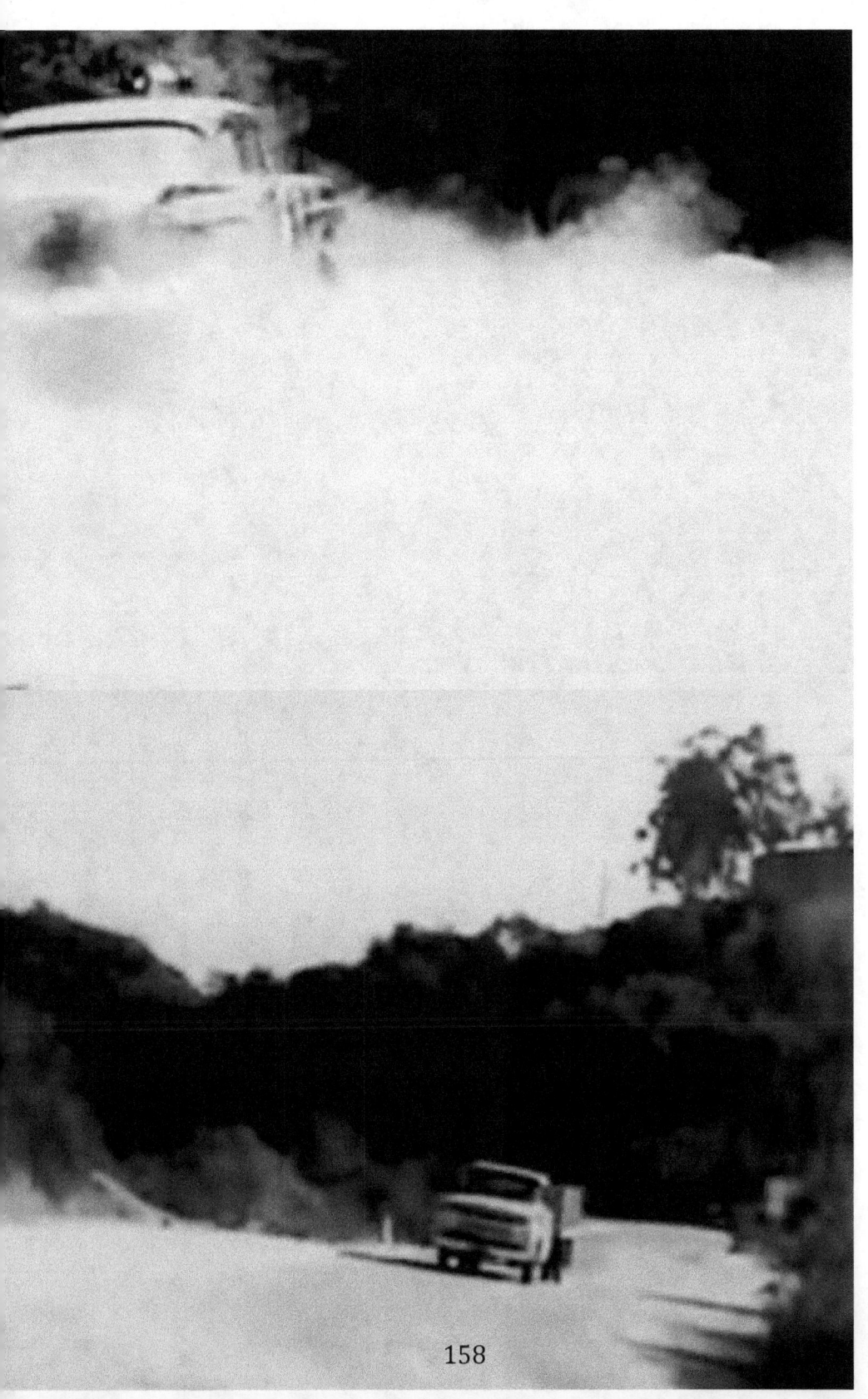

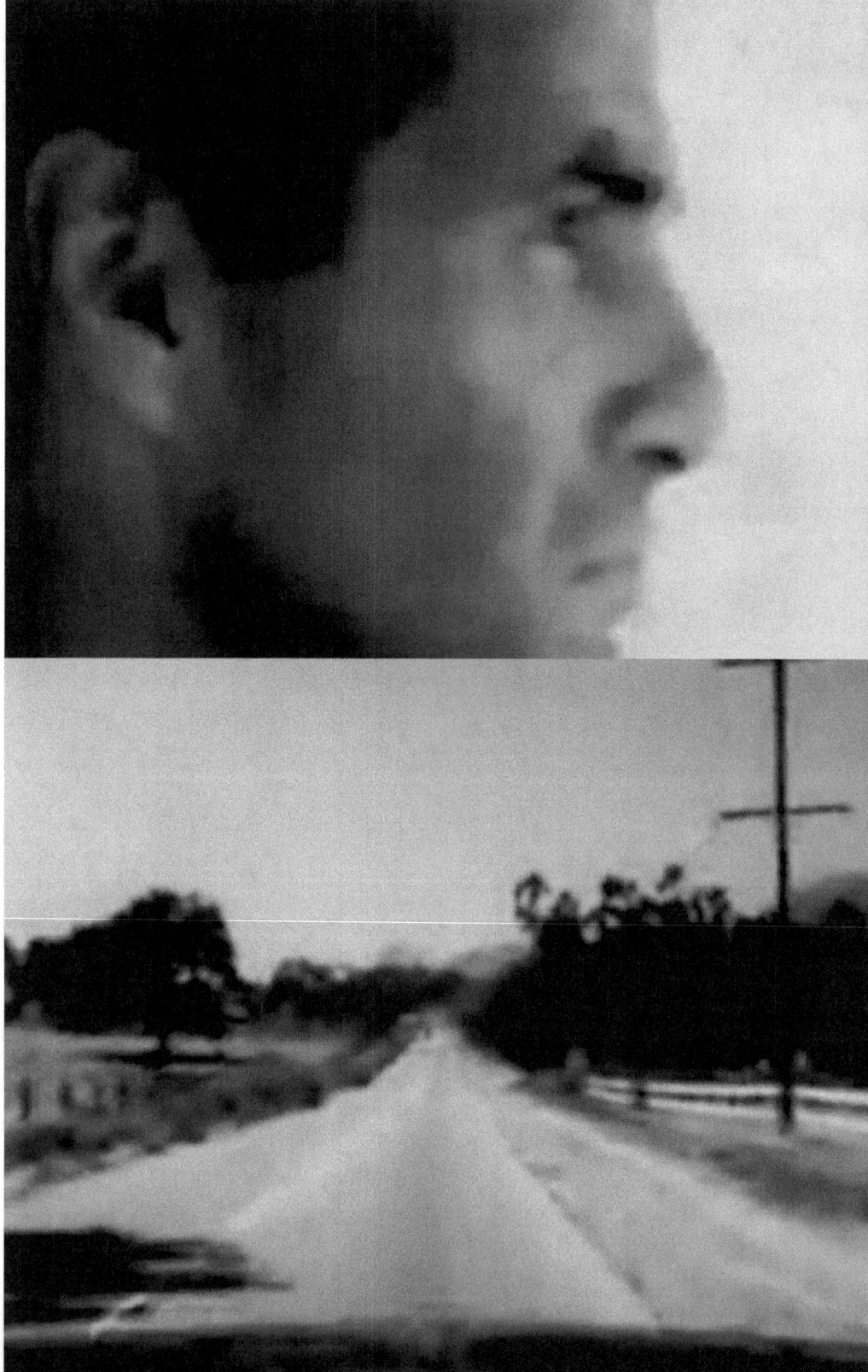

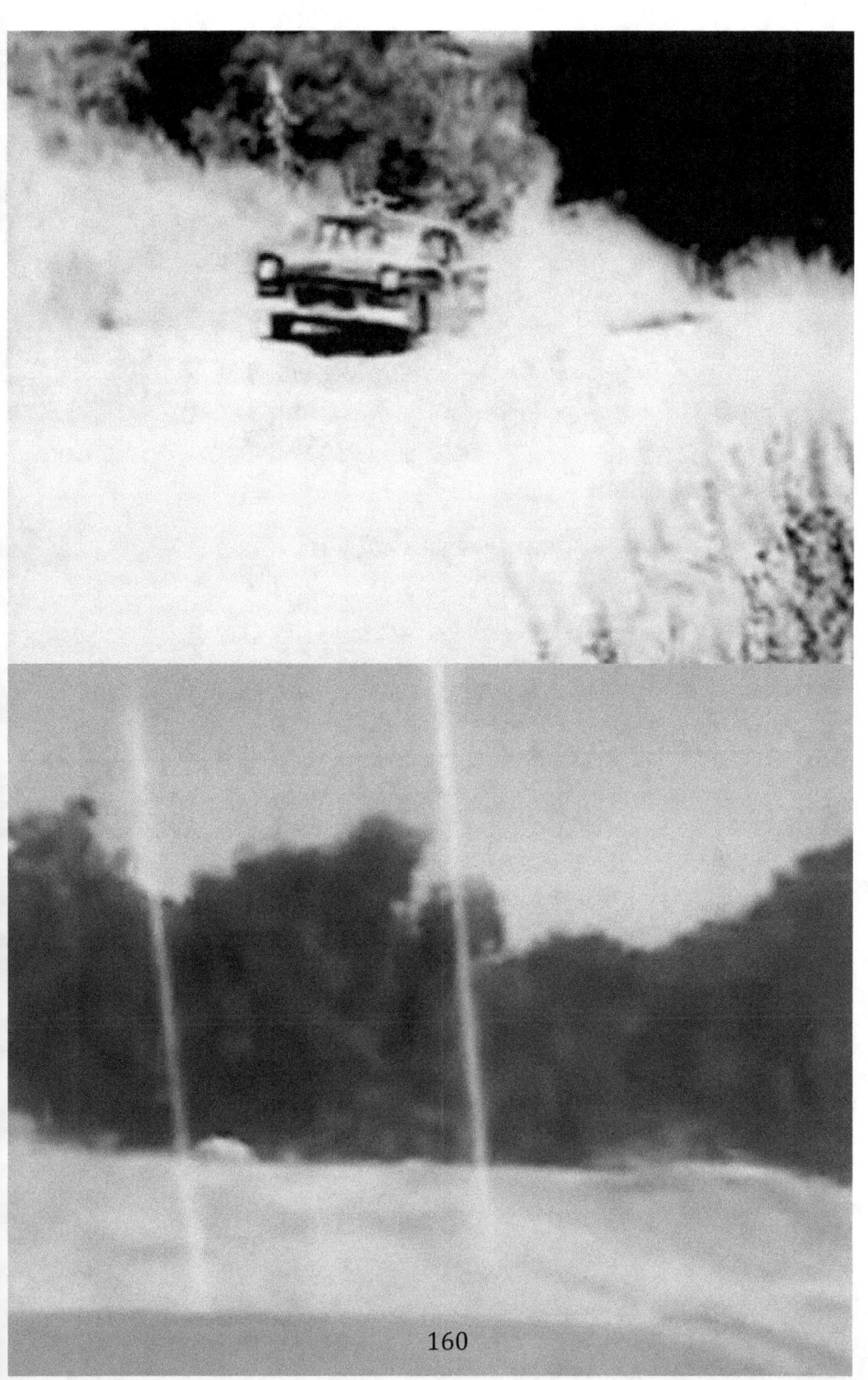

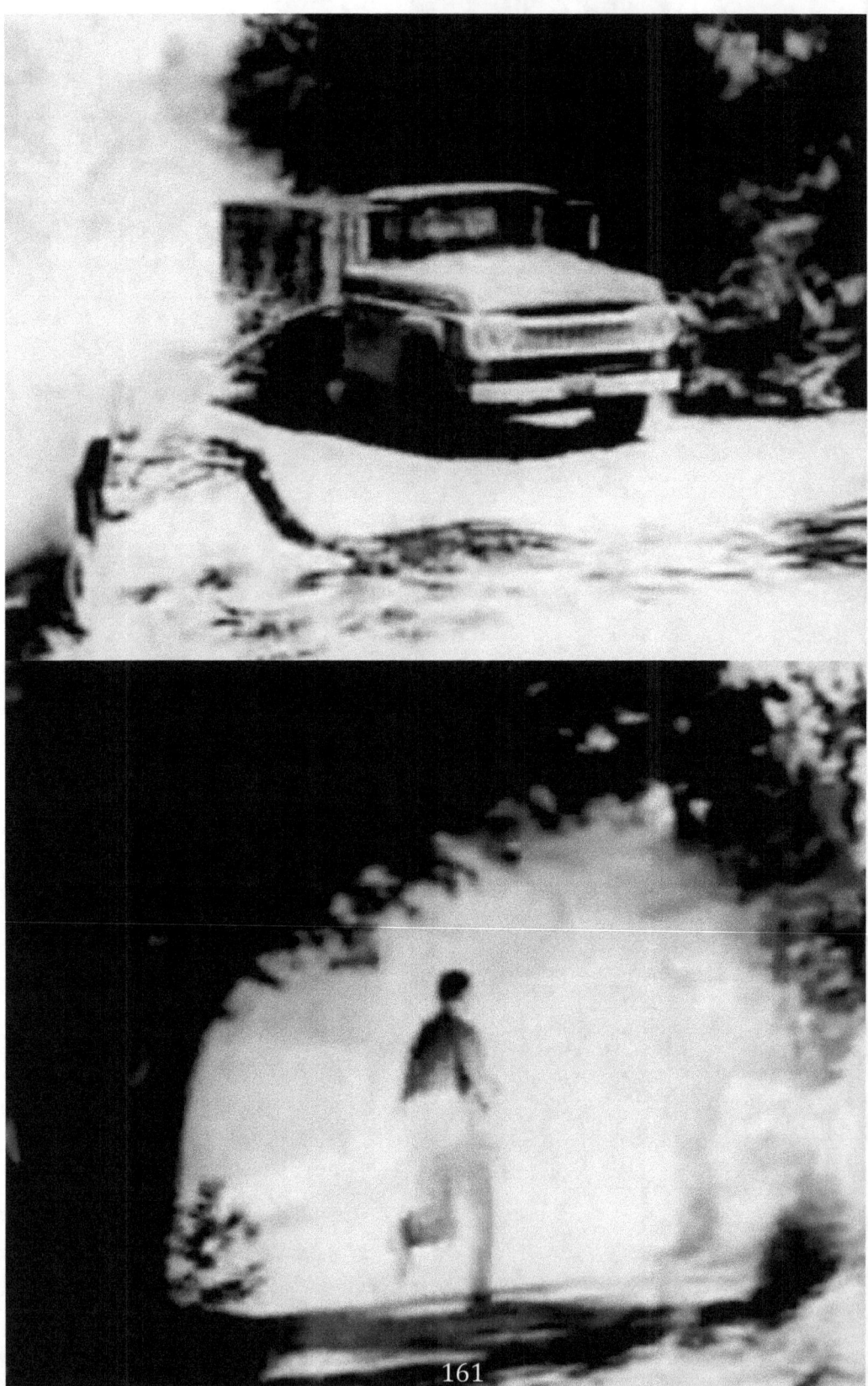

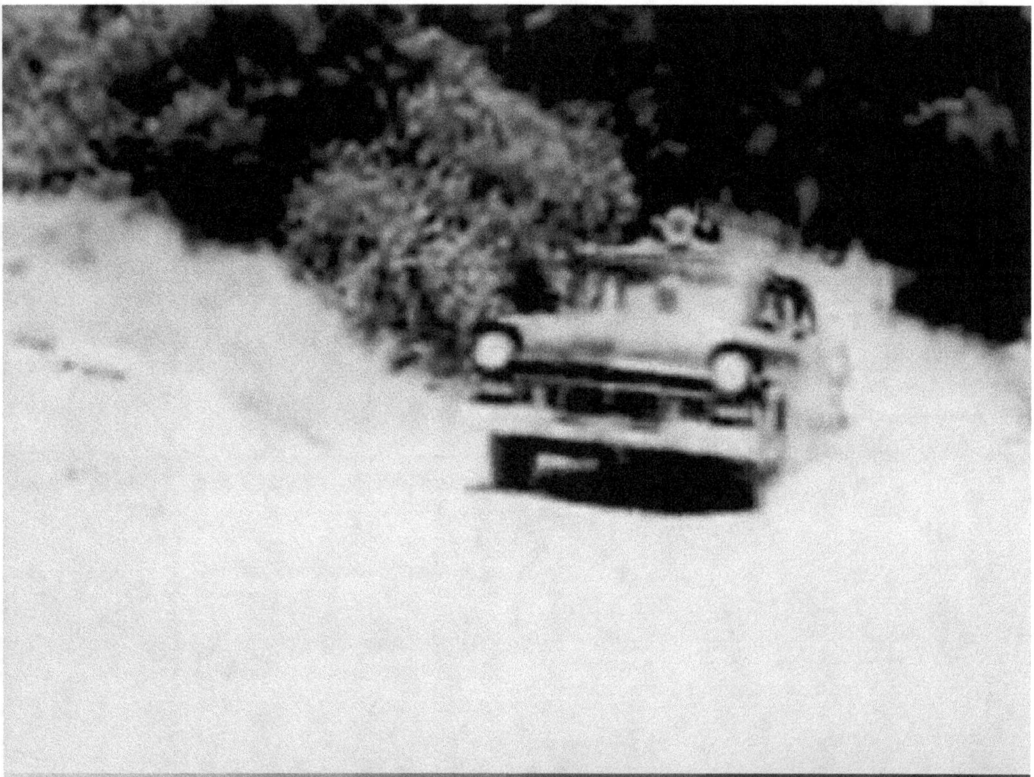

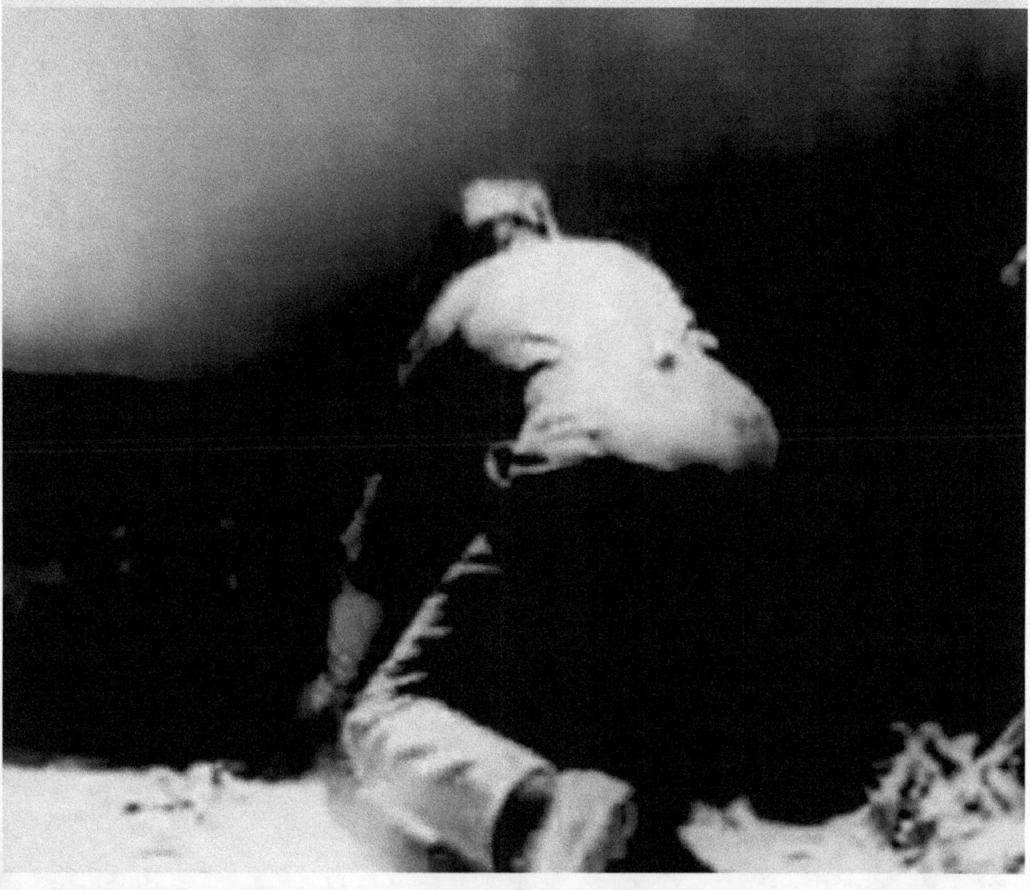

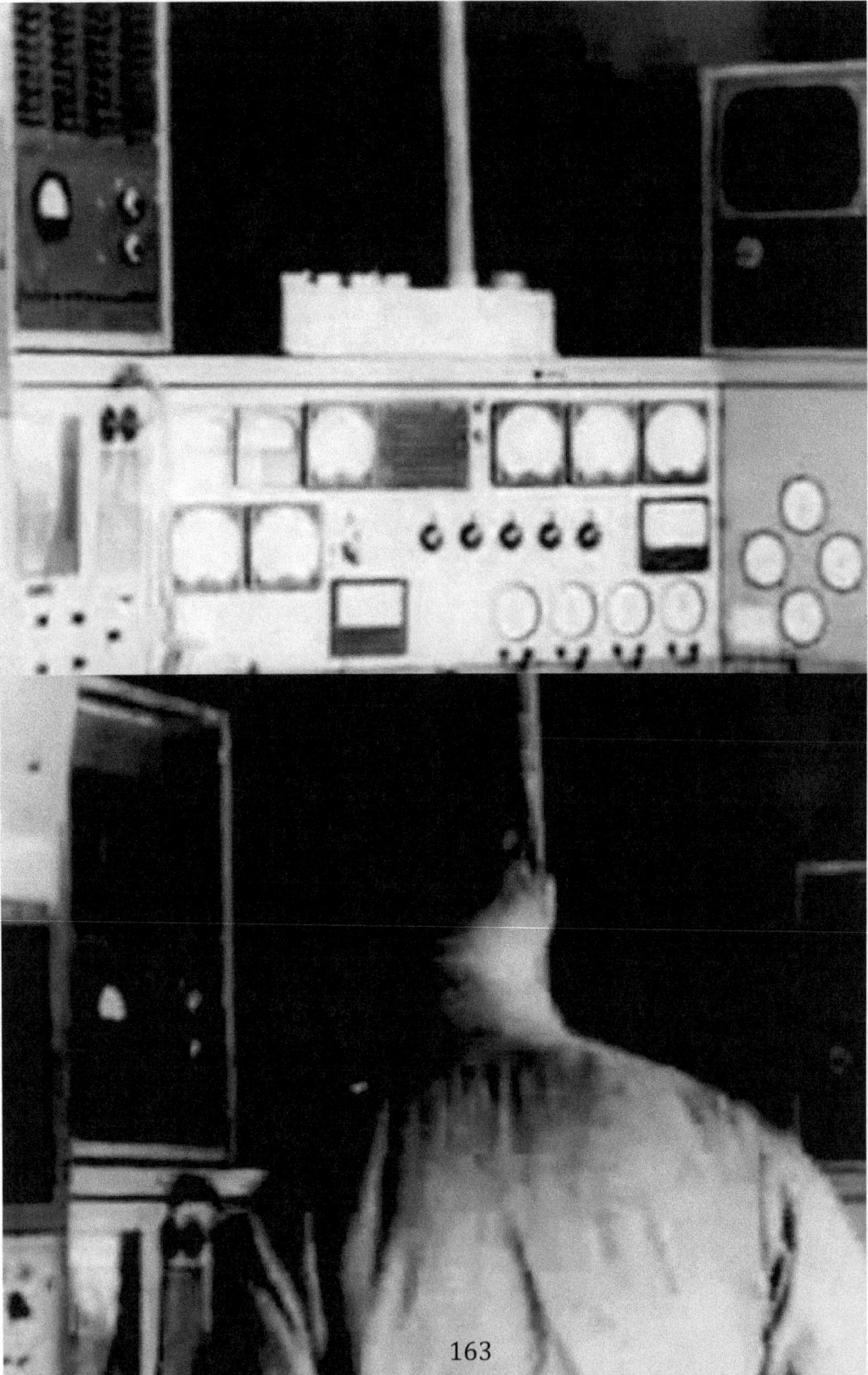

163

THE EXPLOSION LOOSENED
THE HARNESS ON THE
MONSTER AND ALLOWED IT
TO ESCAPE

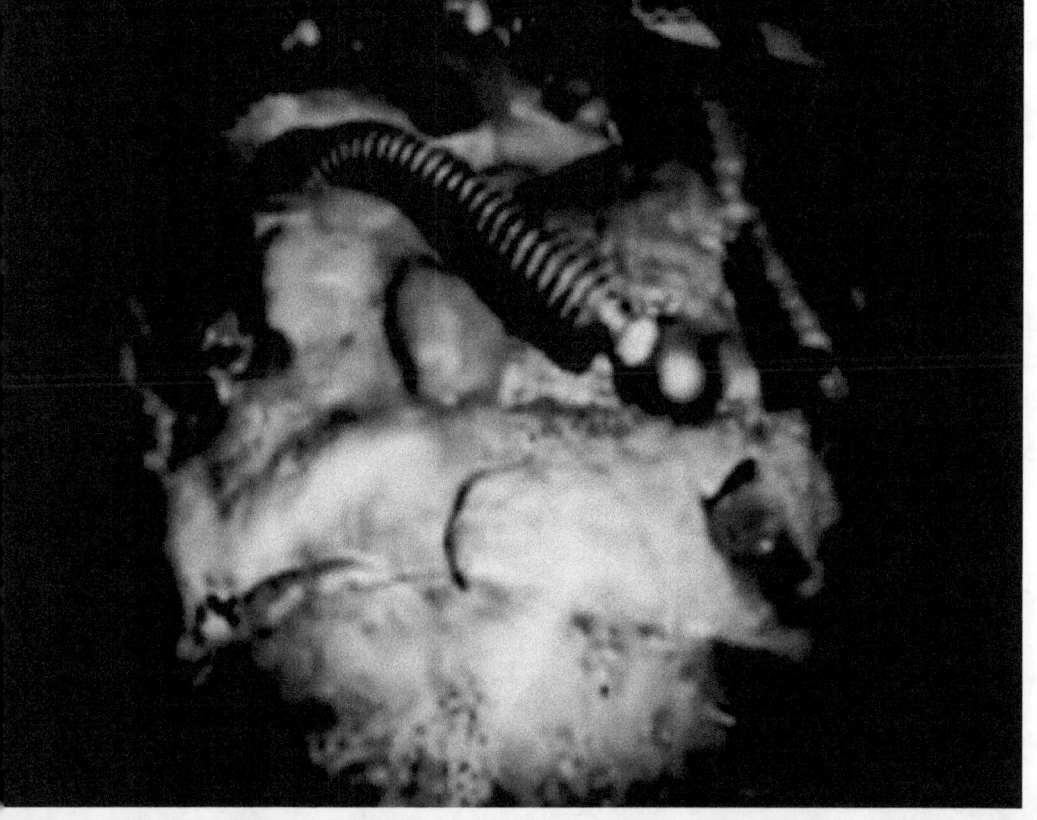

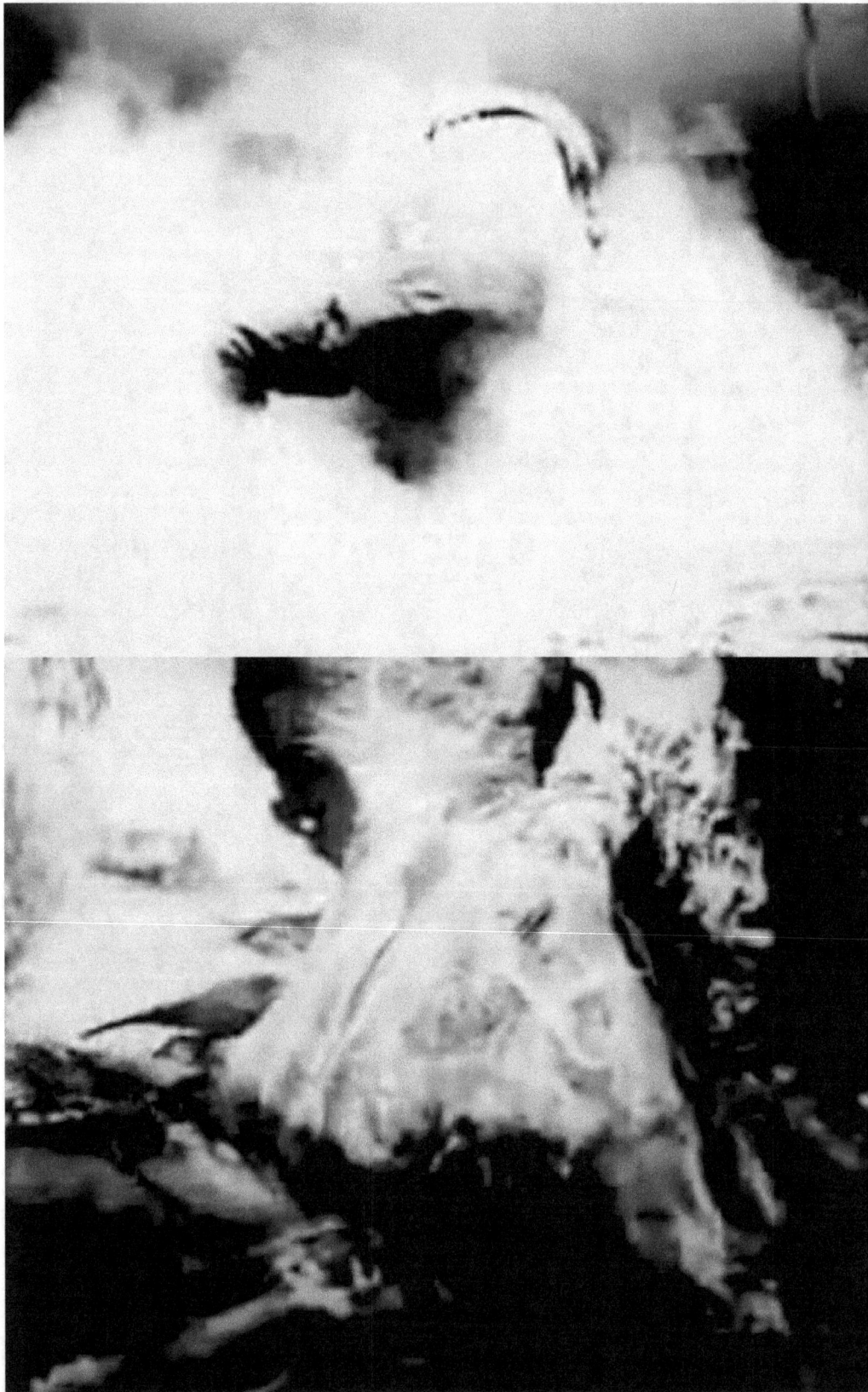

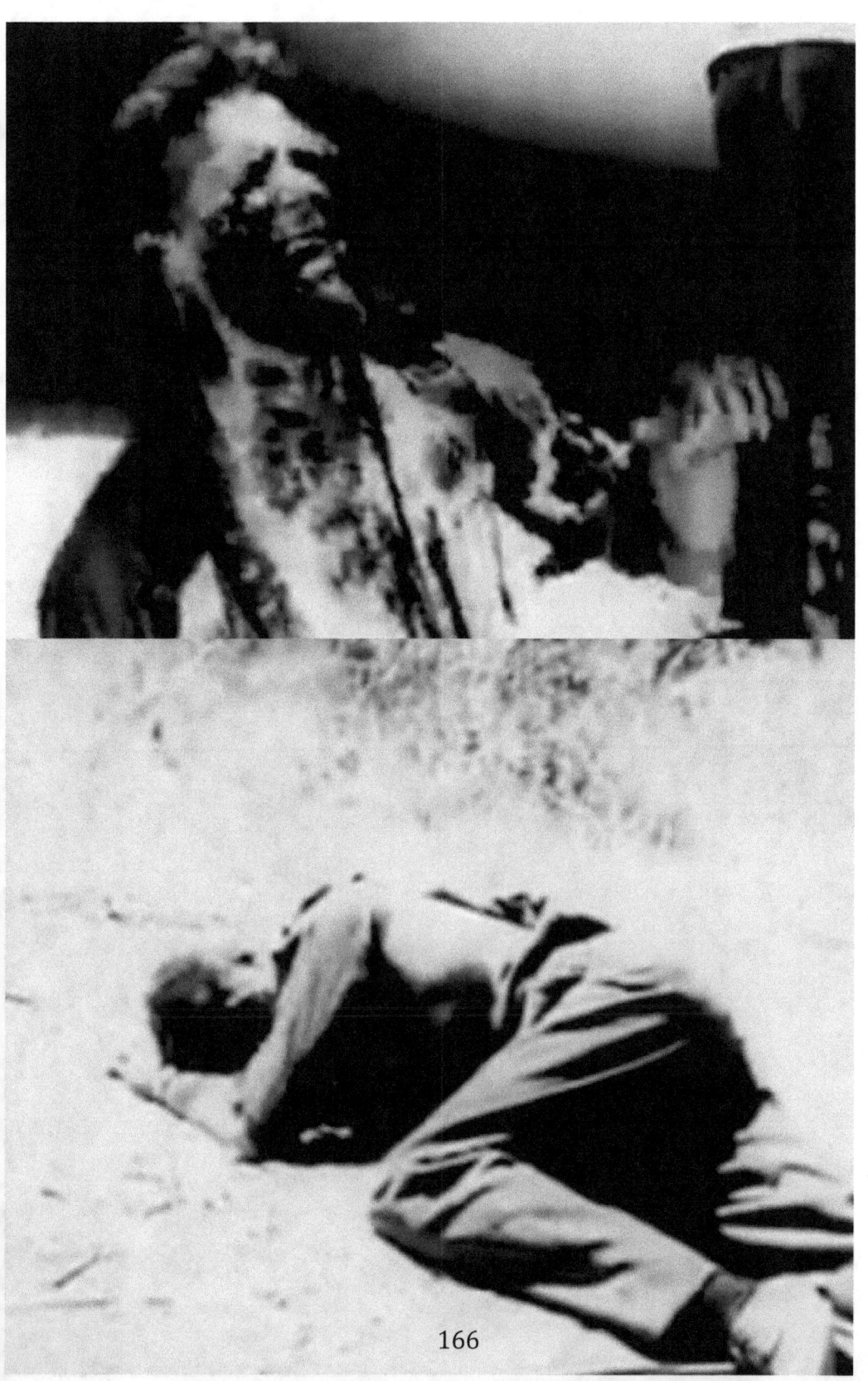

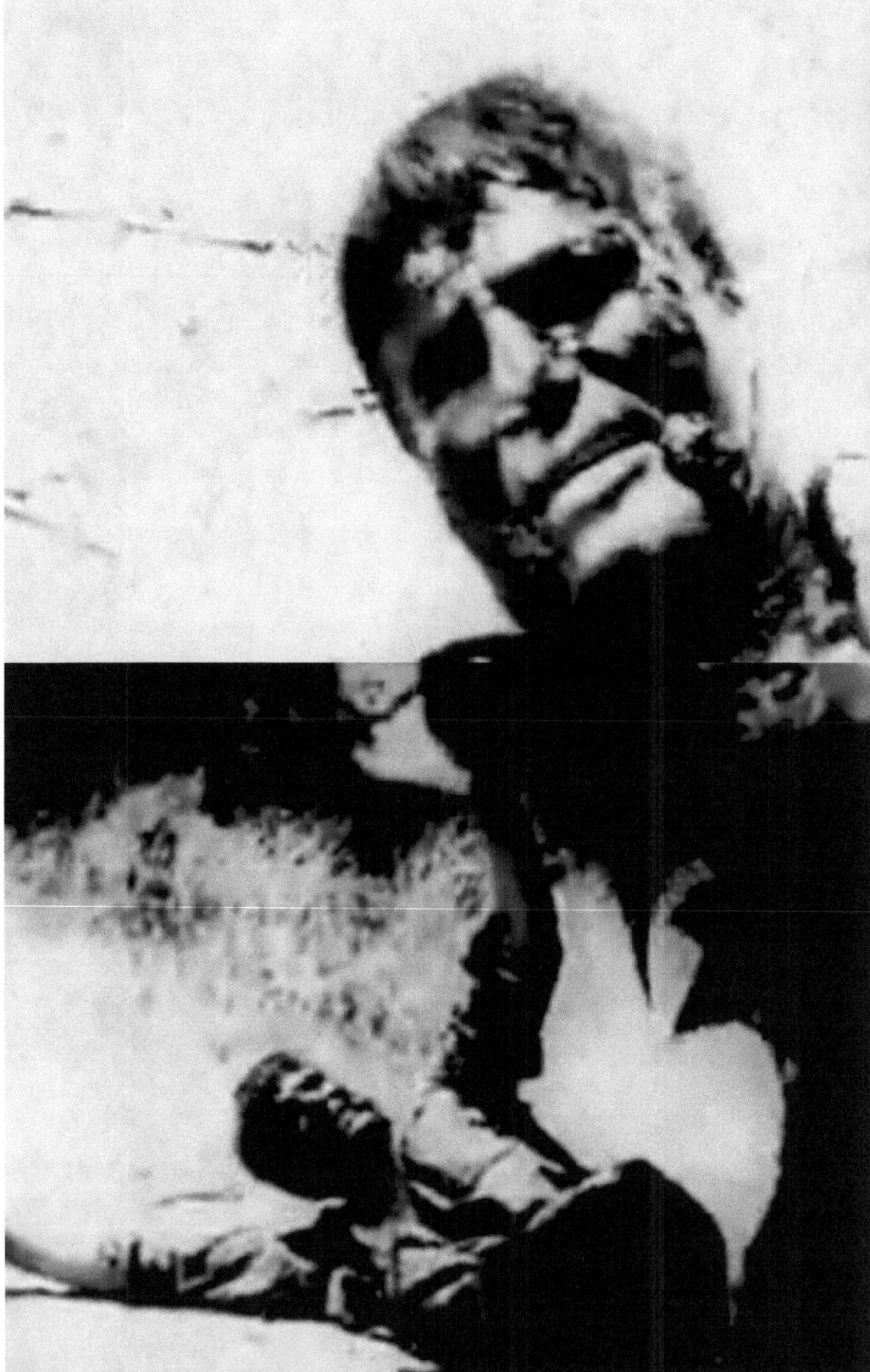

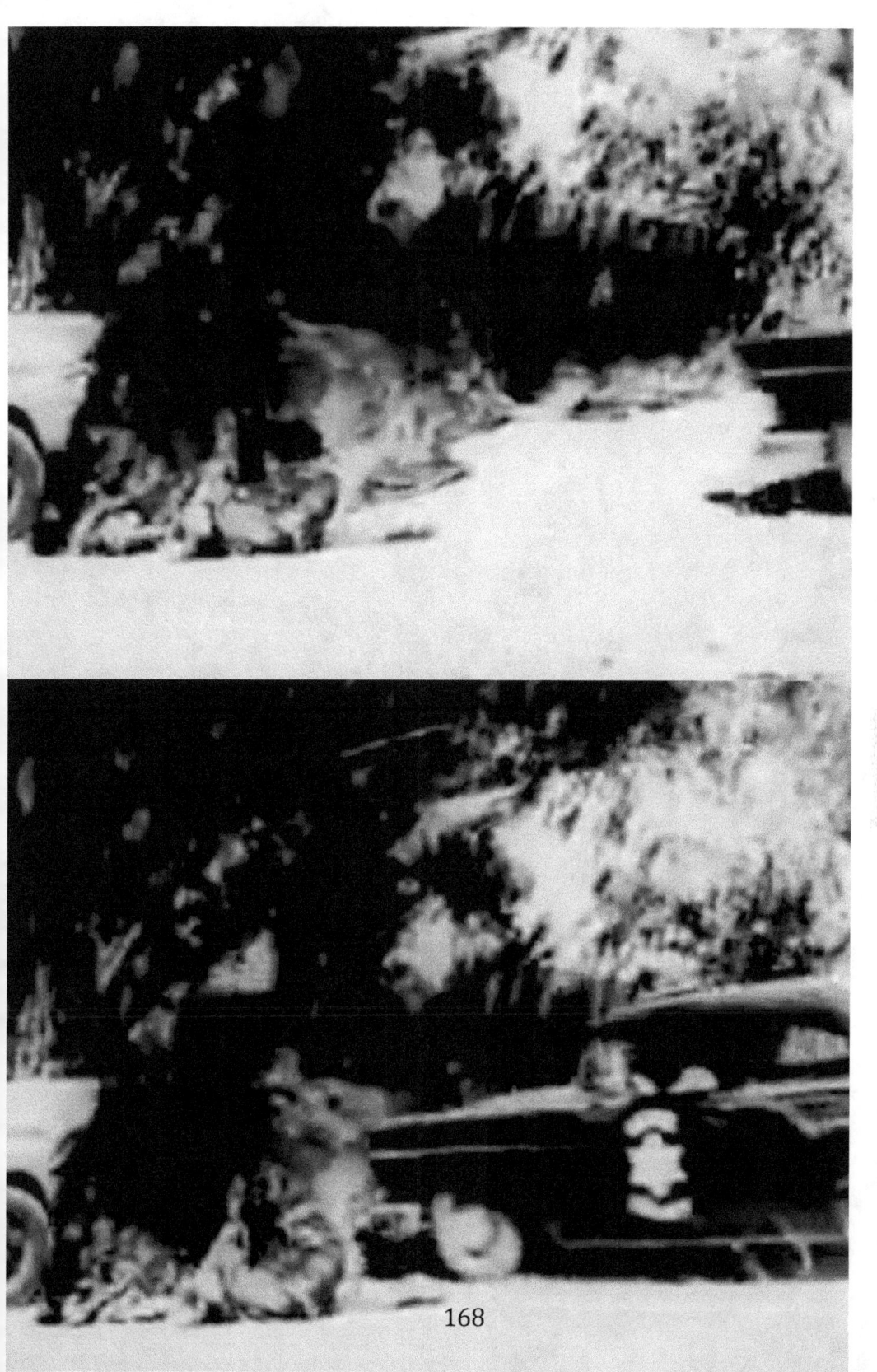

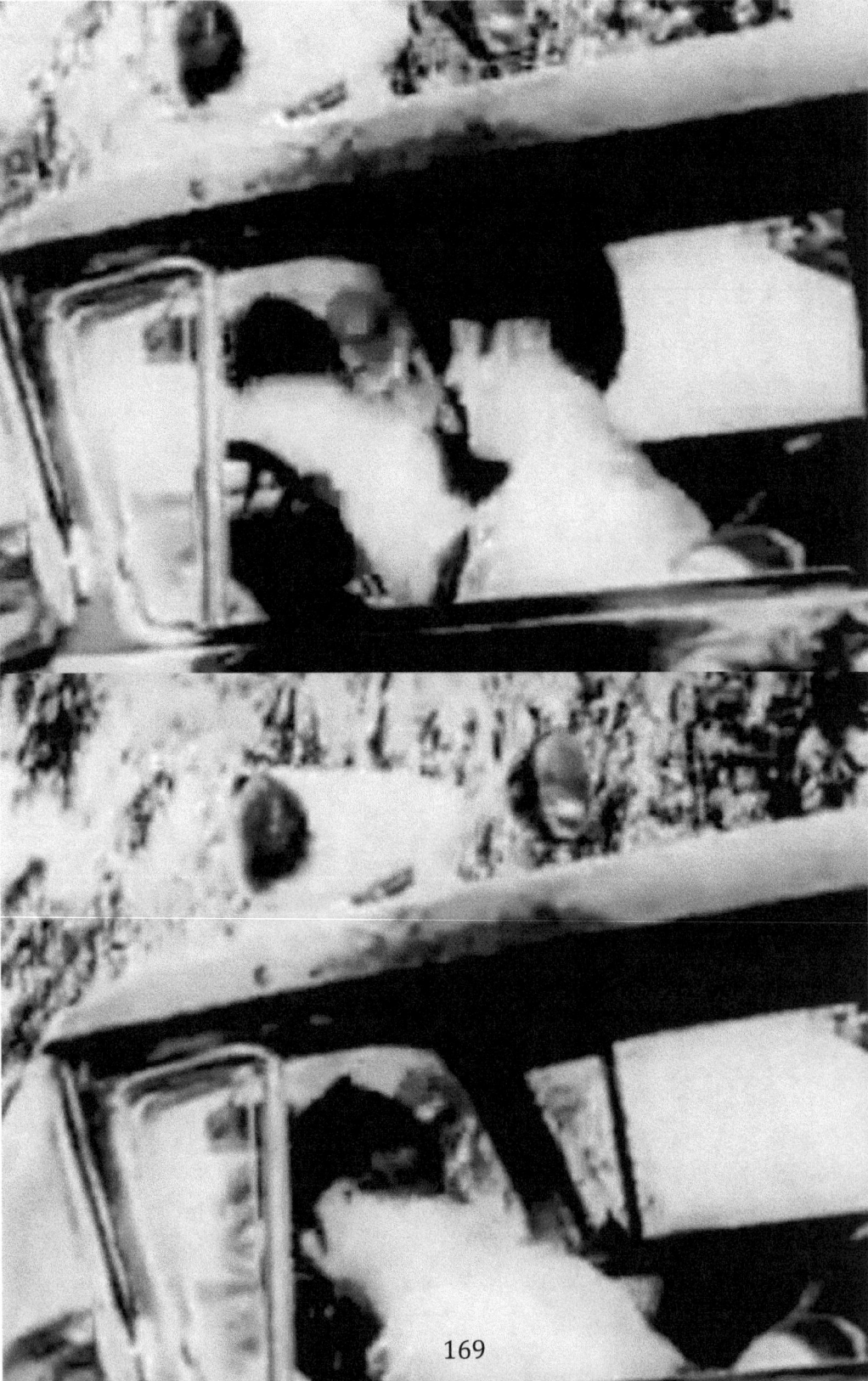

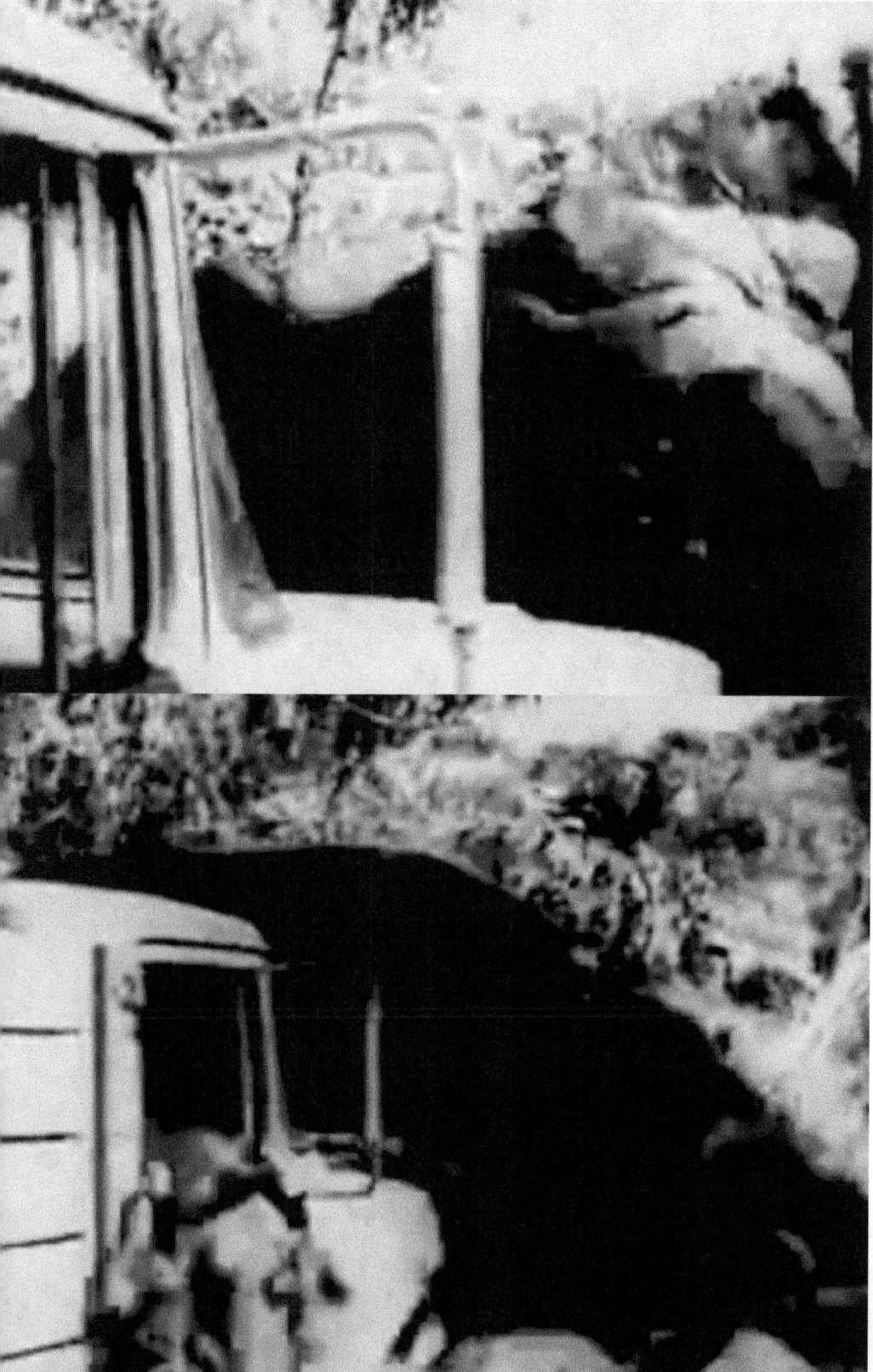

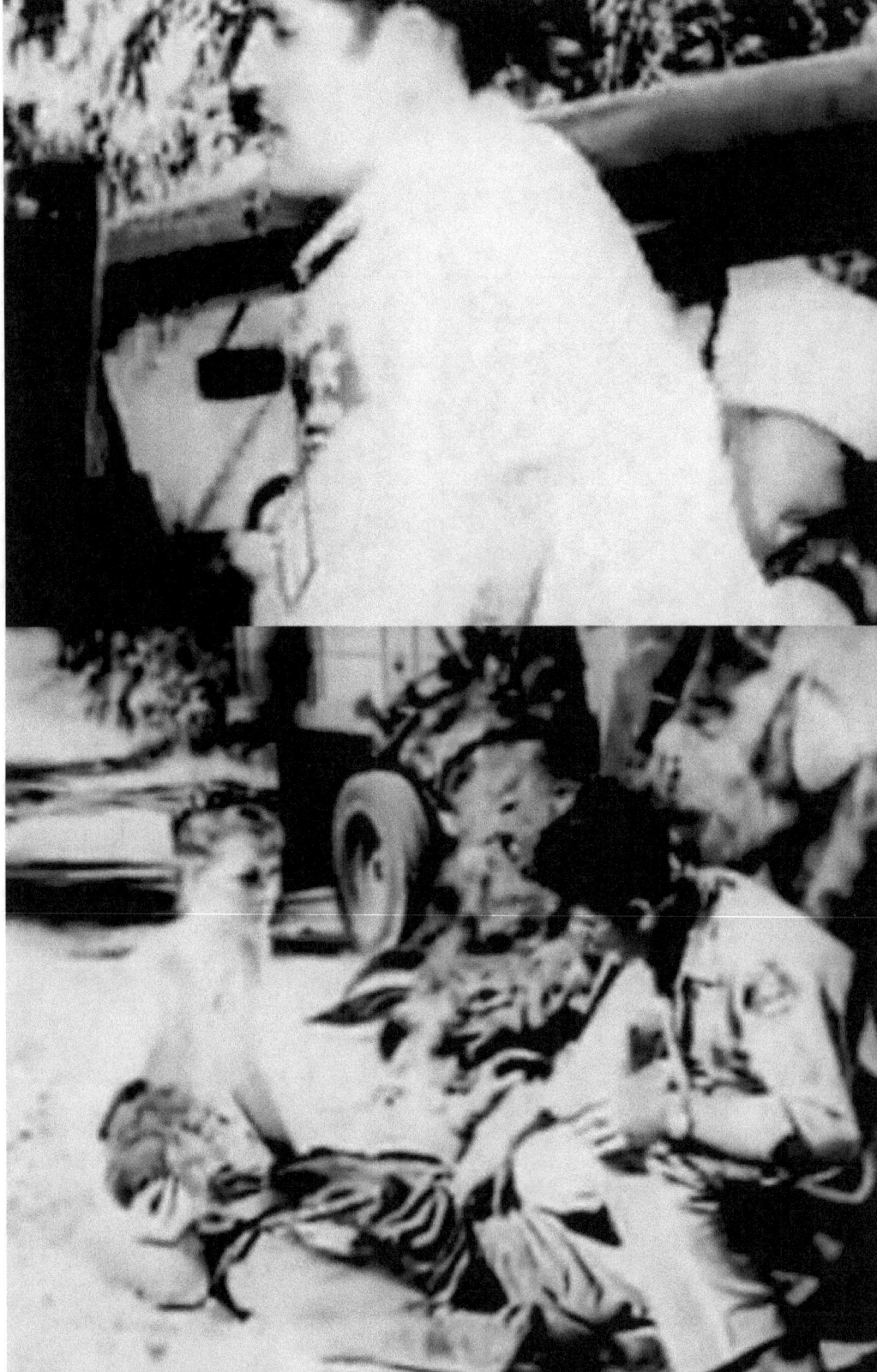

MARTIN TRIED TO HELP THE DR.
BUT THERE WAS NO TIME.
BRADFORD TOLD MARTIN WHAT
HE HAD JUST CONFIRMED.
THESE MONSTERS WERE HIGHLY
SPECIALIZED TEST ANIMALS.
THEY WERE IN FACT, MOBILE
LABRATORIES THAT CONSUMED
HUMAN BEINGS IN ORDER TO
ANALYZE THEM CHEMICALLY,
UNDOUBTEDLY TO DETECT
WEAKNESSES IN THE HUMAN
SPECIES. HE TOLD MARTIN THAT
THE INFORMATION FED INTO A
COMPUTER IN THE SPACECRAFT.
FURTHER HE ADDED, NOW THAT
HIS FACE WAS MELTED AND BOTH
MONSTERS WERE DEAD, THE
COMPUTER WOULD ACTIVATE A
TRANSMITTER THAT WOULD SEND
THE RESULTS INTO OUTER SPACE.
MARTIN KNEW WHAT HE HAD TO
DO. 172

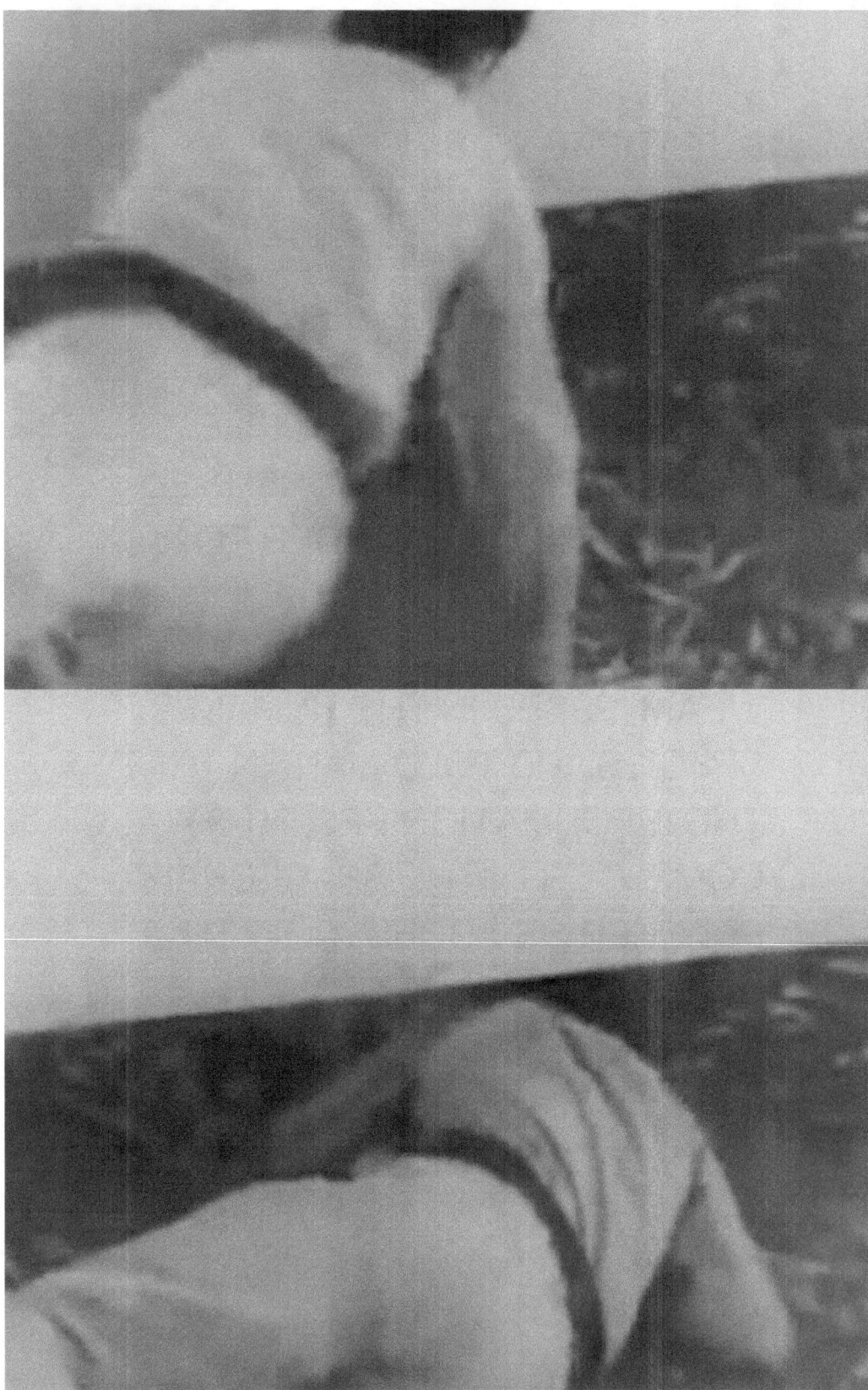

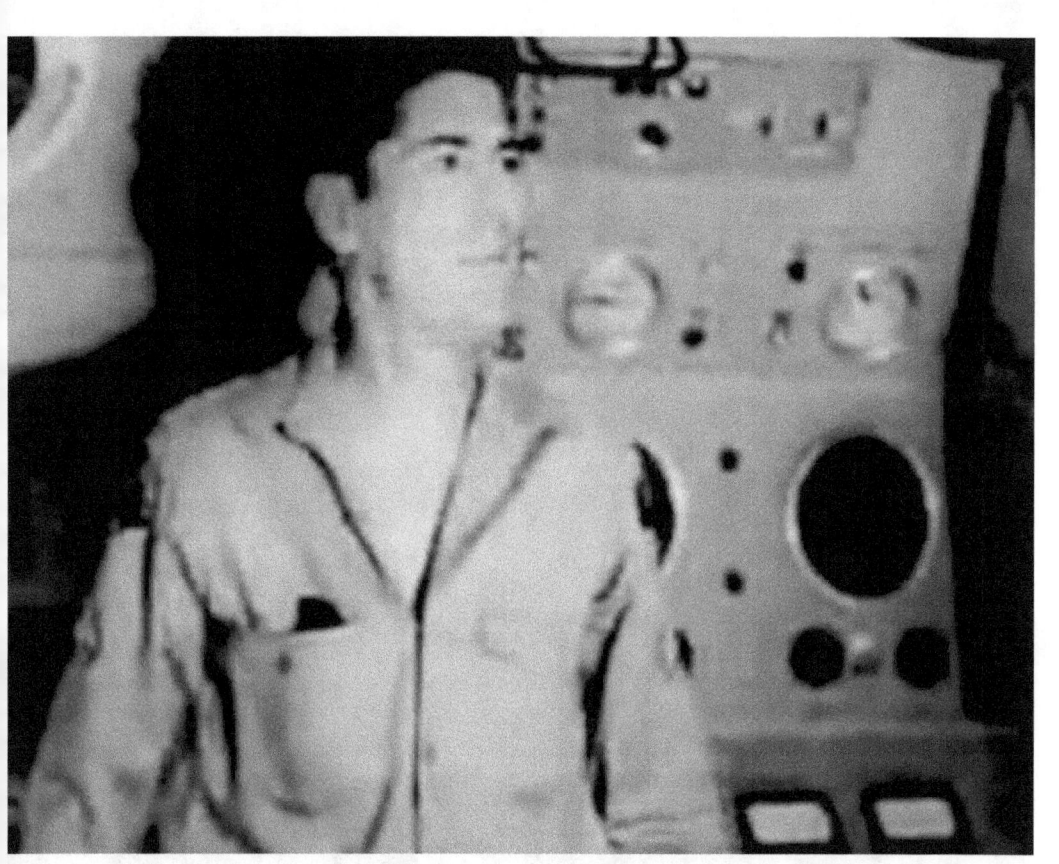

AS MARTIN ENTERED THE
SPACESHIP, HE HEARD THE
TRANSMITTER GENERATOR
KICK ON.

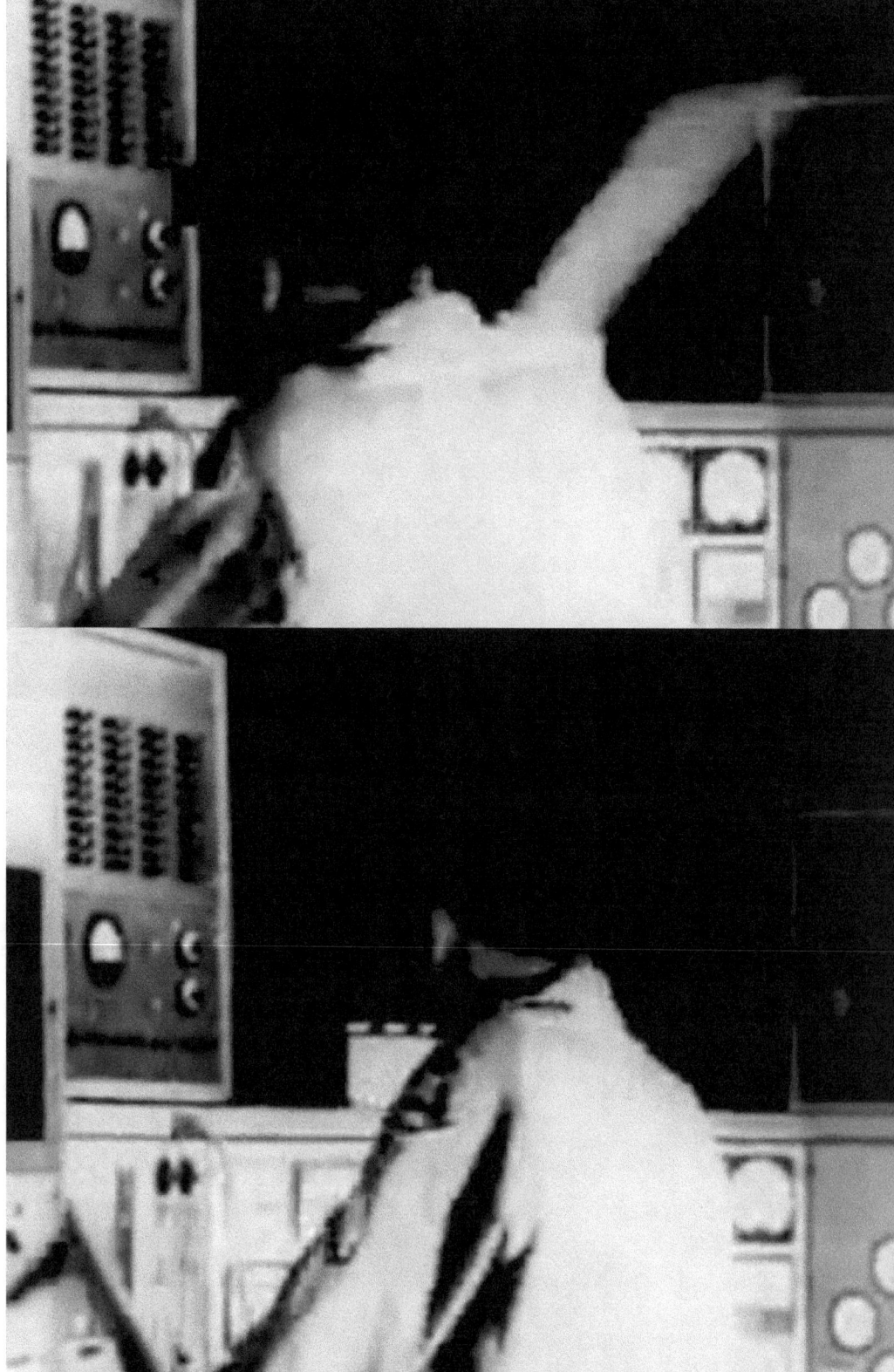

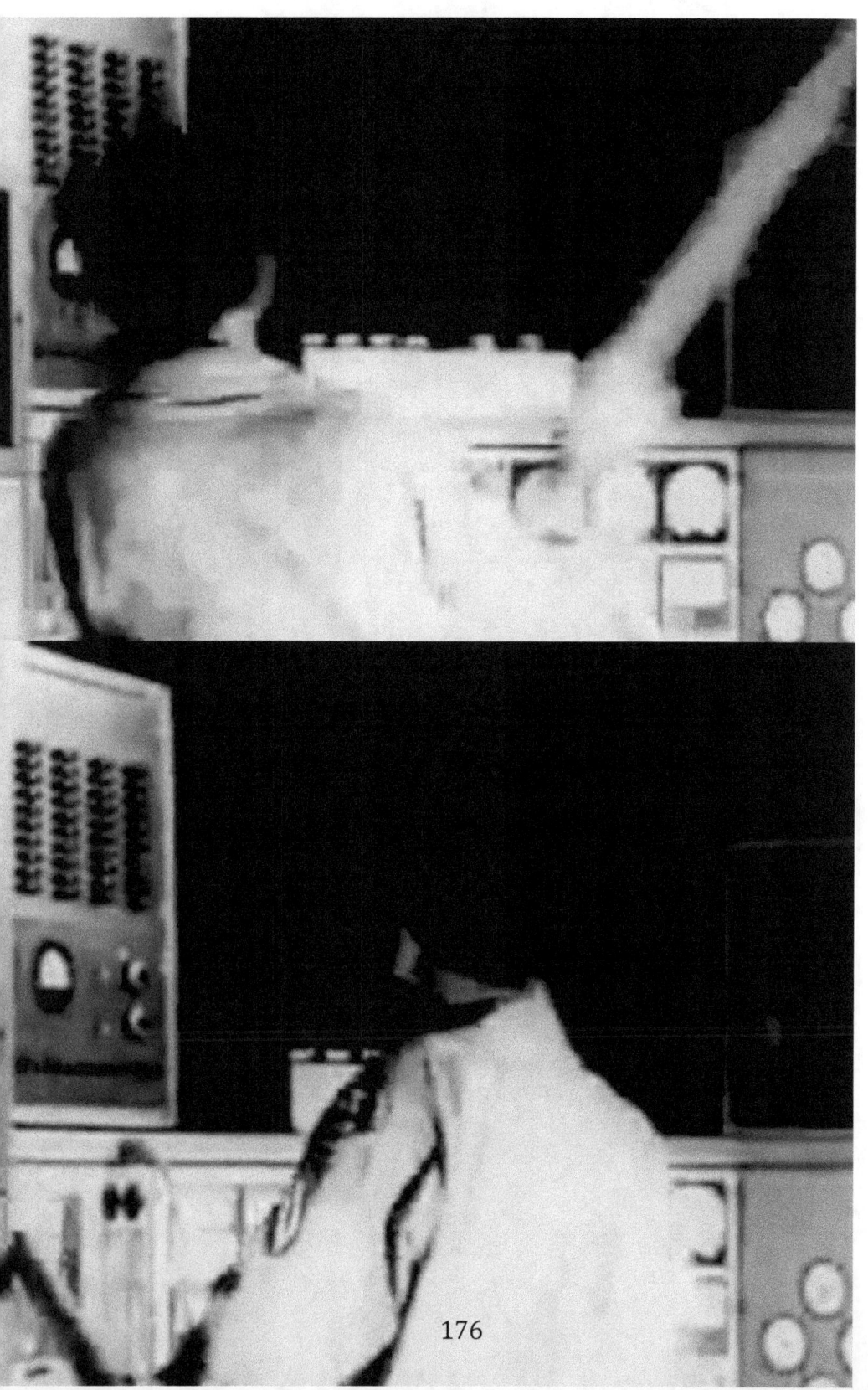

176

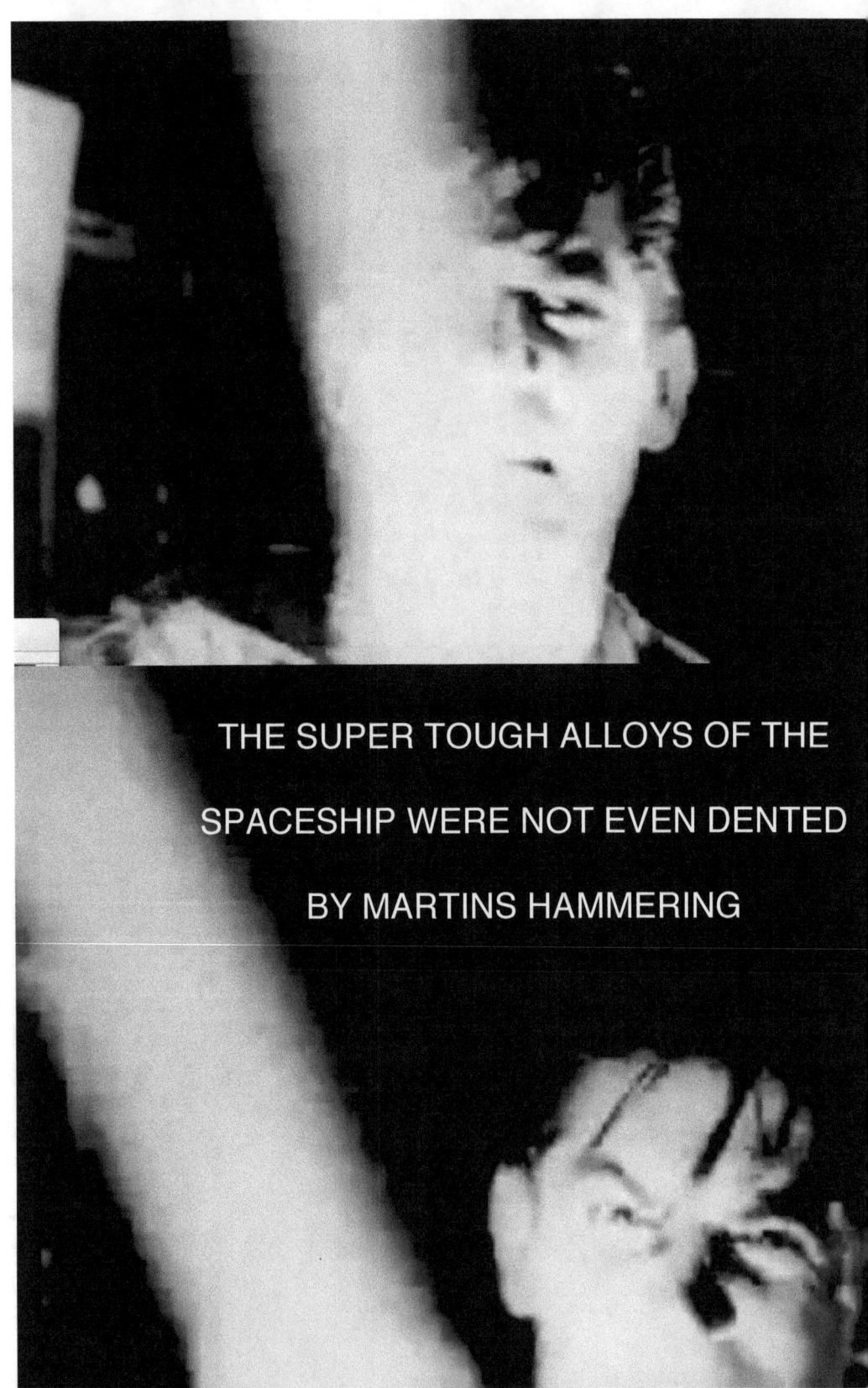

THE SUPER TOUGH ALLOYS OF THE

SPACESHIP WERE NOT EVEN DENTED

BY MARTINS HAMMERING

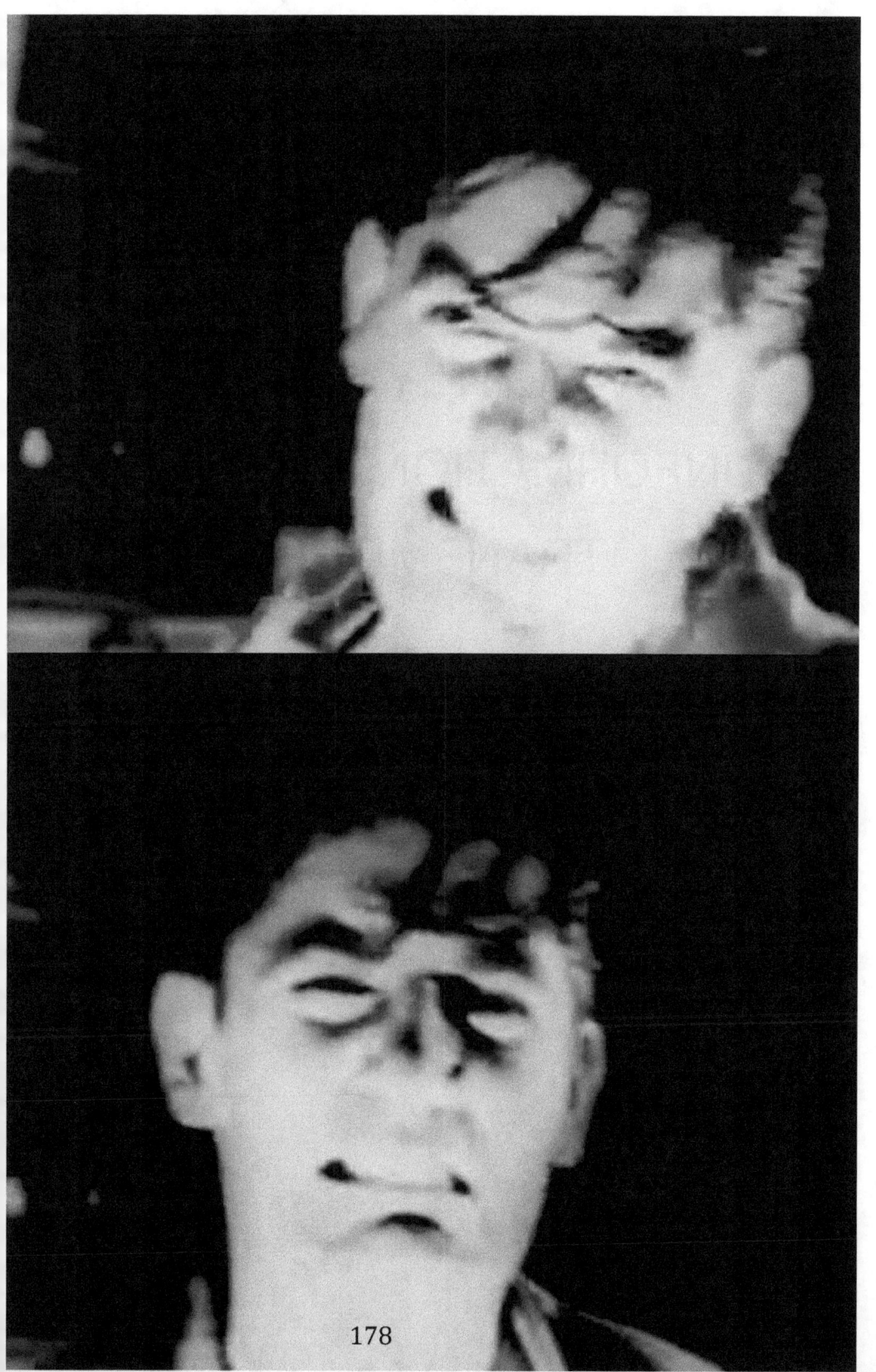

178

AS THE TRANSMITTER
STOPPED MARTIN FELT SICK.

EVIDENTLY ALL THE
INFORMATION HAD BEEN
TRANSMITTED.

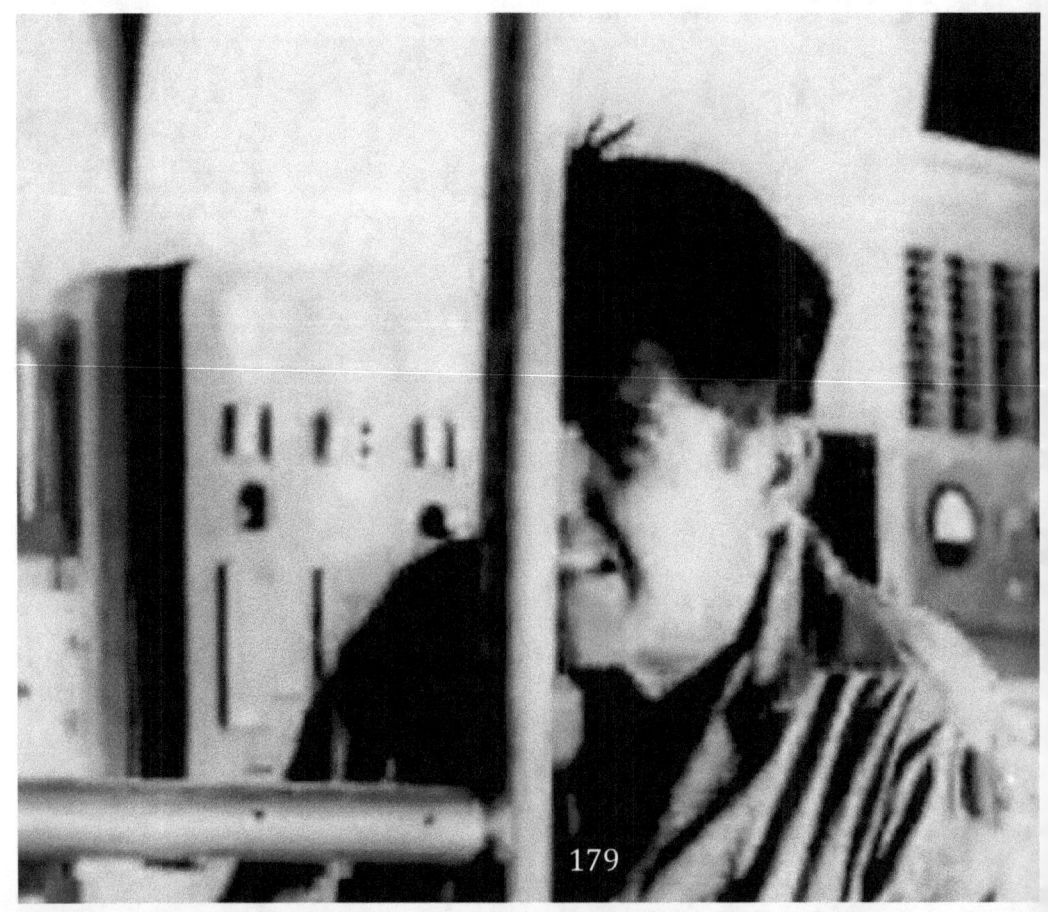

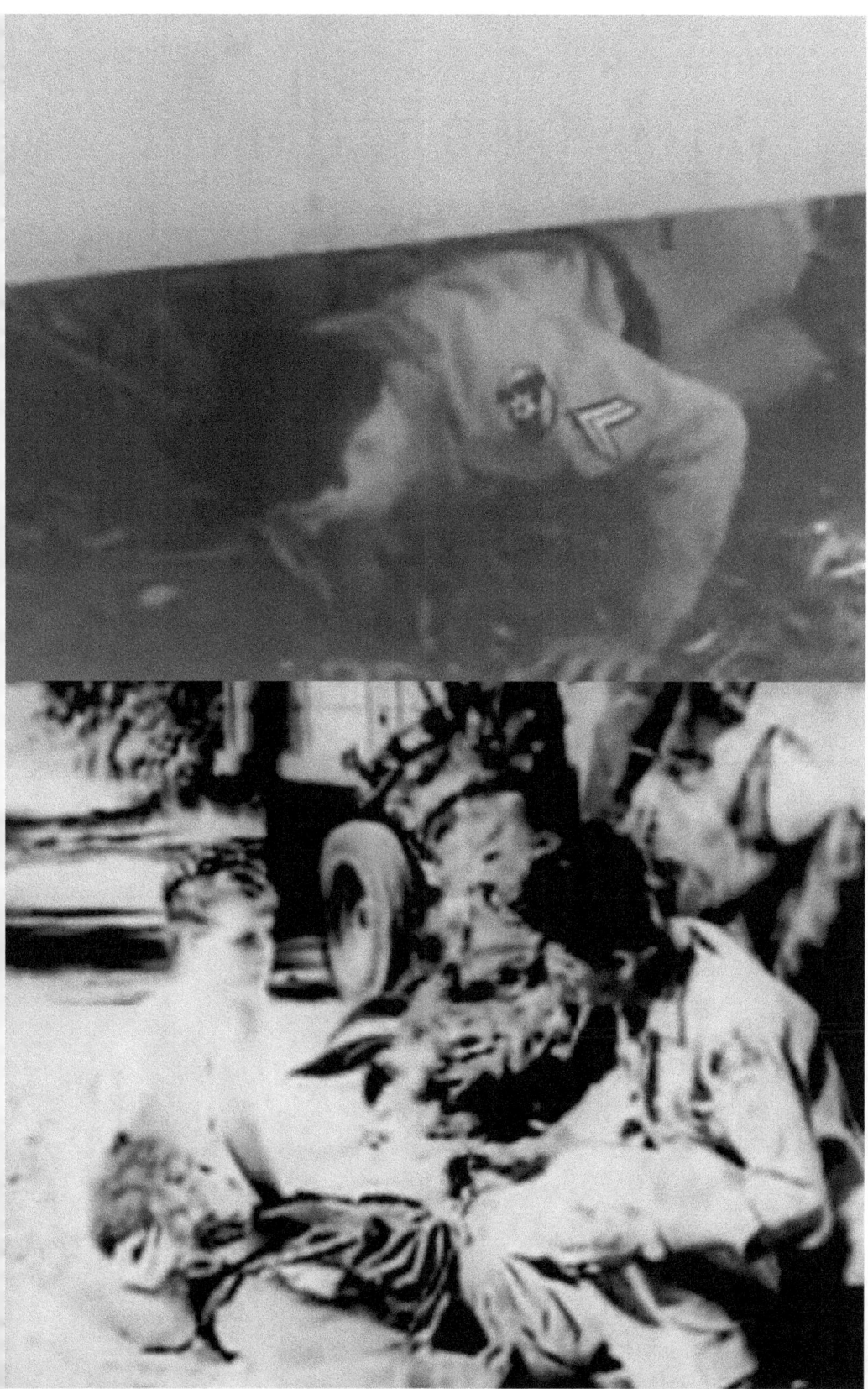

ON MARTINS RETURN HE
CONFESSED HIS FAILURE.
HE SLOWLY ASKED
BRADFORD WHAT WAS IN
STORE FOR HUMANITY

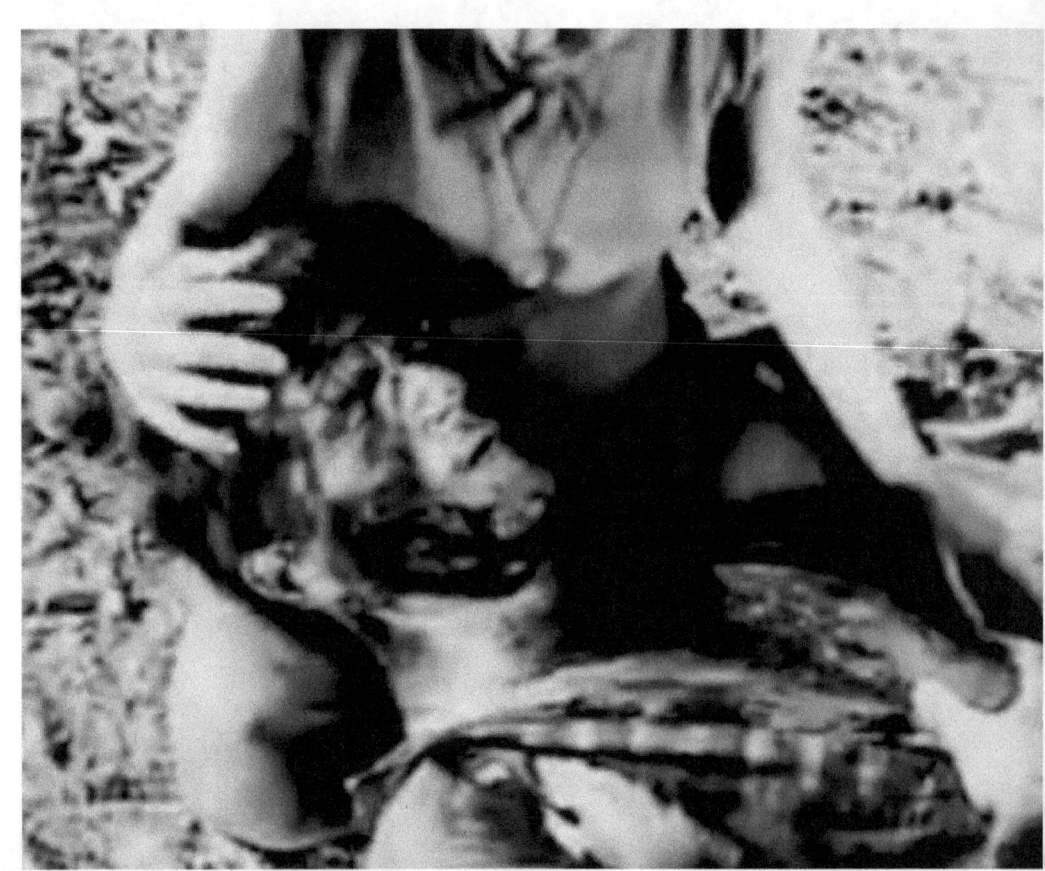

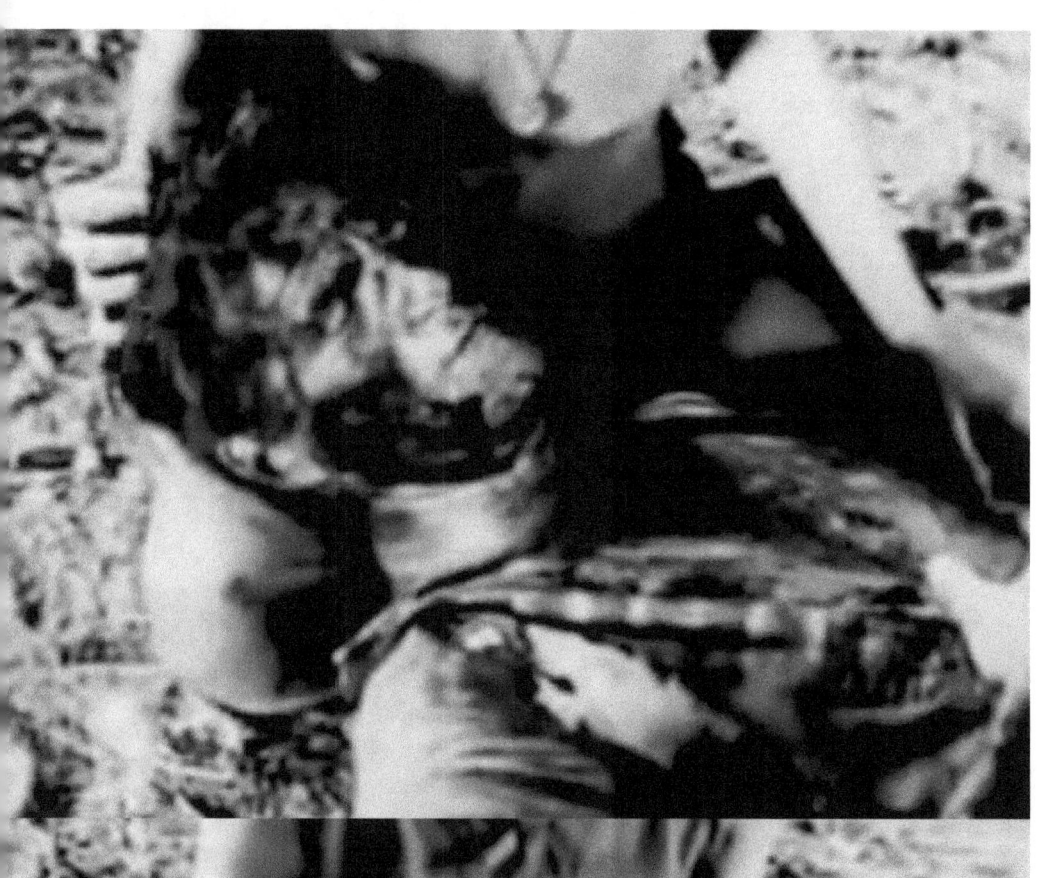

BRADFORD WAS PESSIMISTIC

BUT IMPLIED MAYBE NOT ALL

WAS LOST, AFTER ALL HE SAID,

THE VASTNESS OF UNIVERSE IS

INCREDIBLE.

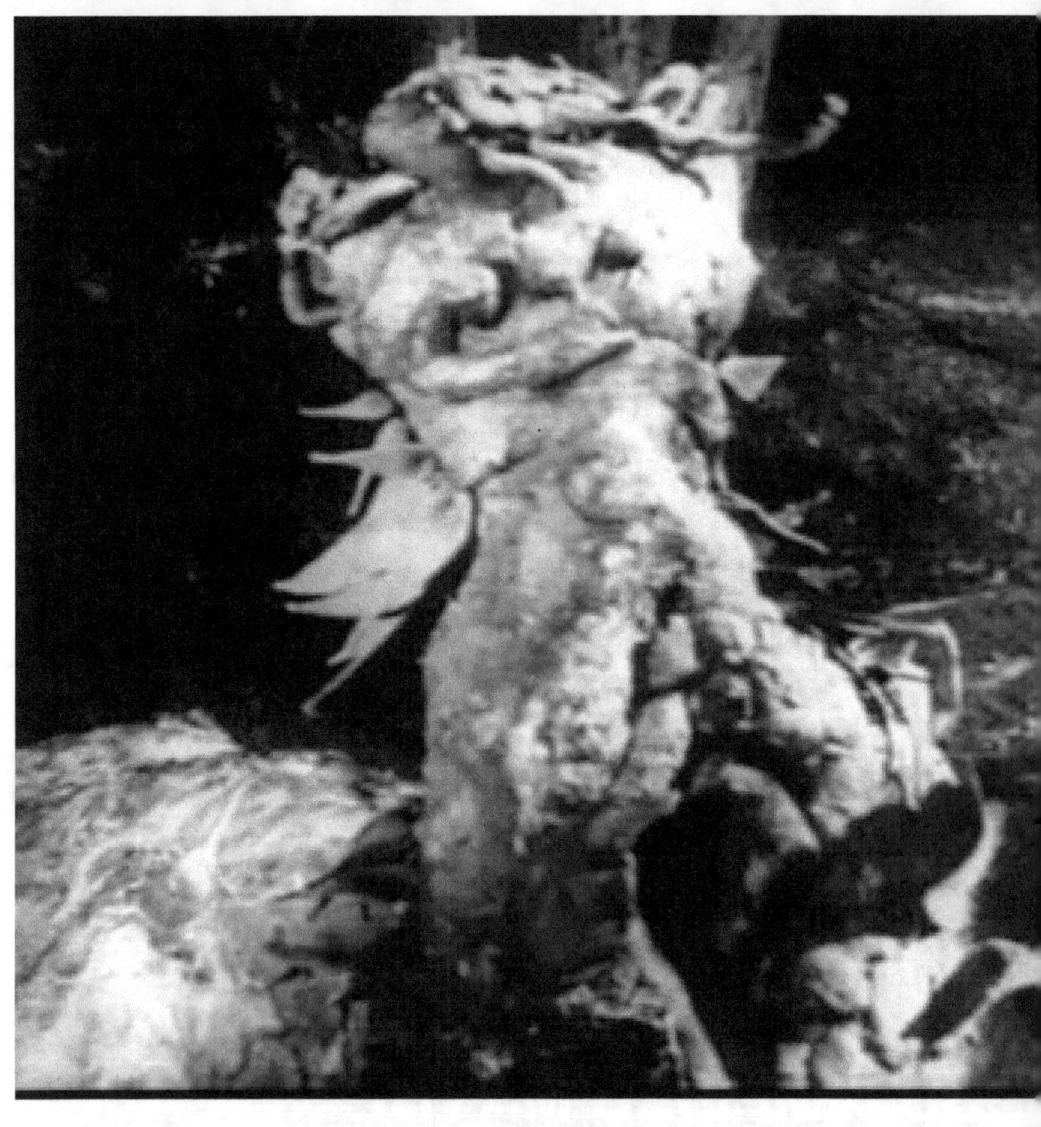

IF THESE MONSTERS HAD COME FROM ITS OUTER

LIMITS, THIER HOME MIGHT EVEN NO LONGER EXIST, OR

IF THEY DO COME AGAIN, PERHAPS MAN WILL HAVE

ADVANCED ENOUGH TO COPE WITH THOSE WHO MADE

THEM. "ONLY GOD KNOWS FOR SURE" WERE

BRADFORD'S LAST WORDS TO ANYONE ON THIS EARTH.

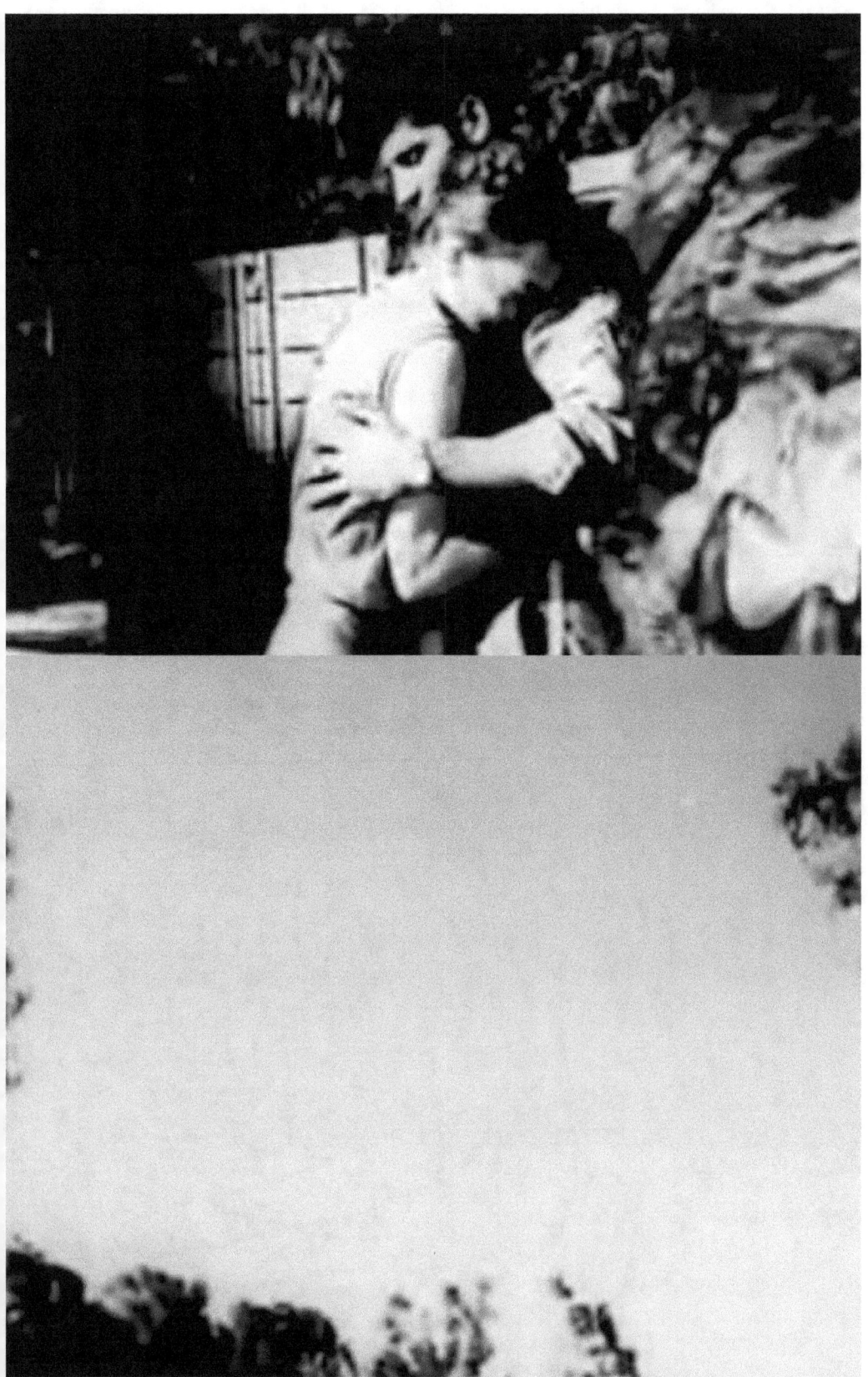

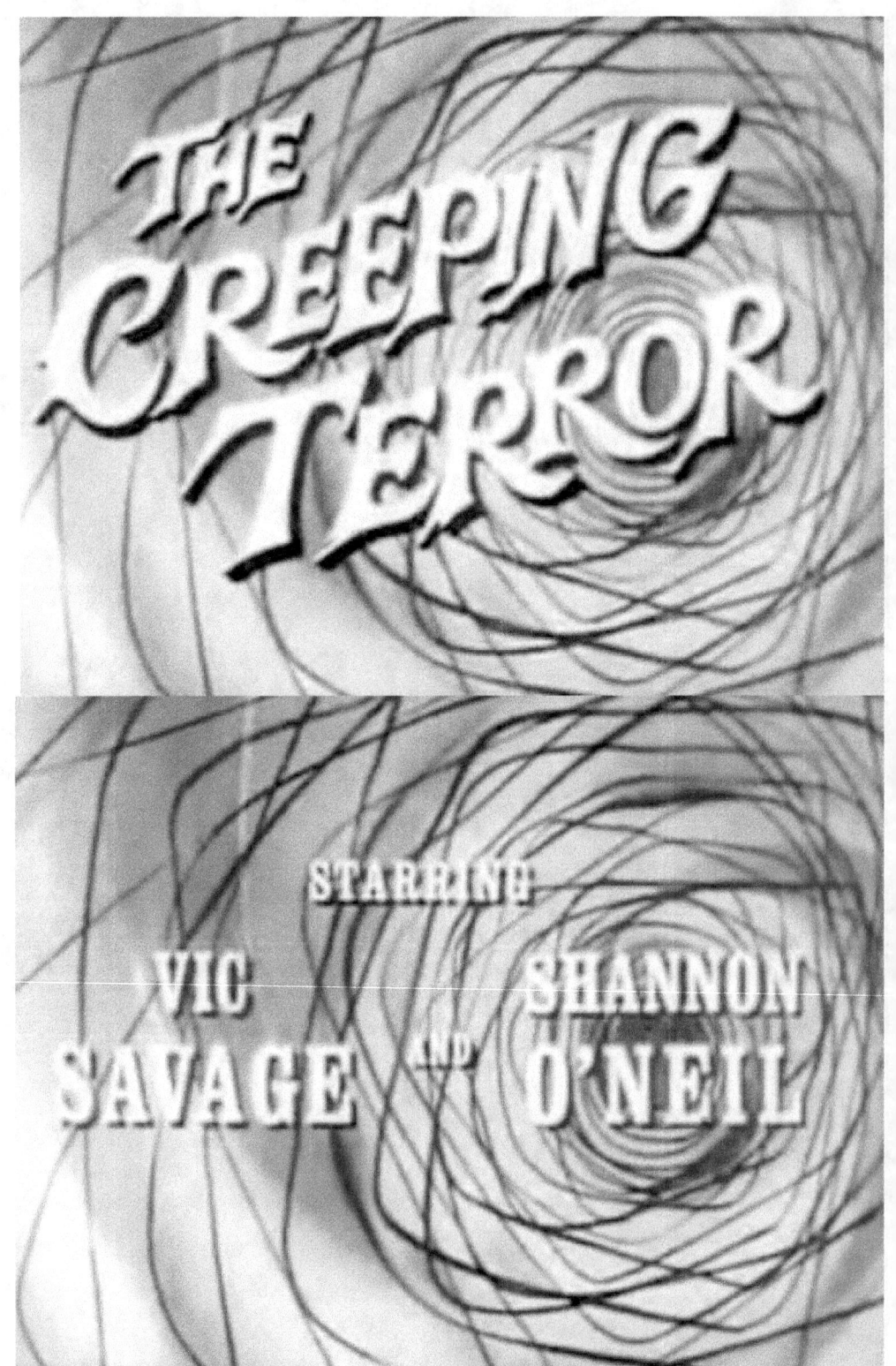

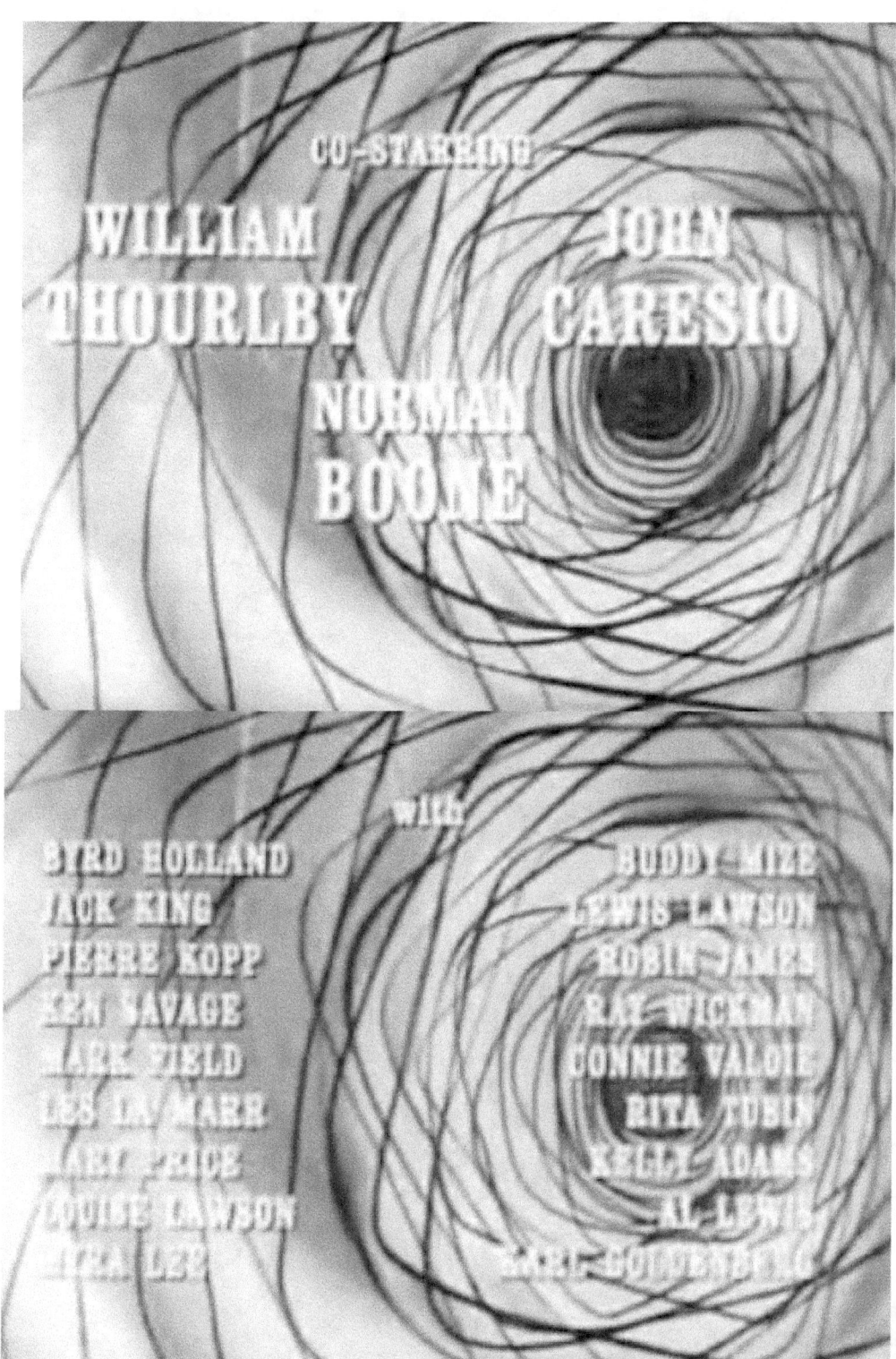

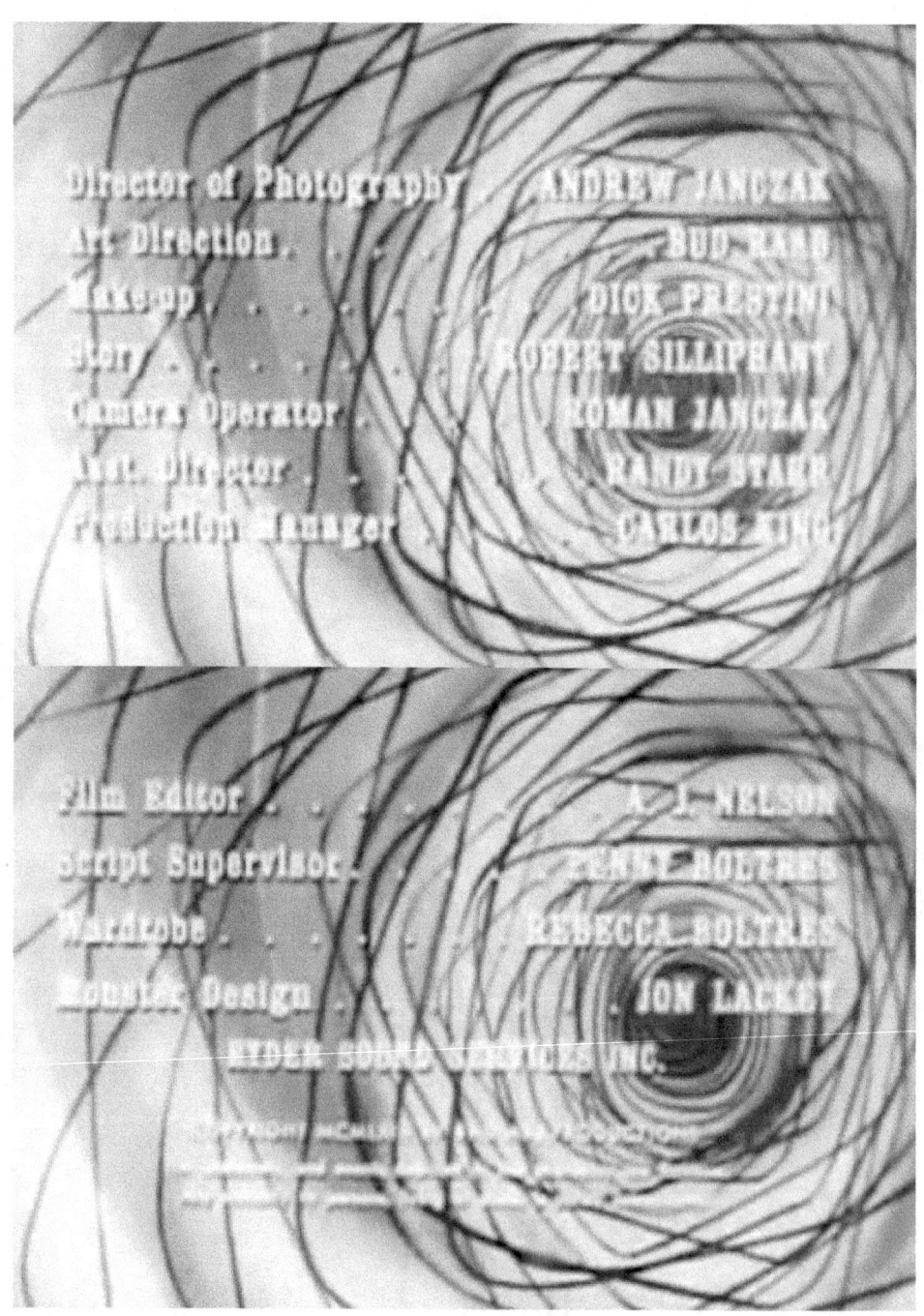

Director of Photography . . ANDREW JANCZAK
Art Direction . . . . BUD RAAB
Makeup . . . . DICK PRESTINI
Story . . . . ROBERT SILLIPHANT
Camera Operator . . . . . ROMAN JANCZAK
Asst. Director . . . . . . RANDY STARR
Production Manager . . . . . CARLOS KING

Film Editor . . . . A. J. NELSON
Script Supervisor . . . . PENNY BOLTRES
Wardrobe . . . . REBECCA BOLTRES
Monster Design . . . . . . JON LACKEY
RYDER SOUND SERVICES INC.

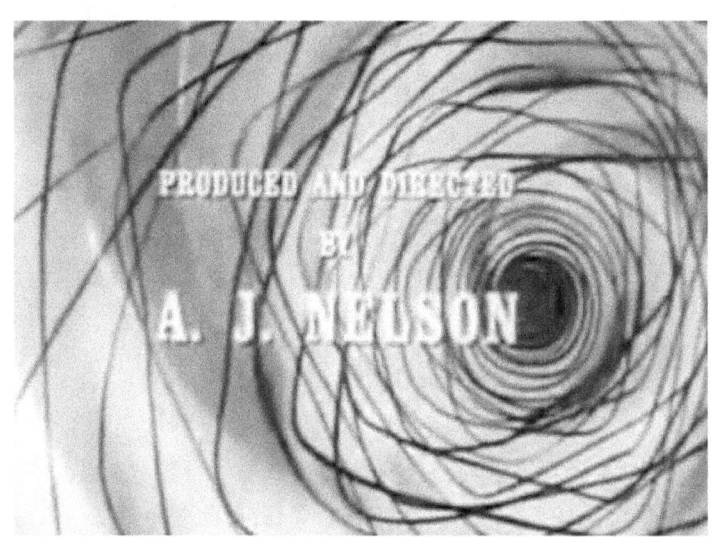

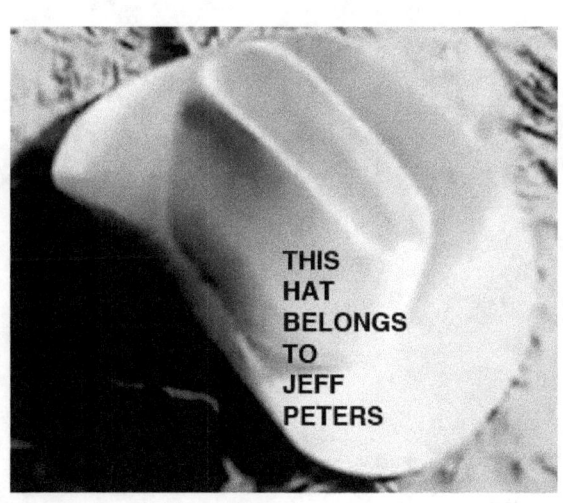

THIS
HAT
BELONGS
TO
JEFF
PETERS